Comparative and International Education

Comparative and International Education

Issues for Teachers

Edited by
Karen Mundy, Kathy Bickmore,
Ruth Hayhoe, Meggan Madden,
and Katherine Madjidi

CSPI ✹
Canadian Scholars' Press Inc.
Toronto

Teachers College
Columbia University
New York and London

Comparative and International Education: Issues for Teachers
edited by Karen Mundy, Kathy Bickmore, Ruth Hayhoe, Meggan Madden, and
Katherine Madjidi

First published in Canada in 2008 by
Canadian Scholars' Press Inc.
180 Bloor Street West, Suite 801
Toronto, Ontario M5S 2V6

First published in the USA in 2008 by
Teachers College Press
1234 Amsterdam Avenue
New York, NY 10027

www.cspi.org

www.tcpress.com

ISBN 978-55130-333-8

ISBN 978-0-8077-4881-7

Canadian Scholars' Press Inc. gratefully acknowledges financial support for our publishing activities from the Government of Canada through the Book Publishing Industry Development Program (BPIDP).

Library and Archives Canada Cataloguing in Publication
    Comparative and international education : issues for teachers /
edited by Karen Mundy ... [et al.].
Includes bibliographical references and index.
ISBN 978-1-55130-333-8
    1. Comparative education. 2. International education. 3. Education--Cross-cultural studies. I. Mundy, Karen E. (Karen Elizabeth), 1962-
LB43.C666 2008   370.9   C2008-900507-4

Interior design and composition: Brad Horning
Cover design: John Kicksee/KIX BY DESIGN
Cover art © René Mansi. "Stack of books," istockphoto.com

08   09   10   11   12   5   4   3   2   1

Printed and bound in Canada by Marquis Book Printing Inc.

Canadä

This book is dedicated to the memory of

Professor David N. Wilson,

our colleague, mentor, and friend.

Table of Contents

How to Use This Book

This anthology grew out of a collaborative effort among faculty involved in the Comparative, International, and Development Education Centre at the Ontario Institute for Studies in Education of the University of Toronto (OISE-UT). Convinced of the value of introducing educators to comparative and international educational research, we set out to produce a text that would offer broad exposure to international issues and explore education in diverse cultural settings. Through vivid portrayals of global educational practices and contributions from pre-eminent comparative education scholars, we hope to stimulate readers to think comparatively and critically about their own educational practices and experiences.

The book is designed as a teaching resource for teacher education and graduate education programs. Each chapter introduces major issues within the field of comparative and international education, highlighting significant research contributions, educational practices, and implications for teachers within each topic. The authors draw on comparative research from the Americas, Australia, Africa, Asia, Europe, and the Middle East. We have used the Canadian context as a case study in a few chapters; however, the concepts presented are easily extended to a broadly North American and even global context.

In Chapter One by Ruth Hayhoe and Karen Mundy, we begin with a discussion of the history of comparative education as a field, asking the key question, "Why study comparative education?" Chapter Two by Hayhoe and Chapter Three by Mundy encourage students to consider theoretical and foundational aspects of comparative education, touching upon the philosophical development of the field in comparative East-West perspective, the sociology of schooling, and the right to education. In Chapter Four, Katherine Madjidi and Jean-

Paul Restoule introduce readers to a rich alternative set of foundations for comparative education, drawn from an exploration of Indigenous worldviews and perspectives on knowing and learning.

Chapters Five by Joseph P. Farrell and Six by Sarfaroz Niyozov look at schooling and pedagogy in comparative perspective. Farrell presents a number of "radical alternatives" from the developing world, while Niyozov examines the contested and complex nature of teaching and pedagogy in the context of rural Tajikistan. Two subsequent chapters look at shifts in policy that are shaping everyday practices of schooling. The history of school improvement and effectiveness reforms are introduced in Chapter Seven by Stephen Anderson, while Chapter Eight by Mundy and Farrell looks at the increasing role played by international assessments and indicators in the field of comparative education.

Our final three chapters expand the scope of the text by touching upon important current issues in comparative and international education. In Chapter Nine, Kara Janigan and Vandra Masemann consider the role of gender in education, drawing on case studies from Canada and Eritrea. Kathy Bickmore examines approaches to conflict resolution and peacebuilding in plural societies in Chapter Ten. We conclude the volume with a chapter by Mark Evans (with contributions from Ian Davies, Bernadette Dean, and Yusef Waghid) presenting diverse perspectives from Canada, England, Pakistan, and South Africa on educating for global citizenship.

Instructors who wish to use this book as a class text may choose to follow the assigned order of chapters, or to change the order according to specific course objectives. There are cross-chapter references throughout the text to link learning across the various chapters and to highlight common themes.

At the end of each chapter, key questions for reflection and discussion, along with a list of suggested readings, are intended to stimulate discussion about the chapter contents. Three of these readings are starred with an asterisk (*), denoting that these are good short articles for group assignments and discussion. Each chapter is also paired with a suggested audio-visual resource, carefully selected to provide students with an opportunity to "experience" education in other cultures without having to leave the classroom. In our piloting of this course at OISE-UT, the films provoked animated debate and discussion, offering the students a visceral feeling for the challenges and rewards of exploring educational issues through a comparative lens. Appendix A provides a description of each film, suggested questions for discussion, and details on how to obtain the recommended resources.

We have also produced a website of audio-visual resources to support and enrich the use of this text: cide.oise.utoronto.ca/resources_ for_teachers/textbook.php. On the website you will find short clips of the authors introducing their respective chapters, and for some chapters a full-length video of the authors' lectures and PowerPoint presentations. Links to relevant websites and online curriculum and teacher resources are provided on the website, as well as being listed at the end of this text in Appendix B.

Acknowledgements

This book is the result of many individual efforts. We are particularly grateful to the faculty and students affiliated with the Comparative, International, and Development Education Centre (CIDEC) at OISE-UT, who along with its director, Karen Mundy, played a fundamental role in crafting this project. We received editing and research support from many CIDEC students, including Kirk Perris and Kara Janigan. Sylvia Macrae, CIDEC's administrative officer, provided important logistical support.

The Initial Teacher Education staff at OISE also deserves thanks for giving us the opportunity to pilot this text through teaching a course on Comparative Education in the autumn of 2006. In this course, we had the pleasure of getting to know 23 initial teacher education students who enthusiastically gave us their critical and insightful feedback.

We are also indebted to CIDEC alumna Annick Corbiel for the superb research report that she compiled in 2005, which helped build the foundation for this anthology. Student participants and professors in faculties of education across Canada were surveyed as part of this initial report. Specifically, we would like to acknowledge Ali Abdi, Zahra Bhanji, Clive Beck, Jennifer Chan-Tiberghien, Reva Joshee, Eva Krugly-Smolska, Brian O'Sullivan, and Mary-Lynn Tessaro for sharing their thoughts about the content of and need for such an anthology. Comments from our external reviewers, Ali Abdi from the University of Alberta, Eva Krugly-Smolska from Queen's University, Suzanne Majhanovich from the University of Western Ontario, and Paul Fossum from the University of Michigan–Dearborn were very valuable to us; we thank them for their time and for their frank evaluations and encouraging responses to the text.

Finally, we were fortunate to receive support from the University of Toronto's Instructional Technology and Course Development Fund, which allowed us to develop short films of the authors and to integrate these films onto our website and CIDEC Research and Development Database. We wish to acknowledge the Education Commons staff at OISE-UT for their professional expertise and advice in producing these fine films. We also wish to thank Scott Wallace for drafting original maps that provide visual geographic context throughout this text.

List of Acronyms

Acronym	Definition
AIDS	Acquired Immune Deficiency Syndrome
ALL	Adult Literacy and Lifeskills Survey
ASEAN	Association of Southeast Asian Nations
BRAC	Bangladesh Rural Advancement Committee
CARE	Christian Action Research and Education
CEDAW	Convention on the Elimination of All Forms of Discrimination against Women
CIDA	Canadian International Development Agency
CIES	Comparative and International Education Society
CIESC	Comparative and International Education Society of Canada
CMEC	Council of Ministers of Education Canada
CSOs	Civil Society Organizations
CSR	Comprehensive School Reform
DfID	Department for International Development (United Kingdom)
DoE	Department of Education (United Kingdom)
EFA	Education For All
FPE	Free Primary Education
G8	"Group of Eight." This group consists of eight industrialized countries: United States, Canada, Russia, United Kingdom, France, Germany, Japan, and Italy.

GCE	Global Campaign for Education
GCSE	General Certificate of Secondary Education
GDP	Gross Domestic Product
GER	Gross Enrolment Ratio
GNI	Gross National Income
HIV	Human Immunodeficiency Virus
HRSDC	Human Resources and Skills Development Canada
IBE	International Bureau of Education
ICCES	International Civics and Citizenship Education Study
ISCED	International Standard Classification of Education
ICCS	International Civic and Citizenship Education Study
ICT	Information and Communication Technology
IEA	International Association for the Evaluation of Educational Achievement
IK	Indigenous Knowledge
IMF	International Monetary Fund
MDGs	Millennium Development Goals
NAFTA	North American Free Trade Agreement
NARC	National Rainbow Coalition (Kenya)
NCLB	No Child Left Behind (United States)
NGO	Non-governmental Organization
OCR	Oxford Cambridge and RSA Examinations
ODA	Overseas Development Assistance
OECD	Organisation for Economic Co-operation and Development
OREALC	UNESCO Regional Office for Latin America and the Caribbean
Oxfam	Oxford Committee for Famine Relief
PER	Public Expenditure Review
PIRLS	Progress in Reading Literacy Study

PISA	Programme for International Student Assessment
PLCs	Professional Learning Communities
SACMEQ	Southern and Eastern African Consortium for Monitoring Educational Quality
SAPs	Structural Adjustment Programs
SAT	Scholastic Aptitude Test
SBM	School-based Management
SES	Socio-economic Status
SITES	Second Information Technology in Education Study
StatsCan	Statistics Canada
TIMSS	Originally, Third International Mathematics and Science Study, now Trends in International Mathematics and Science Study
TRC	Truth and Reconciliation Commission (South Africa)
UIS	UNESCO Institute for Statistics
UN	United Nations
UNESCO	United Nations Educational, Sciencific, and Cultural Organization
UNICEF	United Nations Children's Fund
USAID	United States Agency for International Development
USSR	Union of Soviet Socialist Republics
WINHEC	World Indigenous Nations Higher Education Consortium
WIPCE	World Indigenous Peoples' Conference on Education
WOMP	World Order Models Project
WSIP	Whole School Improvement Program
WTO	World Trade Organization

Chapter One

Introduction to Comparative and International Education: Why Study Comparative Education?

Ruth Hayhoe and Karen Mundy

INTRODUCTION

Why study comparative education? The answers to this question are rich and varied, as we hope you will discover through this introduction to the field. For centuries, educators have acted on what we might call the "comparative" impulse: attempting to understand and improve their systems of learning by looking at others. This impulse is captured in the title of one of the most popular and enduring books in comparative education, *Other Schools and Ours*.[1] Throughout the 20th century, the comparative impulse fed wide-ranging efforts to solve problems of economic development, social conflict, and social inequality through educational reform. It also spawned important critical comparisons of such efforts, leading to pioneering work on the role played by education in the construction of global and national social systems. At its most basic, comparative education offers a starting point for improving our educational systems and our classroom practices. It also challenges us to think broadly about the link between local practices and global issues and to explore the overlapping values and social systems that underpin the educational enterprise itself.

Comparative education has developed over a period of nearly two centuries, and its rich literature constitutes a resource for teachers that is now more accessible than ever before. In this introductory chapter, we begin with an overview of the early history of comparative education, then look at how the field developed in the 19th and 20th centuries and how it expanded to include international education after World War II. We also look at the contributions made by educators and international organizations to the comparative study of education.

THE EARLY HISTORY OF COMPARATIVE EDUCATION

Comparative education developed along with other social sciences such as sociology and psychology in Europe in the early 19th century. However, the field had many early antecedents across regions and civilizations. Plato's famous masterwork, *The Republic*, drew upon the ideas of education and society he found admirable in the city state of Sparta, which he saw as having greater discipline and order than his native Athens. The Greek scholar and general Xenophon introduced Persian education to Greece through the biography he wrote of the magnanimous King Cyrus. Subsequently, during the Roman Empire, the famous scholar Cicero made a comparison of Greek and Roman education systems, and concluded that a state-controlled education system was superior to a family-centred private system, since it nurtured bonds with the state that were important to a democracy.[2]

Over the same period, Chinese thinkers developed educational ideas and texts in the "Five Classics," compiled by Confucius and later philosophers, that formed the core of a uniquely Chinese approach to education. While teaching and learning took place largely in family or clan-based schools at the local level, the imperial government administered examinations at prefectural, provincial, and national levels to select the most knowledgeable and talented young people for government service. This very early meritocracy attracted attention from such nearby states as Japan, Korea, and Vietnam, resulting in profound educational and philosophical influences from China on these societies, including the adoption of the Chinese ideographic script. China also remained open to learning from its neighbours to the west, sending numerous emissaries to India to bring back ideas and texts from Buddhism. Hundreds of texts were translated into Chinese and had a long-lasting influence on education and society in the whole East Asian region for many centuries.[3]

The medieval period saw the beginning of travel and interchange between Asia and Europe, over the fabled Silk Route and by sea. Marco Polo's account of China in the 13th century tells little about its education system, since the civil service examinations had been halted under the Mongol dynasty. Later European visitors, such as the Jesuits of the 16th and 17th centuries, however, wrote admiring accounts of Chinese education that had considerable influence in Europe. One result was the development of highly selective examinations in France for entry to the Grandes Écoles, which in turn assured employment in the nation's civil service. While the Enlightenment and the emergence of modern science and industrialism are often regarded as European achievements, comparative education explorations make it clear that diverse educational contributions, such as mathematics from India and optical and medical science developed by Arabic scholars, were essential foundations for European science.[4]

COMPARATIVE EDUCATION IN THE 19TH CENTURY

Marc Antoine Jullien, who is often regarded as a founder of the field of comparative education, was born in 1775 and experienced the French Revolution as a teenager. Always a democrat in spirit and orientation, his liberal ideas were unacceptable to Napoleon, and he was given low-level positions in the inspectorate that required travel to Holland, Germany, and other countries of Europe. He became more and more interested in education, visiting progressive educators such as Johann Pestalozzi and Philipp von Fellenberg in Switzerland, and corresponding with leaders as distant as Czar Alexander of Russia and Thomas Jefferson of the United States.

After years of travel, observation, and writing, Jullien developed a plan for comparative education, which he published in 1817. In it, he called for the establishment of a Normal Institute of Education for Europe to educate teachers in the best-known methods of teaching on the continent. The institute was to publish a regular bulletin to encourage periodical communication among "all informed men engaged in the science of education."[5] It was also to stimulate the writing of "elementary books… in the different branches of science, which can direct childhood and youth from the first elements to the most advanced steps of human knowledge … by a continuous series of well-linked exercises."[6] Finally, education itself was to be developed into a "positive science" through the collection of facts and observations from different countries and their arrangement in analytical charts, which "permit them to be related and compared, to deduct from them certain principles.… " This would ensure that teachers were not "abandoned to narrow and limited rules, to the caprices and to arbitration of those who control [education].… "[7]

Jullien died in 1848, at the age of 73, never having realized this dream of an international institute for comparative education. Those who did carry forward the work of comparative education were mainly educators involved in developing new state systems of education, who looked to societies other than their own for ideas that would help in this process. Victor Cousin, who became minister of public instruction in France in 1840, found inspiration in the Prussian system of primary education and in approaches to technical education in Holland.[8] Horace Mann, who was the first secretary of the board of education of Massachusetts, made a six-month tour to Europe in 1843 and wrote a report comparing educational systems in Scotland, Ireland, France, Germany, Holland, and England. This report greatly influenced the development of common schools for all children in the United States.

K.D. Ushinsky, a Russian reformer who lived from 1824 to 1870, wrote extensively on educational practices in European countries and the United States, seeking to identify principles that would facilitate educational reform. Sir Michael Sadler, a British scholar and educator, was responsible for an Office of Special Reports for the British government between 1897 and 1903, which published studies of education in Germany, India, and many other countries. Sadler is best known for his insistence that educational institutions need to be understood first in relation to the culture and society in which they are found.[9]

While European, American, and Russian educators had a degree of freedom in their search for educational ideas outside of their own societies, Japanese and Chinese educators worked to create modern systems of education under a tremendous sense of threat and pressure. They saw modern education as essential for strengthening their nations from within, so that they could resist the forms of colonial domination and control that they saw imposed on many other regions of the world. In 1870, the Japanese government drafted a policy for sending students abroad that identified those areas of

> "We cannot wander at pleasure among the educational systems of the world, like a child strolling through a garden, and pick off a flower from one bush and some leaves from another, and then expect that if we stick what we have gathered into the soil at home, we shall have a living plant."[10]
> —Sir Michael Sadler

strength that Japan wished to emulate—engineering and commerce from Britain; medicine, economics, and some basic sciences from Germany; mathematics and basic sciences from France; architecture and shipbuilding from Holland; and agriculture from the United States.[11] This pragmatic form of comparative education laid a sound basis for Japan's economic development, while maintaining fundamental aspects of the Japanese spirit and cultural identity.

A few decades later, Chinese thinkers and educators also tried to study the educational systems of countries they might emulate and select those patterns that would help them establish a strong modern nation. Unfortunately, their political and economic progress was hindered by Japanese as well as Western imperialism. Nevertheless, they had the opportunity to experiment with educational patterns from Europe, Japan, and the United States. By contrast, places such as India, Vietnam, the Philippines, and much of Africa had modern education systems imposed by Western colonizers. A darker side to comparative education emerged through the increasing use of comparative research in the design and reform of colonial education in the early 20th century.[12]

COMPARATIVE EDUCATION IN THE FIRST HALF OF THE 20TH CENTURY

Only in the 20th century did comparative education begin to be taught in universities as an academic field of study, in spite of the fact that Jullien had laid a foundation for the field even earlier than Auguste Comte's work in founding sociology as a discipline. Many of the pioneering scholars of comparative education were either refugees or émigrés, who had personal experiences of education in several different societies. In England, Nicholas Hans wrote one of the early textbooks, in which he emphasized the importance of understanding factors such as religion, language, geography, and economy, which shaped the educational patterns of each nation differently. Hans had left Russia and moved to London at the time of the Soviet revolution of 1917. He maintained a great interest in Soviet education and society, nevertheless, and his comparative analysis of national education systems included England, France, the Soviet Union, and the United States.[13]

The counterpart to Hans in the United States was Isaac Kandel, who was the leading comparativist at Teachers College, Columbia

University, from 1921 to the early 1950s. Kandel was born in Romania and completed a master's degree at Manchester University in England. He then emigrated to the United States and completed a doctorate under John Dewey at Columbia University. Like Hans, Kandel hoped to see comparative education develop as a positive science, with appropriate use of statistical data on education in various countries of the world. He emphasized the importance of understanding the contexts of education in different societies, especially the impact of different political systems on educational development. He felt the distinction between highly centralized systems of education, such as that of the Soviet Union, and decentralized ones, such as that of the United States, was of great significance. His comparative education yearbook, first published in 1933, covered education in England, France, Italy, Germany, the Soviet Union, and the United States.[14]

Kandel also identified what was to become a central issue within the study of comparative education: the importance of education in the construction of world peace (dealt with by Kathy Bickmore in Chapter Ten of this volume). At the end of World War I, women's suffrage organizations, international teachers' associations, and progressive educators each advocated the formation of an educational body within the League of Nations, to promote peace through international understanding and the expansion of educational opportunity. Among them were two women, Beatrice Ensor of England and Elisabeth Rotton of Germany, who went on to found the International League for New Education in 1921, and to promote the Geneva Declaration for the Rights of the Child in 1922. Comparative and progressive educators on both sides of the Atlantic were convinced that educational systems had played a part in the development of what Kandel described as the "sinister" forms of nationalism that lead to war.[15] British and American governments, however, rejected an educational role for the League, arguing that education was a purely national concern.

Despite the absence of a footing inside the League of Nations, progressive educators went on to build the first international educational organization. Founded in 1929 and based in Geneva, the International Bureau of Education (IBE) came into being as an independent professional organization whose goals included the promotion of public education for all and the enhancement of education for international understanding. Operating under the leadership of noted Swiss psychologist Jean Piaget from 1929 to 1967, with Spanish comparative educator Pedro Rossello as vice-director, the IBE gained the status of an intergovernmental organization and developed many of the functions later taken on by UNESCO after World War II. It hosted an annual conference on public education that brought together leaders from national educational systems, and collected and published educational statistics from as many nations as were willing to contribute information. In 1933, it launched an *International Yearbook of Education* as well as four bulletins per year.[16]

Published histories of comparative education between the two World Wars have tended to focus on prominent scholars in Europe and North America, yet in this period comparative education was also being developed and taught in other parts of the world. The first comparative education textbook in the Chinese language, for example, was published in 1928, five years before Kandel's famous textbook. It was written by Zhuang Zexuan, a professor of education at Zhejiang University. Three other books on comparative education were published in China between 1930 and 1934, showing the great importance this field was given in Chinese universities of the time.[17] Like Hans and Kandel, Chinese scholars were trying to understand the broad principles of education that could be learned from comparative study. They also had urgent concerns about China's survival as a modern nation. Many Chinese educators had studied with John Dewey at Columbia or at other American universities, and there was huge interest in progressive child-centred education, with many experimental schools established in the Chinese coastal regions. However, it was extremely difficult for these ideas to be widely disseminated in circumstances of national economic collapse and a looming military invasion by Japan.

Chinese educators were also interested in the centralized French system of education, since France had succeeded in spreading educational facilities throughout its country. This was a matter of great concern for China, where most of the modern schools were located in coastal areas and hinterland areas lagged far behind. At the same time, educators feared their nationalist government would use educational centralization as a means to suppress freedom of thought and to exert direct political control over schools. Comparative education studies provided important contextual analysis to help them wrestle with these difficult questions.

COMPARATIVE AND INTERNATIONAL EDUCATION IN THE SECOND HALF OF THE 20TH CENTURY

After World War II, comparative education developed very rapidly as a field of research and practice. The development of the United Nations Educational, Scientific, and Cultural Organization (UNESCO), founded in 1945, and the gradual inclusion of education in the work of other international development organizations, such as the World Bank, UNICEF, the United States Agency for International Development, and the Canadian International Development Agency, created a new demand for comparative educational research. The Comparative and International Education Society (CIES) of the United States was founded in 1956, and many other national societies came into being in subsequent years. In 1970, the first World Congress of Comparative Education Societies was held at the University of Ottawa, with the official founding of the World Council of Comparative Education Societies that same year.[18] In addition to the many national societies that belong to the World Council, regional comparative education societies such as the Comparative Education Society in Europe and the Comparative Education Society of Asia are also members. Many national societies have their own academic journals, and participate actively in various kinds of international work, including liaising with such international organizations as UNESCO. Because they give equal importance to the academic work of comparative education analysis and to active involvement in international development concerns, many have broadened their description of the field by using the term *comparative and international education.*

The intellectual development of comparative education after World War II reflects the developments that one can see in such major social science disciplines as sociology, political science, and anthropology. From 1945 to 1970, its focus was almost entirely on the relationship between education and national development. Great attention was given to ensuring that comparative education be made fully "scientific," given the availability of more reliable and comprehensive educational statistics and the possibility of large-scale quantitative analysis using computers. This positivistic phase gave rise to lively debates about the purpose and method of the field.

By the mid-1970s, however, it became clear that many of the findings of comparative education had limited relevance for developing nations of the Third World. Though most had gained political independence, their educational systems were still dominated by the ideas and influences of former colonial powers. Dependency theory or world systems theory, both rooted in neo-Marxist scholarship, helped to identify barriers to independent and culturally authentic educational development in the context of a world capitalist system.

In more recent years, processes of globalization, along with the collapse of the Soviet Union in 1991, have spawned a new era of contention in the field of comparative education. For two centuries, comparative education tended to draw its analytic frameworks from Western civilization. In the most recent period, however, comparative education has emerged as a stage for an enhanced dialogue among peoples and civilizations. Examples of this are evident in many chapters of this textbook, which bring forth perspectives from Indigenous peoples, women, and multicultural communities, as well as different geographical regions, such as Africa, Asia, and Latin America. Current debates are coloured by theories of postmodernity and post-colonialism, as well as by heightened awareness of global topics such as equality, peace, and cultural and ecological sustainability.

The brief overview of three widely debated approaches to comparative education that follows offers a critical perspective on its literature.

Comparative Education as Science?

One of the most influential comparative educators of the early post-war period was George Bereday, an immigrant from Poland, who succeeded Isaac Kandel at Teachers College, Columbia University. His 1964 textbook, *Comparative Method in Education*, laid out a systematic approach to collecting facts about different educational systems, juxtaposing them in tables or diagrammatic representation, and then identifying principles or laws of education and societal development through inductive logic. Bereday recognized the difficulties of collecting comparable data and emphasized the need for comparative education researchers to learn the languages of the societies they studied and to limit their analyses to four or five countries. His book included comparative analyses of educational issues in Poland, the United States, the Soviet Union, England, France, Germany, and Columbia.[19]

Bereday stimulated others in turn to reflect on how comparative education could become a science. In 1969, Harold Noah and Max

Eckstein, two scholars who had emigrated to the United States from the United Kingdom, published an influential book entitled *Towards a Science of Comparative Education*. In this book, they proposed an approach to comparative education using educational data from a large number of countries to discover causal relationships between desired educational outcomes and the educational and societal inputs that were responsible for them. The more countries whose data could be used for these large-scale studies, the more "scientifically" reliable would be the findings, they suggested. With the dawning of the computer age, it was believed that the essential data about education and its relation to societal development could be quantified and expressed numerically, with lessening importance given to studying the languages and historical contexts of different education systems.[20]

Two major questions have occupied the attention of comparative educators working in this positivistic mode from the 1960s to the present time. The first explores the relation between education and economic development. What kinds of investment in "human capital" will produce the highest "social rates of return" (benefit to the economy) or "individual rates of return" (income for the individual)? (See Chapters Three and Nine for further discussions on human capital.) Economists are also interested in cost-benefit analysis and what are called "production function" studies, in which the unit costs of inputs are weighted against the outputs of schools. For example, is teacher training or the purchase of textbooks a better investment? These types of study are of particular importance for development agencies, such as the World Bank, whose educational loans are premised on successful economic outcomes and the ability of the borrowing country to pay back the loans over time. In spite of increasingly sophisticated scientific techniques of analysis, however, these studies are far from precise.

The second question, which is of even greater interest to educators, is what factors in both school and society have a significant causal relationship with higher levels of educational achievement. What teaching styles produce the best results in mathematics? What size of class is optimal for high achievement in physics? What types of curricular organization result in most effective language learning? Beginning in the 1960s, the International Association for the Evaluation of Educational Achievement (IEA) began a series of studies to address these questions. Over the years, more and more countries have participated, and alternative international studies of achievement, such as the Programme for International Student Assessment (PISA) have been developed. Chapter Eight of this text, by Karen Mundy and Joseph P. Farrell, introduces the methods and findings of these large-scale cross-national studies.

Not all comparativists of the 1960s and 1970s agreed that comparative education should try to become "scientific" in its methodology. British scholar Edmund King believed that human society could not be compared with the workings of a machine. He proposed that it was more like the exchange of ideas in a conversation than the interaction of forces in a physical system. Thus, he put great emphasis on a comparative understanding of core concepts of education in different societies and nations.

> "It is not only the top-level planner who is so engaged nowadays, but the teacher in the classroom too, and also the parent or politician or employer who may be no expert in comparative studies per se, but who has an experiential contribution to make to the world's comparative analysis."[21]
>
> —Edmund King

King's textbook, _Other Schools and Ours,_ was first published in 1962 and reappeared in five subsequent editions. He dealt with Denmark, France, the United Kingdom, the United States, the Soviet Union, India, and Japan in this text.[22] In his approach to research, King rejected the ostensible neutrality and objectivity that characterized scientific method, and emphasized subjective understanding of the hopes and expectations of teachers, students, and administrators as vitally important inputs for educational policy. In the early 1970s, he carried out a large-scale comparative study of schools, teachers, and students in England, France, Germany, Italy, and Sweden, with a focus on gathering ideas for a new approach to post-compulsory education. This was a time when universities were still highly elitist institutions admitting only about 2 percent of young people aged 18 and older.[23]

Although King was not an anthropologist, his attention to the ways in which students and teachers understood and constructed their social worlds anticipated the kinds of approaches to social theory associated with phenomenology and ethnography. One of the most influential comparative educators of a later period, Canadian scholar Vandra

Lea Masemann, developed an ethnographic approach to comparative education, which attends to the ways in which human beings create meaning through education in different cultural contexts.

> "[A]ttempts to equalize educational opportunity on a global scale have led to the ignoring of local cultural values and traditional forms of knowledge and ways of thinking, which are in danger of becoming extinct."[24]
>
> —Vandra Lea Masemann

Masemann describes her approach to comparative education as critical ethnography: she views neo-Marxism as an essential frame for a critical analysis of oppressive structures in the global economic system whose influence reaches right down to local schools.[25] In recent years, there has been increasing attention given to what actually happens within schools, including the organization of learning, teaching practices, and efforts at school improvement. This can be seen in Chapter Five by Joseph P. Farrell, Chapter Six by Sarfaroz Niyozov, and Chapter Seven by Stephen Anderson.

Another challenge to comparative education as a "science" came from Brian Holmes. He did not reject scientific method, but claimed that Bereday, Noah, and Eckstein were following too absolute an approach to the discovery of scientific fact. Holmes developed what he described as the "problem approach" to comparative education, which followed Karl Popper's idea of science as a series of imaginative conjectures that are subjected to rigorous ongoing testing in the specific conditions of the laboratory experiment. Hypotheses that survive rigorous testing can be considered tentatively true until such time as they are proven false.[26] Holmes felt comparative educators should identify important problems in education, look for solutions in the experiences of different societies, then predict which solutions would produce desirable educational results in the specific conditions of one society. These predictions would be tested not in the laboratory, but in the future unfolding of educational developments. For Holmes, the most significant elements in these specific conditions were cultural. He suggested ideal types as a sociological tool for taking into account deep-rooted religious and cultural beliefs about human persons, the nature of society, and the nature of knowledge. He thus developed a methodology that he regarded as scientific in a post-positivist way and that gave great importance to nonquantifiable religious and cultural values.[27]

Lê Thàn Khôi and Gu Mingyuan challenged the limited notion of comparative education as science from a different direction by demonstrating the deep historical and cultural roots of non-Western educational systems — systems that could not be simply re-engineered through positive science. Both come from East Asia: Lê from Vietnam and Gu from China. Whereas Lê has spent much of his career in France and has written mainly in French, Gu studied in the Soviet Union in the 1950s, then returned to China to revive the field of comparative education there, beginning in the early 1960s.

Lê's work suggests that comparative education could make possible a general theory of education derived from an in-depth study of the reciprocal relations between education and society in different types of civilizations over human history. Such a theory would achieve a universalism that acknowledges how the achievements of modernity were derived from multiple civilizations, not only that of Europe. Lê's approach to comparative education thus looks back into history and recovers aspects of human heritage that have been forgotten in the rush to constitute comparative education as a science.[28]

Gu's approach to comparative education developed in a very different context. He entered university in the year of China's successful Communist revolution. After two years of study in Beijing, he was sent to study in the Lenin Normal College in Moscow for five years. On return to China in 1955, he was full of enthusiasm for all that Soviet ideas could offer to China's socialist educational development, only to face disappointments and setback as China's new leaders rejected Soviet assistance as social imperialism in 1958 and threw the country into turmoil by unleashing a cultural revolution in 1966. The centre and journal that Gu had established for the study of foreign education in the early 1960s were closed down, and he was sent for hard labour in the countryside. Only after Deng Xiaoping came to power in 1978 was he able to draw upon his extensive comparative knowledge of education systems in different parts of the world to advise China's leadership on educational reforms that would make possible the modernization of China's economy and society.[29]

Gu's first approach was to introduce human capital theory to China, showing how this concept was relevant to socialist as well as capitalist countries and could be traced back to *Das Kapital* by Karl Marx. Gu presented a comparative analysis, drawing on extensive empirical data, of the modernization experiences of Western countries and the Soviet Union. On this basis, he persuaded the Chinese government to invest heavily in education.[30] Gu's scientific approach to comparative education proved liberating to Chinese educators who had long felt themselves the victims of political movements outside of their control. They were delighted to be freed from "the caprices and ... arbitration of those who control education," to use a phase from Jullien's *Plan for Comparative Education*.[31]

Gu was not satisfied, however, to stay with this Western approach to comparative education. He developed a long-term research project to explore China's own cultural and educational traditions and to identify educational patterns and ideas that would provide an indigenous basis for China's educational modernization.[32] He has also stimulated Chinese educators to reach out to the world and explain the unique educational ethos of East Asian countries where Confucian traditions have been strong, and what this ethos can offer to educators elsewhere. Chapter Two of this volume, by Ruth Hayhoe, deals with this topic from a comparative philosophical perspective.

Comparative Education, Imperialism, and the World System

In 1974, a book entitled *Education as Cultural Imperialism* by Martin Carnoy exploded like a bombshell in comparative education circles. Up to this time, the main units of comparative education analyses had been nation-states and national systems of education, with educational systems in Europe and North America tending to dominate the literature. Carnoy's book showed how difficult it was for nations in the Third World to develop modern schools to serve their own social, political, and economic development.

Carnoy believed that much that went on in schools in Africa, India, and Southeast Asia was not decided by their own educators but was determined by the languages, curricular patterns, and approaches to school organization that had been left behind by their colonizers. Educational policy was also shaped by ongoing dependence on development aid, which was described as a form of "neo-colonialism."

Dependency theory is a form of neo-Marxism that was developed by economists in Latin America to explain the widespread experience of underdevelopment or distorted development in countries of that region. Underdevelopment, they believed, was caused by their countries' peripheral roles in a world economic system controlled by centre countries in Europe and North America. Education systems, dominated by the European concepts they had inherited, served to make this subservience appear a normal and unavoidable stage of development. The Brazilian educator Paulo Freire was one of the first to challenge this educational imperialism. With his idea of "conscientization," he sought to stimulate Latin American young people and adults to see with their own eyes

> "Neo-classical development theory views schooling as being a 'liberating process,' in which the child is transformed from a 'traditional' individual to a 'modern' one…. But in dependency theory, the transformation that takes place in school cannot be liberating, since a person is simply changed from one role in a dependent system to a different role … The kind of economic structure able to absorb all the educated is not possible under conditions of the dependent situation. Thus a system of schooling which complements all people's social utility is also not possible."[33]
>
> —Martin Carnoy

and to struggle for independence, dignity, and self-determination.[34] Freire's work has had wide-ranging influence, most notably among educators interested in transformative and liberatory approaches to learning.[35] The spread of Freirean pedagogy illustrates an important development in the field of comparative education: the expansion of South-North flows of educational ideas.

Scholars such as Robert F. Arnove, Philip Altbach, Gail P. Kelly, and Nelly P. Stromquist all contributed to this more critical approach to comparative education. Arnove worked to relate comparative education to world systems theory, another form of neo-Marxism that is based in a historical analysis of the development of the capitalist world system, and which looks at the way core, semiperipheral, and peripheral regions are shaped by economic and capital flows.[36] Kelly is recognized as one of the early women pioneers in the field of comparative education. As co-editor with Altbach of the important book *Education and the Colonial Experience,* she built on her early research on education in Vietnam and French West Africa, where one could see the persisting influence of French colonial influences, to develop a critical approach to education in Third World countries.[37] She also became a leading figure in feminist approaches to comparative education, editing several important studies on women in education in different parts of the world.[38] Similarly, Stromquist sought to blend dependency and feminist theories, documenting the nature of gender inequality in education first in Latin America and later at the global level.[39] Grace Mak has carried forward this work in Asia, with titles such as *Women, Education and Development in Asia: Cross-National Perspectives.*[40] Chapter Nine of this vol-ume, Gender and Education, by Kara Janigan and Vandra Lea Masemann deals with this literature.

Another critical approach to problems of education and imperialism came from a group of scholars who initiated the World Order Models Project (WOMP) in the late 1960s and described themselves as non-Marxist socialists. Johan Galtung, a Norwegian who held one of the world's first chairs in peace studies, developed a structural theory of imperialism. He identified structures of domination in political, economic, communications, and cultural arenas and proposed ways of countering them through solidarity among Third World nations.[42] Galtung's pioneering work on peace was also picked up by comparative educators, as can be seen in Kathy Bickmore's Chapter Ten in this volume.

"For feminist scholars of education in the third world, our goal is to find ways in which schools can be made a force to better women's lives."[41]

—Gail P. Kelly

The loosely organized group of sociologists, educators, and political scientists associated with the WOMP created space for visioning a more just and sustainable world order. They brought ideas from the civilizations of India and Africa into the mainstream of Western social sciences. While there were not many comparative education scholars among them, one article that became a classic in the field was Ali Mazrui's "The African University as a Multinational Corporation."[43] The more recent scholarship of George J.S. Dei, with its focus on understanding the roots of African culture and spirituality as a source for educational innovation, is another important contribution to the goal of intercivilizational dialogue and sustainability envisaged by the WOMP scholars.[44]

Globalization and Comparative Education

Perhaps more than any other theme, globalization has provoked expanding interest and lush debate within the field of comparative education. Most definitions of globalization begin with the idea that the integration of human societies across pre-existing territorial units has sped up, assisted in part by the development of new information, communication, and transportation technologies that compress time and space.[45] For some authors, the main motor of integration is economic — the expansion of truly global chains of commercialized production and consumption and the development of a knowledge economy. Others focus on the cultural and political drivers that transcend and subvert nation-state borders. Whatever the focus, central to all theories of globalization is the notion that interregional and "deterritorialized" flows of all kinds of social interaction have reached new magnitudes in recent history. Conceptually, globalization challenges comparative education's traditional focus on national systems of education. It also creates new opportunities for understanding those aspects of the educational enterprise that transcend national borders.

Several dimensions of engagement with the issue of globalization in the field of comparative education are worth highlighting. First, comparativists have been at the forefront of scholarship that shows how economic globalization has contributed to increasing fiscal constraint among states — with profound implications for the funding and organization of national systems of education.[46] Escalating pressures for the expansion of free trade and global competition have forced national governments in all parts of the world to reposition their economies. They find themselves under pressure to view education more as an investment in human capital for competitiveness than as part of a range of measures of social provision and protection to ensure the welfare of all citizens. Economic globalization raises demand for skills and qualifications, but reduces the state's capacity to meet it. This creates new openings for the expansion of private educational services, particularly at higher levels, and new incentives for efficiency reforms at lower levels. Reduced budgets and increased migration and cultural exchange have also challenged the state's ability to use education to achieve social cohesion.[47]

Many scholars in comparative education have begun to document how a common set of educational reforms, organized around goals of market-like accountability and efficiency, have spread around the world.[48] In this volume, Chapter Seven by Stephen Anderson and Chapter Eight by Karen Mundy and Joseph P. Farrell explore two aspects of these global reform agendas—the heightened effort to engineer school effectiveness and improvement, and the expansion of international testing regimes. Comparativists have also studied the expanding influence of key intergovernmental organizations, such as the Organisation for Economic Co-operation and Development (OECD), the World Bank, and the World Trade Organization (WTO), as well as regional organizations such as the European Community and the Association of Southeast Asian Nations (ASEAN).[49] They have begun to make sense of transnational movements—for example, the growth of transnational social movements, teachers unions, and non-governmental organizations (NGOs) advocating for a universal right to education,[50] and the implications of expanding transnational flows of students and transborder delivery of services in higher education.

The infusion of postmodernism and post-colonial theories into the field of comparative education has profoundly shaped the field's engagement with the concept of globalization. Postmodern and post-colonial theories challenge the assumption that globalization is mainly an economic process. Instead, globalization is understood as a cultural process, in which Western modernity, science, and rationality play a powerful role in the subjugation of other peoples and cultures.[51] In turn, postmodern and post-colonial scholars focus attention on the subversive and hybrid nature of local responses to cultural globalization, using ethnographic and subjective approaches to research.[52] In the recent work of Kathryn Anderson-Levitt, Michel Welmond, Anne Hickling Hudson, and Amy Stambach, among others, we see how local communities engage and reshape globalization in the everyday practices surrounding the school.[53] In comparative education, postmodern and post-colonial scholarship has promoted the inclusion of diverse perspectives and ways of knowing, drawing upon Freirian pedagogy, transformative learning, and the experiences of Indigenous cultures. Chapter Four by Katherine Madjidi and Jean-Paul Restoule and Chapter Nine by Kara Janigan and Vandra Lea Masemann will bring forth some of these perspectives by highlighting the comparative study of Indigenous ways of knowing and learning and of gender in education.

Today, most research in comparative education still acknowledges the importance of national governments in shaping the educational destinies of the world's people. However, globalization has stoked interest in what Arnove and Torres have described as the "dialectic between the local and the global."[54] The field is now animated by questions of whether and why systems of education are homogenizing or retaining their local characteristics,[55] and whether national educational systems can enhance social equality and social cohesion in the context of globalization.[56] Mundy (Chapter Three), Farrell (Chapter Five), and Niyozov (Chapter Six) each tackle these questions in this volume by looking at the rise and spread of a global "Education for All" movement, alternatives to traditional schooling, and the influences of developing country cultural contexts on teaching practices. We will also learn how East Asian countries have shaped their response to globalization in Chapter Two, by Hayhoe.

Comparativists remain deeply concerned with the role that education can play in the normative construction of society both globally and locally. They continue to explore educational practices that can enhance opportunities for dialogue among peoples, cultures, societies, and civilizations, and pedagogies to prepare active, self-reflexive global citizens. The growing comparative study of civics and moral education, conflict and peace education, and education for global citizenship has reached an all-time high, as illustrated in Chapter Ten by Kathy Bickmore and Chapter Eleven by Mark Evans.[57] Here, the heritage of Freire, Galtung, and the children's rights activist Beatrice Ensor are taken up alongside complex issues of globalization, global conflict, and global inequality.

●———————————●

QUESTIONS FOR REFLECTION AND DISCUSSION

1. What experiences of cross-cultural learning are you aware of from ancient or medieval history? In what ways is comparing a natural aspect of human learning? Compare this to the ways cross-cultural learning might arise in today's classrooms and news media.

2.   What role has human immigration played in comparative educa-
     tion? What role do you think it plays in the present period? Why
     or why not?
3.   Which names of educators and educational issues in this chapter
     were already familiar to you? Which of those new to you attract
     your interest, and why?

SUGGESTED FILM: *GOING TO THE SEA*, BY JOCELYN CULLITY AND PRAKASH YOUNGER

This film is a documentary about two Canadians living in Dalian,
China, in 1993. As English instructors to future teachers at Liaoning
Normal University, Jocelyn Cullity and Prakash Younger find during
their year-long stay that the university and the city are undergoing
major economic and social changes. The shift from Maoist Marxism to
a market economy in China plays a serious role in the futures of the
students and fellow faculty at Liaoning Normal University.

SUGGESTIONS FOR FURTHER READING

Anderson-Levitt, Kathryn. *Local Meanings, Global Schooling: Anthropology
    and World Culture Theory* (New York: Palgrave Macmillan, 2003).
Arnove, Robert F. and Carlos A. Torres, eds. *Comparative Education:
    The Dialectic of the Global and the Local* (Lanham, MD: Rowman and
    Littlefield, 1999).
*Arnove, Robert F. "Comparative Education and World Systems
    Analysis." *Comparative Education Review* 24, no. 1 (1980): 48–62.
Ball, Stephen. "Big Policies/Small World: An Introduction to
    International Perspectives in Education Policy." *Comparative
    Education* 34, no. 2 (1998): 119–30.
Dei, George J. S. "Learning Culture, Spirituality and Local Knowledge:
    Implications for African Schooling." *International Review of Education*
    48, no. 5 (2002): 335–60.
Hickling-Hudson, Anne. "Cultural Complexity, Post-Colonialism and
    Educational Change: Challenges for Comparative Educators."
    International Review of Education 52, no. 1 (2006): 201–18.
* Lê Thàn Khôi. "Toward a General Theory of Education." *Comparative
    Education Review* 30, no. 1 (1986): 12–29.

Masemann, Vandra. "Culture and Education." In *Comparative Education: The Dialectic of the Global and the Local*, edited by Robert F. Arnove and Carlos A. Torres. Lanham, MD: Rowman and Littlefield, 1999, 115–33.

*Mundy, Karen. "Globalization and Educational Change: New Policy Worlds." In *International Handbook of Educational Policy, Volume II*, edited by Nina Bascia, Alister Cumming, Kenneth A. Leithwood and David Livingstone. Netherlands: Springer, 2005, 3–17.

Schugurensky, Daniel. "The Legacy of Paulo Freire." *Convergence* 31, no. 1–2 (1998): 17–29.

Chapter Two

Philosophy and Comparative Education: What Can We Learn from East Asia?

Ruth Hayhoe

INTRODUCTION

This chapter begins with some reflections on philosophy and comparative education. The philosophical ideas of East Asia are taken as an "other," from which to look comparatively at some of the fundamental values that underlie educational thought in the West. Given the history of European colonization, and the attraction European models had for modernizing countries that were never colonized, these values became the foundations for modern systems of education. State schooling systems were first put in place in newly emerging European nations of the 18th and 19th centuries, as we have seen in Chapter One.

Ideal types will facilitate this comparative reflection on Europe and East Asia. They were developed by German sociologist Max Weber, as a way of identifying and reflecting on the distinctive contributions of differing religious and philosophical value systems to the process of social change. Weber defined ideal types as "an attempt to analyse historically unique configurations ... by means of genetic concepts."[1] He suggested that they should be constructed with a high degree of logical integration for adequacy of meaning. Brian Holmes pioneered their use in comparative education as a way of probing the value orientations of different education systems.

Part one of this chapter gives a comparative overview of ideas of society, knowledge, and the human person in classical China and Europe. It highlights the profoundly different implications of these philosophical traditions for education. The underlying values of two important models of modern education, the American and the Soviet, are also presented.

Part two traces the historical development of modern educational systems in East Asia, showing how they absorbed the Western patterns that had been borrowed or imposed. Japan was the first to surprise the world, with its remarkable recovery after World War II and the development of a strong economy and democratic polity. It was followed by the "four little dragons" of South Korea, Taiwan, Singapore, and Hong Kong, whose development stimulated lively debates over an emerging East Asian model of capitalism.[2] Subsequently, mainland China and Vietnam adopted the idea of a "socialist market economy" and achieved remarkable reforms.

Part three offers reflections on East Asia's modern educational experience within the three paradigms of comparative education that have been introduced in Chapter One: comparative education as a science, comparative education and imperialism, and comparative education and globalization. In taking each framework as a lens to analyse the East Asian experience, we will discover similarities and differences with education in other parts of the world. We will also explore some fascinating paradoxes that reflect philosophical differences between East Asia and the West.

Part four addresses the important question of what the West can learn from the educational ideas of East Asian societies, which have developed under diverse experiences of imperialism, colonialism, capitalism, and socialism, yet shared a common Confucian heritage. With the end of the Cold War, and the beginning of a dialogue among civilizations, there is finally space for the inheritors and admirers of East Asian civilization to introduce its educational values to the global community. The same is true for other civilizations, such as those of Africa (Chapter Three) and the Islamic world (Chapter Six). Later chapters of this text will explore some of their unique contributions to educational thought.

COMPARING CHINESE AND WESTERN EDUCATIONAL VALUES

Holmes suggested the use of ideal types as a way of identifying contrasting values about society, knowledge, and the human person. In his 1983 textbook, he sketched out ideal types for comparing European, Soviet, and American education by summarizing the views of Plato,

Karl Marx, and John Dewey on these three subjects.[3] Holmes was fully aware of the extreme generality of these types. His purpose was not to simplify complex educational phenomena, but rather to identify differences, and interpret educational debates at a profound level.

Here we will give brief consideration to the ideas of the Greek philosopher Plato (427–347 BCE), which had a long-lasting influence on the development of European education. We will view them in comparison to Chinese classical thought, which was shaped primarily by Confucius (551–479 BCE), Mencius (372–289 BCE), and Xun Zi (340–245 BCE); also by the moderating influences of Lao Zi, the founder of Daoism; and by the ideas of Buddhism, a religion that was introduced to China from India in the first century CE.

In his wonderfully reflective volume, *The World of Thought in Ancient China*, Benjamin Schwartz explains the ideas of society, knowledge, and the human person in the dominant Chinese tradition, showing how different they were from parallel ideas in Europe. In Confucian thought, the ideal family is "the ultimate source of those values which humanise the relations of authority and hierarchy which must exist in any civilised society."[4]

In the family, human beings learn those virtues that redeem society. Authority comes to be accepted and exercised through the binding power of religious, moral sentiments based on kinship ties. The rites or ceremonies established by the classical texts thus hold together an entire normative order, which is derived from the relations of the ideal family. This concept of social order was accepted and embraced across the entire Chinese mainland, as well as emulated by such nearby societies as Korea, Japan, and Vietnam.

By contrast, in the city states of Greece, Plato outlined the good society as one that was ruled by guardians or "philosopher-kings." They belonged to the highest of three classes of people, with warriors maintaining order and workers seeing to the mundane needs of society. The philosopher-kings accepted a pattern of life having no place for the family, which was viewed as particularistic and limited in its moral value. They were devoted to a vision of good that was attained through abstract mathematical thought rather than practical life experience. By the same token, the good society was to be regulated by impartial laws, ensuring the fair and just treatment of each individual according to their place in a fixed social order.[5] Schwartz suggests one of the reasons for this fundamental difference in emphasis lay in the character and size of the Greek city state, as against the size of the Chinese empire.[6]

Confucius viewed knowledge as beginning with the empirical cumulative understanding of masses of particulars, then linking these particulars to one's own experience, and subsequently to an underlying unity that tied everything together. By contrast, Plato saw knowledge as created through mathematical reasoning and the perception of eternal abstract forms, something that only philosopher-kings could do, through a rigorous process of deductive logic. Knowledge had to rise above the limits of ordinary human experience for Plato. For Confucius, knowledge "does not rise from the chaos of the world of particulars to a world of eternal forms, since ... the way remains indissolubly linked to the empirical world."[7]

As for the human person, Confucius called for a lifelong pursuit of human heartedness, a learning for the sake of the self. The self, however, was viewed as a flowing stream, and human development as a way of harmonizing the self with the family, society, and the world of nature.[8] Traditional Chinese society had four classes — scholar-officials, merchants, craftspeople, and farmers — yet Confucius made the important statement that in education there are no class distinctions, and stressed the unlimited potential of each person for development through education. Later philosophers debated whether human nature was fundamentally good, as proposed by Mencius, or basically evil and needing to be controlled by law and punishment, as taught by Xun Zi. Nevertheless, all agreed on the importance of education. "The concept that everyone is educable, everyone can become a sage, and everyone is perfectible forms the basic optimism and dynamism towards education in the Confucian tradition."[9]

By contrast, Plato's view of the human person put more emphasis on innate characteristics, and suggested that human beings were born to be philosopher-kings, warriors, or workers, and should be educated to fulfill their ordained role, in order that a society of justice and order could be maintained. Intelligence was not only inborn, but also passed on by heredity. The philosopher-kings were therefore given favourable conditions to ensure the continuance of a line of "superior" leaders. The ideal society maintained the distinction among the three classes, and there was no encouragement to educate either workers or warriors in ways that would enable them to become leaders.[10]

Plato's ideas were challenged almost immediately in the work of his disciple Aristotle (383–322 BCE) and that of many later educators. Yet they expressed an idea that has persisted in Western educational thought—that there are certain innate qualities and abilities that no amount of education can change. By contrast, the Confucian view of the human person emphasizes the perfectibility of each person, if maximum effort is put into learning, and with full support from family and community.

This Chinese conviction about human potential was further strengthened by Daoist ideas put forward in Lao Zi's *Classic of the Way and Virtue*, which emphasized the relationship between human persons and the world of nature.[11] (For a discussion of similar educational worldviews from an Indigenous perspective, see Chapter Four in this volume.) Buddhism was later introduced to China from India and strengthened the Daoist understanding of the interconnection between human psychology and the natural world. It envisions a society where there are neither social nor cultural identities among its members.[12]

The main motivation for learning in Chinese culture was an intrinsic one, learning for the sake of the self, to develop one's full humanity. See Figure 2.1 for Confucius' autobiography. There was also an extrinsic motivation for learning in the famous civil service examination system. It offered the opportunity for all male children to demonstrate their knowledge and ability through a series of written examinations held at local, provincial, and capital levels throughout the empire. Those who succeeded in these examinations were given the opportunity to serve as scholar-officials. The competition for such opportunities was fierce, yet

---

Figure 2.1
Confucius' Autobiography[14]

At fifteen, my heart and mind were set on learning.
At thirty I took my stance.
At forty I was no longer of two minds.
At fifty I understood Heaven's place for me.
At sixty my ear was attuned.
At seventy I could give my heart-and-mind free reign without
    overstepping the mark.

---

there was a significant record of social mobility in traditional Chinese society. Nearly every village had at least one historical example of a boy whose study efforts had enabled him to reach the top.[13]

By contrast, oral rather than written examinations were used in traditional European education. The medieval universities gained papal charters for a degree of autonomy and academic freedom, but their students were largely male clerics. Only with the Protestant Reformation were opportunities for literacy and self-advancement opened up to wider populations, beyond the land-owning aristocracy. When European Jesuits went to China in the 16th century, they were greatly impressed by the Chinese system of government. They wrote admiring accounts of educational practices that enabled the emperor to draw upon talented people from all classes who had been educated to a very high level.[15]

To complete the circle of comparison between East Asia and the West, we will consider two other ideal types. Dewey's idea of society, knowledge, and the human person gives insight into the fundamental values underlying American education, which would influence Japan, South Korea, and Taiwan. Marx's ideal society found expression in the patterns of modern Soviet education, and from there influenced such socialist countries as China and Vietnam.

In contrast to Plato's static view, Dewey saw society as being in continuous change, and democracy as "a mode of associated living, of conjoint, communicated experience."[16] Human beings, as members of society, should jointly find solutions for the problems that emerged in social development through the application of a scientific understanding of the natural and social worlds. Dewey believed that intelligence could grow, as the individual grew, and that "the basic freedom is the freedom of mind and of whatever degree of freedom of action and experience is necessary to produce freedom of intelligence."[17] Dewey saw the future as open, for people to create according to individual or shared visions.

Dewey viewed the human person less as an individual with intrinsic rights and abilities than as "an organism continuously interacting with a natural environment." "The individual and the social should not be set against each other as separate entities, for without one the other has no existence. Therefore, under changing circumstances individuality takes on new forms, and in doing so, further modifies the circumstances."[18]

Holmes defined Dewey's ideal person as a reflective individual in a changing environment.

Dewey's idea of knowledge was strikingly different from Plato's. Knowledge is advanced through problem solving in the social or natural world, and predictions about the most effective solutions to problems are tested by experience. There is no authoritative body of knowledge, but established disciplines should be taught "in connection with [their] bearing upon the creation and growth of the kind of power of observation, inquiry, reflection, and testing that are the heart of scientific intelligence."[19]

Marx's view of human society also emphasized change, a process of movement from capitalist to socialist to Communist forms of society determined by a science of history. With the revolutionary overthrow of capitalism, it was thought possible to construct a socialist polity under working class rule, with the Communist party as its vanguard. The abolition of private property and the shared ownership of the means of production was to make possible an egalitarian society, in which all worked according to their ability and had their needs provided for collectively.

Within Communist society, human persons were to be educated and re-educated, until their consciousness was freed from the exploitative social relations of the prior capitalist society. Each person could then serve the best interests of the collective in the distinctive roles and functions assigned to them by the state, and enjoy the benefits of an equitable set of social relations. The human person was thus seen as part of a collective that was defined by class identity, rather than by a relationship within family, community, or the world of nature.

Within Soviet Communism, knowledge was seen as encyclopedic, embracing all of the subject matter developed over human history. Thus, the major subject disciplines developed in 19th-century Europe were preserved in the curricula of secondary and tertiary institutions. This knowledge was to be applied to the many-faceted task of socialist construction, and the model for education was described as polytechnical. Substantive knowledge of the basic scientific theories underlying a wide range of technologies was to make possible an understanding of the entire cycle of production.[20]

We can see how these three ideal types — the Platonic, the Deweyan, and the Marxist — interfaced with Chinese ideas in distinctive ways.

Plato's picture of a fixed hierarchical social order, with distinct classes having their differing functions, has some resonances with classical Chinese society in terms of the social order. However, the Chinese had quite a different view of knowledge than that of Plato, emphasizing learning through observation and experience rather than rational deduction and theoretical understanding. They also had a different view of the human person, as having infinite potential for transformation through education and as integrally connected to family, community, and nature, rather than an individual with innate characteristics.

We can also see the resonances between Chinese ways of thinking and those of Dewey and Marx. Dewey's ideas of the human person in relationship to community, of society as changing with problems being solved collaboratively, and of knowledge as advancing experientially are particularly close to Chinese ways of thinking. Some aspects of Marxism also appealed to Chinese thinkers: its sense of historical evolution from one type of society to another, its ability to explain the

causes of imperialism in the extension of capitalist economic dynamics to a global arena, and the priority it gave to the collective over the individual good.

MODERN EDUCATIONAL DEVELOPMENT IN EAST ASIA

The term *Confucian heritage societies* is often used for East Asia, including Japan, mainland China, Taiwan, Vietnam, Korea, Singapore, Hong Kong, and Macau. Historically, Japan was the earliest to develop a modern education system, while China followed shortly afterwards. Both Taiwan and Korea were colonized by Japan for lengthy periods of time, and Vietnam was under French colonial influence up to 1939. Hong Kong and Singapore are both essentially city states colonized by Britain. Singapore became an independent nation in 1965, but Hong Kong's decolonization took place in 1997 when it was reunited with China under the formula of "one country, two systems." In 1999, the former Portuguese colony of Macau was reunited with China under the same formula. The whole region can be seen as a kind of laboratory, where European, American, and Soviet educational values interacted with shared Confucian traditions, in colonial, post-colonial, and non-colonial settings, under conditions of capitalist modernization and socialist construction.

Education in Japan

Japan's written history began in about the seventh century CE when it developed a writing system based on Chinese characters and imported many texts of Confucianism, Daoism, and Buddhism while developing its own religion of Shintoism. In the period known as the Meiji Enlightenment (1868–1912 CE), Japan began to selectively introduce Western educational models in an effort to achieve rapid modernization. By the late 19th century, Japan had its own modern schooling system.

School subjects were defined in similar ways to those in the curricula of European schools, and a whole new vocabulary was developed using Chinese characters to give names to such modern subjects as physics, chemistry, mathematics, biology, and economics. Particular emphasis was given to the study of foreign languages, mainly English, French, and German, to make possible the rapid absorption of scientific knowledge from the West. Japanese was the medium of instruction, and in 1890 an imperial rescript was passed that called upon Japanese people to maintain absolute loyalty to the Emperor and preserve traditional values of family harmony and service to the public good. In this spirit they were to "pursue learning and cultivate arts, and thereby develop intellectual powers and perfect moral powers."[21] Within Shintoism, the symbolism of the emperor was particularly important, since the sun goddess was seen as the ancestor of Japan's first ruler.[22]

Japan's success in modernizing began to be evident in the early 20th century with a military victory over Russia in 1905 and remarkable industrialization and self-strengthening. This economic success was accompanied by increasingly aggressive behaviour towards China, however, as Japan sought to secure raw materials for its industrialization. It also copied Europe in the acquisition of colonies. Taiwan was colonized by Japan from 1895 to 1945 and Korea from 1910 to 1945.

After experiencing defeat in World War II, Japan was occupied by the American military for seven years. A new constitution passed in 1947 committed the country to peace, democratization, and the decentralization of education. Under American influence the education system became less hierarchical, and provision was made for the majority of young people to complete secondary education and for an increasingly large percentage to enter higher education. Japan was the first Asian society to achieve mass higher education, in the same time period as the United States, Canada, and the Soviet Union, and well ahead of Western Europe.[23]

Before 1945, the majority of teachers for primary and lower secondary education had been educated in normal training colleges that did not give degrees. After the war, most of these colleges were upgraded to university status, and Japan became the second country in the world, after the United States, to require that all teachers have university degrees. Professional courses for teachers are offered in both public and private universities, but certification is under the control of prefectural authorities. They select the very best of those who are academically and professionally qualified for positions in their schools. This means that only about 20 to 30 percent of those who have the necessary educational qualifications for teaching are able to gain teaching positions. Teachers are civil servants, with a high social status and remuneration that is 30 to 40 percent higher than other public employees with equivalent qualifications.[24]

The main direction of the post-war reforms in Japanese education was to reduce central control over the education system and give greater autonomy to teachers and greater responsibility to local educational authorities. The Ministry of Education nevertheless retained strong control over the national curriculum, and there was a continuing concern with moral education and education for patriotism. Some educators have been highly critical of this, wishing to emphasize children's individuality and right to learn, rather than the state's concern for shaping loyal citizens. Japan's major teachers' unions also have tended to be strongly oppositional to government and left leaning in their orientation. Thus lively struggles over educational policy are ongoing. Horio Teruhisa's writings give many interesting insights into these debates.[25]

There is nevertheless widespread agreement that Japanese children learn well and have comparatively high achievement from early childhood up through primary and lower secondary education. The upper years of secondary education are clouded by the intense pressures of competitive examinations for entry to the top universities, with a sense that the university one enters will determine one's career chances far more than the subjects studied, or the academic grades achieved. This is sometimes described as Japan's "examination hell" and is part of a widely shared Asian heritage.[26] William Cummings, one of the best known comparative educators writing on Japan, has commented on the striking difference between Japan and the United States in the degree of importance given to higher education by the United States as against basic education by Japan.[27]

Education in Mainland China and Taiwan

China was greatly influenced by Japan's Meiji enlightenment reforms and shared a sense of pride in Japan's success in defeating Russia in 1905. From the 1890s to China's Nationalist Revolution of 1911, when the last imperial dynasty was overthrown, China's leaders tried to emulate Japan in creating a modern education system. Hundreds of Chinese teachers studied in Japan, and there was a strong belief that the Japanese model would enable China to absorb Western science and technology for national strengthening. At the same time, they could retain their Confucian identity and embrace gradual change through the establishment of a constitutional monarchy, along Japanese lines.[28]

It soon became evident that this approach would not work for China. With the collapse of the last imperial dynasty in 1911, China launched itself on a journey of change that involved radical experimentation with a range of Western models of education and an overt rejection of its Confucian heritage as a value system antithetical to science and modernity. From 1912 to the early 1920s, European models were most influential in China's modern educational development, due to the leadership of scholars who had studied in Germany and France. Efforts were made to lay a foundation for basic education of five to six years, then to develop a small number of academic secondary schools that would open up entry to a few newly established national universities. Other specialist secondary schools offered programs in teacher education and various forms of vocational and technical education.

The May 4th Movement of 1919 was sparked by the decision of the victorious leaders of France, the United Kingdom, Italy, and the United States to give Germany's possessions on China's east coast to Japan after World War I. Students and professors in China's major universities, led by Peking University, marched in protest against this decision. Both progressive thinkers and Marxists came to believe that China's evident weakness on the global stage was a result of its Confucian heritage and that education for science and democracy was the only way forward. In a situation where the political leadership was weak and divided, educators and local leaders made vigorous efforts to expand basic education and many specialist colleges were upgraded to university status.

An educational law of 1922 adopted American patterns of decentralized educational administration and community responsibility for schools.[29] This was shortly after John and Alice Dewey had spent two years in China, travelling throughout the country to lecture on education, science, and democracy.[30] An American-style schooling structure was also adopted at this time, with six years of primary education, three years of lower secondary, three years of upper secondary, and four years of tertiary education. While Dewey's ideas about education, child development, and democracy were widely appreciated by educators and scholars, China's economic conditions were such that progressive education developed in only a few relatively prosperous cities and regions. Illiteracy was widespread in most of the country, and no means were available to develop a comprehensive modern schooling system.

In 1928, the Nationalist Party came to power and established a national government with Nanjing as the capital. In the brief nine years it had before the invasion of Japan in 1937 and the outbreak of World War II in 1939, great efforts were made to develop a national education system. The American structure was retained while European ideas were drawn upon to create a national curriculum and establish national standards in all the main subject areas.

World War II was followed by a civil war between China's Nationalist and Communist forces, with a definitive Communist victory in 1949. The Nationalist forces retreated to Taiwan and there gained American support in developing Taiwan into a modern scientific power that built upon the infrastructure left by Japanese colonizers. The schooling system had a structure similar to that of the United States, but conscious efforts were made to recover aspects of the Confucian heritage of emphasis on family and community support for children's learning.[31] While Taiwan was ruled by martial law under the Nationalist Party up till 1987, multi-party democracy gradually emerged, and there have been several peaceful changes of government through national elections since the mid-1990s. The one highly sensitive issue still outstanding is Taiwan's relationship with mainland China, which regards it as a renegade province that should be reunited with the Motherland.

From the successful Communist revolution of 1949, China's education developed in an entirely different direction from that of Japan and Taiwan. Chinese Communist leaders felt their only recourse under the conditions of the emerging Cold War was to turn to the Soviet Union for advice and assistance. Therefore the Chinese education system was reformed in the early 1950s to follow Soviet patterns, with a strong emphasis placed on basic education for all, then a highly academic secondary schooling system open to a small percentage of youth, mainly those in urban areas. This included those academically capable and those selected from the working class to move into leadership positions.

The school structure remained the same as before 1949, with six years of primary schooling, three years of lower secondary, three years of upper secondary, followed by unified national examinations to select those who would enter higher education.[32] The higher education system was fundamentally reformed according to Soviet patterns, with many Soviet experts helping China to design monotechnical institutions that would serve the planning needs of the state for specialists in such fields as engineering, agriculture, medicine, and teacher training. Most university programs required five years of study. Entrance was highly competitive and all graduates were assigned positions as state cadres in the new system.[33]

This system trained experts to serve the rapid development of a strong socialist economy, yet contradictions soon emerged. On the political side there was concern that the majority of children and young people, especially those in rural areas, had little opportunity to advance beyond basic education. On the cultural level, there was a reaction against the narrow specialization and segmentation of knowledge and the top-down centralized control. This went against China's holistic knowledge traditions and patterns of community involvement in learning. There was thus an intense reaction against Soviet influences in the Great Leap Forward of 1958 and the Cultural Revolution of 1967. The length of schooling was shortened from 12 to nine years, five at the primary level, and four at the secondary level. The curriculum was greatly broadened and access was opened up to the majority of young people to complete secondary education. While there were only nine million students in general secondary schools in 1965, by the end of the Cultural Revolution there were 58 million.[34]

Political struggle reached an extreme in the Cultural Revolution, as Mao Zedong encouraged young people to rebel against all forms of authority, and parents, elders, and teachers were subjected to extreme and often violent forms of criticism. There are many interpretations of this period. The most common attributes the violence to a power struggle between the radical and conservative factions of the Chinese Communist Party. It can also be seen as a reaction against the imposition of patterns from the Soviet Union that were hierarchical, centralized, and highly restrictive in the Chinese context. When Mao died in 1976, and the infamous "Gang" of four leaders who had supported him fell from power shortly afterwards, a new period of development in Chinese education opened up under Deng Xiaoping.

Deng was a veteran Communist leader, yet he was also a pragmatist. He focused on providing conditions for China to modernize and open up to the world, with education as the key to successful modernization. It was a great relief for Chinese educators, teachers, and students to see increasing investment in education, greater autonomy for teachers, and forms of educational planning that were focused on supporting the nation's economic and social development. At first the curricular patterns of the 1950s were restored but they were soon broadened to respond to the changing needs of the modernization process.

Particular attention was given to respecting teachers and ensuring they had adequate academic and professional training to nurture creativity as well as academic excellence in their students. Educational research included classroom-based studies carried out by working teachers who tried to make learning more effective and more enjoyable. There were lively debates over Soviet, American, and European educational theories, and many experimental partnerships and projects. One elderly educator has described this period as "spring time for educational science."[35] It was a great relief that education was no longer seen as a tool for class struggle, but instead as a process of learning, growth, experimentation and change. It was also a time for recovering some of the positive values of the Confucian tradition, which had been negated and neglected ever since the May 4th Movement of 1919.[36] The results of China's educational and economic reforms have been dramatic, and the world is now waiting to see what kind of global leadership China may exercise in the future.

Education in Vietnam and Korea

Vietnam and Korea suffered as much as China and Taiwan from the impact of the Cold War on Asia. For Vietnam, French colonialism ended in 1939, but the country was divided into two parts after World War II, with the North under Soviet influence and the South under American influence. After the end of the Vietnam War and the US departure in 1975, Vietnam was unified under socialism and its educational patterns reflected Soviet influence. Even before the collapse of the Soviet Union, Vietnam had begun to adopt its own forms of market socialism, and education has played an important role in invigorating the economy and opening the minds of children and young people to a wider world.[37]

For Korea, the end of Japanese colonialism in 1945 was a great relief, yet Cold War tensions meant the country was divided into North and South, with the South occupied by the United States until 1948 and the North under Soviet influence. The Korean war of the early 1950s ended with an armistice that is still in place. South Korea's development parallels that of Taiwan in many ways, with successful industrialization, the creation of a science-based economy, and the end of martial law in 1988. Education has been influenced by American patterns, yet there are also strong Indigenous elements coming from Confucian and Buddhist influences.[38] Mass higher education was achieved in the 1980s, with a dynamic private sector responding to social demand. Teacher education was upgraded to degree level, and a number of universities of education were created to support teachers in their work. For Korean educators and the Korean people more widely, the most painful ongoing issues are the division of the country and the continuing isolation of the North.

Education in Singapore, Hong Kong, and Macau

Singapore became an independent nation in 1965, after 98 years of British colonial rule. Some elements of the British education system have continued to have influence, and English has been the main medium of instruction. Yet there has been a recovery of interest in Mandarin, as well as the promotion of the Tamil and Malay languages for Indian and Malay minorities. There has also been a gradual move beyond the original elitist education system to a more open one, with three universities and a large number of polytechnics providing higher education for an increasing proportion of the population.[39] Most recently, the Singapore government made the decision to become a hub for transnational education in Asia. It has invited top universities from all over the world to establish branches there, attracting students from India, China, Vietnam, Malaysia, Indonesia, and Sri Lanka.[40]

Education in Hong Kong and Macau developed in completely different ways from China, due to their status as colonies of Britain and Portugal. Because they are located on the western and eastern sides of China's Pearl River Delta, decolonization could only mean a return to mainland China. Negotiations between China and Britain over this began in 1984, culminating in 1997 under Deng Xiaoping's formula of "one country, two systems." Two years later, Macau returned to

Chinese sovereignty under the same principle. Macau's education system had gradually adjusted to its Chinese context over a long period of time.[41]

Hong Kong's return to China meant a re-emphasis on the local Cantonese dialect of Chinese as the medium of instruction in schools, a new approach to citizenship education,[42] and an increasing emphasis on learning Mandarin. It also meant a definitive move away from the British-derived structure of education, with "Ordinary" and "Advanced" level examinations. Reforms undertaken after 1997 were intended to reduce examination pressures so that all students could move smoothly from primary to secondary education and face only one set of competitive examinations for university entry, as in mainland China. The other dramatic change that took place after 1997 was the upgrading of teacher education to university level with the establishment of the Hong Kong Institute of Education, which offers bachelor's and master's degrees for teachers.[43]

COMPARATIVE REFLECTIONS ON EDUCATION IN EAST ASIA

Three approaches to comparative education theory were outlined in Chapter One: comparative education as a science; comparative education and imperialism; and comparative education, globalization, and the dialogue among civilizations. Each provides a distinctive framework for reflecting on the experience of educational development in East Asian societies.

If we begin with comparative education as a science, we can see how the human capital argument has played out in East Asia — with remarkable economic results for the educational investments in Japan after World War II, then similar patterns emerging in South Korea, Taiwan, Hong Kong, and Singapore. (See Chapters One and Three for discussions on human capital.) Given that these are all capitalist societies, this is not particularly surprising. It is notable, however, that mainland Chinese comparative educator Gu Mingyuan argued for human capital theory being equally applicable to socialist societies.[44] He encouraged China's leadership to invest heavily in education after the Cultural Revolution. The resulting economic growth has been nothing short of remarkable. Since the late 1980s, Vietnam has followed a similar model with parallel success. Thus the human capital argument has been extended to include socialist societies, reflecting the flexibility of Confucian pragmatism.

Another aspect of the scientific approach to comparative education in the Asian context is a sense of the liberating power of science. For both China and Vietnam, the move away from the use of education as a tool of class struggle towards education as a science has been an enormous relief for the many who were victims of vicious political struggles. There may be a parallel here with Jullien's early idea of educational science liberating teachers and students from the narrow rules of those controlling education on behalf of the state or the church. While there are good reasons to critique positivistic science for imposing a mechanical model of understanding on the world and for legitimating the domination of the West, the East Asian experience reminds us that science may have different connotations at different times and in different socio-cultural settings.

If we turn to comparative education and the world system, East Asia is a veritable laboratory of different types of imperialism. Both Japan and China developed their modern education systems in order to strengthen the nation in face of imperialist incursions. This worked well for Japan, yet, it became itself an imperialist power, occupying both Taiwan and Korea for lengthy periods of time, in conscious imitation of Europe's colonial adventures.

China was never fully colonized, yet its Nationalist leader, Sun Yat Sen, described it as a "hyper colony" because of its experience of British, French, German, and Japanese imperialist incursions at different times. Hong Kong became a colony of the British, Macau of the Portuguese, and Manchuria in China's northeast fell under Japanese control for more than a decade. What is notable about China's educational development, however, is that educational policies were consciously selected to strengthen the nation's resistance to imperialist influences. Thus, China turned from Japanese educational patterns to American ones in the 1920s, when Japan's imperialist intentions became clear.

It is ironic that China experienced education as imperialism most acutely after its successful Communist revolution. The Soviet Union's assistance in economic, political, and educational development came to be seen by the Chinese as an unacceptable form of social imperialism. China's experience can thus be better understood within Johan Galtung's structural theory of imperialism than Lenin's view of imperialism as the highest stage of capitalism.

Smaller countries of Asia such as Korea and Vietnam experienced the full brunt of imperialism and the Cold War, with both countries being divided for lengthy periods of time. South Vietnam experienced American influence in education under partition, then later replaced this with Soviet influence between 1975 and the late 1980s. Nevertheless, it has found its own road to educational development, and its indigenous values have flourished under market socialism.

North Korea has experienced isolation and severe economic difficulty in striking contrast to the affluence and success of South Korea's capitalist economy. While American educational patterns have had some influence in South Korea since the 1950s, there has also been an active anti-Americanism expressed in various popular movements. Educational development has taken its own unique forms based on Indigenous traditions of Confucianism and Buddhism.

As for Singapore and Hong Kong, they are both prosperous city states, though different in their political standing. The heritage of British common law and colonial administration has been turned to positive ends, and the legacy of British educational patterns has been transformed to suit their particular development needs and interests. Macau has also done well in moving beyond its Portuguese colonial legacy.

We can see how the East Asian experience of education and development challenges a simplistic application of dependency theory or world system theory in comparative education. (See Chapters One and Three for discussions of dependency or world system theory.) These theories are probably best taken as ideal types that are most telling precisely at the points where they are contradicted by the East Asian experience. The most striking failure of these theories has been an underestimation of the resilience of local cultures in the face of external political domination and economic exploitation.

It may be within the context of globalization and the dialogue among civilizations that we can best reflect on the lessons of the East Asian experience. In spite of the dramatic differences in political destiny experienced by each of the eight Confucian heritage societies of East Asia in the geopolitics of the Cold War, there are remarkable similarities in educational processes and outcomes. Children from East Asian societies tend to have high educational achievement in international tests of mathematics, science, and language knowledge. There has also been a largely positive relationship between educational investment and economic development, within both capitalist and socialist political systems. These successes have led to considerable interest in what the West can learn from East Asian education.

East Asian societies have experienced capitalism, socialism, and colonialism and have had diverse interactions with Britain, France, the United States, and the Soviet Union. These historical experiences influenced their educational systems, yet the most profound explanatory factors for their educational ethos and the learning achievement of their children and young people lie in shared views of knowledge, society, and the human person rooted in Confucian philosophy.

WHAT CAN WE LEARN FROM EAST ASIA?

In 1980, social psychologists Harold Stevenson and James Stigler undertook an intensive study of a large number of first- and fifth-grade children and their families in three settings — Minneapolis, United States; Sendai, Japan; and Taipei, Taiwan. In 1987, a second study was done, with the addition of children and schools in Chicago and Beijing. The findings of these two comparative studies give remarkable insights into the learning experience of East Asian children.[45]

Stevenson and Stigler considered home, community, and school environments in studying the lives of East Asian and American children, and took into account the viewpoints of the children themselves, their mothers, their teachers, and their school leaders. In looking at children's lives at home and at school, they found that Asian children spent many more days in school than American — about two-thirds of the days in the year, as against one-half — and that school and home life were more closely connected. Asian teachers tended to stay with one class for two or three years, building close links with the children's families. At home, almost all Asian parents provided a desk for their child and a space to work, even though living conditions tended to be crowded. Asian children spent about two hours more a week on homework, and also had homework assigned during vacations. In addition to school-assigned homework, Asian parents often purchased inexpensive workbooks to help their children with exercises for review.

Overall, both Asian and American children spent considerable time each week watching television, Asian children even more than

American children. However, American children spent much more time in sports and other kinds of play, and this was seen as important both for physical exercise and social interaction. American children also spent more time helping their families with chores, while Asian parents tended to excuse their children from this kind of activity.

At school, Asian classrooms tended to have larger numbers of children than American ones, and discipline was taught in such a way that all children learned to be responsible for classroom order. Asian children had more opportunities for participation in group activities before and after class and in frequent recesses, which allowed for vigorous play. By contrast, American children spent more time in the classroom, with less opportunity for group exercise and play during the day, and more time spent working alone at their desks. The authors suggested that this was the reason American families saw extracurricular sports activities and social interaction as so essential.

A main factor for high achievement in Asian children's lives at home and school was the support from family and school for children's learning in Asian contexts. Children felt very much part of a group, enjoyed learning in a whole classroom situation, and accepted responsibility for order and discipline. In these circumstances, "children gradually develop self-direction, good study habits, and motivation to do well in school."[46] "The ideal day in the lives of elementary school children balances physical, social, and intellectual activity, allows children opportunities for gaining a sense of accomplishment and competence, has both structure and freedom, and gradually evolves — so that what is expected of children follows their developmental progress."[47]

A second factor that appeared to be important for achievement in the Asian context was the approach to socialization of Asian parents and teachers. Children are seen as going through two important states, an age of innocence, from birth to six years, and an age of reason, beginning at first grade. Almost no discipline is imposed in the first stage, but with the second, "the family begins to mobilize itself to provide the kinds of experiences and assistance that will be necessary for the child to become a 'knowing' person."[48]

The Asian school also takes on considerable responsibility for the socialization of children, and three techniques stood out in this study as distinct from American practices of socialization. Role models are consistently used and upheld for children to learn from and admire. Group identification is strongly encouraged, and children become adept at an early age in group problem-solving. Children are also explicitly taught routines relating to the management of their own learning, such as how to keep their desks tidy, how to take notes, and how to organize their clothes when change of dress is required for an outdoor class.

Stevenson and Stigler conclude that "Asian parents regard doing well in school as the single most important task facing their children. American parents seek to balance academic achievement with other goals, such as developing social skills, high self-esteem and broad extra curricular interests. Striving for academic excellence, therefore, may be weaker among American children because of the conflicting priorities held by their parents and the resulting de-emphasis of academic achievement."[49]

One of the most striking differences in the attitudes of Asian and American parents and children towards education is that of the importance of effort as against ability. Teachers, mothers, and children in East Asia have a strong belief that with effort, every child can learn successfully. By contrast, American parents and children had much stronger beliefs in the innate ability of children as the main reason for explaining success and failure in learning. In considering this difference, Stevenson and Stigler point to the widespread use of intelligence testing in the United States.

They also conclude that "many Americans place a higher priority on life adjustment and the enhancement of self-esteem than on academic achievement. They assume that positive self-esteem is a necessary precursor of competence. They forget that one of the most important sources of children's self-esteem is realizing that they have mastered a challenging task."[50] While American mothers are easily satisfied with the achievements of their children, even if these are mediocre, Asian parents set very high expectations for their children.

The second half of Stevenson and Stigler's study deals with the organization of schooling, the teaching profession, and the practice of teaching. While Asian countries consider a national curriculum extremely important for standard setting, Americans emphasize the importance of individual differences and see the goal of education as maximizing children's differential potential. Textbooks reflect this difference, with most Asian textbooks having to be approved by a national ministry of education before being adopted. Asian textbooks also tend to be slimmer and less rich in illustration, but more explicit and coherent in their content.[51] Furthermore, Asian children are expected to learn in co-operation with one another. It is rare that children are separated out for special attention due to learning difficulties.

The teaching profession also functions differently in East Asia and America. American teachers have considerable freedom to decide on curricular issues and teaching approaches, while Asian teachers work to a national curriculum. They typically have fewer classroom hours and more time scheduled for collaborative class preparation work. This is a result of the fact that classes tend to be larger, and children are trained to learn from one another, not only from the teacher.

Different images of the ideal teacher in Beijing and Chicago give an interesting insight. Beijing teachers viewed the most important qualities of the teacher as the ability to explain things clearly, next most important enthusiasm, then standards, sensitivity, and patience. Chicago teachers saw sensitivity as the most important quality, reflecting their concern with treating children as individuals. This was followed by enthusiasm, patience, standards, and last of all clarity.

> In Asia, the ideal teacher is a skilled performer. As with the actor or musician, the substance of the curriculum becomes the script or the score; the goal is to perform the role or piece as effectively and creatively as possible. Rather than executing the curriculum as a mere routine, the skilled teacher strives to perfect the presentation of each lesson. She uses the teaching techniques she has learned and imposes her own interpretation on these techniques in a manner that she thinks will interest and motivate her pupils. [52]
>
> In America, teachers are judged to be successful when they are innovative, inventive and original. Skill presentation of a standard lesson is not sufficient and may even be disparaged as indicating a lack of innovative talent. It is as if American teachers were expected to write their own play or create their own concerto day after day and then perform it with expertise and finesse. These two models, the skilled performer and the innovator, have very different value in the East and West.[53]

CONCLUSION: REFLECTING ON THE PARADOXES IN EAST ASIAN LEARNING

The main point of this chapter has been to consider the philosophical underpinnings of comparative education and to show how important it is to learn about the religious and philosophical traditions of a society or region when seeking to understand educational policy, schools, curricula, and teaching practices. It is also important to see how the dialogue among civilizations can take us beyond national schooling systems and help us to understand ways of learning that are common to a whole region.

The chapter has illustrated how ideal types may be used to clarify core values about the human person, society, and knowledge, identify contrasts, and explore commonalities. Thus the notion of "Confucian heritage societies" can be fleshed out by reference to ideas of the human person as perfectible through education, of society as a macrocosm of the human family, and of knowledge as built up through a cumulative study of experience in both the social and natural worlds.

This can help us to reflect on the puzzles and paradoxes of the East Asian experience of education and development at a level that goes deeper than that of regional geopolitics and national educational policies. We can understand the discourses over the relative importance of ability and effort in educational achievement, the relationship between individual and collective in schooling, and the distinction between internal and external motivation in learning in a less dichotomous way than might be the case in the West. These polarities can be held in balance within the flexible and dialectical thinking process of East Asian educators. Likewise, theoretical constructs such as human capital in a socialist society, social imperialism, and market socialism are understood in relation to the lived historical experience of diverse societies that share the Confucian heritage. They take on connotations that might well be unallowable in the more rigid world of Western theoretical scholarship. Perhaps the most striking characteristic of this heritage is a profound and humane pragmatism that insists on the advancement of knowledge through thoughtful reflection on experience.

QUESTIONS FOR REFLECTION AND DISCUSSION

1. How do the ideal types of Platonic, Deweyan, Marxist, and Confucian values stimulate you to reflect comparatively on learning in North American schools?
2. What was the most significant new fact you learned about education in East Asia in this chapter, and why? What aspects of education in East Asia do you see as similar to and different from your own education?
3. Compare/contrast the development of education in various Confucian heritage societies, in light of the educational theories discussed in Chapter One. Which framework for comparative education best explains East Asian schools? Discuss the relevance of these understandings for teachers' work in North American schools.

SUGGESTED FILM: *PRESCHOOL IN THREE CULTURES: JAPAN, CHINA AND THE UNITED STATES*, BY JOSEPH TOBIN

This video is a supplement to the book *Three Cultures: Japan, China and the United States* by Joseph Tobin, David Wu, and Dana Davidson. Observing a day in the life of preschool children and teachers in Japan, China, and the United States, Tobin explores the similarities and differences between these three cultures. Viewers watch preschool children go about their daily activities and hear Tobin explain how teachers from the other two cultures responded to the structure, discipline, and activities of one another's classes.

SUGGESTIONS FOR FURTHER READING

*Biggs, John B. and David A. Watson. "Insights into Teaching the Chinese Learner." In *Teaching the Chinese Learner: Psychological and Pedagogical Perspectives*, edited by David A. Watkins and John B. Biggs. Hong Kong: Comparative Education Research Centre, University of Hong Kong, 2004, 277–300.

Cummings, William. "The Institutions of Education." *Comparative Education Review* 43, no. 4 (1999): 413–37.

Gu, Mingyuan. *Education in China and Abroad: Perspectives from a Lifetime in Comparative Education*. Hong Kong: Comparative Education Research Centre, University of Hong Kong, 2001.

*Hayhoe, Ruth. "Teacher Education and the University: A Comparative Analysis with Implications for Hong Kong." *Teaching Education* 13, no. 1 (2002): 5-23.

Hayhoe, Ruth. *Portraits of Influential Chinese Educators*. Hong Kong: Comparative Education Research Centre, University of Hong Kong, 2006.

Holmes, Brian. *Comparative Education: Some Considerations of Method*. London: George Allen and Unwin, 1981.

Horio, Teruhisa. *Educational Thought and Ideology in Modern Japan: State Authority and Intellectual Freedom*. Tokyo: University of Tokyo Press, 1988.

*Kennedy, Kerry. "Searching for Citizenship Values in an Uncertain Global Environment." In *Citizenship Education in Asia and the Pacific: Concepts and Issues*, edited by Wing On Lee and others. Hong Kong: Comparative Education Research Centre, University of Hong Kong, 2004, 9-24.

Lee, Wing On. "The Cultural Context for Chinese Learners: Conceptions of Learning in the Confucian Tradition." In *The Chinese Learner: Cultural, Psychological and Contextual Influences*, edited by David A. Watkins and John B. Biggs. Hong Kong: Comparative Education Research Centre, University of Hong Kong, 1996, 29-41.

Seth, Michael J. *Education Fever: Society, Politics and the Pursuit of Schooling in South Korea*. Honolulu: University of Hawaii Press, 2002.

Shimihara, Nobuo K. "Teacher Education Reform in Japan: Ideological and Control Issues." In *Teacher Education in Industrialized Nations: Issues in Changing Social Contexts*, edited by Nobuo K. Shimihara and Ivan Z. Holowinsky. New York and London: Garland Publishing Inc., 1995, 169-79.

Smith, Douglas C. *The Confucian Continuum: Educational Modernization in Taiwan*. New York: Praeger Publishers, 1991.

Stevenson, Harold W. and Stigler, James W. *The Learning Gap: Why our Schools are Failing and What We Can Learn from Japanese and Chinese Education*. New York: Simon and Schuster, 1992.

Tobin, Joseph J., David Y.H. Wu, and Dana Davidson. *Preschool in Three Cultures: Japan, China, and the United States*. New Haven: Yale University Press, 1989.

Chapter Three

"Education for All," Africa, and the Comparative Sociology of Schooling

Karen Mundy

INTRODUCTION

Why do we have publicly provided mass education? How did going to school become a central expectation of children, parents, and communities around the world? Does going to school really provide the degree of opportunity and social equalization that we anticipate from it? And why, given the widespread endorsement of education as a fundamental right, do so many children miss out on schooling or receive an education of poor quality in many parts of the world? These are questions that have engrossed comparative educationists as well as sociologists of education since at least the end of World War II. They are still deeply debated today.

In this chapter, we review these debates with special attention to the historical experience of schooling in two countries in East Africa: Tanzania and Kenya. The first section of the chapter looks at the origins of the notion of a universal right to education, and how schooling became the international standard for childhood socialization. The second section considers various interpretations of the effort to expand mass education in the developing world after 1945. We look at whether the post-1945 expansion of formal schooling was mainly about national economic development, or whether it arose as part of a new thrust by Western countries for "cultural imperialism." In section three, we consider why in the 1980s and 1990s educational opportunity eroded in many of the poorest parts of the world, and ask what this erosion had to do with globalization. Section four reflects on the revival of "Education for All" (EFA) over the past decade, while section five looks at the EFA experiences of Tanzania and Kenya. Through this historical overview and exploration of EFA, we can better understand the ongoing debate about the purposes and effects of mass schooling today.

THE RIGHT TO EDUCATION IN WORLD HISTORICAL PERSPECTIVE

The idea that children have a right to attend school is now so widely accepted that it is hard to believe that schooling was not seen as an essential part of childhood in most parts of the world a mere 100 years ago. Yet in the 200-year period from the late 18th century to the late 20th century, "schooling" — formal, age-graded, classroom-based instruction — spread across Western societies and became the international standard for childhood socialization. Initially designed for the elite, by the early 20th century schooling (at least at the primary level) was increasingly being offered to all citizens, typically in systems run and funded by nation-states. So widespread had the institution of schooling become by the middle of the 20th century that the international community promised to uphold a "universal" right to education: first through the creation of the United Nations Educational, Scientific, and Cultural Organization (UNESCO) in 1944; and secondly through Article 26 of the 1948 Universal Declaration of Human Rights, which states:

> Everyone has the right to education. Education shall be free, at least in the elementary and fundamental stages. Elementary education shall be compulsory. Technical and professional education shall be made generally available and higher education shall be equally accessible to all on the basis of merit.[1]

But why did schooling spread so rapidly and become a universal, internationally recognized entitlement? In the 1960s and 1970s, sociologists and comparative education scholars argued quite heatedly about this. Their arguments are consequential because they continue to shape the way researchers and educators think about the right to education and the consequences of schooling today. Four basic explanations emerged from scholars who focused on the spread of schooling in the West:

1) Functionalist arguments portrayed schooling as a response to the needs of modernizing societies, driven by the demands of new forms of economic and political organization as societies

move from pre-modern to modern stages of development. Functionalist arguments underlie much of what we hear about schooling in the popular media and political discourse, including the idea that schooling produces a more modern and more productive citizen-worker, and thus is essential for economic growth.

2) Marxist and critical sociologists of education argued against this conflict-free view of schooling. Research on the social history of schooling in Britain and the United States suggested that schooling expanded rapidly because it played a role in the development of industrial capitalism during the 19th century. Schooling created a tractable, time-conscious work force for new industries out of agricultural peasant populations. Schooling in this view is part of a larger process of class imposition or social reproduction.[2]

3) A third argument, drawing from the work of Max Weber, emphasized the leadership of newly forming territorial nation states in the spread of schooling.[3] Weberian scholars argued that new state authorities promoted compulsory schooling because it helped create a body of citizens that identified with (and were loyal to) the new territorial nation state. Drawing primarily upon histories of schooling in Prussia and in France, they showed how schools were used to integrate different language groups and promote respect for secular authority. Weberian scholars confronted the class-imposition hypothesis with data showing that many industrialists in Britain and North America opposed the spread of mass schooling in the 19th century. They challenged the functionalist hypothesis by showing that schooling had often spread before economic modernization and industrialization took place.

4) A fourth line of scholarship asked whether schooling was indeed imposed, either by state authorities or capitalists. Here scholars pointed out that popular movements — often including organizations of workers, parents, and social reformers — played a significant part in the spread of schooling. These actors demanded access to schooling and educational resources from national governments, and were particularly successful in the era after 1945.[4] Blending Weberian and neo-

Marxist arguments, these scholars argued that the extension of universal access to schooling played a strong "legitimation" role in modern capitalist states: it met popular demands with promises of equality of opportunity. In turn, the notion that schooling should be equally available to all became one of the guiding norms of the industrial welfare state in the 20th century. In this construction, the expansion of state promises for universal and equitable access to schooling is looked at as part of a "social settlement" that was worked out in specific national contexts between state, capital, and organized social forces.

In addition to these four fundamental arguments, Stanford sociologists John Meyer and Francisco Ramirez have added a fifth, overarching contention.[5] Meyer and Ramirez argue that as schooling became institutionalized in the Western world, it achieved widespread recognition as the standard for childhood socialization in the international community. Schooling became part of a standard world cultural model that spread through processes of diffusion and imitation. This theory, known as world institutionalism, argues that schooling is a fundamental feature of an emergent, single, world culture.

As we shall see below, each of these five arguments has been extended in research on schooling in the non-Western world. In this context, functionalist arguments tend to describe the expansion of schooling as a response to modernization: necessary for national development and the creation of the modern, productive citizen. World system and neo-Marxist scholars view the spread of schooling as part of the extension of a capitalist world order, often describing it as a form of cultural imperialism that displaces local cultures and values while legitimating unequal forms of economic integration. Weberian analysts focus more carefully on the political and bureaucratic features of developing country states and governments, arguing that Third World governments expand schooling in order to consolidate territorial sovereignty and enhance their legitimacy within the international community of states. A fourth group of scholars is interested in the role played by popular movements in the construction of local meanings and local social settlements; while a fifth, drawing on Meyer and Ramirez's work, focuses on the way that schooling has become increasingly standardized, so that even Social Studies curricula look alike.

In general, comparative education scholars agree that if capitalism, the state, and/or popular demand drove the spread of mass compulsory schooling in the West, we might expect that these factors would continue to shape changes in the policies and practices of schooling in the developing world. Most also agree that schooling has become so institutionalized that arguments among these different social actors about schooling no longer focus on whether or not schooling is important, but on what kind of schooling works best. Finally, most comparative education scholars agree that national educational choices are shaped by a transnational or world system, though they disagree on what the most influential features of this system are.

Throughout this book we invite you to examine these arguments by exploring recent policy changes in education. For example, what has driven the rise of school improvement reforms or national testing regimes, topics covered in Chapters Seven and Eight? Have states, popular movements, economic interest groups, or the international community played a part? We will also consider how these different "forces" — the state, capital, organized social movements, and the international system — shape the educational trajectories of children in developing countries today.

EDUCATION, AID, AND DEVELOPMENT

In the 1950s and 1960s, the governments of newly independent countries around the world promised their citizens that they would expand access to schooling, replacing the highly restrictive systems inherited from colonialism with universal access. Universal primary education became a central part of the national development plans of post-colonial societies. Parents and children picked up the baton. Between 1960 and 1975, the number of children in school in developing countries increased by 122 percent.[6] Within years of independence, compulsory school laws were passed in virtually every country.[7]

The international community supported these post-colonial efforts to expand mass systems of public education. Aid to education, provided primarily through bilateral development aid (such as that given by the Canadian and American international development agencies) was used to develop the allegiance of post-colonial states to the West during the

Cold War; it also helped build economic ties to industrialized countries. But this was only part of the story. Educational aid also reflected the enormous commitment to education being made across Western welfare states after 1945, where expansion of access (at secondary and tertiary levels) and equality of opportunity had become central commitments. The idea that education could bridge social inequality was universally accepted, and countries with the most expansive domestic welfare states tended to offer international aid as an extension of their commitments to social equality at home.[8] Large numbers of Western volunteers travelled overseas to teach, reinforcing mounting public support for the idea that rich countries should do their share to ensure that every child would get a chance to go to school.

Substantial research literature on the role of education in the development of the newly independent countries of the South emerged in this period. Sociologists and political scientists carried out careful empirical work on the role played by education in constructing "modern" attitudes and behaviours.[9] Economists seeking to understand economic take-off discovered a residual role for a phenomenon that came to be labelled "human capital," and quickly embarked on rate of return studies to substantiate the claim that education enhances economic productivity.[10] Both modernization theories and human capital theory promoted a functional view of schooling as an essential ingredient for national development. Education was linked to economic growth (greater national wealth); social development (more equitable distribution of wealth or opportunity); and political development (the creation of democratic systems).[11]

By the early 1970s, however, many scholars began to question the ambitions that lay behind the spread of modern schooling systems. Researchers challenged the earlier confidence in education's role in political modernization and economic growth, as well as its positive effects on social equality. Political scientist David Abernathy and sociologist Philip Foster,[12] for example, used their research in West Africa to question the wisdom of expanding education in contexts where economic growth was limited. Without the expansion of modern employment, Foster, Abernathy, and others warned, schooling might lead to widespread political dissatisfaction among the young, an unwillingness to work in agriculture, and subsequent political destabilization.[13] Other researchers began to show that while wealthier countries tend to have better educated populations, the expansion of schooling provides no guarantee of economic growth.[14] The effects of educational expansion are sensitive to context: for example, national political stability and position in the global trading system each structure the effects of schooling on individual, community, and national development.[15]

Questions about the role played by schools in the achievement of social equality were also raised. In the United States and the United Kingdom, educational sociologists such as A.H. Halsey and James Coleman collected detailed data suggesting that schooling had minimal impact in altering the socio-economic status and life chances of children.[16] Family socio-economic background played a much larger role. Initial research from the developing world seemed to suggest that schooling did a better job of promoting intergenerational mobility in poor countries, but again, this outcome relied heavily upon the availability of new jobs, and in turn on high rates of economic growth.[17] Subsequent research showed that even in contexts of economic growth, the equity-enhancing effects of each level of schooling seemed to weaken as it became universally available, passing pressure for access upwards to the next level in the educational system.[18] In most cases, elites manage to maintain their status by getting more education than the masses. Furthermore, although schooling could be shown to have positive effects on fertility (lowering the number of children) and on maternal ability to ensure children's health, it often also reinforced ethnic and gender inequality.[19]

Comparative education scholars were sharply influenced by these research findings, as well as by the rising criticisms of education from intellectuals in the global South. A wave of theoretical and empirical work influenced by neo-Marxism explicated in detail the mechanisms through which schooling fed the reproduction of capitalist social relations on a global scale.[20] Led by Franz Fanon, Ivan Illich, and Martin Carnoy, a countermovement of education and development theories emerged which blended neo-Marxist sociologies of education with dependency arguments to produce a hard-hitting critique of Western education as "cultural imperialism." Comparativists posited that the expansion of education in the South was part of a larger process of neo-colonialism, in which developing countries were integrated into a world economic system as supporting satellites of the West.[21]

Educational systems were thought to be playing several different roles in extending a new form of dependency. In the poorest and most marginal countries, schooling produced elite classes who identified with the values and culture of the West and were willing to exploit their own populations to emulate Western lifestyles. Schooling also acted as a legitimating mechanism that laid responsibility for failure in the world economy on the nation and the individual, rather than on the unequal and exploitative features of the world system itself.[22] Even in countries experiencing economic growth, schooling could still be viewed as producing a form of dependency: in this case habituating workers to competition in a global system of trade.

Alongside these criticisms from the left, the 1970s also saw the emergence of a variety of movements inside the developing world that focused on finding alternatives to dependent development. In Africa, for example, political leaders such as Kwame Nkrumah and Julius Nyerere pioneered the idea of African socialism as an alternative to neo-imperialism.[23] Leading African thinkers, including novelists Chinua Achebe and Ngugi wa Thiong'o, began to expose the cultural dimensions of neo-colonialism and explored African philosophy and indigenous forms of knowledge as alternatives to Western approaches to learning.[24] (See Chapter Four.) The spirit of these efforts is captured in the recent work of George Dei, who argues for

> an approach to African development that is anchored in a retrieval, revitalization, and restoration of the indigenous African sense of shared, sustainable, and just social values. I contend that African peoples must re-appropriate their cultural resource knowledge if they are to benefit from the power of collective responsibility for social development. Indigenousness may be defined as knowledge consciousness arising locally and in association with the long-term occupancy of a place. Indigenousness refers to the traditional norms, social values, and mental constructs that guide, organize, and regulate African ways of living in and making sense of the world. Indigenous knowledges differ from conventional knowledges in their absence of imperial and colonial imposition. The notion of indigenousness highlights the power of dynamics embedded in the production, interrogation, validation, and dissemination of global knowledge about "international

development." It also recognizes the multiple and collective origins and collaborative dimensions of knowledge, and underscores that the interpretation or analysis of social reality is subject to different and sometimes oppositional perspectives.[25]

Such criticisms naturally led to proposals for alternative forms of education. Julius Nyerere, the longtime president of Tanzania (1961–1985), first captured this momentum in his well-known essay, "Education for Self-Reliance."[26] Nyerere's interest in self-reliance shares a great deal with Mahatma Gandhi's approach. He saw the inherited colonial education system in Tanzania as elitist in nature and oriented to Western interests and norms. Nyerere not only promised to make access to primary education free and to introduce universal adult literacy programs, he also envisioned schools as community institutions, supporting farms, workshops, and cultural activities that would help bridge the divide between school and rural society.[27] In a move that attracted international attention, Nyerere expanded opportunities for adult education and initiated a national literacy campaign.[28]

The 1970s saw the South-North diffusion of strong, alternative pedagogical models, emanating from socialist educational experiments in the developing world and from the writing and field-tested curriculum of Paulo Freire.[29] Freire built his approach to education around the concept of "conscientization" (introduced in Chapter One), in which he integrated a commitment to education as the practice of freedom and the idea that a dialogue about the learner's own experience can be transformative. Freire criticized dominant elites for using a banking concept of education that encouraged the passivity of oppressed peoples. He argued instead that:

> [T]he task of the humanists is to see that the oppressed become aware of the fact that as dual beings, "housing" the oppressors within themselves, they cannot be truly human. This task implies that revolutionary leaders do not go to the people in order to bring them a message of salvation, but in order to come to know through dialogue with them both their *objective situation* and their *awareness* of that situation — the various levels of perception of themselves and of the world in which and with which they exist.[30]

As we shall see in Chapter Five by Joseph P. Farrell, such efforts at transformative pedagogy were picked up in a range of efforts to establish alternative forms of primary education for the poor. The development of alternative approaches to education also led organizations as different as UNICEF, USAID, and the World Bank to more carefully target poor and marginalized populations in their development aid, and at minimum to pay greater rhetorical attention to issues of equality, empowerment, and poverty.[31]

GLOBALIZATION AND THE CRISIS OF EDUCATIONAL DEVELOPMENT IN AFRICA

Despite skepticism and debates about the role of education in development, the period from the 1960s to the mid-1970s was characterized by widespread expansion of public educational systems. In nearly all developing countries, where colonially inherited educational systems excluded the majority, changes were profound. Primary school enrolments, for example, increased more than sixfold over a 30-year period in sub-Saharan Africa. While fewer than half of all school-aged children were in school in the early 1970s, by 1980, three-fourths attended schools.[32] In some countries, enrolment ratios, particularly of girls, remained quite low (for example, Francophone West Africa). But across the countries of East and Southern Africa, it was not uncommon to find near to universal access to schooling. In Tanzania, for example, primary school enrolments expanded from 903,000 children in 1971 to 3,500,000 million in 1981: a rate of gross enrolments of close to 90 percent.[33]

However, this dramatic and rapid expansion of schooling stalled after 1980. Some countries, such as Tanzania and Kenya, experienced a severe reversal in the ratio of children enrolled in school. The central government and local communities in these countries re-introduced school fees. Educational infrastructure—school buildings, school materials, trained administrators and teachers—deteriorated dramatically, so that even when in school, children received an education of shockingly poor quality. A 1989 UNESCO report from Tanzania (where primary enrolment rates had plummeted to below 75 percent), describes the crisis:

It is not uncommon to find a teacher standing in front of 80–100 pupils who are sitting on a dirt floor in a room without a roof, trying to convey orally the limited knowledge he has, and the pupils trying to take notes on a piece of wrinkled paper using as a writing board the back of the pupil in front of him. There is no teacher guide for the teacher and no textbooks for the children.[34]

Why did this deterioration in access to and quality of education occur? There are several answers to this question. First, African economies, already the most marginal in the global trading system, became even more peripheral during the great wave of economic globalization that began after 1975, in part because rich countries continued to raise barriers to agricultural and other primary commodities from the South. Many African governments also faced a sharp debt overhang, built up over years of borrowing from the West and its institutions for their development. As African government revenues declined, so, too, did available resources for schooling. Even governments that maintained a strong commitment to education saw per capita spending on education deteriorate by an average of $5 across the continent, to an average level of $85 per capita in 1995.[35]

Second, many governments in Africa were poor stewards of their nations. High levels of corruption and nepotism, weak administrative capacity, a tendency towards war, and relatively undemocratic political systems characterized many of the governments of the continent. In these contexts, intermittent promises of access to schooling were often used to broker patrimonial (father-child) relations between politicians and local communities. Used in this way, schooling divided opposition and created "clients" rather than citizens with common perceptions and commitments to social and political rights. In contrast to rich country welfare states, where a strong national social settlement ensured access to education as a right of citizenship, in African countries education was often perceived as a tool of patronage. The hierarchical nature of many African school systems, as inherited from the colonial era, further entrenched inequalities. Administratively, African school systems tended to be organized in a top-down, centralized manner, with little room for participation or innovation.[36]

Finally, external political and institutional factors lay at the root of this crisis. From the late 1970s, African countries faced an increasingly harsh and punitive international community. The wealthier countries of the West were focused on domestic economic reforms to improve their own competitiveness in a globalized economic system, and were less willing to fund international development activities. Rich country governments refused to provide substantial debt relief or to drop trade barriers to the primary commodities produced by developing world countries. Instead they encouraged countries to adopt a set of "belt tightening" and liberalization reforms, often through their engagement with the International Monetary Fund (IMF) and the World Bank. "Structural Adjustment Programs" encouraged governments to place a cap on public spending, often with severe effects on educational provision. In cases such as Tanzania and Kenya, these caps on spending led to the reintroduction of user fees in health and education.[37]

From the late 1980s, externally influenced educational reforms went even further than the constraints and costs imposed by macro-economic adjustment. Developing countries were hit by a set of educational reform proposals that had emerged across rich countries of the world, where policy-makers had begun to question the sustainability of expansionary trends in public funding for education, and were seeking reforms that might guarantee greater efficiency as well as national competitiveness. The first generation of what we might think of as "globalization-driven" reforms in education began in the mid-to-late 1970s when governments began to introduce "finance-driven" measures (cost cutting and the search for new, private sources of finance, for example). A second generation of reforms focused on "competitiveness": the efficient use of schooling to improve the productivity of the domestic labour force.[38] Such reforms, reviewed by Stephen Anderson in Chapter Seven of this volume, included standards-based reform (principally the introduction of national testing regimes) and experiments in school choice and the privatization of educational service delivery (to increase inter-school competition and parental/student motivation).[39] Finance and competitiveness driven reforms tended to squeeze out the expansive, equity-driven mandates of post–World War II educational systems.[40] In turn, they eroded education's role in extending a social compact or settlement to the citizens of developing world countries.

In Africa, these reform measures were carried forward forcefully by the World Bank, which by the mid-1980s had emerged as the largest single financer of educational development as well as the largest education policy think-tank in the world.[41] The World Bank's 1988 landmark publication *Education in Sub-Saharan Africa: Policies for Adjustment, Revitalization and Expansion* suggested that earlier goals of equality themselves could only be met through a substantial liberalization of educational systems. National systems of public education needed to be protected from elite capture, and returned to public accountability through the introduction of market-like mechanisms. Governments were told that they needed to encourage the private provision of education (directly funded by learners) not only because public finances could not afford universal systems, but also because private provision would enhance efficiency and quality. Governments were encouraged to step back from centralized systems of management and return schools to local control (albeit with new regulatory and accountability controls such as national testing regimes).[42]

The impact of these reforms across Africa and the developing world have been mixed. Macroeconomic reforms have, despite their initially steep human costs, brought about a modest renewal of economic growth in countries such as Tanzania, Kenya, and Malawi. At the same time, they have been decried for their negative impact on social equality, since the beneficiaries of economic growth are primarily in the modern sector of the economy, while producers in traditional sectors, such as agriculture, continue to face trade barriers from the North. Further, without debt relief, governments are hard pressed to fund renewal of productive infrastructure: they simply cannot compete in a global market. These economic constraints create a steep barrier for educational change. Without an expanding labour market, it is unclear whether efforts to reform schooling can actually have a great impact on national productivity. Room for social mobility is also sharply constrained. The impact of structural adjustment reforms in Tanzania, for example, has been to shift pressure for access to the secondary level, where there is also a growth of private service delivery. Competition-driven educational reforms — including the decentralization of education, the encouragement of private service delivery, and the devolution of financing to local communities — have had negative impacts on access and equality. Many reforms have floundered because they are introduced with no new resources for already fragile systems.[43] Most observers agree that inequality of educational opportunity increased considerably in Tanzania between 1980 and 2000, "with a growing gap between those who can afford user fees and other school related expenses, and those who cannot."[44]

THE REVIVAL OF "EDUCATION FOR ALL" AFTER 2000

In recent years, the international context for educational development in Africa and other parts of the developing world has taken a somewhat more positive turn. Between 2000 and 2007, rich country governments substantially increased levels of foreign aid to Africa and made new commitments to debt relief. In addition, for the first time the international community has signalled that it will try to close the funding gap that prevents children in the poorest regions of the world from gaining access to schooling. Education emerged as a priority at the Millennium Summit of the United Nations and within the Millennium Development Goals set by the international community at this summit in 2000.[45] It also has gained renewed attention from the World Bank and the IMF, which now look for the achievement of universal access to basic education in their country lending programs.[46]

These changes are particularly dramatic when placed alongside what has been widely assessed as the failure of the international community to achieve the goals established for education at the World Conference on Education for All in Jomtien, Thailand in 1990.[47] The 1990s saw a precipitous decline in overall flows of aid, and an even steeper decline in aid for education. Instead of the "peace dividend" (expected by many at the end of the Cold War), issues of global poverty and inequality were sidelined as governments struggled to adjust to a rapidly integrating global economy.

The resurgence of interest in Education for All by the global community today is tightly linked to two new developments. First, the high-profile anti-globalization protests in response to the 1999 meeting of the World Trade Organization (WTO) in Seattle brought to the forefront the increasing public concern about the negative impacts of globalization. The growing strength, solidarity, and voice of such movements has placed pressure on rich country governments and major international organizations to recognize and respond to these concerns.[48] Second, the rising importance of the European Union, with its more expansive approach to social welfare, has also contributed to new interest in global poverty within the international community. Thus, after more than a decade of declining aid and neo-liberal policy reforms, rich country governments and their multilateral institutions have begun to develop a consensus about international poverty and inequality that appears to offer a framework for a global "Third Way."[49] This consensus links international development to democracy, good governance, and human rights in a more extensive manner than ever before, while also strongly asserting the primacy of markets and capitalism.

Schooling appears to have re-emerged as a central part of this new international consensus or compact, in part because it fits with both the neo-liberal and pro-economic globalization approaches to development endorsed by the International Monetary Fund (IMF) and the World Bank, and the more equity conscious and globalization skeptic approaches adopted by the United Nations.[50] Education straddles both equity and productivity conceptualizations of development, bridging the divide between the neo-liberal and social welfare orientations to global development. Thus, the World Bank argues:

> The expansion of educational opportunity, which can simul-taneously promote income equality and growth, is a win-win strategy that in most societies is far easier to implement than the redistribution of other assets, such as land or capital. In short, education is one of the most powerful instruments known for reducing poverty and inequality and for laying the basis for sustained economic growth, sound governance, and effective institutions.[51]

Others sum up the consensus about education somewhat more critically:

> A crude characterization of the current approach is to encourage internal and external trade liberalization, and simultaneously invest in health, education and good governance, so that people are able to take advantage of new economic opportunities.[52]

This growing international consensus about education is reflected in the seeming ease with which many development organizations and advocates are now calling for increased global support for achieving the universal right to education.[53] For example, the UN's Millennium Development Project Task Force on Education has argued for a "Global Compact on Education" to parallel the new consensus on global development. These calls demand significant reform of the aid business itself. Building on recommendations for donor harmonization and coordination advanced by the Organisation for Economic Co-operation and Development (OECD), the UN Millennium Project urges donors to "commit new funds [7 billion/year] in a new way through a strong coordinated global effort that rewards and reinforces countries' measurable progress."[54] Rich nations are being asked to provide a long-term, steady, and reliable source of funding for the recurrent costs of schooling in the poorest countries of the world, as well as major improvements in terms of donor coordination, concentration of aid on the poorest countries, and the untying of aid to education. Indeed, since 2002, many donor governments have begun to pool their aid to provide funding for the recurrent costs of schools in the South — a first in the history of international development cooperation, which has generally shied away from directly paying for teachers' salaries and other recurrent costs of mass education. In some countries, such as Zambia and Uganda, upwards of 20 percent of the national education recurrent budget is now being funded by external donors.[55]

Education for All efforts have also been fed by the burgeoning of transnational social movements that have used education as a core venue for advocating for global redistributive justice. The right to education is supported by an increasingly active network of transnational advocacy organizations devoted to such issues as debt relief, Overseas Development Assistance (ODA) reform, human rights, and globalization. These actors have been particularly influential in forcing changes in international policies that reflect stronger commitment to social equality and poverty alleviation. Such advocacy work has included successful campaigns against World Bank and IMF policies on user fees in health and education.[56] In addition, the Global Campaign for Education (GCE), a powerful transnational advocacy network devoted to EFA, has also emerged in recent years. Initiated by Oxfam International, ActionAid, and the international association of teachers unions (Education International), the Global Campaign for Education now counts among its members a large number of national civil society EFA coalitions around the world, as well as some of the largest international non-governmental organizations involved in education (including CARE, Save the Children, and Global March). The GCE has been instrumental in pushing bilateral donors, international organizations, and members of the G8 (Group of Eight)[57] industrialized countries to make concrete commitments of resources for EFA. It acts as policy watchdog at the international and national levels, raising issues of adequate financing and equitable distribution of opportunities in national educational planning exercises and in international fora; producing an annual "report card" on developing country and rich country contributions to EFA; and lobbying at the annual World Bank/IMF meetings to highlight the negative impact of IMF conditionalities.[58]

These international initiatives have meshed with democracy reforms across many African countries to produce a return to ambitious plans for universal primary education in recent years.[59] Beginning with Malawi's first multi-party elections in 1994, a series of newly and democratically elected African governments have made free primary education (FPE) an election promise. It appears that when free multi-party elections are held, governing parties see a strong incentive for introducing universal access to basic services. Such promises in Uganda, Kenya, Tanzania, and, most recently, Burundi have led to an enormous increase of students in the primary system.

Political liberalization has also allowed for the development of an increasingly vocal network of civil society organizations across Africa. These organizations not only advocate for equity-driven approaches to national development; they also work with transnational advocacy groups to ensure that international organizations alter their social policy prescriptions. Thus two of the outcomes of political liberalization — universal free schooling and the expansion of local civil society organizations — have been mutually reinforcing. The concepts of EFA and the right to education have now re-emerged as a central part of the social and political landscape in African countries. Political activism by domestic and transnational groups ensures that EFA is something in which both government elites and the local public share a strong stake.

EDUCATION FOR ALL: THE VIEW FROM TANZANIA AND KENYA

Current challenges and dilemmas of educational development can be illustrated by reference to two East African countries, Tanzania and Kenya. Both countries have recently announced national policies supporting universal, free access to primary education. They share a long history of governmental efforts to use education to support economic and social development. Yet, in both cases, the re-introduction of universal access to primary education has raised many new dilemmas.

As noted above, Tanzania was host to a unique experiment in education during the 1960s and 1970s. Under Nyerere's policy of "Education for Self-Reliance," Tanzania was among the first countries in Africa to achieve universal enrolment of children at the primary level; it also achieved relatively high levels of literacy among adults,

and introduced a curriculum that focused on rural productivity. But because Tanzania was among the poorest countries in Africa, these gains came at a cost: to achieve universal free primary education and adult literacy, the government severely limited access to secondary education to less than 5 percent of the school-leaving population. Nyerere's education initiatives, like many of his government's social policy initiatives, were linked to centralizing processes of village-ization and forced resettlement. Ironically, an authoritarian, one-party approach to governance in Tanzania formed the backdrop for policies meant to support universal access and self-reliance.

Kenya and Tanzania are frequently contrasted in the literature because of the sharply divergent development paths their governments chose after independence. While Tanzania pioneered a form of African socialism, Kenya eschewed efforts at centralized socialism and instead adopted a market-oriented approach to development. In addition, Kenya has been the more prosperous of the two countries, not only because it is endowed with significant natural resources but also because it inherited a more developed market economy and physical infrastructure from the colonial period. As a result, early EFA experiences in Kenya and Tanzania were quite different.

At independence, Kenya began with much higher levels of participation in school than Tanzania.[60] Unlike Tanzania, the Kenyan government did not constrain expansion at secondary level in order to focus on universal primary education. Instead, it encouraged communities to build their own secondary schools through a movement known as *harambee* — Swahili for "let us all pull together." As secondary schooling rapidly expanded in Kenya during the 1970s, the government did little to guide its expansion in terms of either quality or distribution. Kenya, again in contrast to Tanzania, paid little attention to reforming its school curriculum to build a distinct national identity or alternative approach to development.[61] Nor did it enforce its promise of free primary education. Despite announcements ending formal fees in 1974 and 1979, individual schools were quietly allowed to re-institute fees for attendance. Thus, although the central government maintained control over the educational system through a national examination system and school inspections, many aspects of Kenya's approach to education mirrored the laissez-faire, open-market approach to development adopted by its government.

This approach to educational expansion in turn contributed to the development of clientalist politics in Kenya, fed by the *harambee* school movement. Under *harambee*, individual politicians were encouraged to make frequent contributions to local *harambee* schools in order to build political support and patronage. Wealthy communities and ethnic groups were able to build more and better schools than poorer communities, and large geographic disparities emerged in terms of opportunity and quality. At the same time, *harambee* schools helped to deflect attention from central government, offering an outlet for popular educational aspirations without creating binding expectations that government should ensure quality or equity across the school system. Disparities in educational opportunity were rarely blamed on the central government.[62]

In the early 1980s, both Tanzania and Kenya entered a period of severe economic constraint, accompanied by neo-liberal economic and educational reforms.[63] In both countries, primary schooling began to deteriorate. Steep declines in educational quality were accompanied by the stagnation and later erosion of enrolments.

In this context, national policies towards education in both countries during the 1980s began to change. In Kenya, the government tried to reassert centralized control over the educational system and to reign in educational expectations. In 1983, the government introduced a new primary cycle of eight years with a new focus on pre-vocational training for self-employment. It introduced secondary and tertiary quotas, and announced that educational policies would be closed to public debate. However, the Kenyan government continued to respond to popular demands for access to higher education: in the late 1980s it expanded university enrolments, further depriving elementary education of finances. Meanwhile, in Tanzania, the government removed the cap on secondary school enrolments, encouraged communities to sponsor private secondary schools, and opened new university spaces. Tanzania's innovative literacy and adult education programs were neglected, and efforts to create a curriculum reflective of local issues and African socialism fell by the wayside.

By the late 1980s, both Tanzania and Kenya began to experience external pressures to introduce cost-sharing policies into their education systems as part of structural adjustment lending. Neither country received significant increases in external aid, despite their economic crises. Indeed, charges of corruption within the Kenyan government led several donors to cease their external aid programs altogether.

Today, Tanzania is still one of the poorest countries in the world, with a per capita GDP of US$330 in 2004. One of every three Tanzanians lives below the poverty line of 26 cents (US) per day, and more than one out of every 10 children under the age of 18 has been orphaned by AIDS. However, the achievement of multi-party democracy (in 1995) and the election of a reform-minded government have allowed the country to experience renewed economic growth and to receive increased development funding from the international community since the late 1990s.

In 2003, the Tanzanian government abolished user fees for primary education, after a successful campaign launched by both domestic and international advocacy organizations. The process through which this occurred demonstrates how new forms of global and transnational accountability are emerging around universal rights, such as the right to education. In the Tanzanian case, research on the negative impact of user fees in education was produced by the education NGO *Maarifa ni Ufunguo* in 2000. This research was then used by American NGOs to lobby members of the US House and Senate, who eventually passed legislation prohibiting the US government from funding the World Bank if it imposed any form of user fees as part of its loan conditionality. The World Bank subsequently removed user fees from its loan conditions, and the Government of Tanzania declared free primary education (FPE).[64] The Tanzania experience in turn stimulated a number of other African governments to remove user fees in education and declare universal FPE. Today, Tanzania continues to boast a vibrant network of civil society organizations working to monitor their government's educational commitments.

In Tanzania, the public response to the declaration of free education was overwhelming and immediate: overnight, approximately 1.6 million new students entered the primary system.[65] Since FPE was announced in 2003, gross enrolment ratios have risen from a low of 77 percent in the mid-1990s back to levels of more than 90 percent. However, expansion of the country's primary education system is heavily dependent on foreign donors. These donors have encouraged the government to decentralize the administration of the education system, so that today school councils in Tanzania have responsibility for preparing budgets and school plans, managing funds and salaries, and preparing financial reports. At the national level a greater variety of stakeholders participate in education policy setting, including civil society and citizens' organizations.[66]

In Kenya, the announcement of FPE came in late 2002, the year in which the longtime rule of Kenya's African National Union party ended with the election of the National Rainbow Coalition (NARC), a party formed from a number of opposition groups. As in Tanzania, the popular response to this announcement was overwhelming: following the implementation of FPE, 1.2 million out-of-school children were absorbed into formal primary schools and 200,000 into non-formal education centres. There had been little planning for such a large response, and only a very limited budget for it. As a result, the first few years of FPE have been somewhat chaotic. A significant number of civil society groups now monitors the Kenyan government's implementation of FPE, although in Kenya there appears to be less formal coherence in the policies advocated by these nongovernmental groups.

The opening up of access to primary education in Tanzania and Kenya has been viewed positively by the international community. Yet, for both countries, FPE raises a host of questions. In both instances, FPE relies very heavily on international aid. Foreign donors finance a large share of Tanzania's education budget.[67] Kenya, while much less dependent on foreign aid, still requires external funding to meet new levels of enrolment. Such dependency puts the future of FPE in a very vulnerable position: a small change in donor funding would place the education of thousands of children at risk. These high levels of dependency also tend to lead to donor driven policies, rather than local control and ownership.[68] There is little sign, in either country, of efforts to "indigenize" the curriculum or use African knowledge as a basis for educational reform. (See Chapter Four in this volume for a more in-depth discussion of Indigenous knowledge and its relationship to EFA.) In both Tanzania and Kenya, the strength of external influence is amplified by a decision among donors to pool their resources and develop regular measures to jointly monitor government expenditures and implementation of policies.

Table 3.1
National Profiles of Tanzania and Kenya[69]

	Tanzania	Kenya
Total Population	38.3 million (2005)	34.3 million (2005)
GDP per capita	US$330 (2005)	US$442 (2005)
ODA as % GDP	16.1% (2004)	3.9% (2004)
Date of Independence	1961	1963
First Multi-party Elections	1995 (Change of leadership but not of party)	1992 (No change of leadership or party until 2002)
Universal Free Primary Education	• First achieved in 1973 • Re-introduced in 2003	• First promised in 1963; again in 1969, 1973, and 1983 • Removal of fees for first 4 years of school implemented in 1974 • Re-introduced, 2002
Transition to Secondary Education	33.2% (2004)	95.4% (2003)

At the local level, the rapid expansion of access to education in Tanzania and Kenya has had sharp implications for the quality of learning. Even with the increase in donor funding, class sizes of over 100 students are not unusual at the primary level in either country. Materials and classroom equipment are in short supply. While donor agencies have focused their funds on providing school level funds for materials and improved classrooms, there is still a strong belief in public sector constraint. Similarly, although many donors are funding teacher training, there is no related support for teacher salaries; thus teacher shortages are likely to continue.

Perhaps most importantly, it is still not clear what going to school can do for national or individual welfare, at least in the short term. While parents continue to see education as a stepping stone towards modern employment, the availability of formal sector employment in Kenya and Tanzania is limited. In both countries the public continues to demand the expansion of secondary level education, and many observers expect that motivation to complete primary schooling will slacken if access to secondary education and formal employment does not improve. Reform measures that encourage terminal primary education focused on self-reliant skills for production—the core of Nyerere's message in "Education for Self Reliance"—continue to be sidelined by parents and governmental elites whose focus is climbing what Robert Serpell describes as the "narrow educational staircase"[70] towards greater individual mobility. The achievement of broad-based equality through education is in tension with competitive self-interest.

The Kenyan and Tanzanian governments are under enormous pressure today—both from domestic groups and international actors—to maintain momentum towards EFA, even as they face limited national budgets, unreliable aid flows, low levels of formal employment, limited access to rich country markets, and increasing popular demand for access to secondary and tertiary education. The fragile democratic regimes at the centre of politics in these two countries have nonetheless staked their claims for political legitimacy on the promise of universal free education. It is not surprising, then, to see governments in both countries scrambling to find ways of harnessing private sector partnerships to expand education, and endorsing donor-advocated reforms such as the decentralization of school management and budgets. Such reforms deflect attention away from the central government and also offer mechanisms for doing more with less. They add to the heightened complexity and interdependencies that now frame achievement of the universal right to education in these and other developing countries.

CONCLUSION

The Tanzanian and Kenyan examples highlight many of the dilemmas and challenges surrounding the international call for universal primary education. Domestically, an orientation towards greater equity, self-reliance, and public accountability across primary and later levels of schooling promises enormous returns. However, these returns can only be realized if, at the level of the world system, there are guarantees of long-term funding for the poorest countries, cancellation of debt, and access to the agricultural and other product markets in rich countries. The emergence of a transnationally organized global public that is critical of globalization and global economic inequalities, and that views the right to education as an important venue for expressing a commitment to redistributive justice on a global scale, is a hopeful sign. Such transnational networks can help pressure rich country governments to provide reliable, long-term international funding. They can also help ensure that the voices of local civil society groups, closest to indigenous knowledge and the everyday experiences of schooling, are heard by national educational policy-makers.

Overall, the democratization of opportunities for learning in the developing world remains a fragile and easily reversible process. For children in many of the world's poorest countries, access to schooling has been a hollow privilege. While schooling may bring children into a global community of childhood rights and expectations, it often also sorts children into poverty and alienates them from their local cultures in ways that harm local self-reliance. The challenge of offering every child an equal opportunity to learn involves not just more schooling, but better models of schooling that will prepare them for active roles in social transformation.

QUESTIONS FOR REFLECTION AND DISCUSSION

1. What drives the demand for and expansion of schooling at basic and at higher education levels? Are the drivers in Kenya and Tanzania similar to or different from those in your own cultural context?
2. How do you view the chances of success for recent international efforts to achieve EFA?
3. What can experiences of schooling in the South teach us about benefits and challenges within our own educational systems?

4. How does schooling in North America sort children into different
    kinds of life chances? How does this compare with educational life
    chances in countries such as Tanzania or Kenya?

SUGGESTED FILM: *BACK TO SCHOOL*, PART OF THE *WIDE ANGLE* PBS SERIES OF INTERNATIONAL DOCUMENTARIES

Back to School, the second part of the film series, follows the school
experiences of seven children in seven different countries trying to beat
the odds and get an education. The series will document the experiences
of these children to 2015, the year the international community has
targeted for universal access to primary education.

SUGGESTIONS FOR FURTHER READING

Abdi, Ali. "African Philosophies of Education: Counter-Colonial
    Criticisms." In *Issues in African Education: Sociological Perspectives,*
    edited by Ali Abdi and Ailie Cleghorn. New York: Palgrave
    Macmillan, 2005, 25–42.
Achebe, Chinua. *Things Fall Apart.* London: Heinemann, 1958.
*Anderson-Levitt, Kathryn. "The Schoolyard Gate: Schooling and
    Childhood in Global Perspective." *Journal of Social History* 38, no.
    4 (2005): 987–1006.
Buchmann, Claudia. "The State and Schooling in Kenya: Historical
    Developments and Current Challenges." *Africa Today* 46, no. 1
    (1999): 95–115.
Cooksey, Brian, David Court, and Ben Makau. "Education for Self-
    Reliance and Harambee." In *Beyond Capitalism and Socialism in
    Kenya and Tanzania,* edited by Joel Barkan. London: Lynne Rienner,
    1994, 201–34.
Fanon, Frantz. *The Wretched of the Earth.* New York: Grove Press,
    1968.
Freire, Paulo. *Pedagogy of the Oppressed.* New York: Continuum, 1970.
Fuller, Bruce. *Growing up Modern: The Western States Build Third World
    Schools.* New York: Routledge, 1991.
*Lewis, Stephen. "Education: An Avalanche of Studies, Little Studying."
    Chap. 3 in *Race Against Time.* Toronto: Anansi Press, 2005.
Mundy, Karen. "Education for All and the New Development Compact."
    International Review of Education 52, no. 1 (2006): 23–48.

Nyerere, Julius K. "Education for Self Reliance." Chap. 1 in *Ujamaa: Essays on Socialism*. Dar es Salaam, Tanzania: Oxford University Press, 1967.

Samoff, Joel. "'Modernizing' a Socialist Vision: Education in Tanzania." In *Education and Social Transition in the Third World*, edited by Martin Carnoy and Joel Samoff. Princeton: Princeton University Press, 1990, 209–73.

Samoff, Joel. "No Teacher Guide, No Textbook, No Chairs: Contending with Crisis in African Education." In *Comparative Education: The Dialectic of the Global and the Local*, edited by Robert F. Arnove and Carlos A. Torres. New York: Rowman and Littlefield, 1999, 409–45.

Semali, Ladislaus. "Community as Classroom: Dilemmas of Valuing African Indigenous Literacy in Education." *International Review of Education* 45, no. 3/4 (1999): 305–19.

*Serpell, Robert. "Local Accountability to Rural Communities: A Challenge for Education Planning in Africa." In *Education, Cultures, and Economics: Dilemmas for Development*, edited by Fiona E. Leach and Angela W. Little. London: Routledge, 1999, 111–42.

Wa Thiong'o, Ngugi. *Decolonising the Mind: The Politics of Language in African Literature*. London: James Curry, 1986.

Chapter Four

Comparative Indigenous Ways of Knowing and Learning

Katherine Madjidi and Jean-Paul Restoule

INTRODUCTION

Comparative education tends to focus primarily on mainstream national systems of education. These systems are often colonial models imposed on the earlier inhabitants of the country, although that point is not always made explicit by the comparativist.[1] Indigenous epistemologies and pedagogies have garnered little attention in comparative education theory and practice. However, Indigenous peoples have maintained and honoured their distinct ways of knowing for generations, even while experiencing intense colonial pressure. In a time when many are recognizing the limitations of Western, monocultural education systems, Indigenous ways of knowing and learning provide a rich basis for comparative education study. As this chapter will illustrate, these worldviews have much to offer today's Indigenous and non-Indigenous students and educators as we seek sustainable, peaceful ways to live.

This chapter highlights key areas for the comparative study of Indigenous ways of knowing and learning. We begin by demonstrating that an opportunity for comparative education presents itself within nation-state borders, through the study of Western (mainstream) and Indigenous (locally contextual) worldviews. We then discuss the representation of Indigenous knowledge in comparative education, and introduce four areas for further comparative study: the reclaiming of Indigenous ways of knowing, comparative Indigenous-to-Indigenous exchange, Indigenous knowledge and international educational policy, and the relevance of Indigenous ways of knowing for mainstream educational reform. We conclude by discussing some implications of Indigenous ways of knowing and learning for teachers, and suggest ways to incorporate these into today's classrooms.

TERMS

Def.

In this chapter, the terms *Indigenous* or *Indigenous peoples* refer to the original inhabitants of a particular geographic territory or area, as well as to collective Indigenous peoples internationally.[2] The capitalized term *Aboriginal* refers specifically to the First Nations, Métis, and Inuit peoples in Canada, although it can also be used synonymously with *Indigenous*. *Native American* or *American Indian* refers to the Indigenous peoples residing in what is now known as the United States of America.[3] *Western* is used to designate people, customs, and ideas originating from a European context, including countries with majority populations of European descendents such as Canada, the United States, and Australia. Wherever possible, the specific name for a particular cultural group will be used (for example, Anishinaabe, Innu, Swedish).[4] We note that Western and Indigenous, as monolithic categories, are broad generalizations, both comprised of diverse national and cultural groups, each with their own unique traditions, perspectives, and approaches to learning. However, we use these general categories as a basis for drawing out points of comparison between two distinct sets of worldviews and approaches to knowing and learning.

COMPARATIVE WESTERN AND INDIGENOUS WAYS OF KNOWING AND LEARNING

The clash of Western and Indigenous epistemologies can be traced back to first contact, meaning the moments in which colonial and Indigenous cultures first collided. Although it was usually assumed by colonizers that the Indigenous populations were so-called primitive cultures without sophisticated social systems, each Indigenous group had its own developed worldview and corresponding approaches for the socialization and education of its people.[5] For example, Wendy Brady states that her Australian Aboriginal ancestors had systems of education in place for 40,000 years before these were destroyed by 208 years of colonialism.[6] Further conflict occurred as the colonizers attempted to assimilate, subjugate, or "save" Indigenous people by indoctrinating them in Western educational systems. In Canada, this was carried out by forcefully taking Aboriginal children from their families and sending them to residential schools far from home, where they were subjected to foreign belief systems, foods, language, clothing, and religion, and often to physical, emotional, psychological, and sexual abuse. This systematic effort to instill Western knowledge and values and to simultaneously erase Aboriginal cultural ways of knowing and learning is at the root of many of the challenges troubling Aboriginal populations in Canada.[7] This experience was not unique to Canada: systematic, imposed residential schooling for Indigenous children was also implemented in the United States (under the name Indian boarding schools) and Australia (where the children who were taken are called the Stolen Generation). In developing countries such as Guyana, in South America, the boarding school model is still used in rural Indigenous regions, and many of the same practices (including discouragement of Indigenous language, dress, and culture; imposition of Western curriculum; and separation from family and community) continue today.

Western and Indigenous models of education are each framed by worldviews that inform their epistemologies and pedagogies. Epistemology, from a Western standpoint, is the theory of knowledge, and pedagogy, the processes by which people come to learn or know.[8] The essential conflict between Indigenous and imported educational systems arises, as Vandra Lea Masemann describes, "from a basic epistemological difference in the path to knowledge itself; that is, a basic disagreement about how people come to know what they know and why they believe it to be true."[9]

As the primary basis for most colonially imposed systems of education, Western methods are currently accepted as the mainstream approach to education in most countries. This model emerged relatively recently from its own comparative background across Western cultures; for example, we learned in Chapter One that the United States borrowed from the Prussians in developing free and compulsory education in the mid-1800s. This system of schooling has not always been widely accepted or implemented, as we learned from Karen Mundy in Chapter Three. However, Western educational models have converged today to comprise what is commonly thought of as schooling or education, and generally include formal school settings, age-graded classrooms, separation of learning into disciplines, belief in a linear and objective pursuit of truth, and a focus on literacy, numeracy, and science as primary areas for basic education.

Common generalizations comparing Western and Indigenous epistemologies include binary classifications such as linear versus cyclical, objective versus subjective, secular versus spiritual, industrial versus nature- and context-based, and fragmentary versus holistic.[10] To construct a more in-depth comparative picture, the following aspects of ways of knowing and learning can be explored: What are learning and knowledge? Where do people come to learn and know? How do people come to learn and know? From whom do they learn? And, why/for what purpose do they learn? Given the wealth of literature on Western models of education, and the Western educational paradigm in which this chapter is being written, this section will focus on Indigenous educational approaches and perspectives from Indigenous scholars on these five questions. Through an analysis of this literature, we will draw out comparisons between Western and Indigenous ways of knowing and learning.

What Are Learning and Knowledge?

Mi'kmaq scholar Marie Battiste describes Indigenous epistemology as theories, philosophies, histories, ceremonies, and stories as ways of knowing. She offers the following commonly used understanding of Indigenous knowledge: "Indigenous knowledge comprises all knowledge pertaining to a particular people and its territory, the nature or use of which has been transmitted from generation to generation."[11] However, she also claims that rather than being diametrically opposed to Western education, Indigenous knowledge reveals Western limitations by presenting a more holistic, developed form of knowledge that "fills the ethical and knowledge gaps in Eurocentric education, research and scholarship."[12] She provides a fuller definition of Indigenous knowledge, explaining:

> [It] embodies a web of relationships within a specific ecological context; contains linguistic categories, rules and relationships unique to each knowledge system; has localized content and meaning; has established customs with respect to acquiring and sharing of knowledge ... and implies responsibilities for possessing various kinds of knowledge.[13]

Several Indigenous scholars identify two central themes underlying Indigenous worldviews: all things are animate and all things are interconnected. Joseph Couture writes, "There are only two things you have to remember about being Indian. One is that everything is alive, and the second is that we are all related."[14] Willie Ermine articulates the two key concepts in Indigenous philosophy as power and place, "power being the living energy that inhibits and/or composes the universe, and place being the relationship of things to each other."[15] In this worldview, human beings are seen as one element in a greater circle of unity with all Creation. Understanding this relationship is foundational to learning one's place in the world.

The notion of spiritual reality is also central to Indigenous epistemology.[16] Battiste explains, "Knowledge is not secular. It is a process derived from creation, and as such, it has a sacred purpose. It is inherent in and connected to all of nature, to its creatures, and to human existence."[17] Leroy Little Bear states, "In Aboriginal philosophy … all things are animate, imbued with spirit, and in constant motion. In this realm of energy and spirit, interrelationships between all entities are of paramount importance, and space is a more important referent than time."[18] From an Indigenous perspective, it is through the spiritual or metaphysical worlds that one can construct meaning in the physical world.[19] This contrasts sharply with the modern-day secularity of Western education. Although many colonial schools were associated with a church, current Western religious education in schools is primarily externally imposed, prescriptive, and treated as separate subject matter within the disciplinary pursuit of knowledge. Indigenous spirituality is largely personal, sacred, and integrated throughout one's interaction with and interpretation of the world.[20]

The importance of spiritual development is represented in the Indigenous-based framework known as the medicine wheel. Depictions of the medicine wheel are usually divided into four quadrants, representing the four cardinal directions as well as the four areas of human development (physical, emotional, mental, and spiritual). Each of these directions is associated with multiple meanings, such as stages of life, seasons, animals, gifts, or qualities. Some cultures include additional dimensions, such as placing the self at the centre of wheel to mark balance and the spiritual relationships between all things,[21] or two additional directions above and below to represent the spirit world and the Mother Earth. Although its use is primarily associated with North American Plains cultures (such as Cree, Dakota, and Blackfoot), similar concepts are used by Indigenous groups throughout the world, such as the Maori *Nga hau e wha* (four winds) and other models based upon the circle and the idea of four or six directions.[22] Marlene Brant Castellano writes that the medicine wheel "is not a model of rigid categorization … rather it is a model of balance … The medicine wheel teaches us to seek ways of incorporating the gifts of the other quadrants … Through the sharing of diverse gifts, balance is created in individual lives and in society as a whole."[23]

The medicine wheel, as Figure 4.1 depicts, offers a clear basis for Indigenous epistemological frameworks and the development of related pedagogy.[24] *The Sacred Tree* describes the four directions as each holding particular gifts, which an individual has the potential to develop throughout a lifelong journey of learning. Rather than viewing education as the development of intellectual capacity, as is primarily the case in Western education, the medicine wheel frames human

Figure 4.1
Medicine Wheel[25]

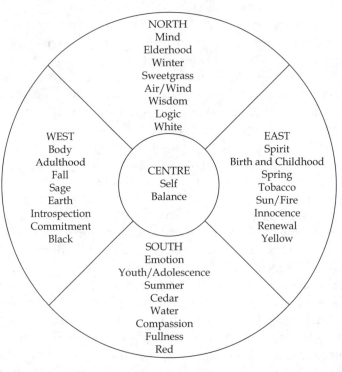

development holistically. With developmental capacities falling within each area of the medicine wheel, corresponding pedagogical practices and educational objectives can be constructed.[26]

Where Do People Learn?
For Indigenous peoples, knowledge is firmly grounded in a particular sense of place. Little Bear writes, "The Earth cannot be separated from the actual being of Indians."[27] This relationship with the earth as Mother, and with a traditional territory as the basis for and source of life, is central to all processes of learning and knowing for Indigenous peoples. Pueblo educator and scholar Gregory Cajete explains, "Indigenous education is, in its truest form, about learning relationships in context."[28] African scholar George Dei also emphasizes the importance of place as the basis for Indigenous spirituality and knowledge,[29] as we learned in Chapter Three. Therefore, when Indigenous peoples are educated in Western school buildings, separate from their traditional land, this decontextualizes their learning and disconnects learners from their base of experience.

The Canadian Royal Commission on Aboriginal Peoples describes the importance to Indigenous peoples of learning from the land:

> The need to walk on the land in order to know it is a different approach to knowledge than the one-dimensional, literate approach to knowing. Persons schooled in a literate culture are accustomed to having all the context they need to understand … embedded in the text before them.… Persons taught to use all their senses — to interpret a complex, dynamic reality — may well smile at the illusion that words alone, stripped of complementary sound and color and texture, can convey meaning adequately.[30]

In this context, Western educational superiority is questioned, and claiming to understand through words alone is exposed as a limited experience of knowing.

Another point of contrast between Western and Indigenous cultures is the relationship of human beings to the earth and other beings. Western, monotheistic religious perspectives place "man" as dominant over all Creation, a concept that has been applied to humanity's search for domination over the earth and its resources.

This belief has also been translated to a search for domination over knowledge itself. In contrast, many Indigenous nations view humans as the last beings to be created and therefore the most humble in relation to the natural world.[31] Similarly, knowledge is viewed not as an area to be dominated but rather as an ongoing experience of understanding one's relationship to the land, community, and all created beings.

In an Indigenous worldview, education is based upon the requirements of everyday life. In this way, education is "an experience in context, a subjective experience that, for the knower, becomes knowledge in itself. The experience is knowledge."[32] Thus, the "where" of learning defines one's experience and happens everywhere. The idea that learning should take place only within the four walls of a school, through the prescription of a fixed written curriculum, is diametrically opposed to the idea that learning is dynamic, experiential, and grounded in a sense of place.

Indigenous epistemology conceptualizes education and learning as both life-wide (happening across formal, non-formal, and informal settings) and lifelong.[33] Traditionally, education from an Indigenous perspective is not conducted through a formal, age-graded system. The importance of different life stages is recognized, represented in the medicine wheel by childhood, adolescence, adulthood, and old age. Different learning takes place at different points in time. For example, the period of adolescence is marked in many Indigenous cultures by rites of passage and initiation. These rites of passage are important for a healthy transition from childhood to adulthood. David Lertzman ties some of today's youths' social struggles to the loss of these cultural practices.[34] Fhulu Nekhwevha describes similar cultural practices that are central to Indigenous education in African contexts.[35] This concept of ongoing learning throughout the different stages of life is distinct from current Western systems, which place learning within a formal age-graded schooling structure. In Western cultures, education is often considered synonymous with schooling. Although this is changing as more emphasis is placed in Western cultures on lifelong learning, the general expectation still is that one must first learn through the intensive accumulation of knowledge over several years of formal schooling, and then "do" once he or she graduates from the formal system. In contrast, in Indigenous cultures, learning has always been viewed as "a life-long responsibility"[36] for each individual, taking place in a variety of contexts.

How Do People Learn?

Indigenous worldviews on the origin of knowledge inform how one learns in an Indigenous epistemological framework. Castellano presents three categories of Indigenous knowledge, each with a particular origin. The first, traditional knowledge, includes the histories, Creation stories, genealogies, rights, and relationships that are passed on from generation to generation. This knowledge is often considered sacred to a particular Indigenous nation, and is passed on through storytelling, apprenticeship, and elaborate ceremonies and rituals to ensure its preservation. The second category, empirical knowledge (such as the healing properties of a particular plant), is most easily related to Western means of obtaining knowledge as it is acquired through testing and observation. However, in Indigenous epistemology this is not considered a linear process in which a particular truth is hypothesized, tested, and then proven as true, as in the Western scientific method. Rather, empirical knowledge is viewed as cyclical, dynamic, and evolving over time through the collaborative observations and inputs of many individuals. The third category Castellano calls revealed knowledge. This kind of knowledge comes from the spirit world, and is acquired through dreams, visions, and intuitions. Whereas revealed knowledge in the Western world is reserved exclusively for prophets of God and miracles, in the Indigenous world each individual has the responsibility to make their own inner journey into the metaphysical.[37] Great significance is attributed to dreams and vision quests as ways for an individual to find his or her purpose of life. Castellano explains, "Sometimes knowledge is received as a gift at a moment of need; sometimes it manifests itself as a sense that the 'time is right' to hunt or counsel or to make a decisive turn in one's life path."[38] This multi-faceted understanding of the origins of knowledge makes learning a dynamic process, going far beyond the limits of an approved curriculum, textbook, or schoolteacher's personal knowledge base.

A commonly cited difference between Indigenous and Western modes of education is of primarily oral versus primarily literate cultures. In Indigenous societies, great emphasis is placed on the oral transmission of knowledge through storytelling, traditionally used to convey Indigenous knowledge, customs, and values.[39] Cajete says that "stories [teach] people who they are so they can become all they were meant to be."[40] Storytelling is described as the oldest form of the arts and thus the basis for the other arts, such as drama, dance, and music.[41] Whereas Western cultures often view storytelling as an activity to entertain small children, in Indigenous pedagogy it is a central tool for teaching and learning.[42]

Equally important to Indigenous pedagogy are the various modes of experiential learning, such as modelling, observation, in-context learning, apprenticeships, and games as methods for learning by doing.[43] "Through observation, experience, and practice children learn the skills, beliefs, values, and norms of their culture."[44] These practices are not exclusive to Indigenous cultures, and were central to most cultures prior to industrialization. However, the introduction of Western schooling marked the separation of children from the community as a base of experience and learning. Lertzman describes the Indigenous context for learning: "Within a community, extended family supplies the social context, along with teachers and individual specialists for these important tasks. Mother Earth provides everything else: classroom, science lab, playground, athletics facility, church, grocery, hardware store, and drug store."[45]

Another important aspect of Indigenous pedagogy is language, which "embodies the way a society thinks."[46] Ermine calls language a "touchstone" for Indigenous culture, saying, "It is imperative that our children take up the cause of our languages and cultures, because therein lies Aboriginal epistemology, which speaks of holism."[47] As has been well documented by anthropologists, language is central to cultural worldviews. For example, in Mi'kmaq culture, languages are verb-rich, process and action oriented, describing "happenings" rather than objects.[48] James (Sákéj) Youngblood Henderson explains that the use of fewer verb tenses in some Indigenous languages does not imply a more simplistic language structure but rather a view of time and space as continuous rather than fragmented.[49]

Other language differences include a varying cadence of speech, commonly known as "wait-time." From an Indigenous perspective, when in dialogue one should take time to internalize and process the other's remarks before responding. Eber Hampton terms this reflective thinking.[50] When Indigenous students do not respond immediately to a question in the classroom, the Western teacher might consider them slow, disrespectful, or unknowing, whereas for the Indigenous student this may be a sign of their thoughtfulness and respect for the other's ideas.

Sacred cultural practices embody ways for knowing and learning that often fall under the spiritual education quadrant of the medicine wheel. Ceremonies help create the conditions necessary for the inward journey towards metaphysical knowledge,[51] "instilling the attitude of expectant stillness that opens the door to full awareness."[52] Ceremonies are also considered opportunities for educational reward, praise, and recognition. Through honoring ceremonies, such as conferral of a name or holding of a potlatch,[53] the community recognizes the individual's movement through the life stages and/or development of certain capacities. Rather than conforming to external rules, as in Western society, in Indigenous societies one is responsible to the group. Ceremonies also confer rights to hold knowledge and authority to wisdom keepers in the community. Sacred practices thus serve as educational markers, points of recognition or "graduation," and award a greater level of responsibility in the community.

Western evaluation of knowledge contrasts with the sacred practices and educational measures of Indigenous peoples:

> Educational philosophy in contemporary education has focused on information to the masses, leading to standardized tests ... and those who can extract information are called educated and intelligent. What this approach ignores is the knowledge that comes from introspection, reflection, meditation, prayer, and other kinds of self-directed learning.[54]

The subjective, such as the experience of participating in ceremonies and cultural practices, is central to Indigenous epistemology and access to truth. This stands in opposition to the Western value of objectivity.[55] This notion of Aboriginal knowledge as personal and sacred leads us into the next discussion, of who teaches or confers knowledge.

From Whom Do People Learn?

In Western educational contexts, the authority of those who confer knowledge is clearly established. Through formal certification, an individual receives the designation "teacher," carrying the defined role and responsibility of educating his or her students. Other sources for knowledge in the classroom include the approved curriculum and pedagogical materials.

In an Indigenous context, the question of who may teach and from whom one learns is much more complex. As previously described, Indigenous knowledge is grounded in the land; therefore, Mother Earth is considered by many as the supreme teacher. Equally important is the spirit world, which includes all Creation and ancestors who have passed on. As all Creation is considered animate, all beings are imbued with Spirit and are therefore potential teachers. Animals or transformative spirit beings, such as the trickster, are characters used to teach children what to do and especially (through their mistakes) what not to do.[56] Rocks are referred to in many cultures as grandmothers and grandfathers and are considered the oldest living teachers.

In Indigenous epistemology, the self is the ultimate teacher. Ermine describes the meeting of Western and Indigenous peoples in 1492 in North America as a clash between peoples destined for two different journeys of discovery: one towards the physical, or "outer space," and the other towards the metaphysical, or "inner space." He writes, "Aboriginal epistemology is grounded in the self, the spirit, the unknown.... [It] speaks of pondering great mysteries that lie no further than the self."[57] Ways of knowing and learning in an Indigenous paradigm are therefore profoundly personal and spiritual, based upon a journey into the inner metaphysical and spiritual worlds of the self.

Indigenous pedagogy assumes personal authority in the search for knowledge, and "values a person's ability to learn independently by observing, listening, and participating with a minimum of intervention or instruction."[58] The Indigenous educational principle of non-interference sets forth the idea of respect for others' wholeness and their independent ability to understand and access knowledge. Although Western educational theorists such as Johann Pestalozzi, Hans Frochel, Maria Montessori, and more recently Paulo Freire have argued for the inherent capacity of the individual and for child/learner-centred dialogic education, mainstream Western education historically has viewed the teacher (and the text) as the authority who holds the knowledge and who has the responsibility to confer this knowledge to students. These contrasting values have been a source of conflict between Western teachers and Indigenous students in the classroom, leading some Indigenous students to rebel when they feel they have been disrespected through the teacher's interference in their personal learning processes.

Conflicts also arise in relation to questions of authority. On the one hand, all beings are teachers in an Indigenous paradigm. Education is considered a collective responsibility that is taken on by the whole community.[59] On the other hand, the right to hold and transfer knowledge is a responsibility endowed by the community based on an individual's earning of that right, as well as by familial and ancestral relationships. Particular individuals are designated as educators in specific contexts; for example, an uncle or aunt is typically chosen to lead a child through his or her rites of passage. Therefore, an Indigenous child entering a Western classroom may question the teacher's authority, since he or she has no context within which to value that authority.

In Indigenous communities, positions of knowledge or respect within the community, such as Pipe Holders, Bundle Holders, or Wisdom Keepers, are obtained through ancestral rights or personal worth, as well as through an elaborate process of apprenticeship and training. These are viewed as positions of service and responsibility rather than of hierarchical superiority. For example, in most Indigenous cultures Elders hold a central role in teaching and guiding children and the community. The designation of Elder (in contrast to "senior citizen") implies gifts of experience and knowledge. Most Elders do not seek status, and position themselves with humility, understanding that they are still learning.[60] One Elder stated, "I am just one day old."[61] Elders traditionally are treated with ultimate respect: if an Elder is speaking, he or she will not be interrupted or questioned critically. This value of respect can create confusion or conflict for the Indigenous student in a Western context, when they are encouraged to think critically and to question those in authority.

Deborah McGregor, an Anishinaabe educator, argues that Indigenous knowledge is governed by rules that are inextricable from Indigenous peoples' traditional relationships to personal and historical identity, experience, land, and ancestral or earned rights. Therefore, Indigenous knowledge is not a subject that can be studied and then mastered: "[J]ust because someone has studied [Traditional Ecological Knowledge] does not mean that one now has it."[62] In contrast, in Western science, the objective is to obtain or possess knowledge by studying it, with an increasing number of years of education directly correlated to one's qualifications as a so-called expert in a field.[63] From an Indigenous perspective, "Knowledge is not a commodity that can be possessed or controlled by educational institutions, but is a living process to be absorbed and understood."[64]

For What Purpose Do People Learn?

The question of why we learn, or what is the purpose of knowledge, is best understood within the Indigenous worldview that all things are related. If all life is interconnected, then the survival of each life form is dependent on the survival of the others. A common Indigenous saying is, "The honour of one is the honour of all; the hurt of one is the hurt of all."

The Western concept of education as a means for the personal advancement of the individual contrasts with the idea that education is a means for the individual to serve the group. According to Eber Hampton, "Education is to serve the people.... The competitive success of the individual is an implicit value of Western schools and, as such, is in direct conflict with the Indian value of group success through individual achievement."[65] In a study conducted on the student experiences in the American Indian Program at Harvard, Hampton found that the majority of Native American students went there with the intention of using their education to help their communities.

The goal of Indigenous education is not individual prosperity or success, but dignity and responsibility to the community. The ultimate purpose of learning is to understand one's place in relation to the web of life, and to gain the skills and knowledge needed to contribute to the advancement of all beings. In this context, the greater one's knowledge, the greater the responsibility that one holds.

THE COMPARATIVE STUDY OF INDIGENOUS KNOWLEDGE

Representation of Indigenous Knowledge in Comparative Education

Within the formal field of comparative education, surprisingly little attention has been paid to specifically Indigenous educational worldviews and contexts. Comparative research has focused rather "on the education systems ... that were superimposed on the earlier inhabitants of the country."[66] The most significant studies addressing Indigenous peoples prior to 1990 are compiled in Philip Altbach and Gail P. Kelly's *Education and Colonialism* and *Education and the Colonial*

Experience[67] (see Chapter One). However, as indicated above, such literature focused more on the effects of colonial systems of education on Indigenous peoples, rather than independently valuing local or Indigenous educational practices.

The notion that Indigenous perspectives could hold equal validity did not significantly enter the field of comparative education until 1990, when Masemann advocated the meaningful inclusion of diverse ways of knowing, including Indigenous knowledge, in her Comparative and International Education Society (CIES) Presidential Address.[68] Since that date, there has been notable movement: the 1996 World Congress of Comparative Education Societies saw the first special Commission for Indigenous Education, and the resulting book, *Tradition, Modernity, and Post-Modernity: Implications for Comparative Education,* included articles on Indigenous education.[69] Robert Teasdale and Zane Ma Rhea's *Local Knowledge and Wisdom in Higher Education,* published in 2000, presents Indigenous perspectives on higher education, in contexts such as Papua New Guinea, Peru, and Australia.[70] Scholars such as Claudia Zaslavsky and Anne Hicking-Hudson have also pioneered comparative research on topics such as ethnomathematics, culturally powerful pedagogies, teacher preparation in Indigenous school settings, and Indigenous teacher identities, thereby deeply enriching the comparative literature with a consideration of Indigenous and local knowledges.[71]

This scholarship is encouraging; nevertheless, our studies suggest that Indigenous ways of knowing are still far from accepted as mainstream. It was not until 1998 that Indigenous knowledge (IK) was included as a subject area in the US-based *Comparative Education Review*; a review of articles since that date reveals very few published on Indigenous topics in the major comparative education journals, with a disproportionate majority in special issues or non-mainstream journals. For example, in 2003 several articles were grouped in a special issue of *Comparative Education,* entitled "Indigenous Education: Addressing Current Issues and Developments." Further, most articles in that issue (as well as in the field) were written from non-Indigenous perspectives, and focused on languages and mother-tongue literacy. While important subject areas, this focus on language demonstrates a persisting interest in the outer (and some would argue, "safer") forms of Indigenous culture, without incorporating a deeper investigation of Indigenous knowledge and underlying worldviews.

In the remainder of this chapter, we therefore suggest four areas for the further incorporation of Indigenous ways of knowing and learning in comparative education studies. We hope that our brief exploration of these areas will both stimulate teachers to consider potential implications for their classroom practices as well as encourage comparative education students to pursue research in these areas.

Rediscovering Indigenous Ways of Knowing and Learning for Indigenous Classrooms

Through the comparative study of Western and Indigenous knowledge, scholars are striving to understand and bring forth models of Indigenous epistemology and pedagogy that have been suppressed and de-validated for years by the imposition of colonial education systems and residential schools. Given the differences illuminated earlier in this chapter, it is not difficult to understand why Western, colonially imposed models of education have been a site of conflict for Indigenous peoples. An essential lack of agreement and understanding between the two worldviews, combined with the forced assimilation of Indigenous peoples into Western school systems, has led not only to Indigenous peoples' disconnection from their own ways of knowing and learning, but also to their perceived failure in the mainstream school system. Documents such as the 1996 report of the Canadian Royal Commission on Aboriginal Peoples have brought this reality to the forefront.

A rift in common understanding between Western and Indigenous cultures in countries such as Canada and the United States continues today. For example, a survey of students in Toronto area schools in 2002 found their knowledge of Aboriginal peoples and issues in Canada greatly lacking.[72] The same year, Indian and Northern Affairs Canada's National Working Group on Education appeared to confirm the trend across Canada.[73]

On a hopeful note, the Indigenous scholars cited in this chapter offer snapshots of the movement by Indigenous peoples to reclaim their ways of knowing and learning. This literature has been growing in strength since 1972 when the landmark document *Indian Control of Indian Education* was presented to the government of Canada, but change has been slow to occur. Reports in Canada and the United States recognize the failure of the Western school system for Indigenous peoples and the need to develop culturally relevant models of education.[74] Although

Figure 4.2
The Thanksgiving Address[75]

Onkwehshon:a *(The People)*
> May we now gather our minds as one and give one another greetings and thanks that we are gathered here in good health and in peace. (All agree).

Iethinistenha Onhwentsia *(Mother Earth)*
> May we now gather our minds together as one and greet and give our thanks to our mother earth for all that she gives us so we may live.

Ohnekashon:a *(The Water)*
> May we now gather our minds together as one and turn to the spirit of the waters of the world. With oneness of mind, we now send our thanks to the waters of the world for quenching our thirst and purifying our lives.

Kariota'shon:'a *(Animal Life)*
> May we now gather our minds as one and give our words of greetings and thanks to the animals.

Okwire'shon:'a *(Trees of the Forest)*
> May we now gather our minds together as one and give greetings and thanks to the trees of the forest for the fruits we eat, for the shade in summer, and for the shelter of our homes.

Otsi'ten'okon:'a *(Bird Life)*
> The Creator instructed the birds to sing upon the arrival of each new day, and to sing so that all life will not know boredom. With one mind we now greet and thank the bird life.

Ratiwe:ras *(Grandfather Thunders)*
> The Creator instructed the grandfather thunders to put fresh water the rivers, lakes, and springs to quench the thirst of life. So with one mind we give our greetings and thanks to our grandfathers.

Ehtsitewahtsi:'a Kiehkehnekha Karahkwa *(Our Eldest Brother The Sun)*
> We are the younger siblings and our brother sun shines the light so we may see and radiates warmth that all life may grow. We now with one mind give greetings and thanks to our eldest brother the sun.

Iethihsotha Ahsonthenhka Karahkwa *(Our Grandmother The Moon)*
> Our Creator placed her in charge of the birth of all things and made her leader of all female life. All babies of all nations are born by her orchestration. May we now gather our minds into one and send our greetings and our thanksgiving to our grandmother the moon.

Shonkwaia"tison *(Our Creator)*
> Our Creator made all of life with nothing lacking. All we humans
> are required to do is waste no life and be grateful to all life. And so
> now we gather all our minds into one and send our greetings and our
> thanksgiving to our maker, our Creator.

---

there is still a gap between rhetoric and practice, educational projects
and programs created by and for Indigenous peoples, which integrate
Indigenous ways of knowing and learning, continue to emerge.
Exemplary models in Canada include the Kanien'kahaka (Mohawk)
Akwesasne science and math program, the Dene Kede curriculum, and
the Innuqatiglit program in the Northwest Territories.[76]

The Akwesasne science and math program is a remarkable three-
year set of curriculum units integrating Western and Kanien'kahaka
thought and methods for learning about the world we inhabit.
Akwesasne is based upon the Thanksgiving Address (see Figure 4.2),
a central spiritual and cultural tradition of the Haudenosaunee (Six
Nations) people, which acknowledges and gives thanks to each aspect
of Creation.

The curriculum follows its structure, moving from the Earth
upward through grasses, trees, animals, to the waters, birds, sky, stars,
and universe. Students learn about these topics from both Western
and Kanien'kahaka perspectives, with neither approach receiving
greater weight. For instance, the children may learn how Western
biologists classify local trees, and at the same time the Kanien'kahaka
words for local flora. Elders are incorporated into the teaching process
and often take the students out on the land to learn the language and
stories containing the traditional knowledge about particular topics.
An early unit provides students with the skills to deal with conflicting
information, a necessary prerequisite to handling information from
disparate worldviews (see Chapter Ten for a further discussion of peace
and conflict education).[77]

Other examples of integration of Aboriginal learning into Western
educational settings in Canada include early childhood education
programs such as Aboriginal Head Start, the initiatives featured
in the Red River College video series *Our Children, Our Ways,* and
innovative elementary schools such as Eel Ground in New Brunswick

where technology and traditions are seamlessly interwoven. At the high school level, some Indigenous students have the opportunity to learn in their language and culture at cultural survival schools such as Kahnawake (since 1978), and Joe Duquette School in Saskatoon (since 1980). At the post-secondary level, Blue Quills First Nations College and Algoma University College have proven that, while a residential school building may remain, Aboriginal peoples can transform those sites with programs providing truly empowering experiences and knowledge. Some movements seek a complete immersion in cultural learning, such as the Mohawk Language Immersion Project at Kanatsiohareke in New York State and the Seventh Generation Education Institute near Fort Frances, Ontario. In a partnership between the University of Manitoba and the Centre for Indigenous Environmental Resources, continuing education is offered to build capacity in Aboriginal communities. Courses embody integration and are team-taught by an Elder providing traditional knowledge, an Aboriginal scholar with university training, and a Western-trained scientist.

Indigenous peoples in Canada have noted the Tribal College system in the United States and the famous language nests of the Maori in New Zealand as models they may want to reproduce locally. This marks an emerging form of comparative education: Indigenous peoples from one region learning from Indigenous peoples in another post-colonial context.

Indigenous-to-Indigenous Comparative Study and Collaboration

Increased possibilities for global travel, communication, and cross-cultural sharing have prompted the formation of <u>international Indigenous alliances and cross-Indigenous partnerships and scholarship.</u> Diverse Indigenous nations from around the world have been meeting, formally and informally, to share their knowledge practices and to form bonds of solidarity in a movement to promote Indigenous knowledge and to demand the recognition of Indigenous rights and knowledge on a global scale. These interchanges are laying the foundation for a new kind of comparative education study, among and between Indigenous peoples.

Many of these cross-Indigenous gatherings do not appear in the formal, documented literature: they have been primarily based upon oral sharing and experiential immersion in the ways of another

Indigenous nation. Although these gatherings are considered examples of non-formal learning, they are often, in fact, quite formal, including strict protocols as to who can participate, what knowledge can be shared, and how the sharing may happen. Examples include various Elders' gatherings that have been taking place throughout the world and meetings premised on the prophecy of the Reunion of the Condor and the Eagle, which predicts the coming together of North and South American Indigenous peoples as a precursor to the achievement of world peace.[78] Cross-circumpolar activities, between the Inuit in Canada, Alaska, and Russia, and the Saami peoples in Norway, Finland, and Sweden, are also gaining momentum through the creation of circumpolar peoples' organizations, research centres, and councils.

Indigenous scholars who have straddled both Indigenous and Western ways of knowing are also engaged in a movement to promote formal, literary scholarship and sharing among Indigenous peoples. Examples include the World Indigenous Peoples' Conference on Education (WIPCE), and a newer body created in 2002, the World Indigenous Nations Higher Education Consortium (WINHEC), which promotes comparative scholarship on higher education from an Indigenous perspective. Articles published in the WINHEC journal are often based on collaborative scholarship between Indigenous peoples from different regions of the world.

Within international and development education, there are a few examples of international exchange programs and development projects based on Indigenous-to-Indigenous sharing of cultural traditions and approaches to learning. In the Nunavut Youth Abroad program, Canadian Northern youth learn to value their own culture through comparative experiences with other Indigenous peoples. For example, a program participant is quoted in *Aboriginal Planet* online magazine: "In Botswana, I learned that the San people or Bushmen lifestyles were very different to our Inuit lifestyles ... I learned that my culture is unique and interesting to other people ... I'm proud of my culture and had fun answering questions that people asked. I found out that our language is similar in some ways."[79] Ghost River Rediscovery's Youth Leadership Program is based upon a similar premise of developing Indigenous youth leadership capacity through the international exchange of culture and experience amongst youth of various Indigenous nations. Aboriginal youth from Canada participate in co-operative learning and development projects in Indigenous communities in countries such as Guyana, Dominica, and Bolivia. Comparative learning naturally takes place in these settings; for example, Aboriginal youth share with Guyanese Amerindian youth about the perils of alcoholism and the ways that it has negatively affected their communities, and the Amerindian youth in turn demonstrate traditional ways of living that have been forgotten by many Aboriginal youth in Canada.[80]

International funding agencies and universities are recognizing the value of promoting official collaboration among Indigenous peoples. For example, the Canadian International Development Agency (CIDA) established the Indigenous Peoples' Partnership Program to fund partnerships between Indigenous organizations from Canada and South America. The University of Calgary's International Indigenous Studies Program focuses on the study of topics related to international Indigenous peoples, often in an "explicitly comparative perspective."[81] The field of comparative Indigenous-to-Indigenous study and collaboration, in its early stages, offers exciting potential for a new kind of cross-cultural comparative learning.

Education for All and the Multilateral Incorporation of Indigenous Knowledge

As "Education for All" is being promoted throughout the world as a Millennium Development Goal (MDG), it is timely to consider the relevance of Indigenous and local knowledge in relation to global educational movements and educational multilateralism. Education for All (EFA), discussed in Chapter Three, sets forth the objective of universal access to formal primary education and literacy. However, most EFA efforts, the targets of which are largely marginalized and Indigenous populations, continue to propagate a Western-based model of schooling and curriculum with little attention to local or Indigenous models of education.

As has been demonstrated in this chapter, vast differences exist between Western models of schooling and Indigenous ways of knowing. Further, attempts to eradicate Indigenous peoples' ways of knowing and to assimilate them in Western systems have resulted largely in failure in those school systems and severe negative impacts on those peoples. In countries such as South Africa and Zimbabwe, there has been a serious backlash against Western neo-colonialist educational models, a warning that EFA and other such movements are destined to fail if they continue to ignore Indigenous epistemology, pedagogy, and values. South African scholar Fhulu Nekwevha quotes Ethiopian Hailom Banteyerga as saying:

> What we see today is that the so-called "modern education" is not satisfactorily addressing the problems of Africa to meet the needs and aspirations of the African people. In other words, it has not done much to boost the material growth and spiritual development of Africa.... If Africa is to regain its place as the centre of culture and civilization, it needs to re-think and reframe its education in the context of Africa—and its problems and aspirations.[82]

Similar concerns are raised in relation to the current world trend towards international standardization and testing measures, such as those discussed by Karen Mundy and Joseph P. Farrell in Chapter Eight. Although these assessments aim to provide a means for comparing education on a global level, they generally promote a presumed universal (Western) standard of knowledge that places value on particular kinds of learning and performance and excludes and de-validates other (Indigenous) modes of learning and knowing. Further, as Stephen Anderson discusses in Chapter Seven, school improvement initiatives increasingly encourage teachers to teach to the test. This suggests that these tests are not only measuring performance, but in fact dictating what knowledge is taught, valued, and promoted. This tension has been well documented within the United States, where it has long been argued that standardized tests privilege a particular model of cultural capital and learning style.[83] As a result of these studies, minor adjustments have been made, such as efforts to remove questions that contain obvious cultural or historical bias. However, contrasting worldview definitions of knowledge (and how that knowledge is demonstrated, assessed, and validated) challenge notions of what constitutes cultural bias, as well as the relevance of these tests for a large percentage of the global population.

In developing evaluation measures or promoting Education for All, meaningful consideration of Indigenous ways of knowing and learning is certainly a more difficult task than simply importing an established Western curriculum. Local perspectives and approaches are excluded not only because Western models are considered superior, but also because inclusion of Indigenous models would be more challenging and time-consuming. If the goal of EFA is to be met by 2015, it may seem more expedient for governments to continue to focus on implementing the dominant Western model of education, including a standard curriculum and teacher training, rather than to develop locally relevant models. However, in our experience, as documented by Nekwevha in this chapter and by Bickmore in Chapter Ten, when international programs do *not* take into consideration local perspectives they are doomed to fail, and worse, they often have lasting negative implications for the participants. In contrast, examples such as those presented by Jospeh P. Farrell in Chapter Five demonstrate that locally relevant methods of education are likely to produce the best learning outcomes for children and the highest chance for success in a developing country or marginalized population context.

On a broader scale, the validity of Indigenous knowledge is slowly being recognized by international multilateral organizations. For example, the World Bank and the United Nations Educational, Scientific and Cultural Organization (UNESCO) have websites dedicated to the collection and dissemination of Indigenous knowledge practices. The World Bank publishes a newsletter called "IK Notes" for the sharing of Indigenous knowledge practices. The UNESCO database collects best practices in Indigenous knowledge and posts them online for anyone to access. The recognition by these agencies of the role of Indigenous knowledge represents a positive shift in consciousness for the international community. However, the way that this knowledge is being treated also raises important concerns about the rights and responsibilities associated with that knowledge.[84] For example, posting forms of Indigenous knowledge in a web-based database suggests that they can be borrowed and applied outside of their human and geographical contexts, which contrasts with the above-cited literature establishing the centrality of place and context to Indigenous knowledge.

As Indigenous educators and practitioners of international development, we suggest that Indigenous knowledge does hold relevance for global education and development practices, particularly where those practices impact Indigenous peoples. This knowledge may even have application outside of local contexts, for example, in approaches to environmental sustainability or more holistic models of education, as we discuss below. However, sharing of Indigenous knowledge must go beyond merely documenting practices; it must be integrated in ways that fully consider underlying worldviews, and provide greater participation of Indigenous peoples as respected partners on their own terms. Further, careful consultations with communities and Elders are necessary to determine what is culturally appropriate and to respect the rights and responsibilities associated with that knowledge. To integrate Indigenous knowledge and perspectives meaningfully, greater exposure to the teachings and greater comprehension will be required.

The Fourth Way

Could aspects of Indigenous ways of knowing and learning be incorporated in mainstream educational reform, not just for Indigenous peoples but for all people? Is there value in this? Could it be done while respecting the rights to and sacredness of that knowledge? What would a curriculum incorporating Indigenous knowledge look like? These questions set the stage for our final discussion.

In her 1990 CIES presidential address, Masemann proposed that forms of Indigenous knowledge were not only valid, but also potentially instructive for widespread educational reform. Referring to the rise of alternative paradigms for knowing, she argued, "What these paradigms have in common is that they are holistic, context dependent, and integrative. They propose ways in which society might be knit together again, not sundered apart."[85]

Although world culture theory (discussed in Chapter One) suggests that we are moving towards a uniform, standardized education model based upon a Western, graded, formal system, there is strong evidence that this model does not work for many of the worlds' peoples. For example, demand is swelling in North America for alternative schooling options such as Montessori and Waldorf, which promote more holistic, child-centred pedagogy. There is also a growing openness to Indigenous practices, as individuals become increasingly dissatisfied with the current trend of world affairs, and with the failed mission of modernity as the elixir for the progress of humanity. Evidence of this shift has emerged in several arenas, notably in health and environmental sciences, as the world looks to Indigenous peoples to share their traditional knowledge in a time of crisis.

For Indigenous peoples, this knowledge is not new; the post-modern debate is merely the recognition by the Western world of paradigms that Indigenous peoples have lived and known for thousands of years. Despite years of oppression, scholars, leaders, and Elders from within the Native world are also reaching out to their non-Indigenous brothers and sisters, offering once again to share their wisdom where the dominant paradigm has fallen short. For most Indigenous peoples, this is the only choice. If education is service, and the hurt of one is the hurt of all, then the sharing of Indigenous wisdom at a time of need is the fulfillment of prophecy and our responsibility as part of the circle.

A leading example of this kind of scholarship is *The Fourth Way: An Indigenous Contribution for Building Sustainable and Harmonious Prosperity in the Americas*. This document, written by Four Worlds International and the United Indians of All Tribes Foundation, originates from nine years of consultation with Indigenous leaders and communities across the Americas. *The Fourth Way* proposes that the time has come for humanity to adopt new ways of learning that will prepare us for a sustainable global future, and that we need to look towards an Indigenous-based, holistic education model to lead the way towards the establishment of world peace.[86] The Fourth Way movement is not alone in this call: organizations such as Global Elders are also offering to share models of Indigenous pedagogy and teachings.[87] Couture writes, "There are those who say that the Native Way holds a key, if not *the* key, to the future survival of mankind."[88]

IMPLICATIONS FOR TEACHERS

It is not difficult to imagine that all people might thrive in environments that value wholeness, spirituality, and diverse modes and means of learning. Indigenous pedagogical methods present a "valuable addition to the present systems of education in any teaching topic, not only when teaching Indigenous peoples. By incorporating observation, experience, introspection, and inquiry during the education process, we will begin to create linkages from the experiences of human beings and transmit them wholly to students in the classroom."[89]

Note that the shift required is not to adopt the "cultural" or "exotic" elements of Indigenous ways. As demonstrated in this chapter, the foundations of Indigenous epistemology are much deeper than this. Investigations of the relevance of Indigenous knowledge for Western or global education must consider the values and philosophical underpinnings informing Indigenous pedagogy:

> Indigenous knowledge presents several goals for educational reform: acknowledging the sacredness of life and experiences; generating the spirit of hope based on experience as a connection with others in creating a new and equitable future; generating the meaning of work as a vocation and as a mission in life; and developing the capacity to do everything to open a new cognitive space in which a community can discover itself and affirm its heritage and knowledge in order to flourish for everyone.[90]

Any investigations of how Indigenous ways of knowing and learning could be applied to mainstream efforts *must* involve Indigenous peoples in their research, design, and implementation. Otherwise, despite the best of intentions, they risk becoming yet another example of colonization, co-optation, and exploitation of Indigenous peoples. As this chapter has demonstrated, Indigenous knowledge is intimately connected to the historical, ecological, social, spiritual, and ceremonial fabric of Indigenous societies and to the Indigenous peoples themselves. Therefore, it cannot be understood outside of those contexts. Through encouraging respectful, collaborative, comparative scholarship between non-Indigenous and Indigenous peoples, and among diverse Indigenous peoples, lies the potential for discerning the path forward for education.

For teachers searching for practical ways to incorporate Indigenous ways of knowing and learning in the classroom, there are many curricular and online resources available.[91] At the end of this chapter, we offer some ideas for incorporating Indigenous ways of knowing and learning into your teaching practice. The way in which you incorporate these suggestions will vary based on your personal interests and expertise, and your classroom and school context. As a start, consider teaching in ways that value every learning style in the medicine wheel: the spiritual, emotional, physical, and mental. In other words, for each topic, find a way to intuit, feel, act, and think about it.

Figure 4.3

Tg Ideas

Ideas for Incorporating Indigenous Ways of Knowing and Learning in Your Classroom

Find out who the traditional inhabitants are of the land on which your school stands. Using proper protocols, invite an elder to come to your classroom and share some of their teachings. Make a field trip to a local teaching facility such as a friendship centre.

Make space for the expression of spirituality in your classroom. Create a regular "spirit spot" or quiet time that students can use for reflection, journaling, art, prayer, or meditation.

Reinforce respect among students for one another
and the world around them.
Demonstrate that same respect towards them.

Post teachings such as the Seven Sacred Teachings
or the medicine wheel in your classroom.

Use circles and interactive modes of sharing,
such as a "talking circle" in which all students have
the opportunity to have a voice and share their emotions.[92]

Incorporate music, art, and storytelling integrally in your classroom
as valid ways of sharing and learning. Invite Aboriginal
and community artists to the class to share these traditions.

Have your class explore Indigenous languages through place names
on the map. Words such as Toronto, Ontario, and Canada all have
surprising and interesting stories behind them.

When studying history, ask students how these events would affect Aboriginal peoples. As part of a local oral history project have students interview community elders (of all backgrounds) to tell the history not represented in textbooks.

Assign groups to research Aboriginal perspectives on all topics covered in a year.

When studying biology, take your students outside to learn the names of the plants around your school. Have students bring examples of Indigenous foods or medicines to class.

Promote a sense of knowledge and learning as a means for service to the greater community.

Use the world as your classroom, and all of its beings as teachers.

A common question from teachers, both Indigenous and non-Indigenous, is, "Do I have the right to teach from Indigenous cultural worldviews and perspectives?" An Aboriginal Studies scholar at University of Toronto has advised reframing this question to ask, "What is our responsibility?"[93] At a time of spiritual, ecological, and social crisis, the opportunity exists to turn towards Indigenous-based holistic frameworks for knowing and learning, to help humanity develop a sense of respect and relationship with all Creation. In this age of rapid globalization and increased interaction and interdependence across cultures, the need to take into consideration Indigenous ways of knowing and learning has never been more relevant.

QUESTIONS FOR REFLECTION AND DISCUSSION

1. Which characteristics or examples of Indigenous knowledge and pedagogy do you think fit in with typical educational practices in your teaching context? How might you use Indigenous knowledge and pedagogy in your teaching?
2. How do you think the need to incorporate/recognize Indigenous worldviews in the classroom can be reconciled with the need to respect the context, rights, and responsibilities associated with that knowledge?
3. What do you consider to be the relevance of Indigenous and local approaches to learning in the context of global educational movements such as Education for All?

SUGGESTED FILM: *THE LEARNING PATH*, BY LORETTA TODD

The Learning Path tells the story of Aboriginal peoples' forced participation in the residential schooling system in Canada, including experiences of racism, loss of cultural identity, and of educational alienation. It then shows how Native Canadians are now regaining control over their education, highlighting the work of three Aboriginal educators in Edmonton, Alberta. Part of a five-part documentary series entitled *As Long as the Rivers Flow*, the feature-length version of this film won a Silver Hugo award at the Chicago International Film Festival.

SUGGESTIONS FOR FURTHER READING

Battiste, Marie. *Indigenous Knowledge and Pedagogy in First Nations Education: A Literature Review with Recommendations*. Report commissioned by the Minister's National Working Group on Education. Ottawa, ON: Indian and Northern Affairs Canada, 2002.

Bopp, Judie, Michael Bopp, Lee Brown, and Phil Lane. *The Sacred Tree*. 3rd ed. Twin Lakes, WI: Lotus Light Publications, 1989.

*Cajete, Gregory. "Indigenous Knowledge: The Pueblo Metaphor of Indigenous Education." In *Reclaiming Indigenous Voice and Vision*, edited by Marie Battiste. Vancouver, BC: University of British Columbia Press, 2000, 181–91.

Cajete, Gregory. *Look to the Mountain: An Ecology of Indigenous Education.* Durango, CO: Kivak' Press, 1994.

Castellano, Marlene Brant. "Updating Aboriginal Traditions of Knowledge." In *Indigenous Knowledges in Global Contexts: Multiple Readings of our World,* edited by George. J. Sefa Dei, Budd L. Hall, and Dorothy Goldin Rosenberg. Toronto, ON: OISE/University of Toronto Press, 2000, 21–36.

Colorado, Pam. "Bridging Native and Western Science." *Convergence* 21, no 2–3 (1988): 49–68.

Couture, Joseph. "The Role of Native Elders: Emergent Issues." In *The Cultural Maze: Complex Questions on Native Destiny in Western Canada,* edited by John Friesen. Calgary, AB: Detselig Enterprises Ltd, 1991, 201–17.

Ermine, Willie. "Aboriginal Epistemology." In *First Nations Education in Canada: The Circle Unfolds,* edited by Marie Battiste and Jean Barman. Vancouver, BC: University of British Columbia Press, 1995, 101–12.

Four Worlds International and United Indians of All Tribes Foundation. *The Fourth Way: An Indigenous Contribution for Building Sustainable and Harmonious Prosperity in the Americas.* Seattle, WA: United Indians, 2006.

*Hampton, Eber. "Toward a Redefinition of Indian Education." In Battiste and Barman, *First Nations Education,* 5–46.

*Lertzman, David. A. "Rediscovering Rites of Passage: Education, Transformation, and the Transition to Sustainability." *Conservation Ecology* 5, no. 2 (2002): 30, www.consecol.org/vol5/iss2/art30.

Little Bear, Leroy. "Jagged Worldviews Colliding. In Battiste, *Reclaiming Indigenous Voice,* 77–85.

Masemann, Vandra. "Ways of Knowing: Implications for Comparative Education." *Comparative Education Review* 34, no. 4 (1990): 465–73.

McGregor, Deborah. "Coming Full Circle: Indigenous Knowledge, Environment and our Future." *American Indian Quarterly,* 28, no. 3 and 4 (2004): 385–410.

Sawyer, Don, Howard Green, Art Napoleon, and Wayne Lundeberg. *NESA Activities Handbook for Native and Multicultural Classrooms,* Volumes 1–3. Vancouver: Tillacum Library, 1984, 1991, 1993.

Chapter Five

Teaching and Learning to Teach: Successful Radical Alternatives from the Developing World

Joseph P. Farrell

INTRODUCTION

As noted by Ruth Hayhoe and Karen Mundy in Chapter One, educational "borrowing" has long been an important strand of comparative and international education. Forms of formal schooling, originally invented in Western Europe in the early 19th century, have spread around the world for reasons introduced by Mundy in Chapter Three. Despite the cultural and civilizational differences highlighted by Hayhoe in Chapter Two, key elements of these forms have become almost universal. Unfortunately, once in place they have generally proven to be extremely difficult to change in any fundamental way, at least on large scale. Meanwhile, starting in the late 1970s, and gaining momentum since about 1990, there has been a quiet revolution in schooling in the developing world, in many cases radically transforming those forms particularly at the primary level, but in some cases at the junior secondary level as well.

These mostly successful radical alternatives are little known and seldom remarked upon among educators and scholars of education in the developed world, and often not known, or if known not well understood, in their home nations. A small published literature about them is beginning to grow, but it consists mostly of individual case studies with few references to other cases, or comparative analyses of small sets of such cases, generally from the same geo-political region.[1]

Some of these programs are still quite small, new (essentially at a pilot stage), and not well documented. Much of the information consists of lore passed informally among practitioners and scholars. Others have several decades of experience, and have grown to systems of thousands (in some cases tens of thousands) of schools, with solid research and evaluation results available. Some operate within the standard Ministry of Education administrative framework; others are operated entirely by non-governmental organizations (NGOs); still others are mixed models with various combinations of government, NGO, and civil society planning and management. In almost all cases these schools fall within what is generally referred to as "community education" or "community schools," with strong organic linkages to the communities in which the learners live. These linkages take different forms in different places, depending upon the local history and patterns of social organization, but are strong and crucial. In most cases that have been seriously evaluated the results are very good, in terms of enrolment, retention, completion, movement to the next level of schooling, and measured academic success. Typically, students in these schools score on achievement tests at least as well as, and quite frequently better than, students in standard schools, including much more privileged youth. On-time primary completion rates range above 90 percent, and the vast majority who complete primary move on to the first post-primary level, generally with excellent results. Considering that the children in these schools are among the most marginalized in their own societies, and in the world overall—the "hardest to reach and hardest to teach" in traditional schooling—such results are quite spectacular.

This chapter is based upon an ongoing comparative analysis of more than 200 of these programs by an international team of scholars, graduate students, international agency officials, and program developers, of which I am a co-leader. This ongoing comparative analysis, best thought of as an international and comparative grounded theory exercise, is still in the early stages of development. There is much that we don't fully understand, and new questions arise regularly. But some patterns and conclusions seem to be sufficiently clear to warrant writing about them, even at this early stage. The first section of this chapter draws upon the overall data set to present some core distinctions between the forms of formal schooling as we have come to know them and the emerging alternative model (called respectively the "bad news" and the "good news"). The next section provides a detailed comparative analysis of three exemplary cases that have been in existence long enough to have accumulated significant bodies of experience and evaluative research, and which collectively represent some of the major differing patterns of alternatives. While there are a wide range of questions and issues that we are examining in this comparative research program, the focus here will be on two key matters: 1) the pedagogical question: how do these young people manage to learn as well as they do? What actually happens in these classrooms to produce these learning results? and, 2) the teacher development question: how do the teachers/facilitators in these programs learn to successfully implement a radically different form of schooling so quickly and so well? In that discussion I note some of the major lessons learned thus far. In the final section I note two major questions, both empirical and theoretical, that remain.

[handwritten margin note: 2 major questions]

The core argument here is that the best hope we have of breaking through the bad news (as outlined below) and eventually providing a better form of learning for this and future generations of young people on large scale, in nations rich and poor, is to try to learn from those people, seemingly small in number in any one place but actually quite large in international aggregate and mostly in very poor places in our world, who have managed to create islands of success where so many others have failed or succeeded only marginally. A subtitle of this chapter could be: Learning from Success. If we choose to try to do that, then we may help to reverse the trend of the past two centuries, in which educational ideas and patterns from the rich North have been so regularly exported to/imposed upon the poorer two-thirds of our world.

THE BAD NEWS AND THE GOOD NEWS: FORMAL SCHOOLING AS IT EXISTS AND EMERGING ALTERNATIVES

As educators we are observers of and parties to a most peculiar pattern. Over the past century or more we have come to learn much about how human beings, young and old, actually *learn* best.[2] Yet almost none of this new knowledge has penetrated into the standard practices of formal schools, which generally carry on the rituals, traditions, and conceptions of how learning occurs and what is most worth learning that were developed well over a century ago, first in Western Europe and then spread around the world. Although I have been making this point for many years, I am certainly not the first to observe it, nor the latest.[3] In 1995, two major books were published that chronicled and

[handwritten margin note: IRONY]

tried to understand a century of failed attempts at educational reform in the United States.[4] The stories told there of dysfunctional formal schooling and of failed reform initiatives indicated that the patterns found in the United States are generalizable to most of the world.

> One general lesson is that planning educational change is a far more difficult and risk-prone venture than had been imagined in the 1950s and 1960s. There are many more examples of failure, or of minimal success, than of relatively complete success. Much more is known about what does not work, or does not usually work, than about what does work.... Moreover, when planned educational reform attempts have been successful, the process has usually taken a long time, frequently far longer than originally anticipated. In recent decades there have been a few examples where an unusual combination of favourable conditions and politically skilled planners has permitted a great deal of education change in a relatively brief period, but these have been rare and idiosyncratic.[5]

In sum, these reviews of international reform experience, explored in Stephen Anderson's Chapter Seven in this volume, all come to roughly the same conclusions. Proposals for educational reform or change are seldom enacted. If enacted (whether via legislation, regulation, or experimental programs), they are seldom implemented well and widely. If implemented, they tend after a few years to fade away as the system slowly moves back to its normal state. If implemented well, widely, and sustainably, there is very little evidence of long-term and wide-scale impact on the primary mission of the schooling enterprise: enabling and enhancing the capacity of young people to learn. What we have come to understand about human learning has almost nothing to do with how schooling continues to be conducted. The forms of formal schooling, set in the 19th century, reflect the misconceptions about human learning of the intellectual and political-economic elites of that very different time and place. But now that we have them, and have set them firmly in place, we do not seem to know how to change them, at least at any large scale. Figure 5.1 outlines those forms of formal schooling.

Figure 5.1
The Traditional "Forms of Formal Schooling"

- One hundred to several hundred children/youth assembled (often compulsorily) for at least a period of time in a building called a school
- from approximately the age of 6 or 7 up to somewhere between age 11 to 16
- for 3 to 6 hours per day, where
- they are divided into groups of 20 to 60
- to work with a single adult, a "certified" teacher, in a single room
- for (especially at "upper grades") discrete periods of 40 to 60 minutes each devoted to a separate "subject"
- to be "studied" and "learned" by a group of young people of roughly the same age
- with supporting learning materials, all organized by
- a standard curriculum set by an authority well above the individual school, which all are expected to "cover" in an "age-graded" way.
- "Adults" assumed to be more knowledgeable "teach" and students "receive instruction" from them
- in a broader system in which the "students" are expected/required to "repeat back" to the adults what they have been taught if they are to go any higher in the educational "system."
- Teachers and/or a central exam system(s) evaluate students' ability to repeat back what they have been taught, and provide formal recognized certificates for "passing" particular "grades" or "levels."
- Most or all of the financial support comes from national or regional governments, or other kinds of authority levels (for example, religion-related schools) well above the local community.

When looked at as a set, this list of characteristics well illustrates the degree to which they have become taken for granted. Who would seriously question them? A striking feature of almost all of the educational reform proposals, whether for a system as a whole or school-by-school, is that they rarely if ever question the basic model, the forms of formal schooling. Typically they aim to alter or improve one or a few bits of it, while leaving the rest unquestioned.

The existence of these forms of formal schooling and their seeming intractability to efforts at change has continued to be a source of great _frustration_ to many individual citizens seeking a better and more productive form of organized learning for their children, to well-intentioned reformers who see their efforts fail regularly, and to scholars of learning who regularly see their hard-won findings knocking fruitlessly on the door of the schoolhouse.

Among the first group, there has been over the past years, especially but not exclusively in North America, a small movement towards alternative schools and home-schooling.[6] These efforts have resulted in some cases in local alternative schools or programs. In 2005 it was estimated that there were more than 12,000 alternative schools or programs in the United States, and that at least a million parents there had opted for some form of home-schooling.[7] But these efforts represent a withdrawing from the formal system among a still very small minority, and have had no perceptible effect upon the broader formal system.

In 2001 Theodore Sizer, a leading figure among the well-intentioned reformers in the United States, noted the following in a forum discussion in _Harper's Magazine_.

> You are assuming that Americans make educational policy rationally. But I think history will show that the system follows a kind of _mindless_ thread … we do what we do because we've always done it. [For example] the basic architecture and ideas behind the high school haven't changed in a fundamental way since Charles Eliot and the Committee of Ten designed it in the 1890s. We know more about human learning. We understand that the culture and the economy have changed. But we are so stuck in what has become the conventional way of schooling that we don't think twice about it. So we still say that the mainline subjects … established in 1893 are the core of the school. We still assume that one can test children's mastery of those mainline subjects in a way that is rigorous and useful. We still persist in thinking that a school is a school is a school. It runs for 180 days. You take English, math, social studies, science in [separate] periods.… The students march forward on the basis of their birthdays, in things called "grades" — like eggs — and we tell ourselves that we can ascertain whether these kids have profound intellectual competence. The system is mindless.[8]

A similar cry of desperation from the psychological researcher side was published by David Olson, a leading cognitive psychologist, in 2003:

> For some time I have been struck by the fact that whereas the psychological understanding of children's learning and development has made great strides ... the impact on schooling as an institutional practice has been modest if not negligible. With most of my colleagues I had assumed that if only we knew more about how the mind works, how the brain develops, how interests form, how people differ, and, most centrally, how people learn, educational practice would take a great leap forward. But while this knowledge has grown, schools have remained remarkably unaffected.[9]

hasn't responded to neuroscience either

The observations noted above should not lead us to conclude that there are not quite a lot of good schools and teachers out there. One finds them often, not only in well-off places but in urban slums and poor villages, and that is like stumbling upon a beautiful blossom in the midst of desolation. The core problem is that, as Michael Fullan and many others have observed,[10] while we are quite good at noting a really good school, and characterizing it, we do not yet have any serious idea about how to *create* such schools, at least in large numbers, nor particularly how to change "traditional" schools in large numbers into places that better match what we have come to know about human learning. That is the bad news.

★★★ we don't know how 2 REPLICATE good schools

It is also now clear that many of the differences between Figures 5.1 and 5.2 can best be seen not as dichotomies but as continua. As described in Niyovoz's Chapter Six in this volume, forms of teaching and learning vary widely based on complex and culturally different local understandings. Successful programs can be variously close to and far away from the characteristics that seem in "pure" terms to differentiate the two core models described (see Ruth Hayhoe's Chapter Two for a discussion of ideal types). But even in this rather generic comparison of Figures 5.2 and 5.1, there are a few points that are of great importance to consider.

COMPAIR TRAD'L + ALT

First, none of the ideas undergirding these alternative programs are particularly new. They have been in the literatures of curriculum,

Figure 5.2
The Emergent Model: Common Features of Alternative School Programs

- Child-centred rather than teacher-driven pedagogy
- Active rather than passive learning
- Multi-graded classrooms with continuous progress learning
- Combinations of fully trained teachers, partially trained teachers, and community resources — parents and other community members — are heavily involved in the learning of the children and the management of the school
- Peer-tutoring — older and/or faster-learning children assist and "teach" younger and/or slower learning children
- Carefully developed self-guided learning materials, which children, alone or in small groups, can work through themselves, at their own pace, with help from other students and the teachers/facilitators as necessary; the children are responsible for their own learning
- Much teacher- and student-developed learning material
- Active student involvement in the governance and management of the school
- Use of radio, correspondence lessons, in some cases television, in a few cases computers
- Ongoing and intensive in-service peer-mentoring for teachers
- Ongoing monitoring/evaluation/feedback systems allowing the teachers to learn from their own experience, with constant modifications
- Free flows of children and adults between the school and community
- Locally adapted changes to the school day and school year
- The focus of the school is much less on "teaching" and more on "learning."

educational psychology/pedagogy, and philosophy of education for a very long time. There are, for example, community schools even in very large cities in some places in North America and elsewhere.[11] Various forms of multi-grading and continuous progress learning have been implemented, out of necessity or intentionally, in many places in the world (see for example the primary school policy of the Government of Quebec from 2000).[12] Many classroom teachers and schools have implemented various aspects noted in Figure 5.2. But, as noted earlier, these have mostly remained relatively isolated examples.

The most important thing these alternative programs collectively teach us is that the traditional model, as seen in Figure 5.1, can be changed, *on a large scale.* And this can clearly be done in very poor places, with very limited resources, with very strong learning results. These programs demonstrate that child-centred, active pedagogy, with heavy involvement of the parents and the community in the learning of their children works. And where this pedagogical model is implemented well, even modestly well, it is producing remarkable learning gains among even the poorest and most disadvantaged young people. Considering the bad news outlined above, that is an extremely important finding. How to accomplish it in any particular place, rich or poor, is always a challenge, and the appropriate solution will differ from place to place, depending on local history and traditions, and socio-cultural and political-economic conditions. There is no one-size-fits-all recipe on offer here. But knowing that it can and has been done even in very poor places is a learning resource available to us, if we choose to use it.

A DETAILED COMPARATIVE ANALYSIS OF ALTERNATIVE SCHOOLS IN COLUMBIA, BANGLADESH, AND EGYPT

Here I present a detailed comparative analysis of three core cases selected from our much larger database of cases: *Escuela Nueva* [New School] in Colombia; the BRAC Non-Formal Primary Education Program in Bangladesh; and the United Nations Children's Fund (UNICEF) Community Schools Program in Egypt. I draw upon extensive and detailed case studies of these programs that were produced in 2004 (cited in the endnotes and highlighted in the suggestions for further reading at the end of this chapter). They were designed to provide not only the facts of the case—for example, history, context, measured learning results, costs, teacher development programs—but also a kind of pastiche narrative account of what actually occurs in the day to day life of the school. These three cases were chosen for several reasons: they are exceptionally well documented and evaluated, including both formal outsider evaluations and insider insights; they are exemplars of different approaches to alternative pedagogy, with a common cross-cultural core of understanding of human learning; they have been widely adapted to other cultural locations; and the authors knew the programs intimately and could thus provide the sort of day-in-the-life-of-the-school accounts we were seeking. Following is some general background on the nations/cultures in which these cases have developed, after which there are brief introductions to the cases themselves.

General Background

All three of these nations are generally classified as poor or developing, but they are differently so in ways it is important to note. Unless you or your family originally came from one of these nations, or you have worked or travelled there or in a nearby nation, your image of them has likely been shaped by brief portrayals in the mass media, which tend to focus on natural and human-created disasters and disruptions. Figure 5.3 below provides some very basic information about the three nations, with data from Canada added as a reference point.

Figure 5.3
Gross National Income per Capita in Four Nations[13]

	Bangladesh	Colombia	Egypt	Canada
GNI per cap	$440.00	$2,000.00	$1,310.00	$28,390.00
%GNI for Poorest 40%	22%	9%	21%	20%
Adult Literacy Rate	40%	94%	56%	99%

In these figures, Gross National Income (GNI) per capita is a very rough index of how much wealth and resources are available per person in a given nation (the numbers are given in equivalent US$). The next line provides rough estimates of what proportion of that total national wealth is available to and usable by the poorest 40 percent of each nation's population, and is thus an indicator of the inequality of income distribution. If one brings together those two lines and adds absolute population figures it is relatively simple, arithmetically, to calculate the average amount of wealth per year available per person, of whatever age, to members of the poorest 40 percent of the population in the nation. Those are: Bangladesh: $97; Colombia: $180; Egypt: $275; Canada: $5678.

Obviously, in all of these three nations the poorer families and their children are vastly poorer than similarly placed people in a place such as Canada, but there are important differences. Bangladesh is generally categorized as one of the poorest nations in the world, and to be poor there is vastly different than being poor in nations such as Colombia or Egypt, which are typically categorized as middle-income nations in the world. This does not mean that to be poor in Colombia or Egypt is necessarily more or less difficult and desperate than to be poor in Bangladesh, but it can't be thought of as being the same either. It should also be noted that all of these nations have long traditions of advanced thought and scholarship, which have contributed much to how we together understand the world and our place within it. The adult literacy statistics in the table above are instructive. Even in a nation as poor as Bangladesh, more than 40 percent of adults are literate, more than 50 percent are so in Egypt, and almost 100 percent in Colombia. Thus, even in extremely poor places there are many people, millions indeed, who are very highly educated, having attended advanced institutions of higher education, and are the inheritors of long traditions of intellectual and spiritual culture, even though they share their national/cultural space with vast numbers of people who are not so fortunate.

Colombia is, like most of North America, an off-shoot of European society. It was colonized by the Spanish in the early 1500s, with much destruction of existing Indigenous populations and their cultures, and quickly became a *mestizo* (mixed) society as in much of Latin America. By the early 1800s, it achieved independence from its European colonial masters, like most of Latin America. This was shortly after the United States achieved independence and decades before Canada, as we now know it, managed the same thing. It is thus intellectually, culturally, and religiously (predominantly Roman Catholic, and thus Christian) an inheritor historically of a long European tradition; in this case, the southern rather than the northern part of Europe. Over those centuries, however, an intellectual tradition, including ideas about teaching and learning, developed in Latin America, which is as unique and distinctive from the former European colonizers as are the intellectual and educational cultures of an off-shoot society in North America, such as Canada. Over many years of living and working in Latin America, including Colombia, I have come to understand that many of the common words and phrases used there to talk about teaching and learning, and about how children develop and hopefully flourish, have no easy translations into the English (or French) language and the ways we in North America think about such things.

Bangladesh and Egypt have grown out of vastly different cultural and religious traditions. Both are now Islamic societies, but they have come to that position over many centuries and from very different historical placements. Bangladesh is an inheritor of one of the very oldest civilizational traditions in the recorded history of humankind. Some of that history is noted, in a general regional sense, by Hayhoe in Chapter Two of this book. Onto that long history of Confucian, Hindu, and Buddhist thought and spiritual tradition, Islam was overlaid in roughly the 12th century CE by a colonial invasion from the central Asian and Middle Eastern Islamic heartland. A few centuries later, the British invaded and colonized the Indian subcontinent, and imposed another, European, overlay of thought and intellectual/spiritual tradition. After World War II, the British Raj was dismantled, with bloody and violent displacements of Hindu and Muslim peoples, leading to the establishment of two separate states in the former colony: India and Pakistan, of which Bangladesh was the eastern section. That partition did not last long and in the late 1960s war broke out, which led to the formation of the new independent nation of Bangladesh.

Egypt is also an inheritor of a very long, but quite different, civilizational tradition; images of pharaohs, kings, great pyramids, and such are well and widely known. It is popularly termed one of the "cradles of civilization." About 5,000 years ago, two previously existing kingdoms (upper and lower Egypt) were forcibly brought together to form what we now think of as ancient Egypt. This new kingdom rather quickly became one of the major centres of knowledge creation and cultural and religious thought in the trans-Mediterranean world. Centuries later it became a core part of the Greco-Roman empires, and remained so for about 1,000 years. Early in the Christian era, sects of the then-new religion established themselves in Egypt and became quite influential and widespread. In the seventh century CE, Arabians invaded and conquered and introduced the then-very-new Islamic faith, to which most of the population converted. Thus in Egypt, Islam was overlaid upon a very different ancient cultural/historical tradition than was the case in what is now Bangladesh a few centuries later. In the centuries following the Islamic conquest, Egypt remained one of the great world centres of knowledge creation and transmission, preserving the writings and knowledge of the Greek and Roman civilizations that had been practically lost in what we now think of as Europe during the "dark ages" following the collapse of the Roman Empire. Egypt helped to reintroduce that knowledge to Europe as it re-awakened from that dark era. In the 19th century CE, Napoleonic France invaded Egypt and established a somewhat tenuous colonial regime, and later in the century the United Kingdom invaded and stayed in control until 1952 when this very old nation, with more than six millennia of history, regained its independent status.

The following three case descriptions from Columbia, Bangladesh, and Egypt are quite brief and introductory. Much fuller accounts are provided in the case studies to which you are referred.

Escuela Nueva (New School) in Colombia.

This is the oldest and perhaps best known internationally of these programs. It started on very small scale in the late 1970s, was carefully grown and nurtured, with constant experimentation and learning from experience, until it had spread to about 8,000 schools by the mid-1980s. After careful national and international evaluation, it was then declared by the government to be the standard model for rural schooling in that nation, and has now spread to most rural schools there (roughly 35,000), with varying degrees of fidelity in implementation. It is currently spreading slowly to urban schools as well. It has been adapted to or adopted in at least 12 other Latin American nations, and there is a recent effort by the World Bank and other international agencies to figure out how, or under what conditions, this model might be adapted to other regions of the world. It is also noteworthy that this model has also, in one region of Colombia, spread upward to the post-primary level of schooling. This allows us to consider how this successful primary level alternative model may adapt as youngsters move to more senior levels of schooling. Thus the comparisons below involve both *Escuela Nueva* Primary and *Escuela Nueva* Secondary.[14]

The Non-Formal Primary Education Program of the Bangladesh Rural Advancement Committee (BRAC).

This program is another of the grandparents of the field. It started in the mid-1980s, has grown to involve about 35,000 rural schools in that nation, and is slowly moving into urban schools and ethnic minority regions of the nation, partly through a diffusion program with other local NGOs. It is also being adapted/adopted, with support from a variety of international and donor agencies, in nations such as Ethiopia, Sudan, Somalia, Uganda, Sierra Leone, and Afghanistan.[15]

The Community Schools Program of UNICEF-Egypt.

This program started in the early 1990s, drawing upon the experience of the two programs noted above, and was adapted to the particular local situation in small hamlets in Upper Egypt, where girls' access to schooling was particularly problematic. It has grown to a core system of about 300 schools, which are referred to as "innovation seed-beds," from which the non-formal pedagogy they are developing is diffused, through co-operation with the Ministry of Education and other donor agencies, to roughly 8,000 government-managed one-classroom schools and then to the broader mainstream school system. Experiments in adapting the pedagogy to other Middle Eastern and Muslim nations are also underway.[16]

RESULTS, COSTS, AND CURRICULUM

There would not be much point in comparing and analyzing these programs and the broader set they represent, unless they can demonstrate that they are producing good learning results not just for a few young people who manage to complete the schooling process, but for most if not all of the young people involved. And the programs must be able to do this at a cost, both total and per student, that is sustainable. It is now well established that among most children in the poorer nations of the world, and among poorer population groups in rich nations, academic achievement tends to be lower, and drop-out rates higher, than hoped for. As noted, all of our cases have been extensively evaluated. The results are noted in detail in the case studies referred to above. Suffice it to say that in all of these cases extremely poor children come to school, stay in school, finish the primary cycle, learn not only the necessary academic material and skills but also develop self-confidence and self-esteem, and in large proportions carry on to the next level of formal education and do very well there. And all of this is generally at superior levels to those of their compatriots in traditional schools, who are usually from more advantaged social backgrounds. Furthermore, the actual costs per successful graduate are lower than in traditional schools.[17]

With reference to curriculum, all of these programs follow the standard national curriculum, if one thinks of that as a set of learning goals/objectives for a particular learning cycle or stage. What these programs do, by altering the pedagogical model fundamentally, is to provide a way for children to learn that curriculum to a generally superior degree compared to traditional schools, sometimes in a considerably shorter period of time. They also provide opportunities for children to learn materials of local relevance, which are typically not included in national curricula, and also to add to the learning such matters as democratic citizenship education (*Escuela Nueva* is particularly strong on this) or arts education (the BRAC and UNICEF-Egypt programs are particularly strong on this).

PEDAGOGY

A sense of the actual pedagogy used in these programs can be obtained by reviewing Figure 5.2. All of these programs have in one way or another moved away from the traditional, age-graded "egg-crate" pedagogical model. This shift both encourages and permits continuous progress learning (children advance individually or in small groups at their own pace, and at different paces in different learning areas—for example, a child may at any given age and stage be really good at reading, but not so skilled at math) and peer-tutoring (older and/or more advanced children assisting younger and/or less advanced learners). Two of the cases (*Escuela Nueva* Primary and the Egyptian Community Schools) are fully multi-graded, with students of mixed ages and grade levels learning together in one classroom. The BRAC program is age-graded in a sense, as the children in any given school go together through Grade One, Grade Two, and so forth, but these grades are not set by the calendar but by the judgment of the facilitators regarding when they are ready to move on to the next stage in a particular learning area. Thus a given class may be working at Grade Three level in reading, Grade Two level in math, and Grade Four level in science at any given time. The class group is composed of children of different ages, and moves together through the primary program, covering a five-year curriculum in four years, with the same teacher(s) from start to finish (which, as noted in Chapter Two, is common in many Asian school systems). This provides many opportunities for a form of continuous progress learning and peer tutoring. It is thus a locally adapted means of accomplishing the core pedagogical objectives. *Escuela Nueva* Secondary is formally age-graded, and classes are divided by subject matter, reflecting the subject-content orientation and testing routines of standard secondary schooling, but they still manage to maintain much multi-grade and multi-age work and peer tutoring as part of the pedagogy. Again we see a locally adapted way of getting at the same core pedagogical changes.

Within this model, children typically spend a large proportion of the school day working individually or in small groups, in learning centres or "corners," using learning materials that are specially designed for such self-guided learning. Standard textbooks are also often used, but only in conjunction with such specially designed materials. Not surprisingly, standard texts, which are designed for age-graded classes, do not work well as a sole learning resource for a multi-grade, multi-age school. When an individual learner, or a small group of learners, encounters a problem, they first ask older or more advanced students for assistance. If that doesn't solve the problem they will ask the teacher/facilitator for help. Thus the adults in the classroom spend much of their time moving about, checking the progress of various learning groups, solving problems and answering questions, and recording the progress and obstacles of various individuals and groups (such as, "Jose and his group need special work in two-column multiplication" or "Tasneem is having real difficulty with verbs in the future tense, but she has just written a wonderful story which she should share with the class — perhaps as a puppet play?") for planning future work.

This does not imply that the teachers don't teach. Rather, they teach differently. They work mostly with individuals or small groups rather than the whole class, responding to learning needs as they arise. They also concentrate effort on teaching each new group of children how to read, using a variety of teaching approaches that would be familiar to most early primary teachers in the world, until the new students have reached a level of decoding and comprehension of written text that permits them to work with self-guided materials. Teachers can concentrate their efforts on such essential learning challenges as they arise precisely because they can depend on the fact that most of the young people are engaged most of the time in their own self-guided learning. Such classrooms are busy places, with much movement and activity, and are generally rather noisy, but not with the disruptive noise of children acting up or acting out but with the productive noise of young people working together on their own learning.

Figure 5.4 compares these programs on a variety of pedagogical aspects that can best be seen as continua rather than discrete categories. Two of these relate to the structuring of the school day and school year: pre-set periods—by subject and type of activity—versus time flowing freely, a standard school day/year cycle versus local adaptations. The next set of continua try to locate these programs on now-standard categories of pedagogical difference: teacher-centred versus child-centred; passive learning versus active learning; and rote-frontal versus constructivist teaching. A caveat should be noted here: these points along the continua should be considered as approximations. All are

---

Figure 5.4
Some Pedagogical Continua

Codes: ENP: Escuela Nueva Primary; ENS: Escuela Nueva Secondary: B: BRAC NFPE program; CS: Community Schools Egypt

Pre-set periods	«----------B---------ENS---------CS-----------ENP»	Time flows freely
Standard cycle	«------------B-----------------------ENP ENS CS»	Local cycle
Teacher centred	«-----------------B--------CS---------ENS ENP»	Child-centred
Passive learning	«--------------------B-----ENS--------CS---ENP»	Active learning

---

based on informed judgments of careful observers of these programs, but they are all based on observations of a (necessarily) small set of the schools in the programs. Moreover, in any program of modest to large scale, there will be much variation, whether intended or accidental, and these programs are not exceptions to that rule. Thus these locations on the continua should not be considered as exact points, but as best approximations with considerable variations around each point. With that caution in mind, the first thing to note is that on each continuum *Escuela Nueva* Primary is at or near the right hand side, as in Figure 5.2. This is the program that, in its full implementation, most completely embodies the emergent model. But it is equally important to note that all of the other programs have moved a considerable distance away from the traditional forms of formal schooling as seen in Figure 5.1. Since all of these programs have achieved considerable success in improving student access, retention, and most importantly learning, this suggests that various degrees and combinations of moves away from that traditional model, suited to local conditions and traditions, can be successful. Again, the emergent model is not meant to be a one-size-fits-all recipe for school success, but rather a tool for thinking about these questions and learning from others' experience.

THE TEACHERS: WHO THEY ARE AND HOW THEY LEARN

Teachers are quite obviously the key to any successful learning enhancement system. (For more on teachers and teacher pedagogy, see Sarfaroz Niyozov's Chapter Six.) So, who are the teachers in these alternative programs, where do they come from, and how do they learn this radically alternative form of working with children in schools? Within our overall data set, there are two distinct patterns in terms of teacher selection. In most of the programs the teachers are not formally certified according to standard systems of teacher selection and preparation (such as university-based faculties of education or normal schools). Rather, they are young people, mostly young women, who have a modest degree of formal schooling, usually junior secondary (that is, Grade 10 equivalent, which ordinarily means that they are among those in the local community with the highest level of formal school achievement available). They are locally known individuals, selected by a local school committee, and trained in the local area to teach in the locality. They are very much "of" the local community and known to that community. They are frequently called facilitators rather than teachers, so as to avoid problems with the national teacher unions or associations. The Egypt and Bangladesh programs exemplify this pattern. The two Colombian programs represent the other common pattern, in which the teachers are university-educated and certified, as are all teachers in the regular formal educational system, and often move regularly from place to place under standard rules of the regional/national bureaucracy regarding fully certified teachers. This has proven to be a problem for the Colombian programs, in that the routines of the teacher profession bureaucracy and Ministry of Education regulations often create such frequent teacher career moves that continuity of teaching in the alternative mode can be a problem, requiring a regular and constant need for teachers to learn the new mode.

2/univ educ'd

What is striking, however, is that whichever model of teacher selection, whether for facilitators with no more than 10 years of formal schooling, or for teachers with up to 16 years (that is, university level) of formal education, in all of these cases the adults learn very quickly how to work in a radically alternative form of pedagogy with excellent learning results for their students. In all cases the pre-service teacher development activities are brief (a few weeks at most), but intensive and involving observation of and practice teaching in successful demonstration schools. This is followed by several years of very intensive in-service teacher-to-teacher mentoring programs and regular supervisory support. In the *Escuela Nueva* system teachers in a given locality are assisted to form and participate in microcentres, where they meet every two to four weeks to analyze problems and discuss results. Talking about accomplishments, sharing doubts, and thinking out loud helps teachers to progress towards specific solutions, to test them, and to share the results of these experiences. The microcentres reduce the uncertainty and fear teachers encounter when implementing new teaching methods.[18] The Egyptian program follows a slightly different version of the same approach. A built-in part of the facilitators' schedule is a one-hour meeting at the end of each school day, which provides time for self-reflection and interchange of ideas about how to improve. In these daily meetings the facilitators note questions and issues that they wish to bring up for discussion at

pre-service training

inservice devt, too (built in time)

the weekly district facilitators' meetings, at which all facilitators from a district meet, along with their supervisor. They help each other in solving problems and exchange experiences and approaches that seem to have been successful. Finally, every two weeks the facilitators in each school, with fairly frequent attendance by their supervisor, meet with the local school committee. These meetings enable them to receive regular feedback from the parents and the community regarding their work, and to discuss collectively how to deal with such problems and issues as will regularly arise. Thus these facilitators are seldom alone in trying to deal with the intense experience of working within their schools.[19] The BRAC in-service teacher formation program is equally intensive[20] and indeed this is characteristic of almost all the cases in our broader data-set.

It is important to note just how different is this approach to teacher development and learning from that typically found in North America and other developed regions, where we generally "front-end load" the process, devoting most of our teacher development resources and energy to the pre-service period. Once the new teachers are trained and hired and in their new classrooms, we essentially abandon them to their own devices. Ongoing professional learning experiences are rare, sporadic, and most commonly devised by authority levels far from the individual classroom. (There are a few exceptions, but the general pattern holds.)

The programs considered here demonstrate that, contrary to a very popular belief around the world, teachers are not obstacles to fundamental school change: one doesn't need to make reforms "teacher-proof," as believed in the "standards and accountability" movements in North American and much of European education. Rather, in these cases the teachers are the promoters and agents of such change, even when they are working in very difficult conditions, are not necessarily formally well educated, and are often very poorly paid. They, like the equally disadvantaged young people for whom they are responsible, can and do accomplish remarkable feats of learning and change in quite short periods. There is an important parallel between the young and older learners here. Just as the success for the young people seems based fundamentally on a focus on learning rather than teaching, so the changes in teachers seem based on the same shift in focus. In these systems the role of the supervisors has changed fundamentally. They are not enforcers or administrators of rules and regulations. Rather they are enablers of and promoters of teacher learning. These successful change programs generally spread or go to scale not by a centrally planned and commanded reform plan with goals and objectives set from afar and agents or supervisors from some national or regional centre going out to teach the teachers about the latest new educational idea or theoretical scheme, but rather by an innovation-diffusion process: teachers learning from other teachers, sharing their "practical professional knowledge"[21] and teaching skills with other teachers, and exploring together how their shared and growing knowledge and experience can help everyone, most importantly the young people in their charge.

QUESTIONS PENDING

There are in this long enterprise many questions, puzzlements, and learning challenges still before us. Here I will highlight just three of them. The first is that the literature available on these alternative programs is generally so highly laudatory as to convey an impression that they are all paragons of pedagogical virtue. They are not. They are all very human institutions, far better on average than traditional schools, but variable among and within the programs. Among the evident successes, mistakes have been made and in the best of cases, corrected. These programs *are* experimental and the people involved are learning as they go, but they are learning. A critical literature reflecting the less–than–perfect as well as the successes has not yet developed, and is much needed.

A second challenge relates to the strain and tension between the global and the local, which is highlighted by Hayhoe and Mundy in Chapter One in this book. All of these cases have drawn upon educational/pedagogical scholarship and traditions that are common, and exported, currency in the North/West of the world. Most people I have talked to and worked with who have developed/are developing these programs are well versed in the standard literature of the North/West regarding education and learning. They have studied and understood such standard icons as John Dewey, Maria Montessori, Johann Pestalozzi, and newer pedagogical thinkers in the North/West tradition (such as Howard Gardner, Nel Noddings, and many others), and generally are well aware of the currents of critical thinking in the North/West. What they have done is to take those globalized ideas and ways of understanding education and mixed and matched them with their own civilizational literatures and traditions of understanding teaching and learning to slowly develop very effective, locally appropriate ways of enabling effective learning among even very poor children. One thing that has struck me often as I hang around schools like these trying to figure out how and why they actually work as well as they do, is that at some level they all feel very similar, but at another level are very different. Rural Colombia is not rural Bangladesh or rural Upper Egypt. But there are commonalities that one can see and sense as an experienced teacher. Sorting all of that out, not in some kind of theory-driven enterprise but through careful, on-the-ground work, is a long-term field research challenge, essential if we are ever to begin to really make sense of the global-local question. For more on local and Indigenous pedagogies, see Katherine Madjidi and Jean-Paul Restoule's Chapter Four in this volume.

A third challenge is in some ways even more daunting. It has to do with the inadequacy of many of our standard terms and categories, derived from the long experience of the forms of formal schooling, to capture well what we are slowly coming to understand about these alternative programs. One such issue is the now-standard distinction between formal and non-formal education. This was introduced into the literature in the 1960s and 1970s and was very important then in denoting that education as an organized intentional enterprise could be and was provided by many means beyond formal schooling, for young people and particularly adults.[22] But what do we do with that categorization when we find, as we are, that many of these alternative programs are bringing into the walls of the schoolhouse the pedagogical models of non-formal education, including methods long advocated by adult educators? Thus our comfortable distinctions between formal and non-formal or adult and child learning seem to be broken by the people involved in these programs. We do not yet seem to have a useful practical and theoretical language to represent this reality.[23] This also applies to such terms as *child-centred* or *active* pedagogy or *constructivist* teaching and learning (as used in Figure 5.4). As we have tried to match these many and varied programs to the terms we usually use in our discussions of schooling and pedagogy, we have found ourselves increasingly confounded: in some deep sense it seems that we do not really know what we are talking about! The standard terms and categories don't fit well with what we are seeing (as discussed by Niyozov in Chapter Six). They are based upon an experience of teaching and learning rooted in the long history of and underlying assumptions of formal schooling as we have come to know it. Breaking out of those traditional intellectual categories and assumptions may end up being even harder than breaking out of traditional ways of practice in schools as we have come to know them. So, there is much to learn; we are in early days. But there is much already available to learn from, if we choose to do so.[24]

QUESTIONS FOR REFLECTION AND DISCUSSION

1. In your experience as a learner, have you experienced learning opportunities that approximate some of the characteristics listed in Figure 5.2? What did it feel like, how did it work? Consider your formal schooling and informal educational experiences such as a sport, music lesson, Boy Scouts or Girl Guides. Note down your experiences and thoughts, as you understood it as a learner, and share them with your classmates.

2. The models described in this chapter suggest that multi-graded classrooms may promote better learning than in age-graded classes. As a teacher you are likely to spend some of your time teaching multi-graded classes, such as split-level classes. Have you had, as part of your teacher education, any preparation for that? Why do you suppose that may be?

3. This chapter argues that the forms of formal schooling are usually very difficult to change. From your own experience as a teacher or learner, have you ever tried (successfully or not) to change some aspect of those forms of formal schooling—for example, trying to get some rule or regulation changed? If so, how did this work (or not), and what did you learn from the experience? Have you

ever had much time for reflection and problem-solving with other teachers/facilitators/stakeholders, as in the alternative education cases profiled in this chapter? If so, what difference did this make?

SUGGESTED FILM: *EDUCATION THROUGH IMAGINATION,* BY ANTONIA ANTONOPOULOS

This short film explains the non-formal educational programs offered by the Bangladesh Rural Advancement Committee (BRAC). BRAC's creative responses to rural community learning emphasize the power of the imagination through child-friendly, gender-empowered, ethnically integrated, and community participatory schooling. Viewers watch the daily school activities while the narrator explains the philosophies behind the many non-formal educational programs that BRAC supports.

SUGGESTIONS FOR FURTHER READING

Ahmed, Manzoor. *The Economics of Non-formal Education: Resources, Costs and Benefits.* New York: Praeger, 1975.

Anderson, Stephen, ed. *School Improvement in the Developing World: Case Studies of the Aga Khan Foundation Projects.* Amsterdam: Swets and Zeitlinger, 2002.

Bransford, John D., Ann L. Brown, and Rodney R. Cocking, eds. *How People Learn: Brain, Mind, Experience and Schooling.* Washington, DC: Commission on Behavioral and Social Sciences, National Research Council, National Academy Press, 2000.

Clandinin, Jean and F.M. Connelly. "Stories to Live By: Narrative Understanding of School Reform." *Curriculum Inquiry* 28, no. 2 (1998): 149–64.

*Farrell, Joseph P. *The Egyptian Community Schools Program: A Case Study.* Washington, DC: Academy for International Development, 2004.

Farrell, Joseph P. "International Lessons for School Effectiveness: The View from the Third World." In *Policy for Effective Schools,* edited by Mark Holmes, Kenneth A. Leithwood and Donald F. Musella.

New York and Toronto: Teachers College Press and OISE Press, 1989, 131–53.

*Haiplik, Brenda. *BRAC's Non-formal Education Program (NFEP)*. Washington, DC: Academy for International Development, 2004.

Olson, David. *Psychological Theory and Education Reform: How School Remakes Mind and Society*. Cambridge: Cambridge University Press, 2003.

*Pitt, Jennifer. *Case Study for Escuela Nueva Program*. Washington, DC: Academy for International Development, 2004.

Rogers, Alan. *Non-formal Education: Flexible Schooling or Participatory Education?* Hong Kong: Hong Kong University, Comparative Education Research Centre, 2004.

Zaalouk, Malak. *The Pedagogy of Empowerment: Community Schools as a Social Movement in Egypt*. Cairo: The American University in Cairo Press, 2004.

Chapter Six

Understanding Pedagogy: Cross-cultural and Comparative Insights from Central Asia

Sarfaroz Niyozov

INTRODUCTION

This chapter presents teaching as a broad, contested, and complex process that cannot be encompassed in simple or dichotomous frameworks. It begins with a consideration of some of the existing portrayals of teachers and teaching in the literature and the ways in which they are expected to contribute to educational reform. Then it turns to the context of Central Asia, where I carried out a sustained study of teachers' lives and work in the Republic of Tajikistan.[1] The context of this country, along with its neighbours, Kyrgyzstan and Russia, is briefly described. The chapter goes on to depict the lessons that can be learned from the changing dimensions of teachers' lives and work in this region of the world.

IMAGES OF TEACHING AND TEACHERS

Whatever may be said about policies, curriculum packages, technological advances, and calls for teacher redundancy and de-schooling, teachers remain at the core of education. What happens in their classrooms, and why they teach the way they do, remains the focus of educational research. They are central to policy and practice about the kind of society and citizens we aspire to have, on both local and global scales.[2]

Portrayals such as moral guardians, effective technicians, professionals, curriculum makers, reflective practitioners, transformative intellectuals, cultural and social reformers, and civil servants are among the many depictions of teachers in the literature.[3] Despite such positive portrayals, questions remain as to whether teaching and schools have really improved and whether changes have made a genuine difference in the lives of students.[4]

It is also becoming obvious that most portrayals depict teaching and teachers in reductive ways.[5] The description of teaching that has emerged is couched in two dichotomized items: content and pedagogy. This dualist conceptualization denigrates important dimensions of teachers' practice, such as their purpose, vision, relationships, ethics, commitment, passion, management, and resources.[6]

Child-centred teaching is increasingly being criticized as culturally inappropriate, politically unsettling, socially and racially biased, and intellectually superficial. Other progressive ideas, such as the whole language approach, co-operative learning, inquiry, critical thinking, and constructivism, are also under question.[7] They are seen as inappropriate for teachers and students in developing countries, as well as for minority students in industrialized societies, due to the demands they make on time and resources. Criticized in the West as being Anglo-American, they are viewed as Western, masculine, elitist, secular, disrespectful of traditional cultures, and "playlike" rather than "serious" in the rest of the world.[8] The fundamental principles of child-centred pedagogy have been problematized in terms of whether a child should be seen as inherently good, whether children's needs are natural and innate or determined by their peers and parents, and whether students' prior knowledge and experience should always be respected and celebrated.[9] Some have also counterpoised the concepts of *teaching* and *pedagogy*, characterizing *teaching* as an act by a teacher, which leads to students' learning, and *pedagogy* as "the performance of teaching with the theories, beliefs, policies, and controversies that inform it."[10]

These debates have some usefulness, but they are limited by narrow dualist conceptualizations, polarized typologies, and imbalanced portrayals.[11] Reductionist and dualist conceptions of teaching exclude much of the complexity that practitioners must deal with. By either idealizing or demonizing teaching, these approaches lead to one-sided solutions that are likely to fail. This, in turn, may lead to cynicism about research, researchers, reform, and reformers.

By contrast, I will try to present a rich, contested, and non-dichotomous portrayal of classrooms, schooling, and teachers' lives in this chapter. This portrayal is drawn from nine months of ethnographic work in three areas of the mountainous Badakhshan Autonomous Province of Tajikistan. The research focused on five core participants, who were observed in their classrooms and interviewed in depth. Three of the five teachers were male, and two were female. Their teaching areas included primary-level history, mathematics, biology, and the Russian language. In the interviews, I asked them about their own life histories, their classroom practices, as well as wider questions of education and society. Interviews were also held with focus groups, school heads, other outspoken and critical teachers, community members, representatives of the school board and education ministry, and members of the international education community.

The data from this fieldwork was analyzed inductively and then linked to other surveys and both empirical and theoretical studies on education in Tajikistan, Kyrgyzstan, and Russia. The analysis was then broadened by reference to a wider literature on pedagogy in developing and industrialized societies.

THE CONTEXT: TAJIKISTAN, KYRGYZSTAN, AND RUSSIA

As part of the rediscovery and reinvention of a glorified past, Tajikistan and Kyrgyzstan claim to be descendants of the Silk Road's ancient civilizations.[12] Tajikistan claims to have been a large and flourishing state ruled by the Samanids, in the ninth to tenth centuries CE, while the Kyrgyz invoke a powerful khanate near the Yenisei River at around the same time. As titular states, however, the two came into being very recently, during the Soviet delimitations of the 1920s and 1930s.[13] Russia's history also goes back to the ninth century, with continuity from Kievan Rus' to medieval Muscovy through the early modern reign of Peter the Great. At that time the state of Moscow was reconceived as imperial Russia and eventually became an empire, annexing the current Central Asia by the end of the 19th century. Since then, the political, economic, cultural, and educational destinies of Tajikistan, Kyrgyzstan, and other Central Asian states have been influenced by Russia.[14]

Considering educational reform as a part of nation-building projects, Russia, Tajikistan, and Kyrgyzstan are unearthing or inventing alternative indigenous pedagogies within their own cultural histories. On the one hand, these pedagogies often appear as appropriated versions of common Western approaches and ideas, camouflaged by local ethno-pedagogy, attributed to indigenous scholars, and appropriated to perpetuate the existing socio-political status-quo.[15]

(See Chapter Five by Joseph P. Farrell and Chapter Seven by Stephen Anderson.) On the other hand, there are many social, political, and cultural factors that make it difficult to introduce genuine reforms that have been dictated by research. For example, group work was banned in one school simply because it caused some students to sit with their backs to the portraits of the country's authorities that hung on the classroom walls. English teaching in some primary schools had to be stopped because of students' limited ability to communicate in their national languages. The English hours were then reallocated to the national language. Such anecdotes illustrate how educational shortcomings are blamed on the very strategies that could remedy them.

While Western Sovietologists have portrayed the relations between Russia and Central Asia as colonial, many Central Asians have willingly emulated Russia as a development model. Different emirates and khanates used Russia in their fights against each other, while smaller nationalities sought Russia's protection from the domination of locally powerful groups. Despite their political independence, as well as some stark demographic differences that are evident in Table 6.1, Central Asia remains under Russian influence 15 years after the collapse of the Soviet Union. The modern education systems in Central Asia were created with Russian and other external help, especially during the Soviet times. Until 1991, these countries all had a centralized education system, following a structurally unified, yet contextually uneven system of three or four years of primary, five years of secondary, and two years of upper secondary education. Post-Soviet system restructuring, including privatization and decentralization, has also largely been similar, with Tajikistan and Kyrgyzstan following Russia's path of educational reform. The structure, culture, politics, and problems of education have remained similar in the three former Soviet states, in each case following a sort of local variation.[16]

In the remaining sections of this chapter, I will illustrate the complex notion of teaching that was introduced earlier through my study of the Tajik teachers and related literature.

TEACHING AS THE USE OF CONTRADICTORY, EVOLVING, COMPLEX, AND MIXED-METHODS STYLES

It became clear in my study that innovative teachers exhibited elements of various teaching styles in their practices. The same teachers moved between teacher-centred, authoritarian, coercive, and transmissive pedagogic modes, on the one hand, and student-centred, democratic, and collaborative styles, on the other. This was often within the same classrooms and subjects. This mixture of practices problematizes the nature of their pedagogies. First, it shows that what is observed cannot be seen as a direct reflection of the teachers' stated principles and intentions; second, neither teacher-centred nor student-centred styles are monolithic or fixed, but rather have shades and degrees; third, it is possible for teachers to change their teaching approaches under the influence of shifting contextual factors; and last, teachers' explanations of their practice may differ considerably from those of the external observer. Therefore, we need to look not only at the teaching methods, but also at the teachers' goals and their ethical stances. Figure 6.1

Table 6.1

Basic Demographic, Economic, and Educational Indicators of Kyrgyzstan, Tajikistan, and Russia[17]

Countries	Total Population (mn) 2004	Area (thousand sq km) 2004	Population Growth % 2004	GNI per capita (US$) 2004	Adult Literacy Rate % 2004	Life Expectancy (years) 2004	School Enrolment 0–18 years, (mn) 2004
Tajikistan	6.3	143.1	1. 4	280–330	98	64	1670
Kyrgyzstan	5.5	199.9	1. 2	460	99	67	1450
Russia	141.3	17000	-0.2	3410	99	65	29809

illustrates the teachers' teacher-centred and authoritarian practices, with the students "passively imbibing the values, skills, and knowledge they impart."[18] Selected quotes from teachers in my study are listed alongside of actions that relate to them.

On the surface, Figure 6.1 illustrates teacher-centred instruction and the transmission mode. The emphasis is on teacher domination of the agenda, memorization, and coercive relationships.[19] The teachers appear as believers in the existence of a direct link between their teaching and the students' learning; they are concerned about covering the curriculum, teaching to the test, and sticking to the textbook. In his study of teaching in Kyrgyzstan, Shamatov's history teacher, Kanybek, was described as follows:

> [He] … predominantly used the lecture method so that he could cover the material within the limited time allotted for history lessons. He commented, "I teach the most important aspects of the theme, and encourage the pupils to study the rest on their own." He dictated his [summary] to his pupils and had them copy the material to read for homework. He said, "If I lecture and have the pupils write my lectures quickly, then it will be very helpful for them when they go to university, because I learned from my university experience that writing a lecture is really tough."[20]

Kerr suggests that the case of Tajik teachers is typical of the situation throughout much of the former USSR:

Figure 6.1
Transmissive, Teacher, and Textbook-Centred/Authoritarian Classroom Practices

Sayings	Actions
Because there is too much information to cover in a short time, I must make it short, simple, and concrete, and lecture that to them.	Warn; stand in front; always have serious face.
Due to lack of textbooks, I have become the source of knowledge and have made them parrots.	Make sure students do not move ... and follow the rules of behaviour (for example, raising hands, sitting, and standing).
Because they and I are not used to group work, I cannot switch to it right away.	Emphasize the years, dates and names; repeat and explain the same thing more than once.
The teacher should be like an encyclopedia, [and] know everything possible.	Maintain close relationships with parents, but strict relations with students; threaten students with their parents.
How can you call it indoctrination when I tell them the good side and bad side of an issue?	Interrupt when students are not on the point.
I am more experienced and tell them so that they do not make my mistakes; I tell them the correct answer so that they do not fail; no one has become something without a teacher.	Ridicule; point out mistakes right away.
	Correct the language use immediately; do not allow use of the mother tongue.
	Tell the students to move out of classroom, stand still, or move to corner.
The younger need to listen to wise people and seek their advice.	Lecture, tell, and explain.

Their language and vocabulary are too weak, and I cannot use their mother tongue – I am not allowed.	Daily plan and develop a conspectus; ask students to copy it.
Due to cold-related winter break, we need to move fast to cover the topics, so I have to tell them the most important points.	Evaluate students at the end of each class. Use moralist poetry and verses from authoritative texts and figures.

> Instruction from the first grade on was characterized by a fairly rigid pattern of rote mastery of text, oral recitation by students, and teacher dominance of classroom activity ... the typical Soviet school was often a dreary place: a decrepit building with few textbooks, out-dated equipment, alienated students, bored teachers, and authoritarian administration. Students graduated with little understanding of the concepts or principles they had studied, or with narrow, outdated occupational training that was often useless in practice.[21]

Avalos extends this to developing countries in general:

> Most classroom activities are directed to the whole class, with the teacher appearing as a "benevolent dictator." The teacher solicits, requests, or orders responses from pupils who in turn must render such services. The children's personal experience is seldom used as a learning input. The provision of feedback to pupils' responses is often arbitrarily decided by teachers who might "ignore" a child's response or treat a child's error as personal insult ... teaching of norms and rules overshadows other teaching activities ... even though a great number of questions are asked, most of them are either recall or simple direct questions mostly initiated by teachers.[22]

Sirotnik states that such teaching and learning situations exist in most industrialized countries, including the United States, where there is:

a lot of teacher talk and a lot of student listening ... almost invariably closed and factual questions ... and predominantly total classroom instructional configurations around traditional activities—all in a virtually affectless environment. It is but a short inferential leap to suggest that we are implicitly teaching dependence on authority, linear thinking, social apathy, passive involvement, and hands-off learning.[23]

The above portrayals are honest, yet they become problematic when they stop at showing one type of pedagogy. If teaching is a lived practice, and if as such, it is a contradictory and complex, contingent, and dynamic experience,[24] why do we discard what we may think is insignificant and why do we ignore the alternatives that may not fit into our agendas and arguments? I believe it is within this complexity that the language of possibility and hope for better practice and sustainable reform exist.

not seeing + bad?

It is also important to note that even these so-called teacher-centred practices have a complex nature. For example, warning and telling of bad and good aspects of one's society by using living examples from one's surroundings and by problematizing a topic in the history textbook illustrates a departure from the "pre-cooked text." It also implies that transmission should not always be seen as bad, monolithic, and fixed. Sometimes it may impart critical and balanced thinking, raise students' consciousness, implant doubt in their minds, and keep them from being fooled by information. In other words, it may well be "a standard fallacy to presume that whole class direct instruction equates with transmission or that collective discussion respects children's capacities as thinkers."[25]

Nevertheless, my participants often acknowledged that the coercive nature of their teaching and attitudes, their bullying of the students, their lecturing, their use of elevated academic language, and their teaching of unrelated topics could be counterproductive and harmful. They saw these practices as stemming from their own disempowerment in the face of the increasing intensification of their working lives:

admit practices but rationalize them

I become rude because life and work conditions make me get out of control, when I prepare myself and my students don't. My wife makes me angrier when she, instead of appreciating my struggle, also curses me, "Why do you kill yourself for teaching and school, when no one cares about you and your family?" I feel she is right.[26]

Figure 6.2 illustrates practices and attitudes that seem to represent forms of transactive and transformative teaching. Transactive education emphasizes a curricular process in which students reconstruct knowledge through dialogue and interaction. Transformational teaching concentrates on an integrated, holistic change in individuals and society. It rests on a humanistic commitment to social change. "In this position, the student is not just viewed in a cognitive mode, but in terms of his or her aesthetic, moral, physical, and spiritual needs."[27]

In Figure 6.2, the same teachers appear to believe in the students' ability to contribute, have knowledge, think, and take responsibility. They ask questions and engage their students in a series of activities. They agree with the kind of activities the students suggest, such as role-play and word guessing. Here, the students are perceived not only as knowledge receivers, but also as emulators, appliers, thinkers, and even producers.[28] These teachers augmented their methods by humane approaches and more engaged pedagogy. Some of this they had personally experienced as students during their schooling. Other ideas they had gained from refresher courses or from reflection on their personal practices and traditional cultures. They allowed their students to move, recite poetry, dance, sing songs, lead the lessons, ask questions, laugh, disagree with each other and the teacher, cooperate and compete, and make noise, although to a limited degree. They sat with their students, made jokes, agreed with their views, listened to their comments, and asked questions relating their curricular and extracurricular lessons and topics. The teachers mentioned the progressive theories of Pestalozzi, Rousseau, and Krupskaya, such as the project method, group work, socialist competition, and problem solving. They cited proponents of the Soviet era pedagogy of cooperation, such as Shatalov, Amonashvili, Lysenko, Davidov,[29] and their counterparts in Tajikistan and Kyrgyzstan.[30] In Russia, while the dominant mode promotes acquisition of facts, strict principles and rules, memorization, and rote learning, there is also a scaffolding of students' knowledge and skills, a pedagogy of co-operation, and other forms of active learning on the part of students.[31]

Figure 6.2
Transactive and Transformative Teaching Practices

Sayings	Actions
I wanted them (11th graders) to conduct the lesson; they lived through perestroika and glasnost, so they know about the topic.	Students discuss and provide feedback to teaching.
Once in two weeks I prepare my good students to teach the whole class.	Students dance and sing during the relevant topics, and also celebrate their talents and successes.
I agree that teachers may not know everything and students may know something that we teachers do not know. Our students travel, meet many people, and see a lot of movies.	Pose problems to do independent work; ask students to question one another. Field trips; ask them to work in large groups and arrange competition between the groups.
I want the children to explain the past so as to imagine a future.	Assign creative homework.
I expect them to create something new.	Hug the smaller children when they come to the front.
I could have lectured, but I know you (students) all have learned a lot of poetry, so I left it to you, and you did very well.	Students select activities such as roleplay for some of the sessions. Bring up social issues and let the students talk about them.
I can prove to the inspector that I am doing the right thing.	Use brainstorming and puzzles.
	Invite the silent students to speak up.
I am a friend of my students, and they share with me more than with their parents.	Relate the topics to the students' lives;

I am there for my students when they need me.	ask the students to assess one another.
It is better to ask questions than tell them.	
I use Shugnani and Wakhi [local languages] from time to time to help my students understand the topics.	

In Chapter Five, Joseph P. Farrell emphasizes interactive learning as the distinguishing feature of the alternative education movements in Latin America, Asia, and North Africa. Others observe many teachers in the mainstream schools in Africa and elsewhere who move between various teaching styles and argue that it is not appropriate to simply judge these styles by externally defined indicators.[32] In China, teachers struggle to implement communicative methods when teaching English. This struggle reveals not only the importance of political will in the spread of learner-centred pedagogy, but also why and how some teachers are capable of bringing about classroom change despite tremendous obstacles.[33] In France, examples of didactic exposition and teacher-centred direct instruction were not always dull and "dead" transmission; some were appropriate and necessary for important learning, awareness, and even inspiration. In sum, there is extensive research that makes it clear that all societies at all times have had interactive, learner-oriented potential that has become predominant or subordinate depending on the conjuncture of various forces.[34]

Subject Matter: More than Facts and Inert Ideas

Teaching, however, is more than methods and styles. While the teachers deeply cared about knowing and imparting the factual material in their subject textbooks, subject matter was not confined to the classroom or considered as a set of generalizations, principles, and objective facts to be transmitted in a detached manner within a particular block of time. Rather, subject matter defined the teachers' identity and status in the school and the community. For example, participants were always addressed as teachers of specific subjects. The devaluation and rewriting of Russian and history as a result of the collapse of the USSR created the toughest emotional, epistemological, and ethical crises for the teachers. These resulted in an identity crisis for these subject teachers, as facts, concepts, and principles that had been considered universal truths during Soviet times turned out to be ideological and political lies. The hidden agenda and the promotion of Russification were suddenly revealed, and debates arose about the educational relevance of these subjects to the mountainous regions of Central Asia. Although times have changed, the local languages, history, culture, and nature itself still wait to become real parts of the school curriculum.

This ideological tension occurred in science subjects also. The biology teacher's belief in evolution was challenged by a student's assertion of divine creation. The teacher's rejection of the student's opinion spilled over to the parents who were conservative, with the father being an active *mujahideen* leader in the area. They warned the teacher not to teach any atheistic or anti-Islamic topics. "Now, I do not become emotional in such situations. I say evolution and creationism are two options. You can choose the one you want."[35] According to the history teacher, the Soviet lies have been replaced with new "truths," which differ in scope, but not in nature and purpose. The re-emergence of political and religious indoctrination and aggressive nationalism in the region clashes with these teachers' internationalist visions of education and citizenship in Central Asia.

Teaching as Relationships

Relations and caring were also evolving and influenced by multiple factors and contexts. Changing times were reflected in the relationships among teachers and students:

> Ten years ago I was more strict and demanding with my students. Now I let them work according to their interests more than my own. In the Soviet times, I knew the students were fed and clothed. That's why I not only asked the students to study harder but also watched that they did not get spoiled and involved in bad activities. Now if I am too strict things get worse. If a child has not eaten bread for a while and I "twist his ears," he may kill himself because of too much pressure here and at home. Two students

from our Tajik and Kyrgyz schools have tried this already. That is why my expectations have gone down.[36]

Figure 6.3 is an illustration of the complex relationships and the forms of caring in the rural, traditional, and transitional society.

Figure 6.3
Samples of Expressions about the Significance of Relationships

- If students like me, they will accept my style and learn my subject.
- Too much kindness makes students lazy and weak, and too much cruelty makes them stubborn and passive.
- One has to be kind and firm at the same time.
- Sometimes I scold the students, other times I shout at them, yet other times I joke, but they know I care for them. I do that for their benefit, that is why they do not get angry.
- I defend the students from abusive parents when needed.
- We have decided to treat children as human beings. We decided to fight those who pull our students into drugs and guns.
- When I see parents avoiding me, I feel something went wrong in my work with their children. Here, if things go bad, they may go so between families and for generations.
- I give my students a four (a "B") and a five (an "A") just because they still come to school.
- In the Soviet times, our respect was contrived by the Party. Now we need to work hard to earn respect.
- Nowadays, if you don't give the students good grades, their parents won't say salom [hello].
- I may have slapped a younger one, but not the older students.
- I treat children well because I want others to treat my children well.
- I became a Russian teacher because my Russian teachers treated me as a human being, better than my Tajik teachers.
- Nasir Khusraw [a traditional sage] says the purpose of learning is to become mature, nice in behaviour. Others say, "It is easy to be a scholar and difficult to be a human being."
- Like Luqman [a Quranic sage], I learned to be nice by avoiding bad peoples' traits.
- I feel hurt when someone has become rich and disrespects his teacher; nowadays people respect only the rich, mafia, and the merchants.

Relationships are central to the success of any pedagogy, regardless of its type, intention, or sophistication. In this rural context, most of the teachers had personal rapport with the students and their students could confide in them.

Like her Tajik colleagues, Ainura, a Kyrgyz teacher, wanted to focus on important social principles that she felt were in decline: respecting elders, helping others, preserving family and community values, caring, doing what is right, and avoiding the wrong. She commented, "As teachers, we should have ethical sessions or informal conversations with our pupils more often. And we should also be models for them."[37] Caring in this case was not just a female or primary teacher's quality, nor does it end with students. Caring is complex and extends to students' families and communities. It also includes the teachers' need to be cared for.[38]

Teaching as Commitment, Moral Responsibility, and Integrity

Teaching included commitment and moral responsibility, particularly in the context of the decline in teachers' status and their fragile economic situation, and also the increase in pressure for unpaid service by the state and civil society. The following participant's voice is a compelling testimony to the way commitment and responsibility are interconnected with the teacher's identity, larger vision, purpose, and ethical stance.

> Materially this teaching does not give me even 5 percent of what I would do in my farm. I could collect wood for winter and look after my cattle. But I prepare myself and come to teach. I feel I have to care for them and for my community. No one can do that except teachers. The authorities and parents do not appreciate this, which makes me very angry, so much that I cannot sometimes control myself and unleash my anger on my students.[39]

Another teacher added:

> Teachers are a source of spirituality, culture, education, and the future of the society. We work so that the children live better and our community does not fall back to the level of Afghanistan. In the 70 Soviet years we have moved so much ahead and we do not want our people to become ignorant again, get involved in drugs and wars.[40]

A similarly growing commitment was noted on the part of a novice Kyrgyz teacher:

> Kanybek faced the challenge of his pupils' lack of motivation. Initially he focused on only those pupils who wanted to learn. First, he thought why should he bother about those who don't want to learn? However, Kanybek eventually felt uncomfortable that many of his pupils were not learning … Kanybek then began focusing on all the pupils, motivating them to study well to succeed.[41]

Teaching as Relevance

While teachers were aware of the curriculum's failure to provide real, relevant, and meaningful learning, they also did not judge the Soviet curriculum as useless. A history teacher, examining the relevance of the Soviet approach to history, suggested that the post-Soviet researchers and policy-makers learn from that period:

> We learned about USA, Russia, and the Roman Empire, which were too far and too old. But we knew nearly nothing about ourselves, our neighbours, Afghanistan and China. Ultimately, we came to teach our Tajik history. But, because our scholars did not care, we have so many problems with teaching it now. Many important themes need to be included. I would include the view of mountains, the traditions of the people of Badakhshan, the needs of Badakhshan and the problems we face today. I have nothing against the Romans and Russians, nothing against the Sogdians and the Bactrians [ancient peoples of Central Asia], but I want to know about ourselves first and how are we connected to them. Many people do not even know about how our people are divided between Tajikistan and Afghanistan. Here, we should start the history of Tajik people from the history of Badakhshan. We in the school conduct extracurricular activities to teach more about our prominent figures and our place, bring in a veteran of the war or a local scholar, arrange a visit to the Ethnographic Museum. On our own efforts, time, energy, and expenses. No one pays us for these. No one thanks us.[42]

Relevance, however, was not just a content question. It involved the pedagogical skill of linking a topic to students' experiences and starting from where they are. A teacher of Russian, facing this dilemma of authentic teaching in the Soviet times, decided to go with his students' learning pace and interests:

> I said, "To hell with the 'parts of speech' [a part of the mandated program]." I will do everything to enable these students to read and write first, if not to speak. When they start reading and writing, we can move to grammar. I knew that I was violating the directives. In the journal I would write that I am covering grammar, but in reality I was teaching them reading intensively.[43]

Teaching as Vision, Goals, and Context

Reflective of their multiple roles, and worried about the dramatic post-Soviet changes, the participants in this study emerged as responsible citizens, whose zone of praxis went beyond the school walls. For them the concern was about where society was heading, the lack of care for the poor and their neighbours, there being no accountability, and the absence of law and rules of behaviour. A teacher felt as follows:

> Unlike some teachers, I cannot sleep comfortably when I do not tell the students and parents about the wrongdoings around. The children witness in the street how modesty, honesty, hard work, and knowledge fail. Once I talked about Tajikistan being socialist; now we criticize that. Once we talked against religion, capitalism, and private ownership; now we praise all of them. Once I said Uzbeks were our brothers; now some people view them as occupiers of Samarqand and Bokhara. If I talk today about Russians as brothers and friends, the youth of the village and my students do not like it. How can I state that we have a law-abiding, democratic and secular society, when there are drugs, guns, corruption, religious imposition, and nepotism? I do not want to be a liar again.[44]

The teachers envisaged and worked for a society that was to be based on co-operation, sharing, and caring for each other and the poor. One teacher expressed it this way:

I should be pushing a humanistic ideology. You noticed how many nationalities and ethnicities we have got here in Murgab [a site of the study]. We should make it a tradition to celebrate Wakhan language and culture one day, the other for Darwoz, third day a Kyrgyz cultural event, and so on. I should promote education that teaches respect, justice, and internationalism. By internationalism I mean the equality of people despite their geographical locations, languages, races, and religions. I like when there is pluralism of thinking, instead of having an ideology of a party or a clan.[45]

The teachers worked for a Tajikistan that was free from drugs, guns, and corruption, all of which had spread due to the mismanagement of their market economy — the bureaucracy's incompetence and lack of ethics. "[T]he only way to improve this society is to have more people with ethics and knowledge," suggested the teacher of Russian.[46] The teachers joined their school's fight for each child, talking with parents, using examples of those who strayed because of drugs and guns. They avoided drugs and gun themselves, using the sayings of the president, figures from literature and the Aga Khan, who is the spiritual leader of Ismaili Muslims. In his 1995 visit to Tajikistan, the Aga Khan emphasized that the continuance and even tolerance of such activities as drug dealing would only hurt Tajikistan's chances of development in a world becoming increasingly meritocratic. A teacher expressed her disgust for rampant nepotism and corruption:

The more we teach about ethics, the less ethical we are becoming. Imagine a poor child prepares himself all his life, works day and night. Then someone else who did not work hard gets to the university by bribe or connection. I despise those who do all this. I feel humiliated. When you see your good student has failed you curse the earth and the sky.[47]

A Kyrgyz teacher illustrates the regional nature of social injustice: "I cannot convince my pupils to help others when they see how easily some guys are becoming rich and famous by illegal means and by avoiding caring and sharing."[48]

The teachers compared Soviet certainty and relative security with the post-Soviet chaos and conflicts; the relatively open access, employment, and mobility opportunities of the Soviet period with the pre-Soviet and post-Soviet tribalism and ethnic discrimination; Soviet brutal accountability with the current unpunished nepotism in jobs, opportunity, and wealth distribution. They compared the history of their linguistic and religious minorities' sufferings in the pre- and post-Soviet times with their relative prosperity during the Soviet era. In making these comparisons, they challenged the triumphalism of many in the West and East over the collapse of the USSR, suggesting rather that the collapse of the communist ideology did not mean the automatic success of alternative frameworks. Neither does it mean that life will get any better for every one, nor that the existing societies will automatically become free and democratic, as promised. While not wishing for a return of the Soviets, they feared that the post-Soviet societies might lose the positive achievements that had been made and bring back to the young and vulnerable Tajik society only the negative features of the pre-Soviet and Soviet periods.

A MULTIPLICITY OF GOALS AND OBJECTIVES

The teachers showed that teaching is an act with multiple purposes and goals. They had broad educational goals, such as enabling the students to become knowledgeable and ethical, to gain access to higher education, to become creative and internationalist, to work in international organizations, and to become famous. They had subject-pertinent goals, such as enabling students to speak Russian, English, and Chinese, developing a love for their country, helping them to know the importance of consensus and national unity, teaching them to be wary of politicians, and enabling them to use biological knowledge in their daily lives. There were topic-related goals, such as explaining the causes and outcomes of Perestroika, the reasons for rise and fall of the Samainds, and learning the names of fruits and vegetables in Russian and Tajik. There were social and ethical goals, such as teaching children to avoid bad habits related to alcohol, drugs, and guns; encouraging love for the motherland, the president, and the imam; developing a sense of pride in the village's contribution to the development of Tajikistan; and fostering friendship with the neighbouring Kyrgyz. There were logistic and organizational goals, such as attending class regularly and observing hygiene, bringing peers and younger children to school, and carrying wood to heat the classrooms. There were individual student-related goals, such as fostering freedom of expression, instilling confidence, and encouraging particular students by giving them high marks.

Continuing the Soviet tradition, where the moral and ethical aims of education were taken seriously, was important. Every aspect of schooling, including youth movements, labour education, and extracurricular activities, was linked to academic aims. The teachers considered social and moral goals more important and harder to achieve than academic ones. This was evident in local proverbs such as *"Olim shudan oson wa odam shudan mushkil"* [It is easy to become a learned person and much harder to become a human being]. Teachers worried about the ineffectiveness of the newly introduced subjects of ethics, morality, conflict resolution, and peacemaking. Comments such as, "The more we teach ethics, the less ethical we are becoming"; "The street has a stronger influence on students than we do"; "Mafia and drug dealers impress them with cars, good clothes, and money"; and "With dollars in hand, you can buy any kind of education and position" are signs of this frustration. Yet, the teachers could not follow these unethical ways of living. One teacher said, "If we go for drugs, the students will follow us." Another teacher added:

> To become rich everyone does what he wants. *But I cannot tell my students to cheat, steal, kill, or sell drugs.* The values that I talk about never die. I hope we are going to have a country where there is law. The key to this is preparing people with ethics and knowledge. That is what the imam tells us now and that is what the Communists told us before. The problem is to put all these words into practice. Not just talk about them.[49]

The teachers were convinced that their working without salary for years, their bringing in guest speakers, local famous persons, or veterans, their not drinking alcohol and acknowledging to the students that smoking and drugs are harmful, and their use of the words and actions of traditional authorities and local poetry were still the only way to a better future.

Yet, while they fostered respect for hard work, honesty, bravery, and love for one's motherland, their classrooms mostly remained focused on covering the formal curriculum and the textbook. This concern often made them authoritarian, teacher-and-textbook centred, and coercive in their relationships. The rural post-Soviet realities, in which the academic year was reduced to six or seven months, instead of nine, due to cold, coupled with the demands for disciplining and grading, created a panic situation. They felt there was no time even to achieve the academic objectives and cover the textbook. Their educational goals and societal visions were doomed to fail within the current conditions of work, and in face of widespread corruption. They also realized that parents' purposes in sending their children to school had become mainly to get a graduation certificate. Facing these difficult social forces, the teachers found it hard to uphold positive values and the best aspects of the different competing ideologies. History teachers in public schools had to follow the nationally prescribed curriculum, which demanded that they promote ethnic nationalism. They found the intrusion of religion and nationalism unacceptable. They were also uncomfortable with the reinterpretation of the *Basmachis* (Islamic guerrillas of the 1920s) as freedom fighters. They continued to favour the socialism that by now had disappeared.

They felt that being a good human in terms of character, ethics, and values was actually the same as being a good Muslim, a good communist, or a good democrat. Some schools displayed the pictures and sayings of Lenin and Marx, alongside of their national president and various religious authorities. They did this to show the continuity of perennial values in education, such as hard work, honesty, justice, and caring. A teacher observed that, as theories, socialism, democracy, and Islam were great and kind. But at the level of practice, the teachers were wearied by these competing ideological claims. Like their visions, the teachers' noble intentions essentially formed their response to the confusing, chaotic, and unjust environment they faced.

Another layer of the teachers' practices was a certain degree of incongruity with the values and perspectives of their traditional communities, particularly in relation to citizenship education. Throughout the history of Central Asia, whether openly or in hidden ways, schools and teachers have always been assigned the role of reformers of their rural societies. In pre-Soviet times, education aimed to Islamize the local populations. During the Soviet period, schools and teachers took over the role of the mosques, churches, and families in re-moralizing the community and creating Soviet human beings who were to be above ethnic and religious differences. "During the Soviet times, we were scolded for not being socialist and atheist enough; in the post-Soviet times we are reprimanded for not being nationalist enough," commented the biology teacher.[50] States seem to use schools and teachers for changing communities in ways that perpetuate the new social order, which is always presented as the best societal model.[51]

PEDAGOGY AND CULTURE(S)

Culture emerged as a major theme in this study. Figures 6.1 and 6.3 could confirm assertions that traditional educational cultures promote passivity, obedience, unquestioned submission, reverence to authorities, traditions, and elders, and that they are conducive to teacher-centred instruction.[52] They may thus harm a child's individuality and ability to take responsibility in decision-making. However, Figures 6.2 and 6.3 and other voices challenge these assertions. Not all authorities and traditions are oppressive. Nor should respect, acceptance, and submission be seen as based on passivity and blind emulation. Traditional culture can promote active learning, questioning, and searching. Nothing should be accepted without questions of what, why, and how, as the 11th-century thinker Nasir Khusraw advised. "Seek knowledge even in China" is a prophetic saying that promotes an attitude of open-mindedness and active learning.

The teachers used these various cultural authorities pragmatically in order to promote their students' development. Among the authorities often quoted are a ninth-century poet, Rudaki, Nasir Khusraw, and the Aga Khan. Nasir Khusraw's life and work epitomized active inquiry where knowledge, reasoning, quality evidence, and active interpretation were used in a search for truth, social justice, and ethical conduct.[53] He modelled learning from people of different Islamic and non-Islamic perspectives, as can be seen in the following poem:

I began to ask questions from thinking people of their opinions:
From the Shafi'I, Maliki, Hanafi, I asked of what they said.
I began to search for the guidance of the Chosen One of God
But when I asked (my teachers) about the reasons for injunctions of
  the religion, or the verses of Qur'an on which they were based

None proved to be helpful, one resembling the blind and the
    other deaf.
Then I rose from my place and started my journey,
Abandoning without regret my house, my garden, those whom I
    was accustomed to see.
From Persian and Arab, Indian and Turk,
From inhabitants of Sind, Byzantium and Jew, from every one,
From the philosophers, Manichee, Sabean, from an atheist,
Did I inquire as to what interested me with much persistence.[54]

Khusraw believed that submission to authority cannot be based on
a blind imitation or acceptance, but must be based on a conscious
understanding, led by brave questions, which have no limits in scope
or nature. "I could never accept the blind following of the prescribed
practices / *taqlid* without explanations, / The truth cannot be provided
by blind acceptance."[55] Rudaki believed one should take responsibility
for one's learning and should seek the reasons of misfortune inside
oneself. His famous verse endorses active and critical learning: "Those
who cannot learn from the passage of daily life, / Will never learn a
thing from a teacher of any kind."[56]

Rudaki and Nasir Khusraw represent Muslim traditions of active
learning and broad understanding of education where intellectual,
moral, and ethical dimensions are in balance and aim at harmony
among heart, mind, and soul. Trends such as this have existed in Central
Asia across its history, sometimes becoming dominant, but mostly
playing subordinate or oppositional roles. Just before the socialist
revolution, a new movement, *Jadid*, aimed to modernize the society
through active learning, respecting the learner, and making learning
relevant and effective by harmonizing Western and Islamic approaches
to learning.[57] Contrary to the usual negative portrayals of mosques,
madrasahs, and maktabs, several researchers have shown that these
institutions have been sites of active learning, open-mindedness, and
tolerance at certain times.[58]

Similarly, Soviet educational culture provided opportunities
for plural forms of education, in spite of its tendency to ideological
indoctrination. It had the holistic notion of harmony between
instruction (*obuchenie*) and upbringing (*vospitanie*); a dialectic between
the collective and the individual; methods of active learning; and

authorities who inspired teachers and students. The teachers often referred to similarities between the advice of Lenin and Muhammad or Lenin and the Aga Khan on learning, education, and other humanistic values. One teacher made the following comment:

> During Perestroika and Independence, I was worried about the excess of talk about Islam, but then I realized that the major principles of the ethical code of the constructor of communism are similar to those of *javonmardi* (manliness) in Islam. The problem is how to apply them in practice. I don't see that happening with either of them.[59]

This complex, dynamic, and contested notion of culture is vital. Culture is seen as a rich and dynamic construct, which can be used for different purposes. It can provide hope and opportunities for renewal, empowerment, active learning, justice, and humane education. This in turn opens up doors for dialogue and border-crossing among perspectives and cultures (see Kathy Bickmore's Chapter Ten). International educators should identify these aspects of interconnectedness, empowerment, and justice at local and global, historical and contemporary levels.[60]

CONCLUSION AND IMPLICATIONS

The image of teaching portrayed above is neither new nor original. Nevertheless, approaches to reform in teacher education and curriculum development have remained fragmented, mechanical, outside-in, top-down, and effectiveness-oriented. They tend to be based on limited portrayals, easy answers, and quick-fix solutions. This has given people the feeling that education reform rhetoric is less about improved teaching and learning, community, and global justice than about making money, exercising power, and reproducing inequalities.[61] When policy-makers perceive teachers as deficient because they are overly didactic and coercive, the solution is to replace their practice with externally developed "effective" methods. These are crystallized, objectified, and separated from the complex and contradictory features of their contexts.

The alternative to the above bureaucratic approach is to acknowledge teaching, research and development work as professional and ethical endeavours, with implications at individual and societal levels. Listening to teachers' voices makes it clear that teaching entails a plurality of evolving contents and methods. It is a lived experience. Each pedagogical style embodies diversity and reflects complementary and conflicting principles and practices.

> Teaching is situated in relationship to one's life story, present circumstances, deep commitments, affective investments, social contexts, and conflicting discourses. Teaching concerns being, acting, and living in a setting characterized by contradictory realities, negotiation, and dependency and struggle.[62]

Teachers' practices need to be understood because they are the ultimate service providers, for better or worse: "[Teachers'] voices are not only heard but also engaged, reconciled, and argued with. It is important to not only attend to the aesthetics of articulating teachers' voices, but also to the ethics of what these voices articulate."[63] This engagement is required in order to both innovate from within and at the same time not to fall into dogmatic and arrogant traditionalism and racism, idealizing oneself and one's tradition, and rejecting learning from the present and from the outside world. This alternative, however, requires setting up a process by which new learning from internal and external sources can become real, meaningful, and relevant. The acceptance or rejection of ideas should not be based on "ours versus theirs" polemics, rather on the quality of an idea, its validity, effectiveness, and ethical implications at personal, communal, and global levels.

●━━━━━━●

QUESTIONS FOR REFLECTION AND DISCUSSION

1. What are some of the complex understandings of teaching/ pedagogy presented that you noticed in this chapter? Compare this portrayal of teaching/learning values and practices to those in educational and cultural contexts familiar to you.
2. This chapter suggests that despite knowledge of active learning pedagogies most Tajik teachers usually do not use such interactive

teaching practices while teaching the mainstream curriculum. Why do you think this is? How is this similar to dissimilar to teaching/ learning contexts you have experienced? Why?

3. To what extent, in your experience, do North American teachers use active learning practices in their classes? Give some examples of effective interactive classroom lessons you have observed.

SUGGESTED FILM: *THE TEACHERS OF THE KARAKORUMS*, BY ARTHUR HOLBROOK AND THE AGA KHAN FOUNDATION

This video highlights an on-the-job teacher education program supported by the Aga Khan Foundation. Most of the teachers in the Karakorums, a rural and mountainous region of Pakistan, are poorly trained and rarely supervised. For one year, teacher trainers participate in workshops, observe the classroom practices of a master teacher, and gradually teach in the classroom with the support of a fellow teacher trainer and a master teacher. The field-based program helps build participants' confidence, encourages them to use child-centred teaching methods, and supports their preparation for the primary certificate teachers' exam.

SUGGESTIONS FOR FURTHER READING

*Bennett, Barrie. "The Complexity of Teaching." *Orbit* 29, no. 2 (1998): 1–4.

Chapman, David, John Weidman, Marc Cohen, and Malcolm Mercer. "The Search for Quality: A Five Country Study of National Strategies to Improve Educational Quality in Central Asia." *International Journal of Educational Development* 25, no.5 (2005): 514–30.

De Young, Alan, Madeline Reeves, and Galina Valyaeva. *Surviving the Transition? Case Studies of Schools and Schooling in the Kyrgyz Republic since Independence*. Greenwich, CT: Information Age Publishing, 2006.

De Young, Alan and Stephen Heyneman, eds. *The Challenge of Education in Central Asia*. Greenwich, CT: Information Age Publishing, 2004.

*Eklof, Ben and Scott Seregny. "Teachers in Russia: State, Community and Profession." In *Educational Reform in Post-Soviet Russia: Legacies* *and Prospect,* edited by Ben Eklof and others. London and New York: Frank Cass, 2005, 197–220.

*Johnson, Mark. "The Legacy of Russian and Soviet Education and the Shaping of Ethnic, Religious, and National Identities in Central Asia." In Young and Heyneman, *The Challenges of Education in Central Asia,* 21–36.

Khan, Sarfraz. *Muslim Reformist Political Thought: Revivalists, Modernists, and Free Will.* London and New York: Routledge Curzon, 2003.

Long, Delbert and Roberta Long. *Education of Teachers in Russia.* Westport, CT: Greenwood Press, 1999.

Medlin, William, William M. Cave, and Finley Carpenter. *Education and Development in Central Asia. A Case Study on Social Change in Uzbekistan,* Leiden, the Netherlands: E.J. Brill, 1971.

Roy, Olivier. *The New Central Asia. The Creation of Nations.* London: IB Tauris, 2000.

Rust, Val Dean and Per Dalin, eds. *Teachers and Teaching in the Developing World.* New York: Garland Publishing Inc, 1990.

Shorish, Mobin. "The Pedagogical, Linguistic, and Logistical Problems of Teaching Russian to the Local Central Asians." *Slavic Review* 35, no. 3 (1976): 443–62.

Sutherland, Jeanne. *Schooling in the New Russia: Innovation and Change, 1984–1995.* New York: St. Martin Press, 1999.

Chapter Seven

Comparative Perspectives on School Improvement

Stephen Anderson

INTRODUCTION

The impetus to improve schools is as old as the existence of public schools themselves. Teachers working in most public school systems can take it for granted that they will practice their profession under persistent public scrutiny and pressure, not only to do their job and do it well, but to constantly strive to do it better. For years, the conventional approach to improving schools emphasized the development and provision of good curriculum and learning materials; investment in the initial and continuing professional education of teachers and school administrators; and inspection to ensure compliance with externally prescribed education policies. Since the mid-1970s, the focus of responsibility and accountability for the quality of public education has shifted away from individual teachers to the collective actions and outcomes of educators at the school level. The shift has been marked by education policies, practices, and research that target school improvement as a focus for education quality development and accountability. This chapter reviews and comments on the history of school improvement trends internationally over the past quarter of a century.

SCHOOL IMPROVEMENT IN HISTORICAL PERSPECTIVE

Innovation Adoption and Implementation

Most scholars of educational change associate the origins of contemporary school improvement research and practice with the launching of the first space satellite by the former Soviet Union in the late 1950s. This event sparked political concerns about the quality of

American public education. However, this was not the only reason for interest in educational change. Demographically, the post–World War II generation represented the first cohort of North American youth for whom post-secondary education, not just high school completion, was deemed a normal expectation. Increasing government involvement in the provision of social programs to reduce poverty, to eliminate racial and social class discrimination, and to provide equal educational and economic opportunities for all (see Chapter Three by Karen Mundy in this volume) also contributed to a proliferation of educational change policies, programs, and projects in the 1960s and 1970s. Education change researchers characterize this as the innovation adoption and implementation era of change.[1] School personnel were expected to adopt and put into practice new instructional programs, materials, and methods, typically developed by external experts (government agencies, university professors, textbook publishers, etc.). In theory, the quality of education in schools would cumulatively improve as a result of implementing a new math program here, a new social studies program there, new teaching methods now, new instructional arrangements (such as open classrooms or team teaching) then, and so on.

Researchers who set out to document the effects of all this idiosyncratic and uncoordinated innovation activity soon burst the bubble of optimism for this approach to school improvement. They repeatedly discovered that change is an implementation dominant process.[2] The formal adoption of new programs and practices, whether mandated or voluntary, did not mean that school personnel would actually change what they were already doing. Some innovations were simply never implemented (not surprising when support for their use in the form of teacher training and assistance, material resources, funding, time, and supervision was often lacking or poorly planned and executed). More often, the new programs were put into practice, but in the process of implementation local educators made significant modifications to their original design that virtually assured little change in existing practices and student learning outcomes. Improvement tended to be equated with the mere fact of getting new programs and practices into place as per the developers' or policy-makers' design, rather than with the innovations' impact on reliable indicators of the quality of teaching and learning. Researchers found that even when innovations were actually implemented, there was no guarantee that use of those programs and practices would be institutionalized or sustained over time.

Notwithstanding recurrent tales of failure, researchers also reported some cases of successful implementation of new programs and practices in schools and classrooms. The lessons from these positive experiences are well reported,[3] but are not necessarily picked up and skillfully applied by education policy-makers and practitioners. Strategically, however, the idea that the quality of teaching and learning in schools would improve overall and continuously through the incremental and uncoordinated adoption and implementation of multiple innovations targeting specific subjects, students, teaching methods, or management practices was not supported by reliable evidence. While the adoption and implementation of discrete new programs and practices continues unabated, at least in schools within the developed countries of the world, the attention (and resources) of school improvement advocates and researchers has shifted to other more systemic change strategies (reviewed later in this chapter).

Comparative Research

A distinct history of educational innovation in the developing world began in the 1970s.[4] The origins of this activity are rooted in the transition from colonial to independent governments (especially in Africa and Asia); in the world-wide emphasis on universal access to public education (see Chapter Three); and in the rise of international and foreign aid agencies such as UNESCO, World Bank, Canadian International Development Agency, United States Agency for International Development. These organizations have played a key role in funding and promoting the development and improvement of education systems in those contexts.

While the challenges of achieving quality education in the developing and developed world countries differ in many respects, there are parallels in how school improvement has been approached in policy and practice. Educational improvement initiatives in the developing world in the 1970s and 1980s often exemplified the innovation adoption and implementation approach to change previously described.[5] Adriaan Verspoor, for example, conducted a multi-case analysis of the process and results of 21 high outcome education improvement projects selected from a sample of 282 World Bank funded projects between 1963 and 1984 in Africa, Latin America, South Asia, and Asia.[6] Many of the findings from that study echoed findings on innovation implementation elsewhere in the world. In-service teacher training, for example, was a key element in the successful implementation of change. The most effective teacher training designs provided local training (at school or school cluster level) to support implementation of change programs, with regular classroom visits, support, and assistance from supervisors and program staff. Initial and ongoing access to in-service training and support contributed to the development of teacher expertise and motivation to change.

Some of Verspoor's findings highlight differences in the experiences of innovation-focused change initiatives in the developing world that have broader implications for school improvement. For example, the most successful projects combined project-specific assistance with interventions designed to develop the capacity of education systems to plan, coordinate, monitor, and support innovation on a continuous basis.

> "Provision of pedagogical support, training, and instructional materials and equipment are critical to sustaining teacher morale and commitment. Where these inputs are lacking, commitment to the program rapidly disappears."[7]
> —Adriaan Verspoor

Policy-makers and researchers in the developed world tended with little justification to take the organizational capacity to manage change in public education systems for granted at the state, national, or even school district levels. Verspoor found that change projects that focused primarily on a single component of education provision (for example, curriculum, teacher training, school management, or material resources) had lower outcomes than projects that addressed multiple components in a coordinated and aligned approach over time. The relative power of comprehensive change was only recognized later in the history of school improvement in the developed world. Finally, Verspoor described four "pathways to change": progressive innovation (multiple linked innovations introduced over a period of time); incremental expansion (innovation introduced in a small number of settings with a gradual planned increase in the scope of use); discrete change (isolated projects implemented in limited settings, uncoordinated with other projects); and permanent pilot (experimental change program that never gains political support and resources for broader use). Critics of the innovation adoption and implementation approach to school improvement in the developed world point to the frequency of the discrete change approach, and the failure to plan for scaling up of successful small scale changes to the larger system.[8] Comparative research in the developing world during this era had more to offer to policy-makers and educators in the developed world than was realized at the time and vice versa (as discussed by Joseph P. Farrell in Chapter Five of this volume).

EFFECTIVE SCHOOLS AND SCHOOL EFFECTIVENESS

A significant shift in thinking and practice about how to improve the quality of public schools, known as the effective schools movement, developed through comparative education research in North America and England during the 1980s.[9] This originated as a response to an influential large-scale study of factors affecting equality of educational opportunity in the United States that concluded that family background factors (for example, socio-economic status) were the primary determinants of student outcomes, and that schools and inputs to schools (such as funding and materials) made little difference. Critics of this position knew of schools serving socio-economically disadvantaged students where academic performance on standardized tests of basic skills rivaled schools serving higher income families. Education researchers in the United States and in England compared successful and ineffective schools serving traditionally low-achieving pupils in order to determine what differentiated the successful from unsuccessful schools. From this research, a common list of the characteristics of effective schools was identified, including instructional leadership, clear and focused mission, safe and orderly environment, climate of high expectations for success, frequent monitoring of student progress, positive home-school relations, opportunity to learn and time on task. The point was not that schooling wholly determines students' academic success, but that what happens in schools does significantly influence learning outcomes. Failure cannot simply be attributed to student abilities and social background: in-school factors that make the difference are within our power to change.

Critics of this research cautioned against overgeneralization of findings that were based on comparisons of small numbers of exceptionally good and bad schools, mostly at the elementary level, mostly in low-income urban settings, narrowly focused on basic skills performance, and sorted by performance differences at a single point in time, rather than over a sustained period of time[10] (as discussed by Farrell in Chapter Five and by Sarfaroz Niyozov in Chapter Six). Critics also noted that the research did not reveal how the good schools got that way, nor did it provide much insight into teacher and administrator actions underlying the effective schools' correlates. Many of the criticisms were addressed in later research (by sampling typical, not just high and low performing schools; sampling for context differences, such as student social background; and tracking results over time).[11]

The original effective schools research contributed to the evolution of a strand of inquiry known as *school effectiveness research*. Initially, school effectiveness researchers distinguished themselves from school improvement researchers, arguing that while they were concerned with quality and outcomes, school improvement research was more concerned with the processes of planned change in schools and school systems. Eventually, these two strands of inquiry converged in a common search to understand not only the ingredients of effective schools, but how to develop and sustain school effectiveness at the school system level.[12]

Comparative Research
During the 1980s and 1990s, a separate tradition of research on school effectiveness developed among researchers studying education in developing countries.[13] Comparative research on school effectiveness across developed and developing countries reveals differences, but also some similarities.[14] Some of the differences are obvious. In comparatively wealthy countries, variations in school effectiveness are not associated with differences in the provision and quality of material inputs (such as textbooks, facilities, or well-educated teachers), because national and state governments have the capacity to assure that all schools have the basic human and material resources. In economically impoverished developing countries, however, variation in the provision and quality of essential resources for schools is often an enduring challenge for government budgets and education authorities, and

thus a key factor in discriminating more and less effective schools.[15] Marlaine E. Lockheed and Henry M. Levin report that in the 1980s annual government expenditures in developing countries averaged about $30 per pupil versus $1551 per pupil in developed countries.[16] The influence of school inputs on student achievement is greater in developing country schools (for example, statistical analysis of school effects in Third World countries attribute up to 25 percent of the variation in student performance to school inputs, while estimates of school effects in North American and European schools are in the neighborhood of 9 to 14 percent).[17]

Many developing world countries are still struggling to make free public schooling accessible to school age children at the primary school level. Due to endemic basic funding and resource problems, fundamental issues of the quality of education provision in schools persist. Unfortunately, this situation has been exacerbated by the international goal of achieving universal access to free primary education (FPE) by the year 2015 (see Chapter Three by Karen Mundy in this volume). In developing countries at the forefront of this movement, such as Malawi and Uganda, the effect of implementing FPE has been a dramatic increase in public school enrolment that far exceeds the current resource capacity of local governments.[19] In Malawi, for example, primary school enrolment rose from 1.9 million to 2.9 million pupils following the announcement of FPE by the government in 1994, resulting in class sizes ranging from 60 to 140 pupils per teacher (often inadequately trained) according to one study.[20] In Uganda, primary school enrolment increased after the government adopted its Universal Primary Education policy from less than 3 million in 1996 to 7.3 million in 2002, with similarly dramatic effects on class size and school resource capacities.[21] Notwithstanding reported improvements in access to school (especially for girls), major education quality issues at the primary school level in the developing world persist, including

> "We cannot stress this too highly: many factors that make for good schools are conceptually quite similar in countries that have widely different cultural, social, and economic contexts. At the classroom level, the powerful elements of expectation, management, clarity and instructional quality transcend culture."[18]
> —David Reynolds and others

high drop out rates, grade repetition, and failure on school leaving exams.

Comparative research also suggests that there are some features of school effectiveness that are not significantly dependent upon variations in context. Instructional process (such as time on task, opportunity to learn, high expectations, structured teaching, questioning techniques, and opportunities for review and practice), curriculum quality, and school leadership, for example, are consistently associated with variations in school effectiveness in most cross-country comparisons. To the extent that comparative research can help isolate common variables that contribute to the effectiveness of schooling, policy-makers and education leaders can proceed with greater confidence in plans for school improvement that take these findings into account. Comparative effective schools research also exposes and challenges some fundamental beliefs and assumptions about student learning and about the organizational conditions that best support it. David Reynolds and others observe, for example, that in Western countries there is a strong emphasis on shifting the responsibility for learning to the student, on the presumption that student capacity to learn on their own is an essential employability skill.[22] One consequence of this emphasis is to privilege students whose social and cultural capital (related to family background and support) enables this kind of behaviour. In Pacific Rim Asian school systems, however, greater emphasis is placed on the role of the teacher in directing student learning. (See Chapter Two by Ruth Hayhoe in this volume.) As a result, research shows less evidence of variation in student performance by family background. Schools in some Asian countries also provide more time and support for teachers to engage in collaborative professional work during the work day (such as joint lesson planning, mutual observation, sharing, and problem-solving) than is typical in most North American and European schools where teachers spend most of their day teaching, perhaps with a period of individual time for preparation and planning.[23] These kinds of findings highlight the potential for comparative research to question taken-for-granted assumptions about school effectiveness structures and processes.

The effective schools research has had a profound impact on ideas, policies, and practices oriented towards school improvement in public school systems. One such impact is the idea that school effectiveness is more a function of school-wide norms and processes that affect the quality of student learning than of human and material resource inputs, or of the aggregated efforts of well-intentioned teachers and principals acting independently of one another. Second is the idea that school effectiveness can be assessed, compared, and acted upon using measures and indicators of student results and progress aggregated to the school level (for example, standardized test scores and retention rates). Third is the belief that if some schools are capable of creating productive learning environments for all students, then it is reasonable to expect, if not demand, all schools to do the same.

Finally, findings from the effective schools research have contributed to the development of models and projects aimed at replicating the characteristics of effective schools. Typically, effective schools projects involve self-assessments by school personnel of their needs vis-à-vis the effective schools correlates, the development of school improvement plans that address perceived weaknesses, and temporary funding and assistance to implement the plans.[24]

Unfortunately, research on the impact of effective schools projects has failed to produce consistent evidence that needs assessments and action plans tailored to the effective schools characteristics make schools better. A common finding is that school personnel tend to focus their plans on factors with weak links to teaching and learning in the classroom and, echoing findings from the earlier era of innovation-focused school improvement, that the best laid plans often do not play out as imagined in the process of implementation, leaving the results unpredictable. Ultimately, the effective schools correlates provide useful hints for what to look for in effective schools, but little practical guidance in how to (re)create those conditions.

The practice of cyclical school improvement planning, however, has become institutionalized in school systems around the world. Virtually every provincial and state government in North America, for example, requires school personnel to submit school improvement plans to school system authorities on a regular basis (for example, in three year cycles with annual updates). Sponsoring agencies for school improvement initiatives in developing countries now routinely include school improvement planning in training programs for school management and in accountability reporting for project activities.

The effective schools and school effectiveness research crystallized the focus of efforts to improve educational quality on the school as the unit of change. Other approaches to school improvement, however, were developed during the 1990s in North America and Europe. The remainder of the chapter reviews four alternative approaches that have exerted a strong influence on efforts to improve the quality of education in schools around the world: 1) decentralization and school-based management; 2) comprehensive school reforms; 3) school choice; and 4) the imposition of educational standards and accountability systems.

DECENTRALIZATION AND SCHOOL-BASED MANAGEMENT

The effective schools practice of school improvement planning coincided with the development of a decentralization and school-based management (SBM) approach to school improvement. Proponents of this approach, often referred to as restructuring in the 1980s and 1990s, argued that the needs and circumstances of schools were too varied to mandate a single solution and plan for improvement, and that schools were constrained from introducing change by education bureaucracies and policies that required standardization in structure and practice.[25] The solution was to allow school personnel greater freedom to determine their needs for improvement, as well as greater control over the use of resources (such as money, staffing, and time) and organizational arrangements (such as roles, decision-making processes, grouping of students and teachers). Decentralization and SBM advocates argue that this approach honours the professional expertise of those working closest to the problems of teaching and learning to determine what and how to improve. In its commonest form, SBM initiatives in North America amounted to little more than requiring schools to establish school teams of administrators, teachers, and parents (often on a voluntary basis) to produce school improvement plans. Sometimes these requirements were accompanied by waivers that permitted the participating schools to opt out of certain (but not all) school district and government policy regulations and contractual arrangements with local teacher unions.

State/provincial policies mandating the establishment of school councils whose membership is dominated by parent and community representatives, not by teachers and principals, are another common school-based management approach to school improvement. In theory, this strategy shifts greater power and authority over school decision-making to school clients. In practice, many of these policies only assign an advisory role to the school councils, reserving important management decisions (such as hiring and dismissal of principals and teachers and allocating school budget) and educational decisions (such as school goals or program change) to professional educators at the school and school system levels. As noted below, policies and strategies that involve greater local control through parental participation have been implemented with greater effect and influence in many areas of the developing world. (See Chapter Five.)

Although there was a lot of talk about SBM as the new strategy for improving schools in the developed world in the 1990s, the practical reality was that the education bureaucracies and the overlay of external policies and laws regulating funding, equality of educational opportunities, and virtually all other aspects of public school operations were too entrenched to permit dramatic changes in public control and resource allocation. A decade of experimentation and research on school restructuring in North American schools yielded little evidence that school-based management strategies in and of themselves, where enacted, had made any significant difference in school effectiveness on a short- or long-term basis.[26] Some researchers (myself included) reported that rather than serving as an engine for improvement, SBM structures and processes sometimes had the contrary effect of providing school personnel with more power to preserve the status quo. There are, of course, some reported exceptions. In the United States, the Chicago school district is the most widely acclaimed example of successful decentralization. Notably, decentralization in Chicago involved a significant transfer of power over school decisions (such as principal hiring) to parent-dominated school councils (not simply increased control by principals and teachers). Moreover, it was system-wide (not a voluntary option for schools), and occurred in a context of mandatory accountability for school performance results (conditions absent or weakly present in many SBM strategies during the restructuring era). However, analysts of the Chicago experience note that evidence of school improvement on a wide-scale only began to materialize when the school district reasserted its role in providing guidance, pressure, and support for school quality and improvement.[27] The mere act of decentralization and school-based management did not lead to school improvement without a shift and reorganization of direction, authority, and support at the district level.

Comparative Research

The World Bank is an active advocate for decentralization of educational management in developing countries, and a critical observer and funder of research on the effects of decentralization policies and strategies on education quality.[28] While decentralization policies in developing countries may occur as part of a general devolution of social services to sub-national levels of government, such as municipal governments, our specific focus is on the establishment of school-based management systems. Typically, this takes the form of school councils or management committees with considerable decision-making authority over staffing (hiring and firing of principals and teachers), teacher supervision, school finances, school maintenance, and, to a lesser degree, curriculum and instruction. In centralized school systems these kinds of decisions and functions are performed by external education authorities at the school district, state/province, or national levels.

School-based management initiatives in the developing world tend to place more emphasis on parent and community influence on school decision-making than on expanding the scope of authority of school personnel. The arguments for increased local control centre on strengthening parent and community pressure on school personnel to carry out their duties in a professional manner; enhancing parental commitment to sending their children to school; and strengthening parental involvement in managing and perhaps supplementing school funding. Teacher and student absenteeism, and lack of accountability for use of school funds, for example, are commonly reported problems in public schools in the developing world. When the right to hire and fire teachers (and principals) shifts from education authorities to local school parents, research on decentralization effects shows improvements in teacher attendance. When parents take on increased responsibility for the management and upkeep of their children's school, they are more likely to make sure that the kids attend regularly. Use of funds for the purchase of needed school resources is more likely to happen when parents have ways to ensure that principals are accountable for spending. It stands to reason that student achievement is likely to improve if teachers are consistently teaching, if students regularly attend classes, and if school funds are efficiently spent on essential resources for teaching and learning.

Some words of caution are needed about the relationship of decentralized school management to school improvement. First, schools operating under local SBM systems can be run just as ineffectively as schools operating under more centralized policies and systems. It is not the act of decentralization that improves schools, but the quality of implementation at the local level, including the quality of supports such as management training for school committees. Second, most research compares the management characteristics (for example, level of parental participation) and performance (student attendance, teacher attendance, student academic results) of traditional externally managed public schools with that of public schools managed by local councils or committees. Researchers attempt to rule out possible explanations for variations in school inputs and outcomes that might be due to differences in community and family characteristics (such as income and education levels). The best research indicates that decentralized management of schools (both primary and secondary), when effectively implemented, does not harm the academic achievement of students, and may be correlated with slightly better results than for comparable students in traditional schools on standardized tests of basic skills (such as reading and mathematics).[29] There is little research on the impact that decentralization through school-based management has on school quality and improvement over time. Local parent/community management may help raise the baseline level of school performance, but does not guarantee ongoing improvement unless combined with measures that more directly affect the quality of teaching.

> "As more decisions are placed in the hands of individual schools and teacher, this autonomy must be balanced with accountability; schools and teachers must show that they can produce results."[30]
> —Marlaine E. Lockheed and Henry M. Levin

COMPREHENSIVE SCHOOL REFORM

The comprehensive school reform movement (CSR) emerged in the United States in the 1980s and 1990s.[31] The basic idea is that change must be "whole school," involving all participants, and the improvement process must encompass a comprehensive array of related factors, including program (curriculum, materials, structure), teaching methods, school management and leadership, teacher development, funding, parent involvement, and performance monitoring and evaluation. A comprehensive school reform model provides a blueprint, process, and support for school development across multiple components of school operations, teaching, and learning. In the United States, the CSR movement evolved out of a number of university-based whole-school improvement initiatives in the 1980s, including the Coalition of Essential Schools (Brown University), Success for All (Johns Hopkins University), Accelerated Schools (originally associated with Stanford University), and the Comer School Development Program (Yale University). Unlike the effective schools approach, the CSR models did not just point to potential focuses for change (such as lists of characteristics of reportedly effective schools), but provided plans, materials, procedures, and assistance for action. In the CSR approach to school improvement, individual schools voluntarily choose a CSR model. The school pays a fee for the right to implement the model (often made possible by government grants), and in return, school personnel receive implementation training, on-site assistance, and program materials from the model developers. CSR schools join networks of schools using the same model, and the model developers facilitate information sharing and mutual assistance across the network. As a result, within a school district one might find a variety of CSR schools linked to different CSR networks.

By the turn of the century, dozens of CSR models were being actively disseminated in the United States, and thousands of schools were taking part. Several major evaluation research studies compared the implementation and effectiveness (in terms of student performance) of different CSR models. Others compared CSR school performance with that of non-CSR schools. While the evidence shows variable impact of different CSR models, overall, the CSR approach to school improvement fares better than the innovation adoption, effective schools, or site-based management approaches to school improvement in terms of demonstrating measurable benefits for student learning and for growth in teachers' professional skills. As a strategy for system-wide improvement, however, the CSR approach is problematic. Since the decision to adopt a CSR model is made at the school level, the role of the school district or government education agencies is ambiguous. Expertise to support implementation rests with the model developers, and the proliferation of different CSR models in the same school system inhibits school participation in common system-wide initiatives. School districts often encourage lower performing schools to adopt CSR models with the expectation that this will lead to reductions in achievement gaps between schools in their jurisdictions. There is little evidence that CSR adoption and implementation in targeted schools, however, yields system-wide improvements in educational quality and equity.

Comparative Research

Although the CSR school improvement models have received a lot of positive attention in the United States, these school designs have not spread far beyond the US borders to other countries in North America and Europe. Interestingly, however, similar programs of comprehensive school reform with similar tales of success have evolved independently in various regions of the developing world. Several of these are described by Farrell in Chapter Five of this textbook. The two best known are Escuela Nueva, which began in Colombia in the 1970s and has since been replicated in Central America,[32] and BRAC (Bangladesh Rural Advancement Committee) in Bangladesh (see also Farrell's Chapter Five). The BRAC system has grown to more than 30,000 schools. The network is now supported by its own post-secondary education institute, and is being implemented in other countries, such as Afghanistan. Other comprehensive school reform models have emerged elsewhere in the developing world. Anderson describes the evolution of a whole school development approach to school improvement through a series of initiatives sponsored by the Aga Khan Foundation in Kenya, Tanzania, and Uganda.[33] As the Aga Khan school improvement program matured, it encompassed an increasing array of organizational factors that affect the quality of teaching and learning, including: teacher learning, school and school district management, teaching and learning resources, parental and community involvement, funding for school and teacher development, change agent development, assessment and evaluation, and teacher working conditions. In Northern Pakistan, faculty from the Professional

Development Centre, North, of the Aga Khan University Institute for Educational Development, created a Whole School Improvement Program (WSIP) that operates in a growing network of government and NGO-sponsored independent schools in predominately rural and remote mountain communities.[34] Like a CSR model, the WSIP approach encompasses teacher training in new instructional methods, school management and leadership training, support for strengthening community participation in schools, school facilities and resources, and a holistic focus on student development.

As an approach to school improvement, the CSR strategy seems to work and to be replicable on a wide scale. However, comprehensive reform programs tend to depend on external support networks, rather than on support from the school systems in which participating schools are located. Coordination between school systems and the CSR networks can be politically, financially, and logistically problematic in both developed and developing contexts.

SCHOOL CHOICE

School choice is a cover term that encompasses an array of strategies and policies based on the premise that competition for clients (students, families) among schools will compel school personnel to find ways to get better at what they do.[35] The literature on school choice identifies two policy strategies. Public choice refers to the provision of greater choice among different schools within the public sector through such mechanisms as open enrolment among schools within or between school districts; access to alternative schools or programs serving students with special needs or interests (such as arts, technology, or French immersion); and parallel publicly funded school systems based on religious preferences or language of instruction (such as secular public and Catholic separate school districts in Ontario, Canada; French and English medium districts in Quebec, Canada). Market choice refers to the use of funding mechanisms such as educational vouchers, scholarships, and tuition tax credits to create competition between private and public schools for students and government funding. Of these, voucher programs are the most widely known, implemented, and debated. The basic idea is that a government provides parents of school age children with a voucher worth a certain number of dollars per child, that the parents choose where to send their children from an open market of public and private schools, and that government funding follows the child to the chosen school. In theory, a voucher system would lead schools to compete for students and dollars in order to survive and thrive in the education marketplace. School personnel would be motivated to innovate and improve. School choice policies are silent, however, on what mechanism and knowledge schools might use to respond to the pressures to improve.

Although voucher programs have been widely debated in the United States, they have not been widely implemented. During the 1990s, a few school districts (such as Milwaukee, Cleveland, and San Antonio) implemented small-scale voucher programs that targeted poor inner city children in schools where students scored persistently below minimum state and district standards of acceptable performance on standardized tests in basic skills. Overall, public school authorities have not welcomed the idea that parents should be provided financial incentives to turn to private schools when public schools fail. Nonetheless, the idea that parents should have a right to choose among schools (including private schools), especially when the schools their children are attending are of low quality, and that at least a portion of public funds for education should be allocated on the basis of parental choice, continues to generate a lot of political interest and debate as a strategy that might lead to incremental improvement in the quality of schools.

Comparative Research

School choice policies and options have been implemented on a wider scale in some countries outside of North America.[36] In Chile, for example, the government funds a national voucher program whereby a set amount of money is allocated per pupil, and students can elect to attend either public schools or private schools (except those that charge tuition). In New Zealand, the government eliminated school districts, making all schools self-governing entities responsible directly to the central government, and established open enrolment boundaries to create full choice (and competition) among public schools for students and funds. In these two examples, the move towards greater choice was linked to political beliefs that a market-like approach to education provision would lead to higher quality teaching and learning outcomes.

In other contexts, a lack of financial resources has led governments to encourage the expansion of private schools. Thus, in Tanzania, about 60 percent of secondary schools are private schools run by non-governmental organizations or by for-profit entrepreneurs.[37] In Pakistan and Bangladesh literally thousands of schools are independently financed and operated by community and other non-governmental organizations with minimal governmental regulation.

Findings from research on the implementation and outcomes of strategies for school choice (such as vouchers and open boundaries) in the United States and internationally do not generally support the claim that increased choice leads to greater competition and more effective schools.[38] There are no reported cases of schools becoming better as a result of losing students or the threat of losing students to other schools. In fact, the effects of greater choice have been found to exacerbate the problems of low-performing schools. More academically high-achieving students (whose parents tend to be more educated, to have higher aspirations for their children, and to be equipped with social/ cultural capital) are most likely to exercise choice options, leaving the source schools with an even greater proportion of hard-to-serve students, with fewer funds to do it, and with reputations guaranteed to deter recruitment of quality teachers. Likewise, there is little evidence that flight from one school to another leads to any improvement in the quality of education provided by the receiving schools (though competition for admissions may lead higher performing schools to restrict admissions to the best students, thereby creating an illusion of school improvement). Inter-school competition for students (and resources) may lead to reduced co-operation across schools, thereby diminishing the potential for school personnel to learn from each other about effective practices, and lowering the commitment of school personnel and parents to the right to quality education as a common public good. Finally, choice research in multiple countries has demonstrated that given an option, parents do not choose schools solely on the basis of academic quality. They are equally if not more concerned about how their child will fit (racially, socio-economically, religiously) with other children, or about the implications of having their children associate with students that represent the majority in a particular school. The capacity to exercise choice beyond the neighbourhood school is also highly dependent on family resources (such as access to transportation and child care arrangements).

Comparisons of student performance in public and private schools yield inconsistent results. In the United States, research comparing student performance in public and Catholic schools has repeatedly reported higher academic results for Catholic school students.[39] Explanations for the reported differences, however, typically emphasize perceived differences in school climate and culture (the strong emphasis on caring and community in many Catholic schools), and greater school control over student and teacher selection, not the fact of school choice and competition. Comparative research on student performance in public, Catholic, and non-denominational private schools in Chile shows Catholic schools outperforming public schools, but public schools outperforming non-religious private schools. The researchers attribute the more positive results in private Catholic schools to higher levels of resources, not to the market dynamics of choice.[40] As reviewed by Farrell in Chapter Five, students in the non-governmental BRAC school system in Bangladesh achieve better academic results than students in the government school system. But the explanation for these differences does not centre on parental choice and competition with public schools. Instead, it is the quality of teacher development, curriculum, instructional practices, school management, and parent involvement that seems to raise quality. In sum, available research does not support political arguments that increased school choice leads to school improvement, though there are other valid reasons for advocating for increased choice in educational programs and schools. Across North America, arguments about increased choice are framed more in terms of parental rights to choose the kind of education they want for their child and to have their tax dollars support that choice, rather than on choice as a quality improvement mechanism.

STANDARDS AND ACCOUNTABILITY-DRIVEN IMPROVEMENT

The imposition by government agencies of standards for curriculum and for student performance, coupled with mandatory testing and public reporting of student results, are key to the standards and accountability approach to school improvement. Government policies mandating this approach emerged concurrently in the United States, England, Canada, and other regions of the developed world in the 1990s.

The logic of this approach to school improvement is straightforward.[41] Government education agencies prescribe core curriculum content standards, specified in terms of outcomes that all students should achieve by subject area and grade level. Aligned to the curriculum, the government prescribes student achievement standards (often the standards differentiate minimum levels of acceptability from unacceptable and advanced levels of performance). All students are expected to achieve at least the minimum levels of acceptable performance. The government then mandates standardized testing of student achievement in core subjects (reading, writing, and mathematics are the most common) at designated intervals (for example, Grades Three, Six, Nine; annually in some parts of the United States).

Accountability is not just about student testing, but also about the reporting and use of test results. Ideally, school personnel examine assessment results to identify which students (individuals and groups) are having difficulty achieving acceptable performance levels in the tested curriculum areas, and use this information to plan and implement interventions intended to assist those students in raising their performance in those areas. Standards and accountability-driven school improvement does not begin with a particular solution (that is, curriculum program, instructional arrangements or teaching practices) for identified student learning needs relative to the targeted outcomes. The basic premise is that school personnel have the professional expertise to discern what works for the particular students being taught, and to find or to create alternative strategies to replace or supplement practices that are not working. Thus standardized testing tends to lead to a preoccupation with discovering so-called best practices, that is, instructional strategies that are correlated with evidence of student success in achieving expected performance standards under similar conditions (for example, students with similar educational profiles; schools with similar characteristics of size and resources; schools serving similar communities in terms of student and family socio-economic indicators). Government agencies and school district authorities often try to facilitate networking between classrooms, schools, and across school districts in order to enable sharing and diffusion of experiences about what practices work best with which students for particular curriculum and performance expectations.[42]

Government agencies do not typically rely on the professionalism of school system personnel to do all this without additional pressure and, perhaps, support. The pressure can come in several ways. One way is to require schools and school districts to submit school improvement plans that are justified partly in terms of their test results. A second way is to make the test results publicly available in what are often described as league tables. While individual student results are only accessible to teachers, the student, and his/her parents, school results and school district results (that is, aggregated scores by test area of all students tested) are made publicly available through government, school district, and school reports and websites, and often through local newspapers. In some jurisdictions, schools are ranked according to their performance, and even officially labelled (such as in Texas, where the author has done research, schools are labelled each year as Exemplary, Recognized, Academically Acceptable, or Academically Unacceptable in terms of state test results). In theory, school personnel, concerned about the status of their school's academic standing and responding to parental concerns, will be motivated to try to improve where needs for improvement are indicated, and to try to sustain already high performance where that is in evidence. The pressure on school personnel to ensure adequate student performance increases when test results are high stakes for students, as well. In some jurisdictions student promotion (from one grade to another) or student graduation (from high school) is dependent upon the results of their performance on these tests (for example, all students in the province of Ontario, Canada, must pass a Grade 10 Literacy Test to get their high school diploma, in addition to obtaining the required number of course credits). Finally, additional pressure on schools to perform and improve can be applied through the proclamation of government targets for student performance. This occurred with the National Literacy and Numeracy Strategies in England in the 1990s. In 2004, the Liberal government of Ontario, Canada, set a provincial target for 75 percent of all students to achieve acceptable performance on elementary school test results by 2007. In the United States, federal government policy under the Bush Republican administration set the highest target of all: No Child Left Behind, with the official goal being for all students to be at or above performance standards established by each state. By setting these targets (whether practically attainable or not) government agencies increase the pressure on underperforming schools to improve, and on high performing schools to sustain if not improve upon their already satisfactory results over the long term.

> "If standards-based reforms are working according to plan, the primary policy mechanisms are through policy alignment around standards—typing all the major instructional guidance mechanisms to challenging standards—and the creation of performance expectations through accountability systems. If the reforms are working according to plan, there must also be instructional improvement in the direction of the standards."[43]
> —Susan Furhman

Beyond the reputational and emotional effects of ranking and labelling, government agencies may mandate school consequences based on test results. The harshest scenarios require the dismissal or replacement of principals, or even the closing and reconstitution of persistently failing schools with a new crew of teachers and principals. Normally, drastic measures are only taken after a period of intensive assistance by local district or government school improvement teams to try to turn the failing school results around. A central feature of the standards and accountability movement is that schools as organizational units are held accountable for the quality of student learning, that consequences are tied this accountability, and that schools where student results are below par are expected to improve. It is in that sense that the standards and accountability movement represents an approach to school improvement.

The expected process of improvement from standards based reforms resembles Verspoor's previously mentioned concept of progressive innovation, driven by and towards clear and measurable outcomes.[44] With performance targets and continuous assessment data on student results in mind and hand, school personnel should incrementally change or add to existing practices until all students are achieving at least the minimum standards. Given the emphasis on diffusion of best practices in a context of common goals for curriculum and learning, the process, while seemingly school-specific, should not lead to increasing variation in practices among schools, but rather to concurrence and convergence in the use of those practices that are found to work under similar circumstances.

The standards and accountability approach to school improvement is controversial, and space will not permit me to do more than highlight some key points of contention. Does this approach force teachers to teach to the test (the answer is yes), and is this an undesirable effect? The answer to the latter part of that question is debatable. If you agree with the mandated curriculum guidelines, and the tests are well aligned with this curriculum, then teaching to the test is really just teaching the curriculum and not necessarily a bad effect. If you do not like the curriculum, think that preoccupation with the tested curriculum diverts teaching and learning time and energy away from other important focuses of student development such as the arts, social skills, civic and values education, maybe more complex or higher order cognitive skill development), or that prescribed standards for curriculum, learning, and assessment are an affront to teachers' professional autonomy, then you are less likely to regard teaching to the test in a positive light. Is it fair to expect all students to be able to attain the same levels of performance in a limited range of subject areas? Some will argue that this denies the pragmatic reality of students' differing abilities, interests, and strengths as learners, as assumed in North America (See Chapter Two for an Asian perspective of students). Others will argue that setting minimum standards for all students in core curriculum areas (such as reading, writing, and mathematics), and holding school personnel responsible and accountable for student performance provides not only a guarantee of quality, but also a guarantee of equity. After a generation of equal education opportunity policies in the United States (but little accountability for student results), the achievement gaps between students from middle- and higher-income families (mostly White) and students from socio-economically disadvantaged communities (poor, often Black or Hispanic) had not noticeably improved. Ultimately, the standards movement could be interpreted as an expression of confidence, not a lack of confidence, in the professionalism of school system personnel to find solutions to student learning problems. On the downside, advocates of high standards and accountability seem to have forgotten that even the best statistical analyses of school effects on student achievement from comparative studies in the developed countries only attribute 9 to 14 percent of student academic results to school effects. (See also Chapter Eight by Karen Mundy and Joseph P. Farrell.) To hold schools solely accountable for those results and improving the results seems a bit unfair. Still, a number of studies report an intentional change on the part of school system authorities (such as school district administrators and principals) and classroom teachers from attributing failure to student deficits (intelligence, motivation, family background and support), and from accepting the failure of some students as normal, to taking on a firm commitment and belief in the capacity of school system personnel to find ways to help all students succeed in accordance with publicly set standards.[45] Is there any evidence, however, that schools improve under standards and accountability systems?

Comparative Research

Research on the implementation effects of the imposition of mandatory standards and accountability policies and systems on school improvement tends to be more context specific that is, within a particular state or country) than comparative (across states or countries). Furthermore, student outcome data are often aggregated to the district, state/provincial, or national level, rather than to the school level, for purposes of analysis. This leads to conclusions about the impact of standards and accountability systems on student learning outcomes across the targeted system, but not to analyses of school-level effects per se. Yet it seems reasonable to infer that school-level improvement in student learning must be happening when there is consistent evidence of gains in test results across the system. The short answer to the question of whether standards and accountability systems have led to improvements in student achievement (as reflected in standardized test results) is yes, but yes with limitations.

Michael Fullan is a prominent analyst of educational change movements, and has served as government advisor and critic for standards and accountability-driven reforms in England and the province of Ontario, Canada. In both England and in Ontario, he cites analyses of student test scores over time that show overall gains in student performance in basic skills areas (reading, writing, mathematics), and reductions in the gaps between lower and higher performing students (which suggests a reduction of the traditional inequities in student outcomes for socio-economically disadvantaged students, who tend to be overrepresented in the ranks of low achievers). On the other hand, Fullan observes that after a few years the improvements in student achievement results tend to plateau.[46] They do not get worse, but they stop getting better. Skeptics might argue that commonly reported improvements in the first few years are little more than a reflection of school personnel aligning and adjusting what they do in the classroom to new curriculum and testing regimes (not really getting better at what they do). Fullan contends that continuing improvement beyond this plateau will require new kinds of interventions.

National curricula and high stakes standardized testing are common practices in many regions of the developing world. National curricula and standardized testing programs in the developing world, however, are frequently maligned as impediments to, not stimuli for, change and improvement. The curricula are criticized for overemphasizing the content to be covered, as opposed to the knowledge and skills outcomes to be achieved. The tests are criticized for rewarding lower level learning (rote memorization and factual recall, use of standard procedures such as mathematical formulas), as opposed to more complex and demanding learning objectives that require open-ended problem solving, application, and synthesis of knowledge in real-world (not just textbook) contexts. National testing programs in the developing world are often more high stakes for students than for schools. That is, the tests and test results are used mainly as gate-keeping devices to control access to further education (primary to secondary school, lower to higher secondary school, university entrance) and to stream students into education tracks (sciences, general education, vocational education). Schools may use student test results as marketing tools (for example, by advertising the number of pupils scoring high on the tests), particularly in school systems where school boundaries are open and where private school options are common. The public school systems, however, are not typically organized around the use of test results at the school level as a basis for and indicator of school quality and improvement. Results-based school improvement plans are not required. School system authorities at the national or local levels do not invest in developing the capacity of school personnel to use assessment data as a basis for school improvement planning, and do not provide funding, technical assistance, or other forms of intervention (such as dissemination networks) strategically linked to data-based accountability and improvement. Comparative research on the implications and effects of government-mandated external standards and accountability policies and systems on school-level improvement is lacking. International comparative assessments of educational quality, however, constitute another stream of the educational standards and accountability movement, and are the focus of Chapter Eight by Mundy and Farrell in this volume.

SCHOOL IMPROVEMENT: THE WAY FORWARD

This chapter provides an introduction to six major approaches to school improvement: 1) innovation adoption and implementation; 2) replication of the effective schools correlates; 3) decentralization and school-based management; 4) school choice; 5) comprehensive school reform; and 6) standards and accountability-driven improvement. While different approaches have dominated education policy, practice, and research at different times and places over the past half-century, they are not mutually exclusive. The adoption and innovation of best practices, for example, is integral to the standards and accountability-driven approach to improvement.

Decentralization and school choice policies often converge together in system-wide approaches to school improvement. The adoption of a comprehensive school reform model is an example of school choice, and school-based management and instructional

> "Successful change projects always include elements of both pressure and support. Pressure without support leads to resistance and alienation; support without pressure leads to drift or waste of resources"[47]
>
> —Michael Fullan

innovations are integral to many CSR models. Nor is the list of approaches to school improvement provided here exhaustive. There are other approaches that we have not addressed, such as school-university partnerships to create professional development schools on the model of teaching hospitals, and current interest in the development of schools as professional learning communities[48] that manifest the professional disposition and collective capacity to engage in continuous school improvement.

Ultimately, it is not so hard to find schools where a majority of students are succeeding academically, and it is possible to find schools where student results have progressively improved over time. The challenge is to take local knowledge of what makes schools effective and of how to make schools more effective and then replicate those characteristics and processes across many schools, that is, to move beyond islands of excellence to develop excellence in all schools in a school system.[49] Therein lies the fundamental challenge of school improvement. Comparative education research has and will continue to play a vital role in helping determine the conditions and characteristics associated with school success and school improvement. Comparative research is helpful in sorting out that which is common to school effectiveness and school improvement, regardless of differences in context, from that which is relatively unique to specific organizational, political, and cultural contexts. And finally, comparative research is an essential tool in the search for and sharing of education policies and practices that work best for meeting particular educational needs.

QUESTIONS FOR REFLECTION AND DISCUSSION

1. What do teachers and administrators in schools that you are familiar with say about current needs for improvement?
2. How do the various school improvement processes discussed in this chapter compare with those that you have witnessed as a student, citizen, or educator? How do you explain the similarities and differences among contexts?
3. How do school improvement needs and processes reported by teachers in today's schools relate to the major approaches to school improvement described in this chapter?

SUGGESTED FILM: *MANAGING CHANGE,* BY DRS. MICHAEL FULLAN AND JOHN R. CHAMPLIN

Managing Change examines change as a crucial aspect of any effort for school improvement. Highlighting key initiation factors for change, it discusses the complexities of the change process and potential role in promoting school improvement. In this two-part film series, you will explore some of the principles of change management and the dynamics of change as it affects schools.

SUGGESTIONS FOR FURTHER READING

Anderson, Stephen, ed. *Improving Schools through Teacher Development: Case Studies of the Aga Khan Foundation Projects in East Africa*. Lisse, The Netherlands: Swets and Zeitlinger Publishers, 2002.

*Fullan, Michael. *The New Meaning of Educational Change, 3rd Edition*. New York: Teachers College Press, 2001.

Fuhrman, Susan, ed. *From the Capitol to the Classroom: Standards-based Reform in the States*. One Hundredth Yearbook of the National Society for the Study of Education. Chicago: University of Chicago Press, 2001.

*Hall, Gene and Shirley Hord. *Implementing Change: Patterns, Principles, and Potholes, 2nd Edition*. Boston: Pearson Education, Inc., 2006.

Lewin, Keith with Janet Stuart. *Educational Innovation in Developing Countries: Case Studies of Changemakers*. London: MacMillan Press Ltd., 1991.

*Levin, Henry and Marlaine Lockheed, eds. *Effective Schools in Developing Countries*. London: Falmer Press, 1993.

Murphy, Joseph and Amanda Datnow. *Leadership Lessons for Comprehensive School Reform*. Thousand Oaks, CA: Corwin Press, 2003.

Murphy, Joseph and Philip Hallinger. *Restructuring Schooling: Learning from Ongoing Efforts*. Newbury Park, CA: Corwin Press, 1993.

Plank, David and Gary Sykes. *Choosing Choice: School Choice in International Perspective*. New York: Teachers College Press, 2003.

Rust, Val and Per Dalin. *Teachers and Teaching in the Developing World*. New York: Garland, 1990.

Stoll, Louise and Dean Fink. *Changing Our Schools*. Buckingham, UK: Open University Press, 1996.

*Teddlie, Charles and David Reynolds, eds. *The International Handbook of School Effectiveness Research*. New York: Falmer Press, 2000.

Verspoor, Adriaan. *Pathways to Change: Improving the Quality of Education in Developing Countries*. World Bank Discussion Papers 53. Washington, DC: The World Bank, 1989.

Chapter Eight

International Educational Indicators and Assessments: Issues for Teachers

Karen Mundy and Joseph P. Farrell

INTRODUCTION

Statistics about educational achievement and other social issues increasingly influence and drive debates over public policy. Both political actors and media commentators make claims based on such statistics: we have all read headlines about the growth of income disparities and other forms of economic inequality, the growth of secondary dropout rates, or the poor literacy skills of youth. Educational statistics are also regularly used in comparing nations (and in federal nations such as Canada and the United States, to compare provinces/states). You may have noticed media reports on how a country ranks internationally, describing, for example, Canadian or American student achievement in math, science, or literacy in relation to students in other countries around the world. The increasing use of such statistics is separate from, but not unrelated to, the movement to gather more educational data at the district and the school level to assess educational performance.

Why are statistics commonly cited in debates about education? At least part of the reason stems from their ability to lend an appearance of accuracy and science to otherwise complex and contested policy issues. Statistics can provide an easy-to-understand summary of quite complicated issues. They are very useful: statistics can allow us to see general trends and patterns, and raise important questions about how our educational system is functioning. They can tell us how children are doing in different areas of learning, and alert us to groups who may be disadvantaged. But it is also possible to "lie" with statistics.[1] The accuracy of statistical data can be highly influenced by factors such as resources for and methods of collection, and biases in survey design and data interpretation. More importantly, the way such data is reported and used can lead to misguided judgments about educational performance, and poorly developed proposals for reforms in educational policy and practice. Thus, how to use the rising amount of statistical data we have about education is often the subject of serious professional debate.

As citizens, students, and professional educators, there is a pressing need for us to better understand these numbers. This chapter aims to demystify some widely used international educational data, which can and do have an important influence on the careers and day-to-day practices of educators. We begin with a history of various efforts to develop statistical indicators for educational systems. We look first at international indicators that provide cross-national (or cross-provincial/state) comparisons of various core aspects of an educational system. Then we turn to international assessments, or cross-national achievement tests. These are sometimes classified as part of the set of international indicators, but the issues involved in their creation and use are sufficiently different from other indicators that they need separate treatment. We also look at how indicators and cross-national achievement tests can be combined to provide a glance or snapshot of different aspects of a nation's educational system, highlighting in particular what a comparative snapshot can tell us about Canada. Throughout this chapter, we emphasize the importance of looking critically at cross-national data on education.

INTERNATIONAL INDICATORS

International indicators, or international statistical comparisons, have been with us for quite a long time. The first formal intergovernmental efforts to assemble systematic international comparisons of educational systems was undertaken by the International Bureau of Education (IBE) in the early 1930s. Beginning in 1933, the IBE collected basic data about the structure of its members' educational systems, as well as information about specific policies or issues, which was published in an annual *Education Yearbook*.[2] After World War II and the formation of the United Nations, UNESCO (the United Nations Educational, Scientific, and Cultural Organization) assumed responsibility for such cross-national data collection and reporting. UNESCO's first questionnaire-based survey of education received responses from 57 member states in 1950. This seems a small number now, but at the time covered almost all of the independent nation-states in the world. The UNESCO survey collected data on school enrolments by level, public expenditure in education, literacy, and a variety of other features of the educational system. The resulting information was published in a *Statistical Yearbook* (which continues to be published under the title *Global Education Digest*).[3]

To comparative educators in the 1960s, it quickly became apparent that the indicators being reported by UNESCO were, for purposes of comparison, often quite misleading. Beyond questions of accuracy, it was not clear what was actually being counted in any given nation compared to the same statistical indicator in some other nation, since the educational systems of various nations were actually quite different. For example, how would one compare data on various aspects of primary schooling, when some systems end primary schooling after five years and other systems go up through Grade Eight? This concern eventually led to the development in the early 1970s of the International Standard Classification of Education (ISCED), illustrated in Table 8.1, which provided standards for all nations as to what should be counted under what indicator. This classification was updated in 1997 (ISCED97) to incorporate new modes of education (such as the multiplication of forms of vocational education and training), the increasing diversity of education providers, and the use of distance education through the development of new technologies.

UNESCO was intended to be the main gatherer of international educational statistics, and in many respects still is so. However, as budgetary crises and leadership problems developed within the United Nations in the 1980s, the agency's ability to develop and improve such indices declined.[4] Other international agencies began developing their own indicators, often using UNESCO indicators, but adding other sources. For example, UNICEF (United Nations Children's Fund) began publishing an annual report titled *The State of the World's Children*, which includes a wide variety of indicators regarding children, including educational data. The World Bank also publishes an annual *World Development Report*, which includes tables listing a wide variety of economic, social, and educational data from most nations in the world.[5] UNESCO began to regain some of its prominence in this area with the

Table 8.1
Original International Standard Classification of Education (ISCED)[6]

Level	Age Range	Stage	Examples
4	22–25	6	• Postgraduate study
3	21–22	5	• Professional schools • Higher stage of university study • Teacher training
	18–19	4	• Advanced technical schools • Lower stage of university study • Teacher training
2	14–15	3	• Full- and part-time vocational schools • Upper section of high schools • Grammar schools • Gymnasiums • Teacher training
	10–11	2	• Upper section of elementary schools • Lower section of high schools • Grammar schools • Gymnasiums
1	5–7	1	• First six years of primary school
Compulsory School Begins		0	• Nursery and kindergarten

Note: *The stages are illustrated by typical examples; ages stated are also illustrative.*

establishment in 1999 of the UNESCO Institute for Statistics (UIS), located at the University of Montreal, whose task is to gather quality statistical information from and for member states, and to report on the global situation of education.

Most education-related indicators are essentially head counts. These include total enrolment by level of schooling or in some cases grade level, retention or dropout rates by level, enrolment ratios by level (the number of students enrolled compared to the number in the population who are age-eligible for that level), number of teachers and teacher/student ratios, government expenditures on education, teacher/faculty average salaries, and adult literacy rates, and so forth. They are primarily derived from the administrative information ministries or departments of education routinely have to collect and assemble for their own administrative and management activities and obligations, or from censuses that usually occur once every decade.

Several examples of the use of such statistical indicators for comparative purposes can be found in this book. In Chapter Five, for example, they are used to describe the general status and condition of the three nations, Colombia, Egypt, and Bangladesh, and to compare them to Canada. There we find Gross National Income (GNI) per capita, which is a rough measure of the amount of wealth available per person in the nation; a measure of income distribution, which roughly measures the percentage of that wealth available to the poorest 40 percent of that population; and the adult literacy rate. In the accompanying text there is an indication of how those wealth and distribution indicators translate into the actual US dollar value of the annual income available to the poorest 40 percent of the population, per capita. These are approximate figures, with no claim to precise accuracy, but they do provide a general snapshot that can help the readers locate these nations quickly in their own mental maps. Similarly, statistics are used in Chapter Three to compare basic education enrolment rates in Tanzania and Kenya and in Chapter Nine to demonstrate gender disparities in education.

Until quite recently, international indicators have rarely incorporated detailed layers of research (such as on students' family backgrounds, socio-economic status, racial/ethnic identity, family private expenditures on schooling, or the quality of teaching and learning), which would provide context for the indicators surveyed. They have also been limited by the data that governments report. Because governments self-report, some of the international statistical series are of questionable or suspicious reliability and accuracy. One part of the problem is that the quality of the information provided to international agencies depends on the resources available to governments to collect such information. Richer nations have the resources available to collect and analyze reasonably accurate information on all sorts of government concerns — but collecting such information is expensive. Thus statistics from poorer nations are often simply the best guess of government officials. It is not uncommon, for example, to find that Ministry of Education officials in poorer nations have only the vaguest idea of how many students and teachers are in their formal education system. Elaborate procedures and requirements for data collection are in place on paper but the resources to accurately gather this data are not available. Moreover, governments often deliberately misreport, for domestic and/or international political reasons, such as to exaggerate their own accomplishments or minimize the accomplishments of a previous regime.

Beyond these problems, it is difficult to know what some often-cited international indicators actually refer to, and how they are measured. Adult literacy rates are a good example of this. At one level it seems clear what literacy refers to: the ability to read text, and in some cases to write as well. Literacy statistics, however, are much more complicated than that. Scholars of literacy often distinguish among levels or types of literacy, ranging from basic or functional literacy (usually thought of as the ability to read with understanding fairly simple texts, such as local newspapers or instructions for medicines or farming/gardening chemicals), to much more complex forms, such as the ability to read complicated texts such as the plays of Shakespeare. We also now speak about new kinds of literacy, such as computer or mathematical literacy. So it is important to understand what level and type of literacy is being referred to.

Furthermore, it is generally difficult and expensive to actually test people's level of literacy, especially for large population groups. So proxies are used. For example, in many international statistical series, literacy is taken as the proportion of the adult population who have completed primary school, on the assumption that it normally takes at least five or six years of primary schooling to become literate. In other cases, literacy rates are based on self-reporting from censuses, in which people often exaggerate their level of schooling and/or literacy.[7] For instance, Latin America is generally considered to be one of the most-schooled and literate regions of the developing world, with primary enrolment ratios for the most part well over 90 percent. However, a study done early in the current millennium, covering a large sample of adults from the region, found that of the 63 percent who reported completing primary schooling and being literate, only about 50 percent could actually read with understanding a short paragraph taken from the front page of a local popular newspaper.[8]

A case from the province of Ontario illustrates how statistics can be misused (or used in a limited way) for the creation of education policy. Recently, comparisons of secondary school dropout rates indicated that Ontario was not as successful as many other industrialized jurisdictions in retaining students past the compulsory schooling limit of 16 years of age. This led the provincial government in 2006 to increase the compulsory schooling age to 18 years. However, Canadian census data also indicate that by age 24 about 85 percent of people have completed their secondary education or equivalent, which means that about half of the dropouts were actually "stop outs" who left the regular school system after age 16 but pursued their education by other means. So, in effect the government responded on the basis of one statistical indicator, while disregarding another statistical indicator that paints a much different picture of the reality of learners and their lives.

In recent years, advances in information technology and the growth in funding for the collection of international data has led to an ever-wider range of statistical information, and to the development of more robust efforts to clarify relationships among statistical indicators. Detailed information on attitudes and lived experiences is often collected alongside administrative data through methods such as household surveys and surveys of students and teachers. As we shall see in the next section, in education such efforts have led to a sometimes bewildering proliferation of cross-national comparative data, in forms that critics argue contribute to both greater homogenization of educational systems, and greater surveillance and control. On the other hand, such data is increasingly sensitive to questions of inequality and may allow us to see whether formally agreed universal entitlements, such as the right to education, are in fact realized in the distribution of educational opportunities around the world. UNICEF's (United Nations Children's Fund) annual *Report Card* on child poverty and well-being in rich countries and UNESCO's annual *Education for All Global Monitoring Report* exemplify this trend.[9]

THE BIRTH OF INTERNATIONAL ASSESSMENT OF EDUCATIONAL ACHIEVEMENT

The term *international assessments* is commonly used to refer to tests of educational achievement carried out in more than one nation using the same tests and testing methodology. The first such international assessment was conducted in 1964, under the auspices of the International Association for the Evaluation of Educational Achievement (IEA). The IEA went on to undertake more than 30 additional studies of educational achievement, in fields as diverse as mathematics, literacy, and civics.

According to Stephen Heyneman:

> Cross-national education survey research was first just an experiment, born out of a chance visit of Torsten Husen from the University of Stockholm [who was a very eminent professor of comparative education] to the Comparative Education Center at the University of Chicago in the mid-1950s. There he met C. Arnold Anderson, Mary Jean Bowman, and Ben Bloom, whose view was that the whole world should be seen as a single educational laboratory. From this meeting emerged the International Association for the Evaluation of Educational Achievement (IEA), which, for diplomatic purposes, was managed from Sweden.[10]

The IEA faced many early technical challenges, related to test designs, student sampling, and questionnaire designs for students and teachers. A large team of people from various parts of the world was brought together to work on them. Its researchers faced a major difficulty because while the core elements of curricula are generally similar, they are differently emphasized from place to place. Thus within any given subject, different aspects and topics are given different emphasis so that at any given age or grade level, students in various jurisdictions have the opportunity to learn quite different things. Another comparison problem is the differing structures of different systems, for example, differing primary cycles or types of streaming. Deciding which grade levels to test, and what sample of students would produce fair and accurate comparisons, became a major challenge. These technical problems were addressed in a variety of ways: through more careful sampling and selection of test topics, for example, as well as through the publication of detailed reports about mismatches between the test design and the systems it is testing.

Even more important than these technical debates, however, was the debate about the use of such international assessments that arose at the inception of the IEA, and still carries on today. Were such international testing mechanisms to be primarily for scholarly and research purposes? Or were they to be used more instrumentally and directly by educational administrators and policy-makers?

Historically, tests of learning achievement have been carried out primarily for the latter purpose, that is, to achieve administrative efficiency in mass systems of schooling. Indeed, by the early 20th century, testing had become so commonplace that it was inseparable from popular images of schooling. Teachers routinely use tests both for formative diagnosis (to understand if a student may need additional help or enriched activities) and summative assessment (for grades and report cards). Provinces, states, and nations have also long used tests to determine which students are permitted to move from one level of education to the next, or to specific types of institutions. Such tests are often used because they are thought to provide a scientific and objective check on the teachers' (subjective) judgments, even though research suggests that testing often adds less diagnostic value than expected.[11] They also allow educational systems to sort students in administratively efficient ways, and to justify such sorting on the basis of so-called objective standards of merit.

The aim of the originators of international achievement testing was clearly much more nuanced. They wanted a better scholarly understanding of educational practices in their societal context. While this might eventually lead to better policy and practice, understanding was the primary objective. As the IEA website explains:

> The founders of the IEA viewed the world as a natural educational laboratory, where different school systems experiment in different ways to obtain optimal results in the education of their youth. They contended that while different countries give similar definitions of these "optimal results," they tend to employ different methods to achieve common ends. The founders assumed that if research could obtain evidence from across a wide range of systems, there

would probably be sufficient variability to permit the revelation of important relationships that would escape detection within a single educational system.[12]

Perhaps even more importantly, the originators of the IEA studies were opposed to using the test results to create league tables of scores across systems, in ways suggestive of a horse-race among nations. As Torsten Husen, the director of the IEA at the time of its First International Mathematics Study (1964), argued:

> The fact that these comparisons are cross-national should not be taken as an indication that the primary interest was, for example, national means and dispersions in school achievements at certain age or school levels.... The following considerations will, it is hoped, show how meaningless it is to compare only national levels of subject matter performance at various levels. It could be expected that the differences between and within countries will vary not only with regard to outcomes (cognitive and noncognitive) of instruction but also with regard to all of the "input" variables, such as technological level and urbanization of countries, social background of children, education of their parents, training of teachers, money spent on education, years of mathematics and periods a week on the timetable. Of special importance is the structure of the school system, that is, how many children are brought how far up the educational ladder. Comparisons between countries are not to be made primarily in terms of levels achieved.[13]

Later in the 1964 study, Husen re-emphasized the point:

> The IEA study [at this time there was only one] was not designed to compare countries; needless to say, it is not to be considered as an "international contest."[14]

He also pointed out that the relationship between cross-national achievement research and policy is a very delicate one, noting, "It should be clearly stated that the design of this study does not allow for the confirmation of imputed causal relationships."[15] In terms of direct policy relevance, this observation is critical. International assessments are designed to allow us to combine discrete educational statistics and give them a context, to permit comparison between jurisdictions and over time. They show trends and uncover interesting questions, such as why some kinds of pedagogical practices appear to yield better or different learning results. However, they cannot by themselves provide explanations or permit conclusions. To make causal arguments and claims (such as, if we do this, then that will result), requires much more extensive research, using a broad range of variables and statistical methods as well as experimental research designs.[16]

However, the basic design and intention of international assessment studies did not stop their results from being used both as direct evidence for educational policy decisions and as fodder for competition among nations. From the very beginning, IEA studies depended on financing from participating governments. Participation in the earliest IEA studies was stimulated in many nations by the Sputnik Crisis of 1957, when the Soviet Union's ability to put the first satellite into orbit, long in advance of North American or Western European nations, was seen as a threatening indication that the nations of the West were losing to the Union of Soviet Socialist Republics (USSR) in the critical areas of science and technology. The blame for this was laid squarely at the door of the schoolhouse, as evidenced in the popularity of such books as *Why Johnny Can't Read and Ivan Can* (written by a retired US admiral) or *Crisis in the Classroom*. Particularly in the United States, education came to be viewed as an essential weapon in the Cold War.[17] For much of the period between 1960 and the 1990s, international assessment studies were viewed by many national policy-makers as part of a battery of efforts to improve the West's educational arsenal.

Thus, each successive wave of IEA studies was eagerly reported in cross-national league tables in the media with much accompanying commentary by pundits and politicians. For example, the United States did not do well in the second IEA study of mathematics learning, carried out in 1982. This led to the US publication in 1985 of a report titled *A Nation at Risk*, which argued in dramatic Cold War terms that the continuing inability to improve educational performance was equivalent to a form of unilateral disarmament.[18] Along with similar calls to arms, this led slowly to the movement towards higher and more specified educational standards and teacher/school accountability through statewide or national testing programs.

Overall, the IEA has carried out more than 30 assessments of educational achievement. While its studies have included assessments of civics education and second language education, the vast majority of its work has focused on math, sciences, literacy, and second language education—subjects easily and directly linked to the national interest and the race for power among nations. However, recent initiatives have also included studies on information technology use and early childhood education.

GLOBALIZATION, LARGE SCALE ASSESSMENT, AND THE POLITICS OF LEAGUE TABLES

In the 1990s, as the Cold War faded from view, governments around the world began to focus their policies on the challenges of globalization and international economic competition. Human capital—particularly in terms of skills in science, math, and literacy—was increasingly seen as central to national efforts to maintain economic advantage within the world economy (see Chapters One and Three for further discussions on human capital).

In this new policy context, interest in international assessments and indicators, as well as in domestic assessment programs, grew rapidly among governments.[19] Assessments were viewed as a way of improving educational achievement, first by setting in place policies that define acceptable standards of learning acquisition, and then by collecting information about the extent to which these standards were being met. Assessments were also seen as useful in another aspect of globalization-driven reforms: they were seen as improving the efficiency and effectiveness of government spending. As we have seen in Chapter Seven by Stephen Anderson, testing and assessment programs were developed to provide information for more efficient and better targeted educational spending (and sometimes cuts). Insofar as they provide information that can be used by parents and the public to demand better services, they also reflect a new approach to public policy that emphasized a role for competition across educational organizations and systems, and for enhanced consumer or public choice.[20]

Among the most publicized and controversial aspects of this movement towards large-scale assessment programs in the 1990s was their emphasis on the production of league tables or tabular ranks of educational institutions and systems. Such public rankings marked a dramatic shift in the way that assessments were conceptualized and employed by public policy-makers and within international organizations.[21] At the time of their founding, both UNESCO's *Statistical Yearbook* and the IEA achievement studies discouraged attempts to use international data to rank countries. Now, instead of using assessments for scientific analysis or as a starting point for in-house efforts to improve educational policies (as UNESCO and IEA founders advised), new assessments were being produced specifically for the public, in league table format. According to Leithwood:

> Large-scale achievement testing is one of the most heavily used instruments in today's accountability-driven policy toolbox. Debates about the value and uses of such testing overwhelm all other topics of debate about how to improve schools. Results of such tests now have become the basic criteria for selecting programs eligible for federal funding with the passage of the No Child Left Behind Act. School staffs are regularly judged as competent professionals or publicly shamed with the publication of league tables [like the relative standing of teams as reported in the sports pages of newspapers] on the basis of their students' performance on such tests…. There are now examples of politicians pledging to meet targeted improvements in such test results within the four years of their electoral mandates (e.g., the recently elected Premier of the Canadian Province of Ontario) or resign if they fail (e.g., the minister responsible for education in England).[22]

Internationally, the 1990s push for large scale assessment and comparative indicators can be seen most clearly in the work of the OECD (Organisation for Economic Co-operation and Development), an international body with a membership of rich industrialized nations and a growing number of middle income countries. Dissatisfied with UNESCO's statistical capacities (which had always avoided any direct international ranking), and seeking a wider and more consistent program for international assessment than had been possible using the intermittent IEA studies, the 1990s saw Western governments fund both an International Indicators Project and a new Programme for International Student Assessment (PISA) under the auspices of the OECD.[23]

PISA is particularly innovative: although it tests the same domains as many IEA studies (math, science, literacy), PISA assessments (unlike the IEA) emphasize the ability to apply knowledge and skills in lifelike situations, rather than mastery of particular curricular content. PISA is also conducted on a larger scale than any previous international assessment: more than 60 participating governments (OECD and partner countries), representing about 90 percent of the world's economy, have committed to the PISA assessment at regular three-year intervals.[24] PISA assessments are based on a scientific sample of 15-year-olds in each country and involve both a written student test and the collection of a wide range of data on students' attitudes towards their studies, their study skills, and the organization and management of schools.

Both PISA and the OECD's International Indicators Project produce highly publicized international comparative indicators, most notably through the widely cited league table results of PISA, and through the annual publication of the OECD report *Education at a Glance*.[25] The release of these reports receives high-profile coverage in many national media, and is important enough to warrant the publication of national responses by many education ministries.

International assessment and indicator projects have now also become a hot topic within the developing world. As early as 1990, the international community linked better assessment to the achievement of education as a universal right (as described in Mundy's Chapter Three). Article 4 of the World Declaration on Education for All (adopted in Jomtien, Thailand, in 1990 and ratified in Dakar, Senegal, in 2000), states, "It is necessary to define acceptable levels of learning acquisition for educational programmes and to improve and apply systems of assessing learning achievement."[26] Subsequently, many governments in Latin America and some parts of Asia introduced national assessment programs in the 1990s.[27] Regional indicator and assessment programs emerged in Latin America and Southern Africa — most notably the Southern and Eastern African Consortium for Monitoring Educational Quality (SACMEQ) and the Latin American Laboratory for Evaluating the Quality of Education.[28] Many other countries simply joined in the OECD's PISA program: non-OECD countries represent more than half its current participants. These initiatives were heavily supported by the World Bank, which increasingly sees assessments as essential to both the efficient allocation of scarce educational resources, and as providing a key way of mobilizing policy-makers around educational reform programs. Mounting international concern with educational quality (an issue that is sometimes neglected in the push for greater access) has lead to many recent calls for the creation of a single global set of standards and assessments to monitor educational quality. Many developing countries produce shockingly low levels of learning acquisition: basic levels of literacy and numeracy are often not acquired during the full primary cycle. In a move that is suggestive of future trends, many international organizations are now calling for the establishment of a set of Millennium Learning Goals, through the rapid expansion of a standardized assessment scheme for all countries in the developing world.[29]

Scholars of international relations and of education policy continue to debate the political effects and implications of this spread of international assessment efforts. As some have pointed out, such assessments do seem to contribute to the larger trend towards standardization and homogenization across educational systems. They are seen by both educators and academic critics as threatening local forms of autonomy, especially the autonomy of teachers.[30] In particular, critics argue that the move towards the publication of ranked results changes the essential purposes of large-scale assessments, while also intensifying the problems and limits with educational statistics we mentioned earlier.[31] We can sum up their criticisms in three points.

1) First, publicized rankings typically use raw results: they rarely adjust these results to reflect the different socio-economic and cultural challenges faced by specific schools or populations.[32]
2) League table rankings contribute to the undigested use of data: they present data on only a select aspect of learning acquisition, but represent this data as adequate for judging the system as a whole. Can, for example, Ontario's results on the IEA-led Third International Mathematics and Science Study (TIMSS) in 1999 truly reflect learning acquisition in Ontario when the test's questions cover less than half of the content of the Ontario curriculum?[33] Even more broadly, does the focus on math and

science that dominates most international assessment efforts adequately reflect the kinds of knowledge and learning we want our schools to be judged for?[34]

3) Finally, and more generally, it is unclear how well such assessments feed into actual improvements within educational systems. Many scholars have noted that large-scale assessments often produce a tendency among teachers to teach to the test (at the expense of other learning). This is somewhat less true in the case of international assessments (which are usually administered to only a small sample of students). But international assessments can distort the focus of educational systems, by encouraging scrutiny and attention to some aspects of the system over others (as in the science example above). As Ben Levin has pointed out, it is not clear that international assessments allow us to learn from one another — instead they may simply promote epidemic-like adoption of educational reforms.[35]

In recognizing these criticisms, we should also note that many of the most recent international assessment exercises are also accompanied by surveys of school organization and management practices, student and teacher characteristics, and pedagogical practices. Surveys of teachers and students now provide information about attitudes, habits, and motivations. Some studies (for example, the 1999 IEA TIMSS assessment and the 1999 IEA Civics Education Study) have also begun to collect video data that allows for even greater analysis of pedagogical practices. Here the original intention of using data to raise questions is in full display.[36] And because much of this data is now widely available online or in electronic formats, teachers themselves can access and review it. As one recent study concludes:

Teachers would have little difficulty recognizing, in a general sense, what their counterparts in other countries [are] doing.... However, they might also be surprised and interested in the different ways in which familiar practices were sequenced and used.... The opportunities to see the familiar in new light might offer many opportunities for teachers to rethink the taken-for-granted practices and see them as choices rather than inevitabilities.[37]

It is also worth noting that the policy impact of international assessments and indicators varies enormously by country and by topic, and seems to be shifting over time. We have already seen, for example, that governments have been much less likely to participate in or respond to international assessments of civics education than to assessments in what are viewed as core areas for global economic competitiveness (math, science, and literacy).[38] But the geo-political issues raised by the terrorist attacks on the United States on September 11, 2001, and the subsequent wars in Afghanistan and Iraq have also led to much greater interest in the upcoming IEA Civics education study, which looks at formal knowledge as well as attitudes and dispositions to democracy. In a related vein, there has been a surprising emphasis on social cohesion and equality in recent OECD reports. International assessments and indicators are increasingly used to highlight the fact that high levels of national achievement are strongly correlated to more equitable levels of achievement. For example, recent OECD studies have used educational data to promote better learning opportunities for immigrant and minority students, and for expanded opportunities for early childhood education.[39] As OECD Secretary General Angel Gurria recently noted, "By showing that some countries succeed in providing both high quality and equitable learning outcomes, PISA sets ambitious goals for others."[40] Two factors seem to be contributing towards this trend: strong public pressure for greater attention to equity in the context of globalization; and an increase in the perception that social inequalities (especially between immigrants and non-immigrants) pose a threat to public safety.

CANADA AND THE INTERNATIONAL INDICATORS

What implications and issues are raised by the rapid growth of international indicator programs for educators? In this section, we answer this question by first describing Canadian involvement in international assessments, and then looking at some of the findings from these assessments and the policy debates they have stimulated. Our goal here is to provide educators with a practical guide to international indicators, and to encourage greater critical engagement with them, using the Canadian experience as an illustration.

Table 8.2
A Guide to International Assessments in Canada

Title (Organization)	Goals/ Method	Years
PISA Programme for International Student Assessment (OECD)	• Reading, math, and science • 15-year-olds • Tests knowledge and skills, with emphasis on problem solving and application of knowledge (does not test mastery of the curriculum) • Collects data on schools, school system, and student characteristics (socio-economic status, attitudes, and experiences)	2008/9 2006 2003 2000
TIMSS Trends in International Math and Sciences Study (IEA)	• Performance in science and math in Grades 4 and 8 • Written test based on commonly agreed questions drawn from national curricula • Student, teacher, and school questionnaires • In 1995 and 1999, video study to allow comparison of teaching processes	2007 2003 1999 1995
PIRLS Progress in Reading Literacy Study (IEA)	• Trends in reading achievement in Grade 4 • Focus on four main areas of literacy: process of comprehension, purposes for reading, reading behaviours, and attitudes • Written test (80 minutes) plus background questionnaire • Student, teacher, and school questionnaires allow for study of home, school, and classroom influences	2006 2001
ICCS International Civics and Citizenship Study (IEA)	• Trends in civic and citizenship knowledge and attitudes, age 14 • National context survey • Achievement test focuses on	2009 1999

	conceptual understanding and competencies • Student questionnaire on aspirations and attitudes • Teacher and school questionnaires (teaching classroom management, school governance and climate)	
ALL Adult Literacy and Lifeskills Survey (previously International Adult Literacy and Skills Survey) (OECD)	• Literacy and numeracy skills of a nationally representative sample from each participating country • Adults' problem-solving skills and familiarity with information and communication technologies	2003 1998 1996 1994
SITES Second Information Technology in Education Study (IEA)	• How, and to what extent, is information and communication technology used in education, and how does it support and enhance pedagogical practices? • Employs online data collection	2006 1997 1995

Canada (through the national Council of Ministers of Education Canada [CMEC], Human Resources and Skills Development Canada [HRSDC], Statistics Canada [StatsCan], and the provincial Ministries of Education) has been quite an active participant in many of the major recent international assessment exercises. Most provinces (though not all, and not the territories) participate in PISA, and are either currently or have in the past participated in the IEA studies in math, sciences, information technology, and reading. No Canadian province participated in the first IEA Civics Education study, and plans to participate in the 2009 ICCS (International Civic and Citizenship Education Study) have not advanced. Canada has also played a leadership role in the design of a new international assessment on Adult Literacy and Lifeskills Survey (ALL, which builds upon the former International Adult Literacy Survey [IALS]), in a collaboration headed by StatsCan. Table 8.2 lists the various international assessments in which Canada participates.

Funding for international assessments is generally provided by the participating provincial Ministries of Education. However, for PISA, (which is the most ambitious and expensive of the international assessments), direct costs are paid for by the federal ministry, HRSDC, with provinces, CMEC, and StatsCan as collaborating partners. HRSDC's involvement is regarded by some critics as marking a new trend in federal intervention in education (since education in Canada is a provincially mandated responsibility). Approximately 28,000 students from 1,000 schools participated in the 2000 and 2003 cycles of PISA, at an estimated cost of $1.9 million per year (or $11.4 million for the two cycles).[41]

It is important to consider exactly what is tested on PISA, and how student performance across Canada compares to that in other countries. PISA is focused on three domains: math, science, and reading literacy. It defines literacy in each of these domains as follows:

- Mathematical literacy is the capacity to identify and understand the role that mathematics plays in the world, to make well-founded judgments, and to use and engage with mathematics in ways that meet the need of that individual's life as a constructive, concerned, and educated citizen. The focus of the test is on overall skills in mathematics and specific mathematics sub-domains, such as space and shape, change and relationships, quantity, and uncertainty.
- Scientific literacy is defined as an individual's capacity to use scientific knowledge, identify questions, and to draw evidence-based conclusions in order to understand and help make decisions about the natural world and the changes made to it through human activity.
- Reading literacy is defined as an individual's capacity to understand, use, and reflect on written texts in order to achieve one's goals, to develop one's knowledge and potential, and to participate in society.[42]

The OECD encourages teachers to go online to view PISA questions and try them out.[43]

What kinds of trends have international indicators and assessments identified in Canada's educational systems? Overall, the PISA data suggests that learning achievement in Canada in all three domains is above the OECD average. In the 2003 PISA study, Canada ranked third in math (after Hong Kong and Finland); second in reading (after Finland), and fifth in science and problem solving. Thus Canadian students finished in the top tier of all countries in every domain tested by PISA. Canada also stands out for greater equality in learning achievement: it is third in the world for having the lowest proportion of students at the lowest levels of the PISA tests; and it has below average levels of variance in performance between students.[44] Thus, according to the OECD, "Canada is one of the countries in which social background has the smallest impact on students' success."[45] So low is the variance in performance across schools that the OECD concludes "performance is largely unrelated to the schools in which the students are enrolled, and parents can be less concerned about school choice."[46] Canada also stands out as having among the highest levels of performance among immigrant children, second language learners, and the children of immigrants.[47] The OECD concludes that Canada has a cost-efficient system of education to upper secondary level, one in which good performance is achieved at a reasonable level of investment.[48]

However, the OECD and IEA indicators also raise many questions for Canadian educators. In terms of the 2003 PISA findings, for example, why do Canadian students do least well on the mathematics sub-domain of "space and shape" while doing so well on "quantity" and "uncertainty"? What causes students in minority language systems across Canada to perform more poorly than other students in science, reading, and problem-solving? Why are girls doing so much better than boys on reading, and why are women in Canada now acquiring more years of education than men, on average?[49] (See Chapter Nine for a further discussion on this topic.) Why is the growth in university enrolment in Canada lagging behind other OECD countries? And perhaps most importantly, why does public expenditure on education in Canada (as a share of gross domestic product) lag behind the OECD average (3.6 as opposed to 3.9 percent), a level that reflects a drop from a high of 4.5 percent of GDP in 1995?[50] These questions are just a few of the many raised by the PISA and OECD comparisons, selected to illustrate the broad range of pedagogical, equity, and expenditure issues that such studies begin to illuminate.

Beyond reflecting on the data that international indicators provide, it is also important for educators to question neglected areas and limitations in the design and implementation of international assessments. For example, Canadian educators may wish to ask the federal and provincial governments why Aboriginal students, especially those on reserves, are often excluded in the sampling for international assessments. (See Chapter Four for a further discussion on Indigenous education in Canada.) Their inclusion might sharply impact appraisals of equity in the system, perhaps mitigating the high levels of praise for equity that Canada is awarded by the OECD. Educators might also want to look more broadly at the way in which equity is treated in international assessments. Should countries receive praise (as Canada does) just for having lower levels of variation by socio-economic background, or should international indicators set basic standards and benchmarks for equity (in the same way that standards for learning acquisition are established by PISA)? The OECD's *Education at a Glance* notes that Canadian students with the lowest socio-economic status are 2.7 times more likely to be poor performers in math than students in the highest socio-economic status (as compared to an average of 3.5 time more likely across the OECD).[51] What makes this level acceptable?

Finally, it is worth reflecting on how international assessments are generally treated in the Canadian media, that is to say, how they are presented to the public. As in virtually every country, the emphasis in the Canadian media is on the ranking of Canada and its provinces, not on the finer details that pertain to issues of equity and pedagogy. Coverage is heavily focused on Ministries of Education, who typically attribute successes to the educational system, while laying failure at the feet of families or economics rather than their own policies.[52] Few researchers or critics are consulted for comment, and sometimes unwarranted causal relationships are asserted. For example, a recent *Economist* article credits Alberta's success in PISA to its introduction of private charter schools.[53] Furthermore, as Michelle Stack concludes in her study of media reporting on PISA, "interpretations of the test results treated students as one group ... there is no other mention of inequality among groups."[54] Here is one area where the voice of educators and educational researchers can play a very important role.

CONCLUSION: INTERNATIONAL INDICATORS—WHAT TEACHERS NEED TO KNOW

The history of international indicators and assessments suggests that they have long been driven by the geo-political and economic interests of Western nation-states. This should alert us to the fact that the gathering of international educational data is a fundamentally political exercise. Furthermore, many technical challenges plague international comparative data, some so severe that they threaten the validity and reliability of the data. One of the lessons from this chapter is that we should never assume that educational data is objective or scientific, or that its presentation is unbiased by political interests and requirements.

This chapter has also highlighted some of the exciting issues and trends that can be illuminated by the recent development of more sophisticated and wide-ranging international indicators and international assessments. For educators, who have typically been quite skeptical of efforts to use standardized tests as the basis for educational decision-making, international indicator research offers both promises and challenges. International indicators provide an important opportunity for us to learn about differences in pedagogical practice, school organization, and classroom management, and to consider how these differences impact different aspects of learning. They also offer us valuable information about trends in the equality of educational systems, and changes in overall levels of funding and support for schools. In this sense, they give educators and citizens important tools for making evidenced-based claims for change. However, international assessments and indicators are not foolproof;they need to be designed carefully on the basis of a widely shared view of the core purposes of schooling. Current practices in international assessment and indictor programs reflect a highly constricted view of the purposes of schooling, focused primarily on the economic return to education as an investment. Educators can play an important role here, by voicing concerns and suggesting amendments to the scope and range of learning and equity goals addressed in current international assessment and indicators programs.

QUESTIONS FOR REFLECTION AND DISCUSSION

1. Why have governments become so interested in participating in efforts to compare their educational performance?
2. What kinds of limits should we be aware of when assessing information from international assessments and indicators?
3. Why are teachers skeptical about international assessment research?
4. In your view, do international assessments and indicators have offer valuable information for educators? Explain.

SUGGESTED AUDIO-VISUAL RESOURCES

Instead of selecting a film for this chapter, we suggest that instructors explore with students the activities and audio-visual resources provided on international assessment websites. Holding this class in a computer lab would be ideal.

a) Explore PISA questions and questionaires:
pisa-sq.acer.edu.au

b) Take sample questions from the IEA Civics Education Study:
nces.ed.gov/surveys/cived

c) Review a short study, "Highlights from the TIMSS 1999 Video Study," with its video clips, from classrooms in Japan, the Netherlands, the United States, and Hong Kong:
nces.ed.gov/pubs2003/timssvideo/Index.asp?nav=1

d) Explore and manipulate performance data from the TIMSS and PIRLS studies. This website allows users to ask their own questions of TIMSS and PIRLS datasets, creating simple charts and tables comparing various aspects of several countries' performances:
lighthouse.air.org/timss

e) Instructors may also wish to use selected footage from the *TIMSS 1999 Video Study: Science Public Release Lessons* or *TIMSS 1999 Video Study: Mathematics Public Release Lessons* funded by the National Center

for Education Statistics. These two multi-CD sets present video footage from the math and science classrooms of Grade Eight students in Australia, Czech Republic, Japan, Netherlands, and the United States. Distributor: Pearson Achievement Solutions
URL: www.lessonlab.com/bkstore/index.cfm/actiondisplayby category

SUGGESTIONS FOR FURTHER READING

*Council of Ministers of Education Canada and Human Resources and Skills Development Canada. *Measuring Up: Canadian Results of the OECD PISA Study.* Toronto: Council of Ministers of Education Canada, 2003. www.pisa.gc.ca/publications_e.shtml.

Heyneman, Stephen P. "The Use of Cross-National Comparisons for Local Educational Policy." *Curriculum Inquiry* 34, no. 3 (2004): 345–52.

Leithwood, Kenneth A. "Programs and Politics: The Local Uses of International Tests." *Curriculum Inquiry* 34, no. 3 (2004): 363–77.

Moll, Marita, ed. *Passing the Test: The False Promises of Standardized Testing.* Ottawa, ON: Canadian Centre for Policy Alternatives, 2004.

*OECD. "Draft Briefing Note for Canada." *Education at a Glance 2006:* Paris: OECD, 2006. www.oecd.org/dataoecd/52/1/37392733. pdf.

OECD. *Education at a Glance 2006.* Paris: OECD, 2006.

*OECD. *First Results from PISA: Executive Summary. Programme for International Student Assessment.* Paris: OECD, 2003. www.oecd. org/dataoecd/1/63/34002454.pdf.

Smith, Thomas A. and David P. Baker. "Worldwide Growth and Institutionalization of Statistical Indicators for Educational Policy Making." *Peabody Journal of Education* 76, no. 3–4 (2001): 141–52.

*UNESCO. *Education for All Global Monitoring Report: Executive Summary.* Paris: UNESCO, 2007. unesdoc.unesco.org/images/0014/001477/ 147794E.pdf.

*UNICEF. "Child Poverty in Perspective: An Overview of Child-Well-being in Rich Countries." *Innocenti Report Card 7.* Florence: UNICEF Innocenti Research Centre, 2007. www.unicef-irc.org/ publications/pdf/rc7_eng.pdf.

Chapter Nine

Gender and Education

Kara Janigan and Vandra Lea Masemann

INTRODUCTION

Teaching is a highly gendered profession, and learning itself is often heavily affected by gender. Wherever we look in educational systems, we find people occupying particular positions and enacting roles that are strongly influenced by their (biological) sex and societal notions of what is appropriate for girls/women and boys/men. Of all the inequalities that exist within and across different educational systems, gender inequality has perhaps attracted the most sustained concern and attention within the field of comparative education over the last 20 years. Elaine Unterhalter, a British philosopher, captures the issue succinctly: "Throughout the world, gender, often linked with injustice, marks life in schools."[1]

The term *gender* refers to the ways that male and female roles are socially defined in any given society. Gender has two dimensions. In popular usage and in many administrative settings, gender is used to refer to biological sex (that is, whether one is male or female). However, in the field of comparative education and across the social sciences, gender is used in a much more nuanced manner: it refers to the specific roles, treatment, and expectations that accompany one's biological sex. In this meaning, gender refers not just to a fixed or innate power dynamic between men and women, but to the ways that concepts of gender are socially constructed and historically changing.

Gender relationships are fundamentally rooted in the historical division of labour between women and men in society. The closer a person is to the physical, emotional, and social care of young children, the more likely that person is to be a woman (mother or grandmother) or girl (sister), and the less likely he or she is to earn money or receive other tangible rewards for doing so. Intangibles, such as respect, love, honour, and other forms of emotional rewards, are heavily favoured. Mothers the world over carry their children in pregnancy, give birth to them or adopt them, feed them, provide their physical care, and give them the rudiments of education before they go to school, if they go to school. These universal characteristics of human reproduction and child socialization have profound implications for the ways in which the institution of education divides human beings into gendered identities and often produces gender inequalities.

However, since notions of gender are socially constructed, the relationship between gender and education plays out differently within different cultural, political, and economic contexts. This makes issues of gender and education of particular interest to the comparative educator. For example, comparativists are interested in the ways that girls' and boys' socialisation and education are differentiated in various cultures and different historical periods. They compare the career paths of teachers and other educational personnel in different national settings to explore how their experiences are shaped by local gender practices. They also look at how gender differences are affected by economic change and processes of globalization and study social movements that have developed to fight gender inequalities. Comparativists have been at the forefront of efforts to understand how historical shifts and intercultural relationships change gender practices and raise new challenges for equality within educational systems.

In this chapter, we use a comparative and international lens to explore the complex relationships between gender and education in several ways. We begin by examining how gender bias was expressed in the founding years of comparative education, and in leadership within its major societies and journals. We then look at different ways of conceptualizing gender equality in education and explore four theoretical approaches to the study of gender and education. Later, we delineate how large-scale statistical surveys of educational issues such as access, attainment, and achievement provide the comparative educator with valuable insights into the educational circumstances of girls and boys nationally, regionally, and globally. However, we also suggest that it is only through qualitative research, such as small-scale ethnographic studies of schooling, that insights can be gained as to the lived reality of gender discrimination in education. By way of illustration, we present the experiences of secondary school girls in rural Eritrea, in the Horn of Africa. A final section looks at the historical evolution of gender equality in Canada (and more specifically in Ontario), illustrating both persistent aspects of gender inequality and evolving gender dynamics. From the Eritrean and Canadian examples, we draw out the fact that, beyond the overarching issues of outright discrimination and gender stereotyping in education, other important dimensions include the intersection of gender inequalities with inequalities perpetuated on the basis of class, race, and ethnicity.

GENDER AS AN ISSUE IN COMPARATIVE EDUCATION

When Marc-Antoine Jullien wrote his first survey on comparative education in 1817, his series of questions on the education of girls reflected the views of a period in history when a large proportion of the populace was still cultivating the land and when social roles for women and men were strongly influenced by the gender-role expectations of that era. He was interested in the various schools for girls, their teachers, their curriculum, relations between the sexes in the education course, and the progress and results of girls' education. Furthermore, Jullien wanted information gathered on

> "general considerations and various questions of which those related to normal [teacher] education, carried to the goal of forming instructresses and to influencing women, who, well directed, become the *complement of education for men* [emphasis added]."[2]

Chapter One has outlined how the focus of studies in comparative education shifted throughout the 1800s and early 1900s from descriptive and historical studies of systems and their components to what was thought to be a more scientific study of sociological variables that influenced education. Gender or sex was mainly used as a label to quantify the relative numbers of males and females enrolled in schools, or to delineate the appropriate curricula on the basis of differing expectations by gender. Much of this kind of analysis — mentioning but not questioning gender/sex variable — continues to this day.

Gender dynamics can also be examined as part of the history of the development of comparative education as an academic enterprise.

Here it is instructive to look at the roles played by men and women as evidence of shifting gender relationships. For much of the 20th century, men tended to dominate as the leading scholars and researchers, major office-holders in comparative and international education societies, organizers of conferences, and journal editors.[3] If we take the Comparative and International Education Society (CIES) of the United States as an example, there was only one woman president in the first 25 years of its history, from 1957 to 1982.

This situation began to change in the 1970s and 1980s. Between 1983 and 2006, nine women have served as president of CIES.[4] Among them, Gail P. Kelly played an important role, both by outlining a powerful agenda for studying gender and education in comparative education, and by playing a leadership role within CIES. As mentioned in Chapter One, Kelly served as president of the society in 1986.[5] She also contributed to a movement among women scholars that saw the establishment by Vandra Lea Masemann of a gender committee in 1989. This committee continues to organize seminars and workshops on gender issues at annual meetings and monitors the contents of the society's journal to encourage fair representation of women authors and research on gender related topics. Today the field of comparative education boasts an ever-growing number of scholars, both female and male, who conduct and publish research on gender issues. Using an impressive diversity of theoretical and methodological approaches, these scholars continue to use the comparative lens to raise questions about gendered practices in education around the world.

WAYS OF LOOKING AT GENDER EQUALITY

When researchers explore issues of gender and education, the terms *gender parity*, *gender equity*, and *gender equality* are often used. Gender parity refers to the actual number of girls and boys, women and men participating within an institution (sameness) whereas gender equity refers to the treatment of girls and boys, men and women within that institution (fairness).

The term *gender equality* can be used in different ways. In its more narrow usage, the term refers to equal numbers—whether in relation to girls' and boys' relative levels of participation or to levels of resource allocation by gender. However, many others use the term *gender equality* more broadly to refer to issues of fairness. For example, the United Nations Educational, Scientific and Cultural Organization (UNESCO), in its Education for All (EFA) documents, uses gender equality to mean "that all girls and boys have equal opportunity to enjoy basic education of high quality, achieve at equal levels and enjoy equal benefits from education."[6] A broad definition of gender equality is also enshrined in the United Nations Universal Declaration of Human Rights in 1948 and, more comprehensively, in the 1979 Convention on the Elimination of All Forms of Discrimination against Women (CEDAW), in which Article 10 states:[7]

> Parties shall take all appropriate measures to eliminate discrimination against women in order to ensure to them equal rights with men in the field of education and in particular to ensure, on a basis of equality of men and women:
>
> (a) The same conditions for career and vocational guidance, for access to studies and for the achievement of diplomas in educational establishments of all categories in rural as well as in urban areas; this equality shall be ensured in pre-school, general, technical, professional and higher technical education, as well as in all types of vocational training;
>
> (b) Access to the same curricula, the same examinations, teaching staff with qualifications of the same standard and school premises and equipment of the same quality;
>
> (c) The elimination of any stereotyped concept of the roles of men and women at all levels and in all forms of education by encouraging coeducation and other types of education which will help to achieve this aim and, in particular, by the revision of textbooks and school programmes and the adaptation of teaching methods;
>
> (d) The same opportunities to benefit from scholarships and other study grants;
>
> (e) The same opportunities for access to programmes of continuing education, including adult and functional literacy programmes, particularly those aimed at reducing, at the earliest possible time, any gap in education existing between men and women;

(f) The reduction of female student drop-out rates and the organization of programmes for girls and women who have left school prematurely;

(g) The same opportunities to participate actively in sports and physical education;

(h) Access to specific educational information to help to ensure the health and well-being of families, including information and advice on family planning. [8]

Different notions of gender equality have also developed from competing theoretical and conceptual frames for studying gender. Four different theoretical frames have been particularly influential: equalitarianism, feminism and feminist standpoint theories, conflict theories, and postmodernism. Each approach attempts to offer both an explanation for the existence of gender inequalities and possible solutions to reduce or eliminate these inequalities.

The first approach, equalitarianism, is based on the assumption that all human beings are (or should be) essentially equal. Its proponents frame their educational goal as getting equal numbers of girls and boys into schools and all areas of study. Equalitarianism is the foundation of many national and international educational campaigns to enrol equal numbers of female and male students at every level of schooling. It is based on a liberal democratic philosophy in which all citizens have equal rights to social participation and government services, including education at public expense.[9] Equalitarianism is ultimately related to theories of social functionalism that suggest that all parts of society work in harmony or at least in complementarity.[10] The objective then is to ensure the enrolment of more girls and women into educational and other institutions, in the hope that having more females participating will result in gender equality in terms of educational and life outcomes.

A central aim of educational systems has been to increase the numbers of girls in classrooms. An enormous amount of statistical information has been gathered in the present era and historically on school enrolment to illustrate the success of efforts to increase female enrolment. This information is based on an equalitarian philosophy, and sociological survey methods are used to handle large amounts of numerical data. No matter what their prevailing political philosophy, countries submitting enrolment figures to international organizations, such as UNESCO, are required to gather information in this way (see Chapter Eight).

Equalitarianism is also linked to human capital theory, in which human beings and their governments are characterized by economists as investing in themselves through education (see Chapter Three). The writing of Nobel Prize–winner Theodore Schultz on human capital reflects the male-oriented language and embedded assumptions of the 1970s:

> The distinctive part of human capital is that it is a part of man. It is human because it is embodied in man, and it is capital because it is a source of future satisfactions, or of future earnings, or of both. Where men are free agents, human capital is not a negotiable asset in the sense that it can be sold. It can, of course, be acquired not as an asset that is purchased in the market but by means of investing in oneself.[11]

A second approach to understanding gender is that of feminist standpoint theory, which "rejects the notion of an unmediated truth, maintaining that knowledge is always mediated by the individual's position and identity according to race, class, and gender in a particular socio-political formation and a certain point in time."[12] Feminist standpoint theory is based on people's own perceptions of their place in society, not only on what policy-makers or bureaucrats may see as their path to progress. Feminist theory has its roots in the movement for female suffrage in the late 19th century in North America and Europe. Suffragists sought to gain the legal definition of women as persons, rather than as chattels of their husbands. They also fought for women's right to vote in public elections, seeing this as key to gender equality. Later waves of the women's movement in North America have also been based on participants' analysis of their diverse situations as married women, partners in civil unions, lesbians, mothers, caregivers, artists, union workers, racial, linguistic and other minorities, professionals, elected officials, and many other roles.

Educational literature based on standpoint theory problematizes women's relationship to curriculum in schools, to modes of educational administration and decision making, and to the ways people respond to or create knowledge itself.[13] In contrast to research based on equalitarianism, studies based on feminist standpoint theory require a more anthropological approach. For example, in the Eritrean case that follows, students participated in interviews about their perceptions of factors that helped or hindered them in their efforts to gain an education. Anthropological research methods also may be used in pilot studies to ascertain the relevant research question or to clarify certain sources of cultural bias, before resources and personnel are invested in large-scale data-collecting based on the equalitarian model. Sometimes qualitative research is used to respond to quantitative findings. For example, Vandra Lea Masemann responded to Philip Foster's general survey of Ghanaian secondary schools[14] by conducting a two-year ethnographic study of the life of a girls' boarding school in Ghana[15] to investigate questions regarding girls' schooling and women's lives.

However, philosophical criticisms have also been levelled against the feminist standpoint approach. It has been argued that it is too heavily based on a form of gender essentialism, that is, ascribing a certain set of innate homogeneous characteristics to persons based on their sex. For example, early educational writing about women romanticised the mother's role in raising children and removed her by means of that discourse from the public world of men.[16] In terms of development discourse, Chandra Mohanty critiques the representation of "the 'Third World Woman' as a singular monolithic subject in some recent (western) feminist texts."[17]

Conflict theory offers a third approach to gender. Conflict theory may be based either on a neo-Marxist analysis of women's relationship to the means of production—women can be shown to perform some two-thirds of the world's work, including their private and public labour, yet receive a much smaller proportion of the world's monetary remuneration for that work—or on an analysis of the nature of patriarchal domination of women by men. The underlying assumption of conflict theory is that the relationship between women and men is not ultimately harmonious but is a constant struggle of two classes of people with contradictory interests.[18] According to this view, merely adjusting the numbers of females and males in schools is not a solution to this power imbalance. Much broader forms of social transformation are needed, and these can only be achieved through direct efforts to organize and mobilize women. The relationship between feminism and Marxism is very much unresolved, however. The feminist critique of Marxism, as it existed historically, is that its political movements subjugated women. Moreover, the interdependent biological and physical relationship between women and men means that women cannot entirely form a new society without men.

A fourth approach to gender is postmodernist. Here, the narratives of women's and men's lives are read as text, and the very categories people use to describe themselves and their lives are up for interpretation. In this view, even the categories of male and female are seen as socially constructed, with their respective boundaries and implications open to challenge. "The central tenet of the post-modern radical epistemology is that the self-legitimation of the One (the male) rests on and is nourished by the exclusion of the Other [the female]."[19] Postmodern approaches question the dichotomous views of human sexual identity and sexuality. Moreover, the traditional distanced relationship of the so-called objective researcher is called into question, and notions of subjectivity and objectivity are reconfigured. In postmodern research, the very tenets of the scientific canon are questioned, and the researcher finds it necessary to identify her or his personal biographical relationship (point of view) to the research question or the participants in the study. Furthermore, the formulation of research questions may take place in interaction with the participants, rather than in isolation from them and their views. In the conduct of the study, the researcher may play a more participatory role, and the traditional line between subjectivity and objectivity may be deemed irrelevant. In the analysis of the data and the writing up of the study, such an author will attempt to make the participant's voice heard and not to impose his or her views over those of the participant. Postmodern approaches suggest that true social transformation requires more than getting women into positions of power previously occupied by men; "what matters is that women as newcomers into these places be allowed to redefine the structures in such a way as to make them less discriminatory not only for women but ultimately for all people."[20]

These four approaches to gender equality in education are important because they help to shape different conceptualizations of gender equality, and offer different solutions to its challenges. But we can also simplify the message of this section: As comparativists, it is important to remember that our definitions of gender equality, whether narrow and based on numerical equality, or broad and based on the lived experiences of women and men, and whether drawn from a standpoint, conflict, or postmodern perspective, affect the way we assess the gendered nature of educational systems and their degrees of gender (in)equality. Our conceptual starting points affect our analysis in significant ways.

CURRENT EDUCATIONAL STATISTICS FOR GIRLS AND BOYS

The present moment in the history of comparative education is greatly influenced by the EFA movement (see Chapter Three), with its emphasis on increasing the enrolment of girls in schools. National and regional statistics collected and reported by governments and international organizations such as UNESCO, UNICEF (United Nations Children's Fund), and the World Bank provide comparative educators with a tool to compare and contrast what is happening in different countries and regions throughout the world. Educational data are disaggregated (divided up) by sex/gender, enabling us to examine and compare the situation for girls and boys, and women and men, broadly and quantitatively. Efforts of this type draw upon equalitarian approaches to gender equality.

From a comparative perspective, what can the current education statistics tell us about the educational experiences of girls and boys throughout the world? Seventy-seven million primary school-age children are out of school worldwide.[21] Fifty percent of these children live in sub-Saharan Africa, while 19 percent live in South and West Asia.[22] Roughly 44 million (57 percent) of all out-of-school children are girls.[23] Out-of-school children are those of official primary age not enrolled in school.[24] The largest number of out-of-school children are in Nigeria (8.1 million in total, of which 4.3 million are girls), Pakistan (6.4 million, of which 4.2 million are girls), India (4.5 million, of which 3.9 million are girls), and Ethiopia (3.6 million, of which 1.8 million are girls).[25] Seven of the eight countries that have 1 million to 2 million children out of school are in sub-Saharan Africa.[26] An analysis of data on 77 million "out-of-school primary school-aged children" revealed that 7.2 million were children who had dropped out, 23 million were likely to enrol later (when older than the official age to enter Grade One), while "46.6 million were unlikely to ever enrol."[27]

In the past decade, the expansion of access to primary education in developing countries has brought the number of out-of-school children down by more than 20 million,[28] largely because of the elimination of primary school fees resulting from the push for universal primary education and EFA. This policy change has been of particular benefit to girls in developing countries, as evidenced by the steady reduction in the gender gap favouring boys in terms of primary school enrolment. Global initiatives such as the Millennium Development Goals and EFA goals emphasize gender parity and equality in schools worldwide.

When examining enrolment figures, we need to consider certain realities that can negatively affect statistical accuracy. Firstly, in some countries, a child can remain registered at school even when she or he is absent a great deal of the time.[29] Secondly, UNESCO estimates that over one-third of out-of-school children live in countries affected by conflict, where sufficient or consistent (or sometimes any) statistical data collection is impossible.[30] (See Chapter Eight by Karen Mundy and Joseph P. Farrell for a further discussion of educational statistics.)

In terms of the composition of enrolment statistics at the primary level globally, gender parity has been achieved by roughly 120 of the 181 countries from which UNESCO was able to collect data in 2004. Of the 26 countries with less than 90 percent of students in primary school in 2000, the gender gaps, which favoured boys, were eliminated in only four countries.[31]

When examining primary out-of-school statistics through a gender lens worldwide, we find that there were 117 girls not in school for every 100 boys.[32] "For every two boys unlikely to ever enrol there were nearly three girls."[33] Regionally, the greatest gender disparities were found in the Arab States, South and West Asia, and Africa. At the country level, the greatest disparities favouring boys were in Yemen (184 primary aged girls out of school for every 100 boys), Iraq (176), India (136), and Benin (136). In contrast, disparities favouring girls can be seen regionally in Latin America and the Caribbean, where 96 girls are out of school for every 100 boys.[34]

Who is out of school? Children whose families are poor and who live in rural areas are most likely to have never enrolled in school or have dropped out. In sub-Saharan Africa and South Asia, rural children account for more than 80 percent of the total number of children not attending school.[35] Whether a child's mother has had some schooling also positively affects the likelihood of the child's attending school. UNESCO found that "on average, a child whose mother has no education is twice as likely to be out of school as one whose mother has some education."[36] When examining why children drop out, UNESCO researchers found that factors relating to poverty and rural location had a greater impact on the likelihood of a child's being out of school than a mother's lack of education or the gender of the child.[37] In a study of eight countries in sub-Saharan Africa, with the exception of Namibia, "girls are more likely never to attend school than boys."[38] Furthermore, children from marginalized groups facing discrimination account for 70 percent of all out-of-school primary-school-aged children.[39] "Excluded subgroups are based on tribal, ethnic, linguistic, or traditional occupation classifications, such as the "untouchable" occupations of the lowest caste in India."[40]

While issues of access to education are important, it is also very important to examine how the girls and boys who do go to school progress through their educational systems. Educational statistics show that while more and more children are entering Grade One globally, many children in some regions are unable to progress through primary school. For example, in sub-Saharan Africa, only 57 percent of children who enrol succeed in making it to the last grade in primary school.[42] Within sub-Saharan Africa, fewer than 40 percent of children who begin Grade One in Chad, Equatorial Guinea, Malawi, Mozambique, Nigeria, and Rwanda progress to the last grade of primary school.[43] In comparison, 80 percent of primary students in the Arab States, and 82 percent in South and West Asia progress to the last grade of the primary cycle.[44]

> The obstacles to female education stem from many factors: national educational policies that affect boys and girls differently; uneven distribution of primary schools, especially in rural areas; lack of schools for girls in systems segregated by sex; shortage of female teachers and general reluctance among females who have their certification to teach in isolated rural areas or in urban slums; perceived irrelevance of primary school curricula to women's employment possibilities; late entry of girls in school and increased likelihood of pregnancy or preparation for marriage; and restrictions placed on the physical mobility of older girls.[41]
> —Mary Chamie

In terms of academic achievement of girls and boys once in school, "girls tend to perform as well as or better than boys."[45] With the exception of sub-Saharan Africa, "girls are also generally more likely to stay in school than boys."[46] While this is the situation in many Latin American and Caribbean countries, gender inequalities favouring girls are particularly acute in Chile, where "poor boys are four times more likely to leave school early and enter the workforce than are poor girls."[47]

Gender disparities favouring boys grow wider at the secondary school level in many developing countries. Only one-third of all the countries from which UNESCO collected data in 2004 reached gender parity at the secondary school level.[48] At this level, gender disparities favouring girls occur in countries where most of the children of the appropriate age group go to secondary school, whereas in countries with low enrolment rates the gender disparities tend to favour boys. Within the sub-Saharan African region, rural girls from poor families account for the greatest proportion of children excluded from secondary school.[49] In Afghanistan, Chad, Guinea, Togo, and Yemen, for every 100 boys who are enrolled in secondary school there are fewer than 50 girls.[50] By contrast, gender disparities in enrolment favour girls in the Dominican Republic, Honduras, Kiribati, Lesotho, and Suriname, where "roughly 120 girls are enrolled for every 100 boys."[51]

Adult literacy statistics reveal similar patterns to those just presented. Women comprise 64 percent (500 million) of the 781 million adults (age 15 and older) worldwide who currently do not have basic literacy skills.[52] According to UNESCO, an illiterate person "cannot read and write with understanding a simple statement from their everyday life."[53] Regionally, literacy rates are lowest in South and West Asia (59 percent), sub-Saharan Africa (61 percent), and the Arab States (66 percent), with fewer literate women than men. Gender disparities favouring men are greatest in sub-Saharan Africa (primarily West and Central Africa), in South and West Asia (notably in Afghanistan, Bangladesh, India, Nepal and Pakistan), and in the Arab States (especially Morocco and Yemen). Lesotho is an exception, where the gender disparity favours women.[54]

When considering these literacy statistics, it is important to note two points. Firstly, despite attempts to obtain accurate statistics, there is a tendency towards overestimation of the number of people who are literate.[55] Secondly, being illiterate adds another layer of vulnerability to women, particularly with regards to the AIDS epidemic. Since biologically "women are at least twice as likely as men to become infected with HIV during sex,"[56] an illiterate woman is unable to read about how to protect herself from becoming infected and, if she is HIV positive, how take care of herself and prevent transmitting the virus to others.

As illustrated in this section, the collection and reporting of educational statistics disaggregated by sex/gender provides critical information enabling comparative educators to better understand certain aspects of educational access and achievement within countries, regions, and globally. Annual publications, such as UNESCO's *EFA Global Monitoring Report* and UNICEF's *State of the World's Children*, enable us to compare statistics over time. It is important to note, however, that without contextual meaning, these statistics can be easily misinterpreted. For example, while statistics reveal that girls in Chile are far more likely to stay in school than boys, who often leave school to work, we cannot assume that these girls are actually considered "equal" within their society or that they have equal opportunities with the education they do attain. Furthermore, statistics can be used negatively. For example, some might consider the problem of gender inequality solved once a country, such as Malawi (see Chapter Three), reaches parity in access at the primary level. But we know that there are other issues at play causing gender inequalities within the education system that need to be addressed. Thus, despite insights gained through the examination of educational statistics, much more information is needed to understand why things are as they are.

Qualitative research studies help to bridge this gap in understanding, by providing valuable insights into the lived experiences of girls and women as we listen to their often-unheard voices. We now examine such a lived reality, in a case study of female students in Eritrea, Africa.

COMPARISON CASE: EXPERIENCES AND PERCEPTIONS OF SUCCESSFUL FEMALE GRADE 11 STUDENTS IN ERITREA

The findings presented in this section are from a study conducted by Kara Janigan in 2001 to investigate factors that enabled some girls to succeed, against great odds, in graduating from secondary school in rural Eritrea.[57] Eritrea is a small country in the Horn of Africa. After a 30-year liberation struggle, Eritrea gained its independence from Ethiopia in 1991. Categorized as one of the least developed countries, Eritrea has some of the lowest social and economic indicators in the world. In 2005, Eritrea's Gross National Income per capita was US$200.[58]

Educational statistics, appropriate to the time of the research, reveal how few female students were able to move up through the Eritrean educational system. According to 1996 statistics, "for every 100 girls starting Grade 1, only 40 will graduate from Grade 5."[59] Even fewer graduate from secondary school. In 1998–1999, the senior secondary school gross enrolment ratio[60] for girls was 13.4 percent compared to 21.2 percent for boys.[61] In that same year, a female student was twice as likely as a male to repeat a grade in secondary school.[62]

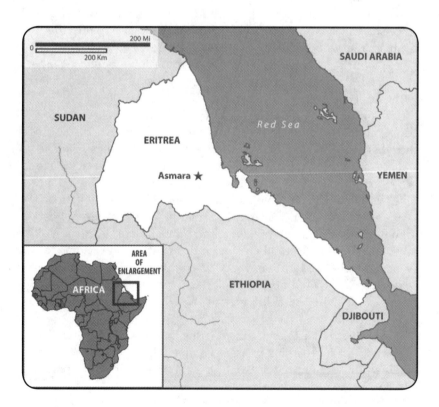

While these statistics are telling, qualitative research is needed to provide insight into the reasons why so few girls are able to successfully complete primary and secondary school. Through individual interviews in the Eritrean study, female students in Grade 11 shared their perceptions of the obstacles they faced, as well as the factors that enabled them to complete their secondary schooling while the vast majority of young women their age had married and left school. By listening to these students and better understanding their lived experiences, we gain valuable insights that can be used by educators to improve the educational opportunities for not only Eritrean girls but also for girls facing similar situations in other countries.

The research was conducted in Debarwa, a rural village 29 kilometres south of the capital, Asmara. While the students interviewed — roughly half of all Grade 11 female students — ranged from 16 to 20, the average age was 19. All were Christian except one, who was Muslim. All were from the dominant ethnic group, Tigrinya. Seventeen students were single, one was married with a child, and one had been engaged since she was 14. Nine students were from Debarwa, while 10 came from smaller neighbouring or distant villages. Two students, from a neighbouring village, walked to and from school daily; the others stayed in Debarwa, two with relatives, three in rented rooms, and three in the local convent.

The students came from relatively similar socio-economic backgrounds, with two-thirds from farming families. The heads of the other students' families worked for the government or were local traders. Just under half of the students' mothers (nine) never attended school, six had received some primary education (Grade Three, Four, or Five), while two had completed Grade Six or Seven (junior secondary). Of the students' fathers, just over one-quarter (five) had never attended school, while six had completed Grade Three, Four, or Five. Unlike any of these students' mothers, four fathers had received some senior secondary school education, with two completing this cycle, and one father had obtained a post-secondary education. Ten students came from a family with five children or fewer, while the largest family had nine children.

This study attempted to uncover the complexity of the students' lives and decision-making process. We now highlight the themes that emerged throughout the research process in relation to supports for and barriers to girls' education.

Parents' Economic Support for Girls' Education

When discussing their experiences, the students identified several issues related to the ways they received support from their mothers and fathers to enable them to be successful students. Economic support, attributed to the father, was predominantly mentioned. One of the most critical factors mentioned by the students was their fathers' and mothers' attitudes regarding the age at which their daughter should marry. These attitudes are intricately linked to their perceptions of the value of education for their daughter. Also of significance was how these daughters expressed the ways their mothers and fathers, directly and indirectly, had expressed their belief in their daughters' academic capability and potential.

Despite the fact that primary education is compulsory in Eritrea, parents decide whether or not to send their daughter(s) or son(s) to school. Parents also often determine at what grade their child will stop attending school. While many different factors could affect this decision, economic factors are often primary for poor families. Economic factors include the direct costs of schooling (such as fees, uniforms, textbooks, and the number of children in the family) and indirect costs (such as time lost which could have otherwise been used for labour).

Several students mentioned the economic support they received, noting how difficult it was for their families to cover school costs, such as books, uniforms, and yearly fees. The greatest economic sacrifices appeared to be made by the families of the three students renting a room in Debarwa. Each student came from a village located one-and-a-half to two-and-a-half hours' walk away from school. Their parents had chosen to undergo economic sacrifices to enable their daughters to have a better chance at academic success by eliminating the difficulties inherent in walking several kilometres daily to and from school. Each student attributed this decision to their fathers, all of whom were farmers. Each of the three girls spoke of their fathers' anger at having been unable to receive more than just a few years of schooling. Despite the economic struggles, all 19 students came from families who sent all their children, girls and boys, to school, though not every sibling progressed as far in school as had these students. For example, one student's sister got married at 18 after completing Grade Seven. This reflects the ways in which parental educational decisions intersect with economic issues, perceptions of appropriate age for marriage, the value of education in relation to aspirations for their child, and the child's academic performance.

Rejection of Early Marriage

Parents play a critical role in the decision-making process regarding the life choices of their children, especially as many marriages are arranged. The age considered suitable for a girl to be married varies among different communities throughout Eritrea. In some areas, marriages are arranged for girls as young as nine.[63] Students in this study spoke of female friends and peers who, as one student stated, were "married by force" when they were 14 or 15. Another noted that "fathers that live outside town, they think a girl should be married at eighth grade." Since it is extremely rare that a married girl or boy continues to attend primary or secondary school, marriage effectively closes the door on a student's further education. Since, on average, males get married at a later age than females in Eritrea, they often have greater educational opportunities.

When speaking of the support they had received, the vast majority of the students noted the importance of their fathers' and/or mothers' rejection of early marriage for their daughter, enabling her to continue her schooling. The married student who participated in this research spoke of how she had been encouraged both by her parents and her husband, who is a teacher, to complete her secondary school education. Some of the students' parents expressed their rejection of early marriage for their daughter explicitly while others did so implicitly. One-quarter of the students mentioned that the head of their family, which in some cases was their mother, had explicitly rejected early marriage for their daughter. Several students spoke of how their fathers had refused marriage offers by telling the prospective husband that their daughter must finish school before getting married. Other parents urged their daughter to finish school, thus implicitly rejecting marriage at that time. One student, whose mother had been married when she was 11 or 12, recalled her mother saying, "At that time I was a child."

The student who had been engaged since she was 14 was allowed by her family to delay her marriage until she completed Grade 11. This student described how, if she were accepted into a post-secondary institution once she was married, her husband would then decide whether she might continue her studies. Another form of rejecting early marriage can be seen in the families who allowed their daughters to live at the convent, since two of the three students living at the convent clearly expressed their plans to become Catholic Sisters.

Four students spoke of how their mother and/or father had told them to decide for themselves who they would marry. One student stated, "My mother says, 'Don't marry. Complete your school. After that you will do whatever you like'." Another, speaking of her father, said "He is always encourag[ing] me to finish my school. After that, by selection yourself, I will do the marriage."

Academic Excellence

It is important to note that these girls were exceptional students, as the majority of them had never repeated a grade, whereas Eritrean educational statistics in 1999 show that, on average, it takes a student up to eight or nine years to obtain five years of primary education.[64] Students may do poorly in school for any number of reasons including absenteeism, lack of adequate nutrition, and/or inability to complete their homework. Repeating a grade or grades can have a particular negative effect on the educational opportunities of female students, when considered in relation to marriage norms for girls. A girl who begins Grade One at age seven and takes eight years to complete primary school will be 15 when she finishes. As evidenced by the students' comments, this is considered by many in rural Eritrea to be a suitable age for a girl to marry and to stop going to school. This calculation helps to explain why, although the average age of both female and male students was 19, only 15 percent of all Grade 11 female students at the Debarwa Senior Secondary School were 20 years old or older, compared with 37.5 percent of all Grade 11 male students.[65]

Parental Encouragement

When speaking of the support they received, the students spoke predominantly about their fathers having enabled them to continue their schooling. As one student stated, "My mother help[s] me but not more than my father." This encouragement is likely due to the traditional role of the father as the negotiator when marriages are arranged. Also the fathers, as often the main and only wage earners, were seen by the students as suppliers of the funds to cover the direct costs of their schooling. According to the students' comments, their fathers appeared to be the ultimate decision makers in the family, with the mothers having a voice in the decision-making process, particularly regarding certain issues such as the arranging of their children's marriage. While the fathers were most often the first to be mentioned, many of the students later said that their mothers shared the same views and attitudes on these issues of marriage and schooling as their fathers.

Integrally linked to parental attitudes regarding age of marriage for their daughters are parental attitudes about the value of education and their aspirations for their daughters. Through their words and actions, the research participants' fathers and/or mothers demonstrated that they believed education was of value for their daughter and, most importantly, that she was capable of succeeding academically. Furthermore, one-quarter of the students noted explicitly that their parents were motivated by the belief that, once educated, they would be able to get paid employment. When speaking about other girls in her very small village, one student said, "Parents [think], for the girls, marriage is useful. They think education is not useful for girls. That is the problem, main problem."

Students' Own Attitudes to Schooling, Higher Education, and Work

As for the students themselves, all were adamant about not wanting to marry until they had completed their schooling and had obtained a job, with the exception of the students living at the convent who, once finished school, intended to become Sisters (and the one who was already married). The vast majority of the students stressed a strong and significant connection between education and employment, as they believed that only by receiving a high level of education would they have a chance of obtaining paid employment in the future. In a typical statement, one student said, "I'm thinking I do not like to get married at this age but after I finished my school and I get a special job. And especially my husband he have to get a job. After that, it is life." Another student expressed her aspirations by stating, "I hope to get … to enter university. It's the only thing I hope with my thinking. I always think when I sleep to go to university only. After I get to university nothing … any work I can take from the university I can work."

Twelve of the students spoke explicitly of their hope to score high enough in their matriculation exams to gain admittance to either the University of Asmara or the Teacher Training Institute. A few mentioned the desire to become a doctor, a teacher, or an engineer. One student said, "In the future, I want to go to the university and I want to be a doctor. I want to help many people to cure." While a few students were very specific about their aspirations, most were not. They spoke about getting a job, any job. One stated, "If you learn or if you study very well you will get any work because in the world there is learning only."

As one student said, "I don't want marriage. I finish school. I get a job. Then I [will be] helping country and family." This desire to give back to their family was commonly expressed. Another student expressed her appreciation for all the help she had received from her family and how she hopes to help them in the future.

The aspiration to get paid employment was also influenced by the desire of some students to remain in the public sphere. These students linked early marriage and a lack of education to young women's being restricted to staying primarily in their home. As one student put it, "If finishing school, I can get job, I can working. I can get money by myself. If I not finishing school only my husband is get job, only staying in the house. That's not good."

Another critical factor was parents' allocation of their daughters' time. Issues related to the availability of time to study are important throughout a student's schooling years, but are most critical for Grade 11 students because their matriculation exam results are the sole determinant of whether they will gain admittance to a post-secondary institution. In addition, high marks ensure a greater likelihood of a student being admitted into a program of their choosing. Although many students throughout Eritrea write the matriculation exams each year, only a very small percentage are able to continue their studies.

Lack of Time to Study

For the majority of the students in this study, a shortage in available time to study was identified as the greatest difficulty they faced. This was attributed to the allocation of their time, particularly in regards to household responsibilities. Students living at home with their families described daily routines that included cooking, cleaning, washing clothes, and fetching water and wood. In Eritrea, these tasks are traditionally considered girls' work. In a typical comment, one student noted how:

> the work in their house [is] totally finished by the girls. Boys [do] not work in the house. That is the problem. For example, my brother in my house, I am work anything in the house, cooking, but he studies only your books, only his books. You do not help me with the work. [She laughs.] I am all, the work is finished by me.

Many students pointed out that although girls' work is usually in the house, during harvest time girls may also be needed to help with the family farming. One student described how "there are some girls who are as clever as boys. But mostly girls are not good [students] ... more work is for girls, especially in the harvest time, all boys and girls are working together but during other free times as we as working in the house boys are playing or studying."

Many students equated their mothers' support with their opportunity to allocate their time by lessening their household responsibilities. This was expressed through students' statements such as "I am in the school. My mother helping me in the house" or "She gives me time to read in the house." Several of the students' mothers had told them explicitly to study and not to work in the house.

Despite their mothers' urging, several students spoke of their personal sense of obligation to work in their home. Even when these students appeared to have the possibility of extra study time, their sense of familial obligation did not allow them to take advantage of this opportunity. As one student explained, there was a strong sense that it was wrong not to help. When describing the work her family was doing at harvest time, she said, "Always we are working all the day because we should help our parents because we are their children. Even when they say 'don't work,' how can we as they are working?"

Seven of the 19 students described a daily routine that allowed for study time at night after completing the household work. One student explained, "After helping my mother, I study." Many students echoed a variation of this statement. Some also mentioned waking up early in the morning, especially during exam times, to study before helping their mothers with housework. A few spoke of waking up in the middle of the night for an hour or two of quiet uninterrupted study time. One student described how, after going to bed at nine o'clock at night, she set her alarm clock to wake her at one o'clock in the morning so that she could study for a couple of hours before going back to sleep. "I like to study in night. There is no ... nothing noise." She explained that, while she set her alarm to wake her up each night, if she was too tired to study she would go back to sleep. Similarly, another student described that at two o'clock in the morning, "that time is very nice, not noisy." She read her notes and books for about an hour and a half before going back to sleep. "If I tired, I sleep but always I wake up."

One student described her seemingly exceptional circumstances. Being the eldest and only girl in her family, she described how her younger brothers were required to take on work, such as fetching water and wood, even though this is considered girls' work. This allowed her more time and energy to devote to her studies.

Students living at the convent and those who lived in a neighbouring village also spoke of a shortage of time to study. Students living at the convent mentioned how similar household responsibilities, along with the responsibility to attend various church services, left them with little time to study. A shortage of time to study was most acute for students living in neighbouring villages, as they had household responsibilities as well as having to walk long distances to and from school daily. Their journeys range in time from one and a half hours to two and a half hours each way.

In contrast to the students living at home or at the convent, the four students living on their own had no difficulty finding time to study. Three of these students were renting a room and one was living on her own, in a traditional house inherited by her family from her grandparents. All four of these students had only themselves to take care of. One student spoke of how her life, renting a room in Debarwa, differed greatly from when she had lived at home while attending the junior secondary school in her village. She described how, when living at home, there was "no time to study." When asked what difficulties she faced at the time of the study, she replied, "No difficulties."

This case study demonstrates many aspects of the difficulties that female students must overcome in order to graduate from high school in an environment such as theirs in rural Eritrea. Factors such as distance from school, place of residence, and other domestic obligations played a strong role. Encouragement and financial help from parents were important supports to give girls opportunities to complete their education.

The key variable in this study was the fact that most of the families lived in rural areas where human labour was needed to work the soil to produce food and to perform domestic duties. In this context, girls' and women's work is necessary for survival. Families need to make a calculation as to what labour they can forfeit in order for their children to remain in school and to eventually obtain employment in the urban sector. But these factors are not unique to Africa. They were also salient in industrial countries within the last few hundred years, as we will see when we look at the history of gender and education in Canada.

GENDER INEQUALITY IN EDUCATION IN CANADA

The historical evolution of gender equality in Canada (and more specifically in Ontario) illustrates both persistent aspects of gender inequality in education and the fact that gendered practices evolve and change over time, and vary significantly across cultural settings. In this section we review two separate histories of education in the 18th, 19th, and early 20th centuries that have shaped gender equality in present day Canadian education. We also look briefly at issues of gender equality in Canadian schools today.

For residents of European origin, gendered educational experiences can be traced back to the voluntary provision of schooling in the early years of British colonialism. European settler children learned from their parents or other adults in the community in a mainly agrarian and extractive economy.[66] Some children had tutors, learned in church or mission settings, or attended small private schools. However, by 1807 government-funded district grammar schools were established in Upper Canada (Ontario), while local common schools emerged in 1816. These common schools were attended by both girls and boys. The grammar schools (forerunners of high schools) were considered more elite institutions: by the 1850s and 1860s there was an attempt to reduce or curtail the attendance of girls there, since it was thought that attendance at grammar schools "ought to be tied to [boys'] academic ambition and ability rather than to [girls'] social status or wealth."[67] In 1871, after Canadian Confederation in 1867, Upper Canada became the Province of Ontario and passed the School Act, under which each municipality had to provide a free common school for girls and boys. All non-Aboriginal Ontario children between seven and 12 were required to attend school for at least four months of any school year. The common school was then called the public school, and was funded with public money to achieve public goals.[68]

Although girls were admitted to common and grammar schools, the design of these schools indicated a grave mistrust of the idea of educating girls and boys together.

> Common school architecture and pedagogy as well as Education Office advice throughout the period insisted on separate entrances, separate playgrounds, separate seating and even separate recitations for boys and girls "except in the primary department and there too when practicable." And where most of the students were adolescents, as increasingly seems to have been the case in the grammar schools, segregation seems more important still.[69]

The greatest barrier to higher education for girls was the passage of a Council of Public Instruction regulation in 1865 that allowed for the admission of girls into the grammar schools on passing the appropriate examinations, but excluded them from taking the classical course that was the prerequisite for entry into the university or the professions. As Alison Prentice explains, it was not envisaged that a "lady" would be pursuing higher education or indeed any form of paid employment. "Significantly, education and power were masculine. The intellectual student grew up into 'masculine maturity and vigour'; the college graduate appeared as '*a man*'; and the purpose of educating boys was to impart to them a 'manly and Christian energy.'"[70] The intersection of social class and gender bias meant that upper class girls were seen as not needing higher education or employment because they were going to marry wealthy men and were, in any case, "ill-adapted for the various professions open to young gentlemen, to the rough games of boys, or even to higher education."[71] On the other hand, girls of the lower classes, who would have had to work for a living, were seen as "low and vulgar"; it was considered "better that grammar school boys not know that girls could be 'pert and bold.'"[72] "The occupations of employed women who were not ladies, or even of employed ladies, were rarely if ever discussed by leading Upper Canadian school promoters. The education of girls in the public system, if referred to at all, was most frequently discussed in very negative terms."[73] By 1869, however, the Education Department had to rescind this provision in order to qualify for the provincial grant to education.[74]

Notions of gender difference also shaped teacher training institutions (called normal schools) in the period between the 1800s and 1930. Strict rules were enforced concerning respectable behaviour for future teachers. "At the Normal School in Toronto, male and female students were not permitted to address each other in the school, let alone meet outside."[75] After graduation, the careers of male and female teachers took different trajectories, with male teachers being much better paid and in positions of administration, while female teachers were relegated to less lucrative positions with less chance for promotion and with stringent rules that forced them to give up their jobs if they married. As late as the 1950s, women were expected to retire from teaching upon marriage. Reflecting the entrenched differentiation of male and female teachers, elementary school teachers' unions in Ontario were divided by gender until 1998, when the Ontario Public School Teachers Federation (for men) and the Federation of Women Teachers' Association of Ontario (for women) amalgamated to create the Elementary Teachers' Federation of Ontario. After secondary schools began to employ women, the Ontario Secondary School Teachers Federation included both genders, although it remained male-dominated until recent years. The history of schooling and the teaching profession in Ontario is inextricably linked to issues of gender, and many of these issues are still salient in the schools and classrooms of today.[76]

Another important dimension of gender inequality in Canada grew out of the colonial education of Canada's First Peoples during the 19th and 20th centuries. In contrast to the dynamics of gender and class highlighted in the education of European-descended Canadians, here it is the intersection of gender, colonialism, and ethnicity that has produced and reinforced gender inequality.

Upon the arrival of the Europeans in what is now Canada, the First Nations of that land had already developed a great diversity of sex-specific cultural practices and beliefs, which had been passed down through many generations. These practices differed according to each Indigenous nation; for example, in Canada, many of the Eastern and West Coast First Nations (such as Mohawk, Haida, and Kwakiutl) had matriarchal societies, in which women held the decision-making power and rights of ownership. A man could act as chief, but only if chosen by the "clan mothers," and he could similarly be removed from power if the women disagreed with his politics. Plains cultures (such as Blackfoot, Nakoda, and Cree) tended to be more patriarchal; however, a close sense of gender interdependence was prevalent as the survival of a society depended intimately on the participation of both men and women in their respective roles (such as hunting versus raising of children).[77]

Beginning in the early 1600s, formal education was introduced to the First Nations through missionary activity. At the end of the 19th century, public authorities in both English and French Canada launched efforts to school their First Nations populations (see Chapter Four for a further discussion of this topic). This process had multiple effects on Indigenous concepts of gender roles, values, and practices, as well as on other aspects of First Nations life. Girls and boys were taken away from their parents to live in residential schools, where European constructs of gender roles were imposed through lessons of domestic servitude for girls and manual labour for boys.[78] Federal legislation enacted after 1869 institutionalized gender inequalities by introducing patriarchal rules for determining Indian status, band membership, and rights to reserve residency.[79] Schooling and the laws meant to "modernize" First Nations communities had the paradoxical impact of eroding important aspects of female authority and leadership that had characterized earlier eras in Canadian Aboriginal societies.

How has gender inequality and efforts to deal with it changed in Canada over the past century? As in many rich, industrialized countries, girls' and women's access to education has steadily improved in Canada over the past 100 years. Today, Canada's federal government reports that women are achieving higher levels of educational attainment than men: they are more likely than men to be high school graduates; they make up the majority of full-time students in most university departments; women in the 25- to 29-year-old age category are more likely than men to have university degrees. In keeping with equalitarian notions of gender, Status of Women Canada proudly notes that "this is a reversal of historic trends and indicates that policies aimed at improving women's educational outcomes have achieved a degree of success."[80]

These gains have been hard won. They are the result of active organizing and advocacy among women's organizations, teachers' unions, and academic researchers, whose efforts were especially important from the late 1960s to the early 1980s. Educational systems across Canada expanded rapidly in this period, and a second wave of feminist organizing swept across North America. During this period, the focus was not only on expanding female access to higher levels of education, but also on changing the content of the school curriculum: efforts to remove sex-role stereotyping from textbooks and courses of study multiplied rapidly. Since the 1970s, sex-role stereotyping has been repeatedly identified as a key educational issue contributing to woman's inequality in Canada as articulated in reports by both the Royal Commission on the Status of Women in Canada in 1970 and the Royal Commission on Learning in Ontario in 1995.[81] At the same time, scholarship and training programs to encourage women to enter higher levels of education proliferated. Teachers' unions have also fought to improve the position of women in the higher administrative levels of education and in implementing employment-equity policies within school boards.[82]

Nonetheless, many of the earlier dimensions of gender inequality have persisted in Canadian education, and feminist scholars continue to raise questions about best approaches for achieving greater gender equality in Canadian schools. An enormous gap exists between men and women in the wages earned for equal levels of educational attainment, and women have only slowly made inroads in male-dominated fields of study. In 1997, women with university degrees earned 74 percent of their male counterparts' income for full-time full-year work; with other post-secondary diploma or certificate, 71 percent; with some post-secondary, 75 percent; some secondary school, 65 percent; and less than Grade Nine, 70 percent.[83] The impact of motherhood on educational attainment remains severe for women: in 1998, for all young women and men, 64 percent of young women aged 22–24 with dependent children left high school before graduating, compared to 28 percent of young men aged 22–24 with children.[84] Gender inequality in educational attainment is also heavily apparent in today's First Nations communities: "In 1996, over 28.8% of Registered Indian women living on reserve had less than a grade 9 education compared to 15.3% of Registered Indian women living off reserve. Furthermore, Aboriginal women with a university degree experienced an unemployment rate of 7.2% compared to a rate of 27% for those with less than grade 9 education."[85]

Many critics have argued that the Canadian gender equality approach has focused too much on the attitudes and aspirations of the *individual* girl or woman as the key factor in her opportunity and capacity to compete for the educational and occupational rewards in capitalist society. This approach, based on liberal equalitarian assumptions, claims to be non-sexist and focuses on adding relevant curricular content and education about non-traditional jobs to redress the imbalance caused by the omission of material relevant to girls' lives. In reality, this approach holds the male model of achievement as the standard, and its influence is still prevalent today.[86] Feminist scholars in Canada take a more structural, conflict approach to issues of gender inequality in Canadian schools: they argue that changes in education need to be matched by broader forms of social transformation. Frustration with equalitarianism has led to the development of "anti-sexist" philosophies and initiatives that focus on building an awareness of the systemic nature of sexism. For example, workshops and conferences for students are conducted that teach a critical approach to schooling and pedagogy, not only in relation to gender but also to race, ethnicity, and social class.[87]

More recently, research on gender and education in Canada and many other rich industrialized nations has taken a turn towards a greater emphasis on the lagging literacy attainment of boys. Canadian achievement results from the 2000 Programme for International Assessment (PISA) (described in Chapter Eight) provided evidence that "girls performed significantly better than boys on the reading test in all countries and in all ten Canadian provinces."[88] A wide number of explanations have been put forward to explain boys' underachievement in literacy. One explanation is that "boys and girls are born with different interests, motivations and abilities."[89] As one 10-year-old Canadian boy remarked, "It's mainly girls in the class that enjoy the reading. It's just not a boy habit to read."[90] Some suggest boys' poor performance is due to differing learning styles of girls and boys.[91] Others argue that boys' academic underachievement is a result of the "feminization" of schools and education.[92] Still others call attention to the need for data disaggregated by race, ethnicity, rural/urban location, and other factors that would reveal specifically which boys were performing poorly and potentially dispel the idea that all girls are performing better than all boys.[93]

Across Canada, policy-makers now widely recognize that sex-role stereotyping can also be discriminatory against boys and men, pressuring them to live up to so-called masculine norms. Sex-role stereotyping not only affects whether students understand reading as a "girl habit" but is often linked to gender-based violence, bullying, and sexual harassment in today's classrooms and schools. (See Chapter Ten for a discussion of conflict resolution and peacebuilding.) Children may become the victim of violence if they don't fit popular definitions of what it means to be a normal girl or boy. Bullying, which includes physical or verbal aggression, is recognized by the Ontario Ministry of Education as "an underestimated and pervasive problem in Ontario schools."[94] In terms of gender differences, some suggest "boys' aggressive behaviour often involves direct physical aggression, yelling, and assertions of status and dominance. In contrast, girls tend to use indirect aggression involving hostile acts that unfold in the context of social relationships (for example, gossiping and manipulating others to exclude a victim)."[95] In Ontario and elsewhere in Canada, safe schools initiatives are being implemented to respond to school violence and harassment. Innovative projects, such as the Roots of Empathy project and the Boys for Babies program, have been undertaken to socialize boys into nurturing and caring roles.[96] Such efforts move well beyond equalitarian notions of gender equity, drawing on notions of caring and nurturing typically associated with women to expand notions of masculinity.

CONCLUSION

In this chapter, we have attempted to illustrate how taking a comparative and international approach to issues of gender and education can be useful for educators. We have reviewed the ways gender and gender equality have been conceptualized and used in research studies of both a quantitative and qualitative nature, and looked at how sex/gender disaggregated statistics allow us to compare educational access and attainment of girls and boys worldwide. The two cases presented, of girls' experiences in 21st-century rural Eritrea, and of the history of gender equality in Ontario, Canada, illustrate some social factors that support and impede diverse girls' opportunities, illuminating how sex-role stereotyping (practices that perpetuate common ideas about what it means to be a girl/woman or a boy/man) have led to discriminatory practices in education. By looking at these two cases comparatively, we can also see that there are both similarities and differences in beliefs about gender roles and education in different cultural contexts. The Eritrea case highlights the educational experiences of the girls themselves at a particular point in time. The Canadian case, which looks at change over more than 100 years, highlights both persistent dimensions of gender inequality, and the important improvement in overall levels of access that were fought for by women. However, the Canadian experience also highlights two paradoxes: first, efforts to "modernize" Indigenous peoples through education have resulted in the erosion of the basis of women's power in First Nations societies. Second, even in a rich industrialized context, the gender equity implications of improvements in women's educational access and attainment are still sharply debated.

From a comparative perspective, some would see the question of gender equality in education as solved in the wealthier countries, but not in the poorer ones, based on enrolment statistics. Many in the Western world probably believe that opportunities for males and females to enter the educational institution of their choice are no longer restricted on the basis of gender, but there is much evidence that widespread gender-based harassment and violence in education still exists.[97] (See Chapter Ten).

Therefore, it is critical to recognize that teaching and learning remain heavily gendered in all parts of the world. One of our challenges, as educators, is to recognize gender bias within our own teaching contexts and practices and take action to address this bias. Exploring comparatively how issues of gender affect the way girls and boys access and experience education, in Canada and elsewhere, helps us to identify challenges and to raise questions about how to ensure that each child is able to learn effectively, in a safe environment, and to the best of her or his ability.

QUESTIONS FOR REFLECTION AND DISCUSSION

1. Think about your own family's experience of gender and education. Describe your own educational background, and trace your parents' and grandparents' experience of education in their lifetimes. What role did gender play in the educational experiences of the three generations of your family? (For example, discuss access to education, reasons for attending and/or dropping out, gender roles, academic ambitions or frustrations, and economic considerations.)

2. Compare the educational experiences of the female students in the Eritrean and Ontario examples presented in this chapter. Which factors were similar in shaping their education, and which were different? How do you think some of those factors operate in your local school system today?

3. Compare this chapter's international perspectives on gender and education with some present-day gender issues that may affect any of the following: your life as a teacher, the experiences of your various students (for example, wealthier and poorer, young and old, culturally diverse), interactions in your classroom, your future career trajectory.

SUGGESTED FILM: *WHAT'S GOING ON? GIRLS' EDUCATION IN INDIA*, PRODUCED BY RCN ENTERTAINMENT IN ASSOCIATION WITH THE UNITED NATIONS

This film explores the educational opportunities typically available to girls in India by telling the story of three girls, Aarti, Geetha, and Leala. Each girl is profiled in terms of her life circumstances and the challenges she faces relating to schooling.

30 minutes

SUGGESTIONS FOR FURTHER READING

Aikman, Sheila and Salina Sanou. "Pastoralist Schools in Mali: Gendered Roles and Curriculum Realities." In *Beyond Access: Transforming Policy and Practice for Gender Equality in Education*, edited by Sheila Aikman and Elaine Unterhalter. Oxford, UK: Oxfam, 2005, 181–95.

Arnot, Madeleine. "Gender Relations and Schooling in the New Century: Conflicts and Challenges." *Compare* 30, no. 3 (2000): 293–302.

Asamoah, Alex, Bagele Chilisa, Máiréad Dunne, Linda Dzama Forde, Nick Kutor, Fiona Leach, Tapologo Maundeni, and Richard Tabulawa. "Executive Summary." In *Gendered School Experiences: The Impact on Retention and Achievement in Botswana and Ghana*. Education Research Report No. 56. London: Department for International Development (DFID), 2005, vi–xiv, www.dfid.gov. uk/pubs/files/genschoolbotsghanaedpaper56.pdf.

Bonder, Gloria. "Altering Sexual Stereotypes through Teacher Training." In *Women and Education in Latin America: Knowledge, Power, and Change,* edited by Nelly P. Stromquist. London: Lynne Rienner Publishers, Inc., 1992, 229–49.

Brown, Shirley P., Alice E. Ginsberg, and Joan Poliner Shapiro. "Gender in Education: Contradictions and Connections." In *Gender in Urban Education: Strategies for Student Achievement*. Portsmouth, NH: Heinemann, 2004, 1–14.

*Coulter, Rebecca P. "Gender Equity and Schooling: Linking Research and Policy." *Canadian Journal of Education* 21, no. 4 (1996): 433–52.

Herz, Barbara, and Gene B. Sperling. "Executive Summary." In *What Works in Girls' Education: Evidence and Policies from the Developing World*. New York: Council on Foreign Relations, Inc., 2004, 1–16, www.cfr.org/content/publications/attachments/Girls_ Education_full.pdf.

Jayaweera, Swarna. "Women, Education and Empowerment in Asia." *Gender and Education* 9, no. 4 (1997): 411–23.

Liu, Jinghuan, Heidi Ross, Vilma Seeberg, and Guangyu Tan. "Grounds for Prioritizing Education for Girls: The Telling Case of Left-Behind Rural China." In *Education for All: Global Promises, National Challenges*, edited by David P. Baker and Alexander W. Wiseman. Oxford: Elsevier Ltd, 2007, 109–54.

Magno, Cathryn and Iveta Silova. "Gender Equity Unmasked: Democracy, Gender, and Education in Central/Southeastern Europe and the Former Soviet Union." *Comparative Education Review* 48, no. 4 (2004): 417–42.

*Raynor, Janet. "Educating Girls in Bangladesh: Watering a Neighbour's Tree." In *Beyond Access: Transforming Policy and Practice for Gender Equality in Education*, edited by Sheila Aikman and Elaine Unterhalter. Oxford: Oxfam, 2005, 181–95.

*Stromquist, Nelly P. "Gender Inequality in Education: Accounting for Women's Subordination." *British Journal of Sociology of Education* 11, no.2 (1990): 137–53.

Chapter Ten

Education for Conflict Resolution and Peacebuilding in Plural Societies: Approaches from Around the World

Kathy Bickmore

INTRODUCTION

Does education contribute to peace or impede its development? How might education help to build capacity for constructive conflict management among individuals and groups in contexts of social diversity? This chapter asks you to examine how the often-invisible, taken-for-granted, everyday patterns of non-violent conflict management and peaceful behaviour may be fostered (or impeded) by formal education (schooling) and non-formal education (other planned teaching and learning initiatives), in various national and cultural settings.

Conflict refers to disputes, distrust, and incompatible interests (among individuals, groups, nations, and the like). These underlying problems should not be confused with the responses they provoke, which include war and other forms of violence as well as a whole range of systemic and non-violent manifestations. Clearly fights and wars are more visible, and more damaging, than other approaches to conflict, but that doesn't mean they're more common:

> Actually, peace is not news because most people live in peace with their neighbors most of the time, and most countries live in peace with neighboring countries most of the time.... Educators must overcome the partial view of the human condition propagated by bad news in the headlines and by histories that emphasize battles and wars.[1]

What people experience as conflict, as well as how they handle it, depends on the social and cultural contexts that shape their learning and their options for responding. Based on analysis of anthropological evidence from many cultures, Marc Ross found that conflicts are rooted both in relatively tangible, socially structured interests (access to resources for fulfilling wants and needs), and in less tangible, culturally shaped narratives and interpretations (beliefs and values, fears and concerns — what matters to people and why).[2] Education alone cannot resolve structural issues that cause conflict, such as resource scarcity or concentration of power. However, it forms an important *part* of the development of conflict and peace, by influencing people's understandings, perceptions, values, skills, and relationships.

Peace and conflict education, like other kinds of comparative international education work described by Ruth Hayhoe and Karen Mundy in Chapter One, speaks to practical action as well as scholarly research. This chapter describes a wide range of educational practices that may influence conflict behaviour and non-violent coexistence, drawing insights from cases in diverse contexts around the world as well as from systematic international comparisons.

EDUCATION AND VIOLENCE

Unfortunately, schooling and other pedagogies may exacerbate and teach violence, at least as often as they teach constructive, non-violent responses to conflict.[3] Schools' hidden and/or explicit curricula often facilitate destructive expression and escalation of social conflict in various ways. These include by being a valued resource that is unequally distributed; by legitimizing national or ethnic chauvinism, blame, and intolerance of some peoples towards others; by disadvantaging some groups through language or grouping practices; by perpetrating physical punishment or not interrupting harassment; and by normalizing aggression and militarism. Such violence often disproportionately targets girls (see Chapter Nine by Kara Janigan and Vandra Lea Masemann) and marginalized groups, thereby deepening social inequality.[4] For example, Aboriginal peoples in North America were forced to attend residential schools, where physical, sexual, emotional, spiritual, and cultural violence were often inflicted, thereby deepening an ongoing legacy of oppression (see Chapter Four by Katherine Madjidi and Jean-Paul Restoule). Another example is the "Jim Crow" segregation of White and Black populations in the United States (and to some degree in Canada) in the 19th and 20th centuries, which supported and taught structural racism. Educational perpetuation of destructive conflict can become a vicious cycle because escalated conflict can make people less open and able to learn: "Conflict tends to reduce people's willingness to learn as well as what might be called agency — the capacity of individuals, families, communities, collectives, and systems to care for themselves."[5] Thus, education for non-violent conflict resolution and peacebuilding is not a simple matter of adding new learning activities; it often requires changing existing pedagogical practices.

Armed conflict (war, terrorism, and so forth) disrupts educational opportunities in all kinds of ways — for example, school buildings and equipment may be destroyed or redeployed for other uses, and teachers and/or students may be abducted, killed, missing, or forced to flee.[6] Furthermore, schools and teachers, because of their relationship to human rights as well as to their nation-state employers, may be specifically targeted in terrorism and war, as occurred for example in the United States–backed *contra* war against the Nicaraguan government during the 1980s.[7] Conversely, after Costa Rica abolished its army in 1948 and allocated the savings to public education, it became the most prosperous and peaceful country in Central America.[8] By 2005, 28 countries had followed suit by decommissioning their standing militaries.[9]

Paradoxically, even though education can exacerbate harmful social conflict, educational initiatives and changes can form essential parts of peacebuilding solutions. In addition to facilitating the development of skills and confidence, education can increase people's awareness of the nature and extent of a conflict, its negative consequences for weaker parties, and the possibility of change. This learning can then motivate people to act to shift the balance of power in unpeaceful relationships.[10] Conflict resolution education is likely to be easiest during the calmer phases of a conflict cycle (in long-range prevention, and in reconstruction after a peacemaking process has begun to work), rather than during outright violence. That said, the examples below show a wide range of educational initiatives, some of them applicable in even the most difficult and threatening situations.

Traditionally, international comparisons of education systems have seldom attended to conflict or peace issues but have focused instead on measuring generic educational outcomes such as literacy and numeracy, estimating economic benefits of schooling expenditures, and examining policy alternatives for issues such as school access, attainment, and cost. However, some recent research, using national-level statistics from 37 countries, suggests that these broad system factors — in particular, equity in opportunities to succeed in school — may be related to the incidence of violence within schools.[11] Motoko Akiba and her colleagues showed that schools' rates of violence are not necessarily determined by the violence or crime rates in their countries: First, schools are sometimes considerably safer than their surrounding environments. Second, they showed that the strongest statistical predictor of violence inside schools was a wide variation in academic achievement between the most-successful and least-successful students. School systems that offered support and remediation for students having difficulty tended to have lower reported rates of violence than more competitive systems that allowed some students to fail. The authors speculate that improving inclusive opportunities to succeed may reduce the frustration and negative competition that sometimes provoke violence. As with any large-scale, transnational scientific studies (see Chapter One), correlation between the imperfect indicators chosen to represent achievement equity and violence in this study does not by any means prove or explain what might *cause* increased or decreased violence. Yet whatever the complex causal links might be, this international study highlights a broad factor (institutionalized support for equitable opportunities to succeed in school) that may help to shape, boost, or limit smaller-scale initiatives for conflict resolution education.

There remains around the world a remarkable hope and faith in education's capacity to help communities to reconstruct and develop after devastating violence. For example, scholars believe that expanding and reforming schooling can help to overcome the "intellectual imperialism" causing violence and economic stagnation in post-colonial African countries,[12] or challenge systems of privilege and urban-rural inequity that could re-ignite violence after the civil war in El Salvador.[13] Often among the first initiatives in emergency assistance for refugees and other war-affected children at times of emergency is to establish schooling, even where there is no functioning nation-state to govern this education.[14] The threats, persecution, and flight that cause people to become refugees completely unravel the usual continuities in childhood socialization. Even in shorter-term refugee camp contexts, education is often seen as a key initiative for normalization and psycho-social wellness of children and as a feasible way to help mitigate the harmful impact and the likelihood of further violence.

Clearly, to transform destructive conflict patterns, it is important that people have access to education, but it is also important *what* and *how* they are taught. For example in Afghanistan, more than four million children returned to school in the first two years of (relative) peace early in this century; however, as of 2005, textbooks and teachers continued "to teach ethnic hatred and intolerance" in those schools.[15] Sobhi Tawil and Alexandra Harley (citing Ernest Gellner) argue that a "monopoly of legitimate education in modern nation-states may be more important than the monopoly of legitimate violence." In other words, public education may be more effective than military or policing measures in improving social cohesion, peace, and security.[16]

VALUES IN PEACE/CONFLICT EDUCATION

Peace and conflict education is unique in that it explicitly intends to change the world, to make it more humane. While education for peace may take a multitude of forms and particular objectives, it is the explicitly value-laden goal, to promote social change by nurturing a frame of mind, "a prism through which the pupils learn to view and evaluate topics and issues raised in the various subjects," that distinguishes it from other education.[17] This makes the implementation of peace and conflict education particularly dependent on the conditions, cultures, and levels of consensus in the environment where it is carried out.

Johan Galtung's theory of structural violence, mentioned in Chapter One, has had a pivotal impact on international peace/conflict education. This theory explains that systemic factors (such as repression, or poverty arising from inequitable trade relations) can be just as harmful as visible, overt violence.[18] Further, Galtung uses the term *cultural violence* to describe attitudes and inclinations, embedded in the individual and collective subconscious, that support and assume the legitimacy of such structural violence.[19] Galtung called the absence of overt physical violence at a given place and time *negative peace* — not meaning a bad state of affairs, but rather that there has been no sustainable resolution of the factors causing harm.

Peacekeeping security measures are designed to achieve negative peace (sometimes as a prerequisite to longer-term, more complex problem solving). In contrast, *positive peace* refers to the regularized presence of justice and non-violent conflict resolution processes (that is, mechanisms and support for sustainable, ongoing redress of

> "Peace research is about violence, a major form of violence is structural violence, the fight against structural violence is called liberation, and a good place for peace researchers in particular, and social scientists in general, to start is to start with oneself." [20]
> —Johan Galtung

structural violence as well as individual disputes). In the peace and conflict education work that builds on Galtung's theory, *peacemaking* (negotiation to identify creative, mutually acceptable resolutions to conflicts) is a necessary part of creating positive peace, but positive peace also requires *peacebuilding,* which involves long-term, complex processes of overcoming exploitation, marginalization, and dehumanization through building structural and cultural peace.[21]

Galtung's work foregrounds the unique yet complex role of values, imagination, and emotion in peacebuilding research and practice, and their ramifications for education. While some other research may appear neutral because it does not question the legitimacy of the status quo, research and practice in peace and conflict education assumes that the (violent) status quo is not acceptable, and facilitates re-imagining, building, and sustaining alternative, constructive approaches to conflict. Education can build participants' awareness of conflicts and alternatives, their skills and understanding of how to facilitate non-violent problem solving, their inclinations to delegitimize dehumanization and exploitation, and their experience with healthy and equitable relationships.[22] Thus, education about conflict inevitably embeds values, which may be explicit or implicit.

Richard Merelman's review of research in political socialization suggests how such values might be caught or taught differently in different kinds of social environments.[23] In relatively contested regimes (contexts of escalated inter-group conflict such as revolution or civil war, in which a large proportion of people do not support the legitimacy of the existing governance structure, such as in Northern Ireland, Israel-Palestine, or Somalia), children grow and learn in the context of highly visible value conflicts. In these contexts, they may develop little fear of conflict and some understanding of how conflicts work, although they may need to learn how to re-humanize and communicate across differences. By contrast, in relatively uncontested regimes (in which groups disagree but the stability of the existing government is not threatened, such as in Canada), Merelman suggests children also learn about conflict through the informal processes of growing up, as well as in school. But in this case, value conflicts and their roots in inter-group relations are less visible, and not necessarily viewed as legitimate by the adults in the community. In relatively uncontested situations, young people may have little experience with recognizing alternate viewpoints, and even may learn to view conflict as abnormal and dissenters as bad. In either case, peace and conflict education is value-laden, but these values may be more visible (contested) or more hidden (assumed, uncontested), and have different ramifications for people in different positions of social identity and privilege. People growing up in these different social contexts may glean from their environments, and consequently need from their schooling, different sets of skills and understandings.

Some peace and conflict education initiatives, including the international *Hague Agenda for Peace and Justice for the 21st Century*,[24] emphasize the importance of persuading people to accept core values such as non-violence, tolerance, justice (cross-cultural equity, non-sexism, non-racism, etc.), solidarity, human rights, and environmental sustainability.[25]

This "culture of peace" work embodies a maternalist approach, an intellectual descendant of the International League for New Education mentioned in Chapter One. One of its influential proponents is Betty Reardon, of UNESCO and Columbia University Teachers College. She argues that women's roles in many societies demonstrate that peaceful, nurturing behaviour occurs as naturally among

> "A culture of peace will be achieved when citizens of the world understand global problems, have the skills to resolve conflicts and struggle for justice non-violently, live by international standards of human rights and equity, appreciate cultural diversity, and respect the Earth and each other. Such learning can be only be achieved by systematic education for peace."[26]
> —Hague Agenda for Peace and Justice for the 21st Century

humans as does aggression, and that positive peacebuilding requires people to develop love for the "other," including the others each of us carry inside ourselves.[27]

By contrast, Galtung argues that too much value consensus would stifle diversity and creativity: "The line between education and indoctrination in this field is a very fine one."[28] Thus values are inescapably embedded in peacebuilding education, and correlated with the achievement of peaceful environments, but the road from here to there is not straightforward. To simply teach non-violent values, disconnected from the social-structural problems that give rise to violence, could be impositional.

There is remarkably little evidence that teaching values can reliably cause changes in behaviour.[29] Based on a review of research on anti-bias workshops and other social learning studies, Clark McCauley argues that "feet first" education (practising small changes in behaviour) is more likely to change hearts and minds. For example, McCauley shows that people have unlearned racism by engaging constructively in de-segregated situations where there was institutional support and sanction for non-discrimination—"head" following "feet," rather than the other way around. It is clear that peaceful and just behaviour is associated with different values from discrimination. However, it may not be very effective to teach the values of peace in isolation from support to practice peaceful behaviour.

The work of Paulo Freire has had a profound influence on peace and conflict educators' efforts to find ways to redress structural violence.[30] Campaigns to empower poor and marginalized people, through Freire's model of "conscientization" (discussed in Chapters One and Three) were mounted in contexts such as revolutionary Cuba (1960–61), El Salvador during its civil war (1980s), Nicaragua during the Sandinista regime (1980s), and Guinea-Bissau, West Africa, after its independence (1980s). The objective of these campaigns was to engage literacy learners in expressing the reality of their own oppression, so that they could rise up and transform their situations.[31] In practice, the stresses of ongoing violence, resource scarcity, and insufficient teacher training tended to reduce the capacity of some of these literacy campaigns to facilitate dialogue-based learning that would build upon the local cultural knowledge of participants, and led to top-down processes that took power back out of the hands of the people and left little room for conscientization to occur.

For example, it was easier to prepare standardized teaching materials, which also introduced and legitimized the new government regimes, than to elicit and encode wisdom from the lives of each local community.[33] However, other

> "Founding itself upon love, humility, and faith, dialogue becomes a horizontal relationship of which mutual trust between the dialoguers is the logical consequence."[32]
>
> —Paulo Freire

attempts to implement Freirian-based participatory learning to address structural violence have been more successful, for example in the *Movimento Sem Terra* (Landless Movement) in Brazil.[34] Thus, depending on context, underlying intentions, and modes of implementation, educational initiatives may help to alleviate elements of structural violence or may reinforce existing power structures.

IDENTITY-BASED CONFLICTS

Most escalated armed conflicts today are intrastate (civil and involving non-state insurgent groups), not interstate. These situations are very often understood as ethnic, or identity-based, conflicts.[35] Thus, a particular concern, which international comparative study is especially well-suited to help us understand, is how people develop antagonistic or oppositional group identities, how (in contrast) they learn to get along, and how education can facilitate or impede social transformation towards non-violent coexistence. Unfortunately, as previously mentioned, formal and non-formal education can, and often does, encourage people to hate the "other." Clive Harber describes the ways curriculum and textbooks used on different sides of many inter-group conflicts, such as in Bosnia and Herzegovina, Kosovo, and Cyprus, teach completely different narratives of identity, history, causation, and blame.[36] For example, Greek Cypriot teachers' nationalistic discourse in the classroom presents Turks and Turkish Cypriots as barbarians, and discourse about Greeks and Greek Cypriots in Turkish Cypriot classrooms is just as adversarial and dehumanizing, thereby building a culture of violence and exclusion.[37] Bosnia and Herzegovina and Lebanon have essentially separate parallel school systems and curricula teaching incompatible, mutually exclusive ideologies, and "national" identities in their various ethnic communities.[38] Violence against lower caste and Sinhalese or Tamil people has been legitimized in Indian and Sri Lankan schools; similarly, many Rwandan schools' and teachers' active support for dehumanization, and for unquestioning deference to the authority structure, paved the way for genocidal violence there in 1994.[39]

Since the cessation of escalated violence, Rwanda's government and educators have sought to promote national unity and reconciliation through eliminating the most egregious elements of the pre-1994 curriculum; most proposed new curriculum had not yet been implemented.[40] As of 2003, it has been illegal to classify students ethnically as Hutu, Tutsi, or Twa. However, Rwandan history was still not taught at all, "despite official encouragement to teach those elements of history which are not in dispute."[41]

Zsusza Mátrai shows how some school systems, such as in Greece, Hong Kong, and Hungary, emphasize nationalist identity in ways that deny or avoid conflictual questions of social diversity, leaving students unprepared to handle identity conflict challenges.[42] At the same time, Mátrai shows how other school systems, such as the German school curriculum teaching about Nazism and the Holocaust, explicitly teach the importance of solidarity across nations and minority groups by emphasizing the historical impact of identity conflict and intolerance. Confronting or silencing painful conflicts are opposite approaches to educating for peace. It is easy to understand how people in power, seeking calm and stability, would choose to silence discussion in school of intractable conflicts. However, young people would still learn elsewhere about those conflicts and axes of dehumanization in ways that could be even less responsible than what they might get in school. Illustrating his ideas through analysis of three Israeli civics textbooks, Hillel Wahrman suggests that, despite the inevitable risks, questions of identity and identity-based conflict should be discussed more explicitly in relation to democratic politics, to encourage student engagement.[43]

Schools may exacerbate identity-based conflict in other ways. Clearly, inequitable resource access, irrelevant curriculum, and constrained autonomy for minority education can increase minority populations' sense of relative deprivation and antagonism towards the majority, as well as exacerbating dominant populations' ignorance and discrimination towards that minority. Beyond these basics, comparative educators disagree about which approaches to curriculum might help or hinder inter-ethnic conflict. For example, an official discourse of secularism might leave no space for expression of cultural or religious diversity, whereas integration of religious content could help to alleviate problems by including what people find meaningful in their education.[44] On the other hand, teaching any particular version of religious education in public school curriculum for minorities, as for example Islam is taught in Palestinian schools in Israel, could repress within-minority-group differences.[45]

This question of how schools should respond to religious differences is alive with controversy in North America as well. Gita Steiner-Khamsi, applying Nancy Fraser's citizenship theory to questions of education in protracted-conflict contexts, suggests that anti-racist multicultural education would work better if it were to recognize complex, multifaceted diversities rather than bipolar differences, and include conflict resolution education (foregrounding equality demands) to help facilitate redistribution of resources between "have" and "have not" groups.[46]

NARRATIVES AND HISTORY IN CURRICULUM AND TEXTS

In human cultures, we organize a lot of our thinking and feeling about conflict through stories or narratives. The re-telling and re-invention of those narratives can be a powerful element of conflict transformation.[47] History education in schools is often hotly contested because it is where those narratives are at their most visible. Interviews with over two hundred diverse secondary students in Northern Ireland, for example, showed strong community influences on students' ideas about their identities in relation to that conflict, and showed (as Merelman's research, previously cited, would have predicted) that they were comfortable with competing narratives about the conflict. However, these students also explicitly expected that the history they learned in school would have provided a more balanced and reliable version of events.[48] Similarly, Orit Ichilov found that Israeli Palestinian Arab and Orthodox and non-Orthodox Jewish Israeli youth had developed different notions of ethnic and national identity, and different narratives of the citizenship roles that might be possible for various parties to that conflict.[49] He describes attempts to bridge these rifts in a pluralistic manner, such as a new civics curriculum implemented in Israel in 2001. In the recent past, narratives such as the history of the 1967 war in six Israeli secondary textbooks (in use from 1987 until at least 2002) emphasized Israeli politicians' attempts to avoid war, blamed Arabs for provocations starting that war, and presented the nation-state as hero.[50] A content analysis of the subsequent new history textbooks found "a more open and complex perspective" than prior textbooks, but found that the mainstream Zionist master narrative still organized the majority of the texts, leaving negligible space for meaningful multicultural education or for considering or legitimizing Palestinian narrative.[51]

Similarly, Sri Lanka has been embroiled in conflict over history education and textbooks: as in Israel-Palestine, a few pilot peace and human rights education/national integration education projects, at various grade levels, have attempted to create workable alternative curricula.[52] Along similar lines, some Russian history textbooks have been revised. While the new texts present a very critical narrative about the Soviet regime with a reconstructed patriotic overlay, they pay little or no attention to the emergence of new conflicts since 1991, in particular social inequality.[53] A joint commission of Japanese, Korean, and Chinese scholars has created a new history text that more openly addresses Japan's imperialism and violent incursions in East Asia, although their hope of wide dissemination in schools has not yet been realized.[54] Where these 50 scholars could not reach agreement about how to represent a particular situation, their book presents three parallel narratives representing alternate views of those events. Thus, history texts and other curricula are created by human beings with differing perspectives, in ways that may escalate or mitigate social conflicts. Although it is not easy, these narratives can be re-created to facilitate peacebuilding.

Clearly, the challenges of history education are especially acute, and difficult to resolve, when that history includes serious injustice, human rights violation, or genocide by one people towards another within the "same" nation. For example, the newly intercultural curriculum in Guatemala purports to integrate universal and Indigenous Mayan values and to recognize multiple cultural identities and Aboriginal languages.[55] However, some scholars see such intercultural education as a gentle form of assimilation, even cultural genocide, that substitutes surface recognition and incorporation into the mainstream instead of true recognition of sovereignty, cultural context, and harm done (see also Chapter Four in this volume).[56]

Where formal public education represents the heavy weight of the nation-state, informal popular education through the media may offer alternative openings for eventual conflict transformation, for example by acknowledging harm committed in the past. For example, a mass popular education effort in Australia commemorated and apologized for shameful practices towards Australian Aborigines.[57] Public events such as the Truth and Reconciliation Commission (TRC) hearings in South Africa are pedagogical, as particular truths are encoded and mediated in order to shape the management of conflict in the future.[58] The majority of South Africans were not included in the definition of victims who could testify before the TRC about their memories of human rights violations and murders during the apartheid period, and the process legitimated the existing government transition process. Since only some people testified, and testimonies were not verified, there is disagreement over whether TRC achieved either truth or reconciliation. Yet some voices were heard through the TRC that otherwise would not have been, and some instances of reconciliation were achieved. This admittedly imperfect reality could offer a model for peace learning that would begin to address the competing narratives surrounding complex conflict and violence.[59]

LEARNING TO HEAR THE OTHER: INTER-GROUP CONTACT, DIALOGUE, AND PREJUDICE

The most widely practised and studied form of education designed to reduce inter-group prejudice in social conflict situations is the "inter-group contact" dialogue model. Planned inter-group contact encounters take many forms, but generally involve non-formal programs that bring together individuals from two or more adversary groups, face-to-face, for facilitated sharing, co-operative activity, and dialogue about the participants' understandings of the conflict between their groups. Contact groups are typically small and voluntary, primarily attracting participants who are already more open to peacebuilding than some of their neighbours. Although such programs affect far fewer people than would broad public schooling reforms such as desegregation or significant revision of curriculum materials, contact program participants often report profound, life-changing personal impacts. Further, international research on such initiatives sheds light on broad questions of prejudice reduction and peacebuilding that are relevant to a range of contexts, including North American schools.

Inter-group contact or other anti-bias education is by no means guaranteed to reduce enmity. Often there is a remarkable amount of prejudice and misinformation to unlearn. For example, American peacebuilding scholar Mohammed Abu-Nimer, in a 2002 speech, recalls how, when working with Israeli and Arab children in a contact program, he saw the children inspect one another, looking for the tails they each had been led to believe would be part of the other's anatomy.[60] Gordon Allport's 1954 "contact hypothesis" articulated certain conditions under which inter-group contact would be likely to reduce prejudice and increase openness to the other side's perspectives: a process and participant selection designed to equalize status between the groups; close and prolonged contact; cross-group co-operation towards common goals; and institutional environments that support co-operation and prejudice reduction.[61] Unfortunately, these conditions are often not fully met in many programs. As in other anti-bias education in North America and elsewhere, such prejudice reduction initiatives are often marginal efforts of short duration, undertaken without much social-institutional support for status equalization or behaviour change.

A great deal of inter-group contact education research and practice has been conducted in Israel and Palestine (sometimes including people from nearby countries such as Jordan), and in Northern Ireland, involving Catholic and Protestant children. In Israel, the Arabic- and Jewish-Israeli school systems are completely separate, with different curricula and language of instruction; in Northern Ireland, schooling is more than 90 percent segregated by religion and very often by social class.

Emergent alternatives to the inter-group contact approach are single identity or common identity approaches: these attempt to reduce the reliance on bipolar identities, through de-categorization (helping participants to view people as individuals rather than merely "one of them") and by teaching superordinate shared identities that cross-cut the adversary identities.[62] It is not surprising that these approaches are attractive to nation-states, since the superordinate identities encouraged are often national identities (such as "multicultural Canada"), and sometimes connected with state-sponsored pluralistic citizenship education initiatives.[63]

A typical example of an inter-group contact initiative is the Let's Talk dialogue program, involving young people from the Republic of Ireland, Northern Ireland, England, and Australia. It includes activities such as discussion of contentious issues in workshops and conferences, and youth referenda. While Ed Cairns and others caution that contact encounters do not necessarily overcome prejudice (participants may come to view the other participants as exceptions, rather than typical representatives of their groups), Lynn Davies presents an optimistic assessment of Let's Talk, based on student participants' apparent development of openness, political awareness, and hybrid (less adversarial) identities.[64]

A similar kind of contact dialogue program in Israel included teacher professional development, internet dialogue, and limited face-to-face time between Israeli Jewish and Bedouin minority high school students. A pre- and post-test of participants' feelings and attitudes towards their own

> "Education on its own will not create world peace. Nor will a school be able to heal and control children living in violent or drug-related communities.... I do think schools can interrupt the processes towards more violence."[65]
>
> —Lynn Davies

and the others' ethnic identities demonstrated small positive effects, although the average Bedouin student participant felt more strongly, and changed their attitude less, than the average Jewish student participant.[66]

A similar but more comprehensive program in Northern Ireland, connected to ongoing public school programming and the Education for Mutual Understanding curriculum requirement, is the Speak Your Piece pilot project conducted in 1996–97. This program employed youth worker facilitators, television programs, teaching of conflict resolution skills, and class discussion, mostly in identity (home school) groups, but also including some opportunity for positive contact with the other, directly and via computer conferencing. The leaders/researchers believed they were fairly successful in facilitating open, forthright, and inclusive dialogue on controversial issues, to "generate respect for the right to express points of view and to show sensitivity to personal biographies."[67]

An example of a related type of program, primarily involving adults, has taken place in a small Slovenian town in Croatia. A series of mixed dialogue groups using an open-ended interview listening approach, sustained over a period of years, appeared to result in a breakthrough in inter-community communication in that town.[68] A similar effort involved a sustained series of cross-group forums and co-operation to reform education in an Israeli city with a mixed Palestinian and Jewish-Israeli population. Here, professional development was provided for school principals, some of whom formed an interest group that successfully engaged the wider community in mixed-group peacebuilding and problem-solving activities.[69]

Many inter-group prejudice reduction programs use popular culture, electronic technology, and other creative approaches to give people incentive and opportunities to engage. In one creative effort, a conversation started by an accidental wrong number, in which an Israeli Jew called a Palestinian home, led to the initiation of a telephone dialogue project sponsored by Families Forum, an organization of Israeli Jews and Palestinians whose family members had been killed in that conflict.[70] This initiative, called Hello Peace, included a broad public promotion effort, encouraging people to call a special number, through which a computer connected them to a person on the other side of the conflict who also had expressed willingness to talk. The program logged over 480,000 calls between October 2002 and October 2004. Many participants reported significant impacts on an inner circle (active participants), a middle circle (their friends and relatives), and to some degree on a third circle who had been exposed to the media campaign or indirectly to participants.

Another approach to prejudice reduction in conflict-ridden regions involves the many *Sesame Street*–type children's television programs.[71] An assessment of one such program, designed for ethnic Albanian, Macedonian, Roma, and Turkish children ages seven through twelve, found that this program was very popular and had significant positive effects on children's understandings of themselves and others.[72] Beyond the anti-bias education effort aimed at children, such initiatives represent sustained cross-party co-operative efforts among the diverse adults who design and implement the television programs.

One way to make inter-group contact and cooperation more sustained, involving shared, daily experiences over time, is to create integrated schools. As of 2006, about 6 percent of Northern Irish pupils attended the 57 voluntary integrated schools that exist in various parts of the six-county region, led by either a Catholic or a Protestant principal. Integrated schooling is even rarer in Israel: there are a total of four integrated Jewish-Palestinian schools, two of which were opened within the last few years. Each school has two principals, one Jewish and one Palestinian, working together and offers bilingual as well as bicultural education. A recent comparative study found that parents' motivations for putting their children in these integrated schools did not necessarily emphasize peace, but instead sometimes focused on the schools' perceived academic excellence (including, in the Palestinian case, Hebrew language practice).[73] Based on interviews with relevant government officials and the principals of six typical Northern Irish integrated schools and all four Israeli-Palestinian schools, Claire McGlynn and Zvi Bekerman found that inter-group differences were typically managed differently in the Irish integrated schools, which emphasized *individual* differences and *common* identity, compared to the Israeli-Palestinian integrated schools, which emphasized development of mutual understanding while *maintaining* and affirming each *distinct* ethnic identity. The authors found three basic approaches to inter-group conflict in integrated environments: passive (no confrontation of inequity), reactive (sporadic response to harmful disruptions), and proactive (critical pluralist peacebuilding). They argued that the latter, the more sustained and critical anti-racist approach, was likely to be more effective.[74] Research on the impact of inter-group contact in Northern Ireland found that considerable inter-group contact, albeit usually informal and shallow (for example, interacting in shops or on buses), did occur naturally for many people, even though Northern Ireland remains quite segregated.[75] While some inter-group contact initiatives may have effects on attitudes for some participants, they reported that so far it had had negligible impact on tangible behaviour such as housing segregation, cross-group friendships, voting patterns, or willingness to participate in integrated (cross-community) education.

There are various kinds of dialogue processes. The goal in people-to-people peacemaking and inter-group encounters is generally to facilitate participants' development from positional (adversarial) dialogue, towards efforts to understand the other through human relations dialogue, and eventually to more comprehensive activist and problem-solving dialogues that also function to plan and implement joint action.[76] Edy Kaufman highlights many of the same dimensions articulated previously in the contact hypothesis, showing that small, marginal contact and dialogue initiatives can stimulate creativity and sometimes have an important impact on the prejudices or motivations of a few individuals, but that lasting change in attitudes and behaviour generally requires more sustained, repeated, and ongoing opportunities for participants to co-operate on mutually meaningful projects. In many protracted-conflict situations, such opportunities for constructive inter-group contact of any depth do not arise naturally in the course of regular life. Thus, despite the fact that success is by no means guaranteed, people continue to create special bridge-building opportunities such as contact and anti-racism dialogue programs around the world. There is no magic reliable solution to intractable conflict, but comparative international study offers many hopeful examples and insights that can strengthen such efforts, domestically and internationally.

RE-IMAGINING RELATIONSHIPS: COMMUNITY-BASED PEACEBUILDING AND LEARNING

To offer the possibility of reconciliation after very harmful violence, peacebuilding dialogue requires participants to acknowledge harm done, to take initiatives to alleviate that harm, and to rebuild non-violent relationships.[77] Beyond dialogue and reconciliation, sustainable peacebuilding also requires education: development of understanding, skills, and confidence to act, through guided opportunities to practice handling conflict constructively. Whereas negative peace — the absence of overt violence — can be created through a ceasefire and peacekeeping control, positive peace — the presence of capacities, norms, and processes for handling life's inevitable conflicts justly and non-violently — depends upon ongoing education.

Sustained peacebuilding requires broad participation, and thus (reformed) education for whole populations. Defined educational initiatives reviewed above, such as revising history curricula or organizing inter-group contact encounters, help to remove obstacles, to generate learning from successes with committed participants, and to build some people's capacity for peacebuilding participation. Peacebuilding and conflict learning also may be infused throughout communities, in informal and non-formal learning settings as well as schools — for example, through regular opportunities to practice discussion of controversial issues, decision-making deliberation, and mediated conflict resolution. Through these processes participants may develop values and attitudes conducive to peaceful coexistence and constructive conflict resolution. However, intentions alone are not sufficient; at least as important are the concrete skills and understandings rooted, practised, and reinforced in actual behaviour.

For example, people in West Africa, Northern Ireland, and elsewhere have used arts-based social action, music festivals, grassroots advocacy, and other creative approaches, grounded in local cultures, as catalysts and informal learning opportunities for peacebuilding.[78] Burundi, Sierra Leone, and other sub-Saharan African countries have seen dramatic increases in young populations, and heartbreaking problems with recruitment and exploitation of children as soldiers, so youth-serving and youth-led organizations play a special part in facilitating grassroots peacebuilding learning.[79] Just as people learn about conflict by witnessing and participating in it, people can learn about constructive peacemaking and peacebuilding by practising peace in informal community activities.

Although the forms of restorative justice circle processes that currently are becoming influential around the world have their roots in Aboriginal cultures in New Zealand and North America, many human cultures have ancient traditions of sitting in some kind of circle for dialogue, deliberation, and problem-solving to handle conflict.[80] Peacemaking circles can be effective conflict resolution processes because they accommodate complexity, multiple stakeholders, and power imbalances. Further, such processes may offer participants powerful affective and cognitive learning opportunities through support, guided practice, and constructive feedback.[81]

Conflict resolution and peacebuilding education benefits from insights gained through international and cross-cultural comparison, yet, at the same time, context matters: application of approaches from one social and cultural context in another can be problematic. Many conflict resolution and conflict resolution training methods are often imported or imposed. They are delivered from relatively privileged and less contested contexts, yet expected to work in less privileged, culturally distinct, and more contested contexts. Based on his years of conflict resolution facilitation and training in Latin American and other violence-torn contexts, John Paul Lederach argues that top-down prescriptive training and conflict management processes, rooted in the typically individualistic and rationalistic cultures of the privileged world, are often inappropriate and/or ineffective in particular local conflict contexts.[82] His advocacy for more elicitive training methods, designed to derive and give voice to the implicit knowledge rooted in each culture's experiences, stories, and proverbs, has been widely influential.

Circle processes are good examples of conflict resolution and conflict learning mechanisms that have roots in many cultures, and, due to their inclusive and non-hierarchical nature, can be responsive to the particular social and cultural contexts participants bring into the process with them. However, even this seemingly universal format is conducted in different

> "'Culture' should not be understood by conflict resolvers and trainers primarily in technical terms as a challenge to be mastered and overcome. Culture is rooted in social knowledge and represents a vast resource, a rich seedbed for producing a multitude of approaches and models in conflict resolution."[83]
> —John Paul Lederach

ways, closely tied to particular cultural belief systems and worldviews. For example, in Anishanaabek culture, the circle proceeds clockwise, whereas in Ongwehonwe (Six Nations) culture the circle proceeds counter-clockwise.[84] Consideration of international and intercultural nuances can help to ensure that conflict management and education processes are safe for all involved, and that they contribute to peace building rather than perpetuation or deepening of conflicts.

CONCLUSION

Education for peacebuilding is conflict education. There seems to be no way to get to peace without confronting the problems that have created systemic and/or overt conflict and violence. Positive peace is not an ideal of love or living happily ever after: it is more a process than a destination. Thus, to educate for positive peace is to expect, prepare for, and engage in constructive conflict communication and resolution, not to avoid conflict. While constructive conflict resolution and peacebuilding education are possible even when violence has escalated dangerously, paradoxically, they are easiest and most effective to implement in non-emergency situations when conflict could be avoided.

At its best, conflict education for peacebuilding around the world involves development of wide repertoires of processes, skills, and understandings for handling differences and problems, rather than prescription of narrowly predefined knowledge or procedures. Resources for conflict management are rooted in each culture's and community's narratives and languages, implicit feelings as well as rational thoughts, and in informal as well as formal learning settings. Comparative international study of conflict and peacebuilding education can create awareness of this wide variety of experiences, insights, and questions, to offer a critical perspective on the risks and opportunities in local and global classrooms.

QUESTIONS FOR REFLECTION AND DISCUSSION

1. Consider some of your personal experiences with (global and/or local) peace, conflict, and peacebuilding, and how these may have been influenced by your formal and informal educational experiences.
2. Compare some of the educational initiatives in this chapter to some of the ways peace, conflict, and controversy were addressed (implicitly and/or explicitly, constructively and/or destructively) in your own school and classroom experiences (for example, in higher-conflict and lower-conflict cultural settings). How did your educational experiences affect your personal understandings and ability to handle conflict, controversy, and peacebuilding?
3. In what ways could you, as a teacher, meaningfully introduce peace and conflict: in a culturally homogeneous classroom setting? In a culturally and/or ideologically heterogeneous setting? How might classroom curriculum and pedagogy speak to students' multiple

identities and implicit cultural knowledge (such as national origins/loyalties, religious affiliations, feminist viewpoints, and so on) in ways that hinder peacebuilding? In ways that facilitate peacebuilding?

4. How might students' diversities be a resource for developing their facility and comfort with handling life's inevitable conflicts, uncertainties, and controversial issues?

SUGGESTED FILMS

Teaching Peace: In Time of War, produced by Kent Martin and Peter d'Entremont

Featuring Canadian peace educator Hetty van Gurp, the film takes viewers behind the scenes of her work with a middle school in Serbia. The film shows the problems and processes of transforming teacher-to-student relationships and student-to-student relationships within a particular school into peace-centred ways of learning and interacting. The film highlights the personal life of van Gurp, as well as explores the challenges that the Serbian teachers have to face in adopting this method of pedagogy and practice.

Promises, by Justine Shapiro and B.Z. Goldberg

This film follows four Jewish-Israeli children (from ultra-conservative through liberal-secular) and four Palestinian (citizens in Jerusalem and refugees in a nearby camp) over a period between 1997–2000. The children are interviewed by B.Z. Goldberg about their views of the Israeli-Palestinian conflict. Goldberg eventually brings some of them together for a day of fun/relationship-building and dialogue. The film ends by showing the children two years later to find out their views and whether they kept in contact with the friends they met through the contact program.

The film was nominated for an Academy Award for Best Documentary Film in 2002.

SUGGESTIONS FOR FURTHER READING

Aronson, Elliot. *Nobody Left to Hate: Teaching Compassion after Columbine.* New York: Worth Publishers, 2000.

Bickmore, Kathy. "Education for Peacebuilding Citizenship: Teaching the dimensions of conflict resolution in social studies." In *Challenges and Prospects for Canadian Social Studies*, edited by Alan Sears and Ian Wright. Vancouver: Pacific Educational Press, 2004. 187–201.

Bickmore, Kathy. "Democratic Social Cohesion (Assimilation)? Representations of Social Conflict in Canadian Public School Curricula." *Canadian Journal of Education* 29, no. 2 (2006): 359–86.

Bush, Kenneth and Saltarelli, Diana. *The Two Faces of Education in Ethnic Conflict: Towards a Peacebuilding Education for Children*. Florence, IT: UNICEF Innocenti Research Centre, 2000.

Curle, Adam, Paulo Freire, and Johan Galtung. "What Can Education Contribute towards Peace and Social Justice?" In *Education for Peace: Reflection and Action*, edited by Magnus Haavelsrud. Keele, UK: University of Keele, 1974. 64–97.

Davies, Lynn. *Education and Conflict: Complexity and Chaos*. London: Routledge/Falmer, 2004.

*Lederach, John Paul. *Beyond Prescription: New Lenses for Conflict Resolution Training Across Cultures*. Waterloo, ON: Institute for Peace and Conflict Studies, Conrad Grebel College, 1–18 and 34–40 (also highly recommended: 19–28).

*Luwisch, Freema Elbaz. "Understanding What Goes On in the Heart and Mind: Learning about Diversity and Co-existence through Storytelling." *Teaching and Teacher Education* 17, no. 2 (2001): 133–46.

*McCully, A., M. O'Doherty, and P. Smyth. "The Speak Your Piece Project: Exploring Controversial Issues in Northern Ireland." In *Peacebuilding for Adolescents*, edited by Linda Forcey and Ian Harris. New York: Peter Lang, 1999. 119–38.

Merelman, Richard. "The Role of Conflict in Children's Political Learning." In *Political Socialization, Citizenship Education, and Democracy*, edited by Orit Ichilov. New York: Teachers College Press, 1990.

Milligan, Jeffery. "Teaching Between the Cross and the Crescent Moon: Islamic Identity, Postcoloniality, and Public Education in the Southern Philippines." *Comparative Education Review,* 47, no. 4 (2003): 468–92.

Reardon, Betty. "Militarism and Sexism: Influences on Education for War." In *Three Decades of Peace Education around the World: An*

Anthology, edited by Robin Burns and Robert Aspeslagh. New York: Garland, 1996. 143–60.

Ross, Marc. *The Management of Conflict: Interpretations and Interests in Comparative Perspective*. New Haven: Yale University Press, 1993.

Salomon, Gavriel, and Nevo, Baruch, eds. *Peace Education: The Concept, Principles, and Practices around the World*. Mahwah, NJ: Lawrence Erlbaum Associates, 2002.

Schweisfurth, Michele, Davies, Lynn, and Harber, Clive, eds. *Learning Democracy and Citizenship: International Experiences*. Oxford: Symposium Books, 2000.

Tawil, Sobhi and Harley, Alexandra, eds. *Education, Conflict and Social Cohesion*. Geneva: UNESCO/International Bureau of Education, 2004.

Ware, Helen, Peter Greener, Deanna Iribarnegaray, Bert Jenkins, Sabina Lautensach, Dylan Matthews, Jonathan Makuwira, and Rebecca Spence, eds. *The No-Nonsense Guide to Conflict and Peace*. Oxford and Toronto: New Internationalist Publications/Between the Lines, 2005.

Chapter Eleven

Educating for "Global Citizenship" in Schools: Emerging Understandings

Mark Evans, with contributions from Ian Davies,
Bernadette Dean, and Yusef Waghid

INTRODUCTION

Explicit attention to educating for citizenship continues to expand and deepen worldwide. Many countries now include citizenship education as an important feature of their official curriculum, albeit in variant forms. For some, it is viewed as an opportunity to begin preparing young people for their understanding of, and involvement in, the civic life of their community(ies). For others, it is viewed as a way of responding to a range of existing social concerns (such as civic illiteracy among youth, racism, conflict and violence, and low levels of participation among youth). For whatever reason, there has been a proliferation of research studies, formal discussions, and curriculum initiatives throughout the world, as teachers, policy-makers, and researchers attempt to understand and assess the complex processes by which young people learn about democratic citizenship and its location and representation in school curricula.[1]

Attention to citizenship education in recent years has evoked substantial discussion about its scope and breadth. Differing conceptions of citizenship and citizenship education have led to a certain level of conceptual ambiguity. Dominant views of citizenship—the civic republican (responsibilities-based) and the liberal (rights-based) —offer varied understandings of citizenship education while other perspectives (such as communitarian, social democratic, multi-culturalist, post-national) further complicate the situation.[2] These contrasting conceptions raise questions about which learning goals ought to be to nurtured and create a sense of uncertainty among educators attempting to effectively introduce citizenship education into the school curriculum in a meaningful way. McLaughlin, for example, believes that this situation has led to "minimalist" interpretations of citizenship being encouraged.[3] Heater, in contrast, worries that certain perspectives offer little more than the indoctrination of youth to the purposes of the state.[4]

Educating for the complex and abstract goal of "global citizenship"[5] has been a critical dimension of these discussions and investigations. First, there is growing recognition of the need for a more explicit global focus in citizenship education. Second, there is a growing acknowledgment among education researchers that how we educate, specifically referring to what teachers know and are able to do, is one of the most important influences on what students learn.[6] Comparativists voice similar concerns about the minimal attention that traditionally has been paid to pedagogy in comparative international studies, and have identified this as an important and substantive research direction for the future.[7] This chapter explores evolving understandings of what it means to educate for global citizenship, briefly compares and contrasts directions in global citizenship education in Canada, England, Pakistan, and South Africa, and identifies some common threads and challenges for further discussion.

EVOLVING UNDERSTANDINGS OF THE GLOBAL DIMENSION IN CITIZENSHIP EDUCATION

The idea of conceptualizing citizenship beyond one's national borders is certainly not new. As Ruth Hayhoe and Karen Mundy remind us in Chapter One, distinctive understandings of so-called world citizenship have been present, shared, and survived for at least 2,000 years in different histories and contexts. A sense of kinship with all humankind, recognition of international legal principles, and actions for world governance are some of the distinctive understandings that have underpinned notions of world citizenship. At present, however, there is a growing acknowledgement (and sense of urgency) that many of today's socio-economic, cultural, political, and environmental issues transcend formal national boundaries. Recent shifts in the speed, pervasiveness, and global reach of information and communication technologies, an interdependent global economy, challenges in human rights and social justice, and global broadcast and impact of international tragedies and emergencies, for example, are creating tensions and conditions that require more integrated, worldwide responses.[8] Not surprisingly, understandings of global citizenship are being explored with increased intensity.

As might be expected, there has been a corresponding growth in interest among teachers, policy-makers, and educational researchers in various parts of the world in strengthening the global dimension of citizenship education in school curricula at all levels. Audrey Osler, director of the Centre for Citizenship and Human Rights Education at the University of Leeds, England writes:

> We live in an increasingly interdependent world, where the actions of ordinary citizens are likely to have an impact on others' lives across the globe. In turn, our lives, our jobs, the food we eat, and the development of our communities are being influenced by global developments.... Education for living together in an interdependent world is not an optional extra, but an essential foundation.[9]

Varied characterizations and perspectives about what it means to educate for global citizenship tend to blend themes associated with both citizenship education and global education and advocate particular kinds of classroom and school-wide practices. On the one hand, there is growing attention around the world to themes associated with citizenship education. There is also more inclusion of global dimensions and goals in education, in many school systems. Table 11.1 highlights some of the general and overlapping themes associated with each dimension of education.

Teaching practices are viewed as a central element in each of these dimensions of education. Teachers, wishing to explore and integrate some of the general themes associated with citizenship education and/or global education, are finding a rich array of inquiry-oriented, participatory, and performance-based classroom, school-wide, and community-based ideas and activities to inform and guide their practice. The use of case studies, the infusion of substantive and procedural concepts, public issue research projects, model town councils, peacebuilding programs, community participation activities, public information exhibits, peer mentoring and conflict resolution programs, online international linkages, and youth forums are types

Table 11.1

Core Themes in Citizenship Education and Global Education

Core Themes Associated with Citizenship Education	Core Themes Associated with Global Education
• An understanding of concepts, structures, and processes necessary for informed civic decision making and involvement (for example, rule of law, local and national governance structures and processes)	• An understanding of concepts and the workings of the wider world (for example, interdependence, international legal principles, global systems, sustainable development, peace and conflict)
• Sense of membership or identity with one's varied communities that extend from the local to the national to the global	• Worldmindedness, a sense of membership or kinship with all of humanity
• An understanding of rights and corresponding duties and responsibilities usually within the national context (Charter of Rights and Freedoms)	• An understanding of rights and responsibilities within the global context (Human Rights Act, Rights of the Child)
• An understanding of civic conflict and decisions, personal values, and perspectives that guide citizen thinking and action, and the challenges of governing communities in which contrasting values and perspectives coexist.	• An understanding of global conflict and decisions, respect for diverse perspectives, cross-cultural understanding, and a commitment to global social justice and equity
• The development of a set of virtues and capacities that enable someone to critically explore, reflect upon, and participate in civic questions and issues, mostly of local and national interest and importance	• The development of a set of virtues and capacities that enable someone to critically analyze and actively engage in questions and issues of global interest and concern, in relation to local and national circumstances

of classroom and school-wide activities that are being encouraged. Attention to "fitness of purpose" — that is, the alignment among the desired learning outcomes, the tasks and activities designed by the teacher to achieve those outcomes, learner diversity, and contextual considerations — is of central importance. At the same time, there is increasing acknowledgement that pedagogical practices communicate different messages that are *not* politically neutral. These practices convey important messages about which forms of learning are being given priority (and which ones are being neglected or silenced), and in doing so, may support and/or obstruct the intended learning to take place.

Below are three examples of perspectives on what it means to educate for global citizenship that have emerged internationally in recent years. Note their commonalities and differences, and the ways each perspective foregrounds and backgrounds various themes associated with citizenship education and global education. In addition, consider the teaching practices that are associated with each conception.

Worldmindedness and Holistic Understanding

Canadian and British educators Graham Pike and David Selby emphasize two strands in their perspective on global citizenship education. One strand in their preferred curriculum is *worldmindedness*: an understanding of the world as one unified system, and a commitment to viewing the interests of individual nations in light of the overall needs of the planet. Pike and Selby emphasize the importance of five interconnected areas of learning: systems consciousness, perspective consciousness, health of planet awareness, involvement consciousness, and process-mindedness. They advocate the need for attention to issues raised by "conflicting loyalties" emerging from "plural and parallel" understandings of citizenship. Pike and Selby's second strand is *child-centredness*: a pedagogical approach encouraging children to explore and discover for themselves and addressing each learner as an individual with a unique set of beliefs, experiences, and talents.[10] They recommend a broad and varied program of transformational teaching-learning opportunities, with an emphasis on student involvement, whole-person development, and activity-based learning. They also stress the importance of infusing values — such as respect for rights and freedoms, environmental consciousness, non-violence, and social responsibility — into the day-to-day classroom culture.

Related to Pike and Selby's, though not identical, is American educator Merry Merryfield's perspective. Merryfield advocates a holistic approach to encourage students and teachers to better understand themselves and their relationships to the global community. Her preferred curriculum does this by attending to human beliefs and values, global systems, global issues and problems, global history, cross-cultural understanding, awareness of human choices, the development of analytical and evaluative skills, and strategies for participation and involvement.[11] Like Pike and Selby, Merryfield advocates inclusion of instructional practices that concentrate on "teaching and learning globally oriented content in ways that support diversity and social justice in an interconnected world."[12] Her curriculum conception addresses self-knowledge (identity, heritage, privilege), cross-cultural experience, cross-cultural skills (listening, interaction, co-operation, conflict management), consciousness of multiple perspectives (on a range of local and global issues), analysis of values, beliefs, and attitudes (that underpin sources of public information), and authentic learning (applications). Both of these perspectives, worldmindedness and holistic, identify a number of core themes related to citizenship education and global education, and foreground the importance of self-awareness, values, and global perspectives on issues.

Multiple and Cosmopolitan Citizenship

British scholar Derek Heater argues that the modern concept of citizenship within a singular national context "has burst its bounds."[13] Educating for world citizenship, he argues, implies an understanding of citizenship as "multiple," occurring simultaneously at three distinct levels: the state or national, the sub-state or local, and world citizenship at the supra-state (global or multi-state governance) and/or trans-national level. He connects his idea of world citizenship to notions of cosmopolitanism, in particular the individual's ethical responsibility towards fellow citizens across the planet. In this conception, a world citizen might get involved ("act" as a citizen) in at least three ways: through participation in civil society organizations with a global intent, through involvement in supra-national political institutions, and through various forms of citizen advocacy, to bring attention to world issues. Heater's conception of cosmopolitan citizenship education emphasizes three dimensions of student learning: knowledge and understanding of the social, legal, and political systems in which students live and operate; skills and aptitudes to make use of that knowledge and understanding; and an exploration of their values and dispositions, to put their knowledge and skills to beneficial use.[14] Central to Heater's perspective is his emphasis on knowledge of world systems, and the responsible use of that knowledge in active citizenship roles, enacted locally, nationally, and globally. He recommends the inclusion of experiential teaching and learning practices (such as participation in school councils or involvement in community work). He also points out the crucial importance of flexible and innovative teaching methodologies, age-appropriate learning goals, and supportive classroom and school culture.

Action for Justice

British scholar Lynn Davies argues that characterizations of global citizenship education are very much in flux, but that they all seem to include more of a sense of obligation to act for social justice in transnational contexts, compared with previous conceptions of either citizenship education or global education:

> What seems to happen with education for global citizenship is a confirmation of the direct concern with social justice and not just the more minimalist interpretations of global education which are about international awareness or being a more well rounded person. Citizenship clearly has implications for both rights and responsibilities, of duties and entitlements, concepts which are not necessarily explicit in global education. One can have the emotion and identities without having to do much about them. Citizenship implies a more active role.[15]

Beyond the academy, various international non-governmental organizations are also taking a closer look at what it means to educate for citizenship within the global context. Oxfam, for example, advocates global action for justice. The "global citizen," according to Oxfam, is someone who: is aware of the wider world and has a sense of their own role as a world citizen; respects and values diversity; has an understanding of how the world works economically, politically, socially, culturally, technologically, and environmentally; is outraged by social injustice; participates in and contributes to the community at a range of levels from local to global; is willing to act to make the world a more sustainable place; and takes responsibility for their actions.[16] Oxfam advocates particular attention to knowledge and understanding in relation to social justice and equity, diversity, globalization and interdependence, sustainable development, and peace and conflict. Oxfam's curriculum conception also emphasizes development of skills including critical thinking, the ability to argue effectively, the ability to challenge injustice and inequalities, and co-operation and conflict resolution. Further, Oxfam's preferred curriculum includes a values and attitudes dimension addressing identity and self-esteem, empathy, respect for people and things, commitment to social justice and equity, respect for diversity, and concern for the environment and sustainable development. Oxfam advocates learner-centred pedagogy, infused through specialized subject areas and integrated across the curriculum, as well as including whole-school and community-based approaches. Central to Oxfam's perspective on global citizenship education is an emphasis on civic action to redress social injustices around the world.

These influential perspectives on global citizenship education all include some attention to understanding global interdependence, and some sense of membership, identity, and responsibility in relation to local and transnational actions affecting that interconnected world. At the same time, however, these curriculum perspectives differ in their relative emphases on general themes such as knowledge of world systems, questions of rights and justice, and/or equipping students for political advocacy roles.

EDUCATING FOR GLOBAL CITIZENSHIP: EMERGING CURRICULUM PRACTICES IN CANADA, ENGLAND, PAKISTAN, AND SOUTH AFRICA

Below are four vignettes that briefly characterize the overlapping and contrasting directions in which educating for global citizenship is emerging in different curriculum contexts: Canada, England, Pakistan, and South Africa. Ian Davies (University of York, England), Bernadette

Dean (Institute for Educational Development, Aga Khan University, Pakistan) Yusef Waghid (Department of Education Policy Studies, Stellenbosch University, South Africa), and I present four personal perspectives, each of which attends to the following questions:

1) Where and how is citizenship defined in education policy in your country? Is global citizenship or a similar concept defined?

2) How is global citizenship taught through the school curriculum? Are there materials and resources that have been developed to promote global citizenship?

3) What are some of the key challenges that teachers face as they attempt to educate for global citizenship?

Educating for Global Citizenship in Canada
Mark Evans

Educating for citizenship is a part of the core curriculum for elementary and secondary students in all provinces and territories in Canada. Although variations have been apparent at different times, in different regions, at least three broad contrasting approaches have been noticeable throughout the past century: characterizations that emerged in the early 20th century (and continue today) that encourage social and political initiation and assimilation (foregrounding the study of public institutions and the ascribed roles and responsibilities of citizens), characterizations since the World War II era that expanded citizenship education's purposes and practices (including increased attention to Canada's national civic identity, social cohesion, and cultural diversity), and more recent multi-faceted, transformative characterizations (highlighting civic literacy, active engagement in confronting real civic issues in the political arena, equity and inclusion, and a local-to-global perspective).[17]

As in other parts of the world, education about the world in Canadian curricula has been most prominent in History and Social Studies courses, and has been guided by different perspectives and circumstances, both internal and external. Richardson claims, for example, that school curricula in Canada have largely represented global understanding as a matter of national self-interest, and almost exclusively tied to the civic structures of the nation state. Thus students in Canada are urged to take up their responsibilities and obligations to address significant global issues such as international conflict, environmental degradation, or the protection of human rights as citizens of Canada rather than as citizens of the world.[18]

Educating for global citizenship gained attention in Canada during the 1980s and early 1990s. The Canadian International Development Agency (CIDA), for example, funded a number of Global Education Centres across Canada to promote global understanding among teachers and to assist them in exploring and developing curriculum classroom ideas and practices for the study of global themes and issues.[19] A recent study of current Canadian curriculum materials, *Education for Peace, Human Rights, Democracy, International Understanding and Tolerance*, reveals various ways themes of citizenship and global understanding have been introduced into the curriculum across Canada.[20] These curricula expanded understandings of citizenship to include meaningful civic engagement and complex public issues of local and global proportions.

There has been substantial discussion about the scope and breadth of citizenship education in recent years, in Canada and elsewhere, pointing to a range of critical issues and tensions. Contrasting conceptions of citizenship and citizenship education have led to a certain level of conceptual ambiguity. Understandings of what it means to educate for global citizenship in Canada are often intertwined with these broader conceptions of what it means to educate for citizenship. Like the three sample perspectives offered above, theoretical perspectives such as Will Kymlicka's "multicultural" model,[21] Ken Osborne's "12 Cs" framework,[22] Alan Sears' "Conceptions of Citizenship Education" model,[23] and Veronica Strong-Boag's "pluralist" orientation[24] each acknowledge citizenship's global dimension in varying ways in relation to the particular perspective of citizenship that each advocates.

Recent provincial curriculum policy developments show a heightened attention to the global citizenship component of student learning. In British Columbia, citizenship and global understanding are core themes interspersed throughout curriculum guidelines. One of the four overriding goals represented in the prescribed learning outcomes of the recently introduced Civic Studies 11 program in British Columbia emphasizes the acquisition of knowledge and understandings that assist students to "become more mindful of their connections to the civic world and of their responsibilities as members of various local and global communities."[25] *Education in Québec: An Overview* also emphasizes an "International Dimension" in its curricula:

> At this point in history when the global village is growing at an ever increasing rate, opening up to other cultures and learning about other countries is an essential element of citizenship education. This strategy involves the inclusion of an international dimension in Québec education, student and faculty mobility, exportation of skills and the development of Québec's influence abroad. Within this context, Québec's elementary and secondary schools are being encouraged to emphasize citizenship and intercultural education based on the great diversity of their students' geographical origins, mother tongues and cultural roots.[26]

The Ontario Ministry of Education and Training's Social Studies (Grades One through Six), History and Geography (Grades Seven and Eight), and Canadian and World Studies (Grades Nine through Twelve) curricula introduced between 1998 and 2005 have signalled increased attention across the Social Sciences curriculum to citizenship and its global dimension. The compulsory Grade 10 Civics Curriculum (introduced in 2000 and revised in 2005) requires an explicit focus on "what it means to be a global citizen and why it is important to be one."[27]

Curriculum reform initiatives across Canada also reflect attention on how to educate for citizenship. A host of useful ideas in the form of new websites and resource materials help to inform and guide teachers' work in relation to various aspects of instruction related to citizenship education. For example, CIDA's *In the Global Classroom Initiative*, Classroom Connections' *Cultivating Peace in the 21st Century* and *Taking Action*, Mark Evans and Cecilia Reynolds' teacher's resource handbook *Educating for Global Citizenship in a Changing World*, Craig Kielburger's *Take Action: A Guide to Active Citizenship*, and UNICEF Canada's *Global Schoolhouse* are a few of the many resources that recently have been developed in Canada, offering instructional guidance for teaching and learning about global citizenship. Participatory forms of learning that actively involve young people in meaningful civic engagement with real public issues (such as case analysis, public issue research projects, model town councils, peace building programs, community participation activities, public information exhibits, online international linkages, and youth forums) are receiving more attention in Canadian education. These diverse active learning strategies foreground opportunities for deepened conceptual understanding, personal and interpersonal understanding, the investigation of public issues (from the local to the global), building skills of critical inquiry and practitioner research, and responsible engagement in community questions and concerns.

Canadian teachers face different challenges as they attempt to educate for global citizenship. Conceptions of what is expected and included in global citizenship education, for example, lack clarity. Various learning goals are given priority and depth of treatment, raising questions about what types of learning might be experienced and what types might be silenced or ignored. Similarly, the selection of appropriate pedagogical practices remains an issue. In particular, instructional practices that aim to address beliefs, values, and notions of social justice, and participation in civic life, appear to receive little attention in current Canadian curriculum policies and materials. Lastly, the nature of teachers' work is an important factor. Overload, an overcrowded curriculum, and the reality that most schools, organizationally, tend to reinforce norms of hierarchical control, may undermine the impact of certain types of citizenship curriculum goals.

Educating for Global Citizenship in England
Ian Davies

One could argue that global citizenship is not defined explicitly or consistently in official policy documentation in England,[28] although there are many relevant statements from government departments, agencies, and non-governmental organizations (NGOs). For students aged five through 11, citizenship is part of the non-statutory personal, social, and health education framework. There is flexibility for teachers to develop work in ways that are appropriate for their own contexts, but it is relatively straightforward to see the opportunities for global citizenship in various summary statements. The statement shown below, for example, is an overarching view of what should occur in key stage two (students aged seven through eleven).

> Pupils learn about themselves as growing and changing individuals with their own experiences and ideas, and as members of their communities. They become more mature, independent and self-confident. They learn about the wider world and the interdependence of communities within it. They develop their sense of social justice and moral responsibility and begin to understand that their own choices and behaviour can affect local, national or global issues and political and social institutions.[29]

Since 2002, the National Curriculum in England has included the subject Citizenship for students aged 11–16 years. In key stage three (ages 11–14), it is now compulsory for students to be taught about "the world as a global community and the political, economic, environmental and social implications of this and the role of the European Union, the Commonwealth and the United Nations." For students aged 14–16, this is expanded to cover "the United Kingdom's relations in Europe including the European Union and relations with the Commonwealth and the United Nations," as well as emphasizing the need for students to understand "the wider issues and challenges of global interdependence and responsibility including sustainable development and local agenda." For students older than 16, and who are beyond the compulsory phase of education, there are citizenship initiatives — although these activities are not very detailed and refer vaguely to involvement at international levels.[30]

There are also relevant official statements made about global citizenship by British government departments other than those that deal principally with education. The Department for International Development[31] has produced perhaps the clearest and fullest statement on this field. Interestingly, the term *global dimension* is used and explained as something that incorporates the eight key concepts of global citizenship, conflict resolution, diversity, human rights, interdependence, social justice, sustainable development and values and perceptions. It explores the interconnections between the local and the global. It builds knowledge and understanding as well as developing skills and attitudes and shows how connections can be made with different subjects and aspects within the National Curriculum, although there seems a lack of clarity about the meaning of global citizenship and its relationship with the other seven key concepts.

There is a wealth of material available for English teachers and others on global citizenship education. Some of that material relates directly to work promoted by Department for International Development. The British Council manages a wide range of international programs and professional development activities and uses what it calls *Global Gateway* to help develop international dimensions in schools. The Development Education Association is an umbrella organization in England working with 240 member organizations including a network of local development education centres. One of those NGOs is Oxfam which, among other activities, produces resources for use in classrooms.[32] CitizED, an organization funded by the Training and Development Agency for Schools, produces resources for teacher trainers, trainees, and others on a wide range of issues including global citizenship, sustainable development, international NGOs, and the Commonwealth. The government also publicizes materials that are available for specific age groups.[33] Most commercially produced textbooks and other resources have clear sections on global citizenship or the global dimension.[34]

The development of global citizenship education in England is not straightforward. Among educators, there is a lack of consensus about what global citizenship means. There are competing definitions and characterizations that are at times asserted but are in key ways unclear.[35] There are, beyond this general difficulty of clearly characterizing global citizenship, issues about the specific pedagogical focus that could or should be developed. In this regard, there are at least three challenges that need to be met before we can decide about where to place the emphasis:

- Is students' capacity to act as important as their capacity to *learn how to* act? The latter would mean that teachers would not necessarily want outcomes that were successful in terms of concrete achievement in, for example, the creation of a new resource for a community.

- Is cognitive understanding to be emphasized more than affective responses? How much significance do we place on students' capacity to think critically as well as being able to empathize and perhaps sympathize with others?
- In light of the above two points, what position is (in practice) established in relation to bias and accusations concerning attempted indoctrination? What should a teacher do, for example, if a group of young people decided to protest against the United Kingdom's involvement in Iraq during school time? The response was clear in a number of cases in our recent experience, as young people learned that protest was regarded (rightly or otherwise) as an unnecessary distraction and some policy-makers felt that if teachers had encouraged such action they would have been guilty of unprofessional conduct.

Teachers, in light of the above challenges, have to decide about how to implement global citizenship. Is global citizenship education a discrete school subject or a cross curricular theme? Will it essentially find expression in extra-curricular contexts perhaps in a way that is beyond the taught curriculum and so allowing positively for community involvement or negatively for marginalization? What would this mean for who will teach it, what knowledge and skills would those teachers need, and what status would they have as a result in the school and other communities?

Educating for Global Citizenship in Pakistan
Bernadette Dean

The Pakistan National Education Policy 1998–2010 recognizes the importance of globalization and the need to prepare young people to be global citizens but the policy's main thrust is towards promoting national citizenship. The policy envisions the transformation of Pakistan into an educationally well-developed, politically united, economically prosperous, morally sound, and spiritually elevated nation, able to rise to the challenges of the 21st century. In order to realize the vision, the policy aims to: educate and train young people as true practising Muslims; provide basic rights including free and compulsory secondary education to all citizens; promote national unity; and build the character of young people so that they possess the highest sense of honour, integrity, and responsibility and act selflessly in the service of the nation and Islam.[36]

In the national curriculum, citizenship education is most evident in the aims, concepts, content, activities, learning outcomes, and assessment strategies of social studies. The social studies curriculum aims to develop both national and global citizenship. Specifically, students are expected to the know the contributions of Muslims to the betterment of humanity and to the creation of Pakistan; know the social, economic, political, and cultural aspects of Pakistan, South Asia, the Muslim World, and the rest of the world; understand one's "rights and responsibilities;" develop inquiry and problem-solving skills; and develop a strong sense of interdependence, national integrity, cohesion and self-reliance.[37] The curriculum uses an expanding horizons model of curriculum development beginning with the local. Students learn about themselves and their families, their local community, province, and country in years one to five, about South Asia, the Muslim world, and the world in years six to eight, and in years nine to twelve about Pakistan and its place in the world. The curriculum content, drawn from the disciplines that comprise social studies, suggests knowledge about citizenship and a values-explicit teaching approach.

Pakistani schools are very diverse in school type (international baccalaureate, Cambridge Board, matriculation, *Madrassa*), clientele (serving a particular social class, gender, religious group), and infrastructure and resources (urban schools are better resourced than rural schools). Most students study in matriculation schools that follow the national curriculum. The highly prescriptive curriculum is translated into textbooks that schools are bound to use. Classroom teaching is usually teacher-directed with teachers using lecture or a read-explain-question format to transmit textbook knowledge and regularly testing students to ensure memorization of this knowledge. Given the curriculum and prevailing teaching practices, students learn about the world, the interdependence of communities, and regional and global issues and institutions, albeit from a nationalistic and Islamic perspective. To address the limitations of the national curriculum, a few private schools have developed their own personal and social education curriculum, often including a focus on character education, health education, the study of current social issues, and/or involvement in community service projects.

In addition to classroom teaching, teachers are finding ways to educate for local, national, and global citizenship outside the classroom. Most schools celebrate national and international days. Many use them to further develop students' knowledge and encourage informed action. Earth Day celebrations raise awareness of the need for sustainable development and encourage actions such as cleaning the beaches, recycling and tree planting drives. International Children's Day celebrations focus on educating children about their rights and have children arrange *melas* (fun fairs) to raise money to support rights initiatives for less-fortunate children. A few private schools have students participate in programs designed by non-governmental organizations, which focus on human rights education or environmental education. Moreover, information and communication technologies and exchange programs are being used to connect Pakistani students with students in other parts of the world.

Educators in Pakistan face a number of challenges in relation to educating for global citizenship. Global citizenship is given little attention in the National Education Policy and has a low status in most Pakistani schools. The curriculum's focus is on the acquisition of a narrow body of knowledge, and the teaching practices used in most Pakistani classroom are not conducive to the development of informed and participatory citizens. Examinations, based on prescribed textbooks, tend to reinforce an emphasis on the transmission of knowledge. Lack of adequate teacher preparation further complicates the situation.

There appear to be, however, many opportunities on the horizon that could provide impetus to encourage global citizenship education in Pakistan. Presently, a very participatory process is being undertaken by the government to develop a new education policy and a new curriculum. Proposals call for citizenship education that is based on democratic principles, the use of multiple textbooks, an improved examination system and better pre-service and continuing in-service teacher education. The first private matriculation examination board is leading other examination boards to set examinations based on the curriculum rather than a textbook and move beyond the assessment of facts to understanding and application of knowledge. In the area of citizenship education, Aga Khan University Institute for Educational Development is offering certificate courses in citizenship, human rights, and peace education. The program helps teachers envision a democratic society, suggests a citizenship education program to realize it, and provides school-based support as teachers implement it. While curriculum materials are being designed to support implementation, teachers are assisted with free materials from NGOs operating in Pakistan, international NGOs, UN agencies, and materials available on the Internet.

Educating for Global Citizenship in South Africa
Yusef Waghid

Following the 1994 elections, the transformation of the education system became the top priority of the new government in South Africa.[38] According to Education Minister Kader Asmal, democratic values, as enshrined in the South African constitution, were to be developed and internalized by South Africans, and schools were the most convenient point of embarking upon this project. Since the establishment of the country's new democratic system of government in 1994, every education policy initiative has been linked to democratic principles enunciated in the Constitution and Bill of Rights of 1996.[39] Understandings of what it means to educate for global citizenship in school curricula in South Africa are interwoven in policy documents and frameworks that address the broader goal of democratic citizenship education.

In 1999, the national Department of Education initiated the *Tirisano* (Working Together) project, to ensure that the country's new outcomes-based education system could be successfully implemented commensurate with a spirit of democracy, respect for human rights, justice, equality, freedom, nation building, and reconciliation. Four of the *Tirisano* project's goals were establishing co-operative governance in educational institutions, making schools "centres of community and cultural life," creating an education and training system that could meet the socio-economic demands of the country, and dealing purposefully with HIV/AIDS.[40]

During informal discussions on religious education for the *Tirisano* project, the idea of a Values, Education and Democracy project was taken up, following the international trend of "education for democratic values and social participation." A working group on Values, Education, and Democracy was established by Minister Asmal in February 2000.[41] Under its auspices, a school-based research project was conducted by a consortium of research organizations led by the Witwatersrand University Education Policy Unit to explore the ways that teachers, students, and parents think and talk about values, education and democracy in 97 representative schools across five provinces.

The outcome of this research was a report titled *Values, Education and Democracy: Report of the Working Group on Values in Education*, completed in April 2000.[42] In it, the working group reported its findings and recommended that the democratic Constitution and Bill of Rights provide the frame of reference for a democratic educational philosophy. The working group identified the country's commitment to democratic citizenship education in public schools for learners aged seven to eighteen (grades one through twelve), and stressed the importance of developing the intellectual abilities and critical faculties of learners, establishing a climate of inclusiveness in schools whereby learners do not feel alienated and excluded, and equipping learners with problem-solving abilities. The group also proposed the promotion of six core values — equity, tolerance, multilingualism, openness, accountability, and social honour — which, they contended, would contribute to these goals. The understanding of democratic citizenship education espoused in the aforementioned values appeared to imply a liberal conception of democratic citizenship, by placing an emphasis on, for example, citizens' rights and obligations, equity, and the rule of law.[43]

The culminating Values, Education, and Democracy Conference resolved to implement citizenship education with three additional dimensions:

1) Promoting anti-racism through the teaching of a new history curriculum, which requires that teachers be upgraded appropriately;
2) Integrating the aesthetic performing arts subjects and African languages into the curricula; and
3) Incorporating civics education in the curricula with an emphasis on people engaging critically in inter-subjective deliberation.[44]

Certainly, the anti-racist agenda propounded at this conference resembled a liberal conception of democratic citizenship, whereby people's rights irrespective of race, colour, belief, and ethnicity cannot be violated. Yet, the conference, which culminated in the generation of the Manifesto on Values in Education,[45] put a great deal of emphasis on citizens engaging actively with others in shaping the future of South African society through deliberation, an idea which seems to be attuned with a communitarian conception of democratic citizenship.[46] This Manifesto on Values in Education identified 10 communitarian values in educational institutions: democracy, social justice and equity, equality, non-racism and non-sexism, *ubuntu* (human dignity), an open society, accountability, the rule of law, respect, and reconciliation.[47]

Teachers in public schools are required to acquaint themselves with the Manifesto on Values, Education and Democracy through in-service training offered by the nine regional education departments. The eight learning areas/themes in the Revised National Curriculum Statement are all attuned to the teaching and learning of democratic citizenship education as enunciated in the Manifesto. One of the serious challenges that teachers face, in particular in some township public schools, is how to begin to teach democratic citizenship education in an atmosphere of gangsterism, drug abuse, and domestic violence against women and children.

Can educational transformation be deepened according to this Manifesto agenda? I shall discuss two views on this: the view that a liberal-communitarian conception of citizenship education can deepen educational transformation, and the view that *ubuntu*, an extended liberal-communitarian conception of democratic citizenship education, can bring about meaningful change in public schools.

One can have little doubt that cultivating in learners the values of democracy, social justice and equity, equality, non-racism and non-sexism, *ubuntu*, openness, accountability, respect, and the need for reconciliation, and recognition of the rule of law, can produce a heightened awareness of what it means to be a "good" citizen, which would position them favourably to deal with issues of democracy, accountability, and reconciliation in post-apartheid South Africa. Educational transformation aims to engender in learners a deepened awareness of and appreciation for mutual respect, disagreement, justifiable criticism, critical judgment, rational deliberation, and nation building; it follows from this that the democratic "goods" proposed in the above Manifesto can in fact bring about transformation in education.

Enacting *ubuntu* has become currency in democratic citizenship education discourse in South African public schools, because it opens up possibilities for learners to connect with one another. Why? First, *ubuntu* presupposes a particular way of interacting with people on the basis of mutuality, thus invoking the integrity of all people in the social group, community organization, family, and so on. Second, *ubuntu* in an African humanist sense implies that people develop the capacity to reach out to others, being committed to one another without having to declare such commitment.[48] Third, moral goods such as social justice, human rights, equality before the law, quality of life, and democratic transformation of education are interdependent and can only be realized in community.

COMMON THREADS AND CHALLENGES IN GLOBAL CITIZENSHIP EDUCATION

In this chapter, I have explored some evolving understandings of what it means to educate for global citizenship and, with the help of my international colleagues, described curriculum directions in Canada, England, Pakistan, and South Africa. Below I offer a few concluding reflections as a way of illuminating some of the common threads and challenges that emerge from these examples.

Conceptions of what it means to educate for global citizenship reveal distinctive and overlapping understandings that are both complex and ambiguous.[49] On the one hand, perspectives from the four country vignettes above attend to certain common themes foregrounded in the citizenship education and global education literature. For example, all attend to questions of membership or identity, rights and responsibilities, interdependence, respect for diversity, and to some degree, at least in Canada, England, and South Africa, to cross-cultural understanding. The assorted conceptions described in the four country vignettes each include some attention to capacity-building to enable a young person to effectively engage in, and reflect upon, themes of global civic concern, and notions of social justice (in relation to such issues as human rights, the HIV/AIDS epidemic, global warming, and world poverty). Each country vignette demonstrates increased attention in recent years to citizenship in general, and (in some countries more than others) to democratic and/or global citizenship in particular.

At the same time, the country vignettes highlight divergent kinds of citizenship orientations (such as civic republican, liberal, communitarian). There is remarkable variation in which learning goals are given priority and depth. This suggests ambiguity in understandings of (global) citizenship and the learning it entails. Notions of membership in the global community (beyond that of the local and national), for example, are emphasized in different ways and to differing degrees, raising a range of questions about civic allegiance, identity, and culture. There is an apparent need to consider identity and culture more critically and deeply, balancing unity with diversity and "thinking globally" with "acting locally." Similarly, rights and responsibilities are given varying levels of attention in the conceptions provided above. Relevant international documents and agreements (such as the *Universal Declaration of Human Rights* and the *United Nations Convention of the Rights of the Child*) simply lack "legal and political exactness … when used to describe the status of a person in relation to the state."[50] Further, the country vignettes show differences of opinion (within and across countries) about how (global) citizenship education should approach questions of political action and advocacy for particular viewpoints. Thus global citizenship education, like all citizenship education, is an ambiguous and contested endeavour.

The importance of pedagogy is central to the conceptions of global citizenship education in each of the four vignettes. In some countries, global citizenship is located primarily within the History and Social Studies curriculum area; in others, global citizenship education is co-curricular and/or cross-curricular. Some curricula emphasize cognitive and content goals; others emphasize affective and/or skill-learning goals.

Clearly, pedagogy in any of these settings is never neutral (see Chapter Ten by Kathy Bickmore), and educators need to carefully select pedagogical practices (including instructional strategies, assessment approaches, and establishment of classroom climate) that align with the particular learning goals associated with educating for global citizenship. Critical thinking activities, issue-based inquiries and analysis, sharing of cross-cultural experience, managing instances of conflict, the exploration of multiple values, beliefs, and attitudes that underpin viewpoints on global issues, experiential opportunities for authentic learning, and engagement in one's community(ies) to address various forms of injustice are some of the pedagogical practices encouraged, albeit with differing levels of emphasis in each conception. Underpinning these global citizenship education practices, in many cases, is a transformative intent. Students are encouraged to inquire critically into various social and political themes and issues, and to use their findings to bring about personal and/or social change as active and responsible participants. Personal and social transformation, beyond a narrow set of core knowledge or thinking skills, appears to be central to global citizenship education intentions in various parts of the world.

Our brief consideration of curriculum policy in different national contexts illuminates additional issues. Interpretations of what is meant by global citizenship in policy documents, for example, are often subjective and infused with distinctive contextually rooted perspectives and priorities, what Pike has referred to as "globally oriented models of national education."[51] Certain curricula represent a stronger national orientation; others show a stronger religious orientation. These issues become more apparent when one considers how (global) citizenship is defined in policy documents, in relation to the broader purposes of learning, teaching methods, and assessment practices. These contrasting approaches raise questions about which learning goals ought to be to nurtured, and create a sense of uncertainty among educators attempting to effectively introduce understandings of global citizenship into the school curriculum.

Teachers face a range of challenges as they attempt to infuse global citizenship education into the curriculum. An already overloaded curriculum, inadequate professional preparation, little room for innovation in the official curriculum, or a school ethos that is not supportive are a few of the common roadblocks. Teachers also often have a sense that they will not be supported when attempting to address more complex global issues. While the literature cited above and these country vignettes demonstrate a burgeoning interest and availability of some global citizenship teaching resources from governmental and non-governmental sources, there is rarely consistent support for teacher learning or student materials in this area. The introduction of any curriculum innovation, wherein participants' conceptual understanding is unclear and/or underdeveloped, can be particularly problematic.

These challenges are further complicated by the relatively low status accorded to explicit citizenship education, and especially to global citizenship education, in many schools and school districts. This low status may be viewed in relation to "the deep historical links between citizenship education and the national state" and/or to an imbalance between the curriculum's civic intent and its economic intent. A "radical disjunction between developing perceptivity and world mindedness on the one hand, and preparing students to compete in the global economy on the other, suggests a struggle between two competing ideologies."[52]

This chapter has explored the varied understandings of what it means to educate for global citizenship, in relation to school curricula in different national and cultural contexts. A range of issues associated with area of education become quickly apparent, as do the questions and challenges for the teacher intending to infuse global citizenship into their teaching repertoire. Yet, as Heater suggests, "it is the very importance of the status and activity of being a citizen that commands us, not to neglect the subject, but, on the contrary, to understand the complexities and tensions that do exist and worry them to resolutions."[53]

QUESTIONS FOR REFLECTION AND DISCUSSION

1. Review the three perspectives offered as "Evolving Understandings of Global Citizenship," and consider the following questions:
   a. What key themes of citizenship education and global education are foregrounded in each perspective?
   b. In what ways are the perspectives similar and in what ways are they different?
   c. Which perspective do you find most appealing, and why?
2. Review the four vignettes that characterize curriculum directions in Canada, England, Pakistan, and South Africa and consider the following questions:
   a. What are the main attributes associated with educating for global citizenship in each context?
   b. How do you account for the apparent similarities and/or differences (e.g., historical, geo-political, philosophical/religious)?

    c.   What are some of the key challenges that teachers face as they attempt to educate for global citizenship?

3.   As a teacher, what do you see as being some of the more significant opportunities and/or roadblocks for infusing understandings of global citizenship into your own day-to day teaching? What types of support do you think would be helpful?

SUGGESTED AUDIO-VISUAL RESOURCES

We suggest that rather than showing a film, instructors explore Internet resources on citizenship education. Holding part of this class in a computer lab would be ideal.

a) Explore the Voice section of Taking It Global. This site offers tool kits on youth activism, allows youth to identify the global issues that matter to them most, and provides a list of websites and events that call for youth participation: www.takingitglobal.org/action/voice.

b) Review and perhaps conduct a classroom activity suggested in the document *Educating for Global Citizenship in a Changing World: A Teacher's Handbook*: cide.oise.utoronto.ca/globalcitizenship.php.

c) Take some of the quizzes and games on citizenship aimed specifically for children on the Cyber School Bus website sponsored by the UN for children: www.un.org/Pubs/CyberSchoolBus.

d) Instructors may also wish to use selected footage audio-visual resources on the Australian Broadcasting Corporation website, The Common Good. The website offers several websites on citizenship and democracy and highlights other online resources that may be useful to secondary school teachers: www.abc.net.au/civics.

SUGGESTIONS FOR FURTHER READING

Banks, James, ed. *Diversity and Citizenship Education: Global Perspectives*. San Francisco: John Wiley and Sons, 2004.

Boulding, Elise. *Building a Global Civic Culture: Education for an Interdependent World*. John Dewey Lecture. New York: Teachers College Press, 1988.

Clough, Nick and Cathie Holden. *Education for Citizenship: Ideas into Action*. London: RoutledgeFalmer, 2002.

*Davies, Lynn. "Global Citizenship: Abstraction or Framework for Action." *Educational Review* 58, no.1 (2006): 5–25.

Fountain, Susan. *Education for Development: A Teacher's Resource for Global Learning*. London: UNICEF, Hodder, and Stoughton, 1995.

Gibbs, Jeanne. *Reaching All by Creating Tribes Learning Communities*. Santa Rosa, CA: Centre Source Publications, 2006.

Hicks, David and Cathie Holden. *Teaching the Global Dimension: Key Principles and Effective Practice*. London: Routledge, Taylor, and Francis Group, 2007.

Kielburger, Marc and Craig Kielburger. *Take Action: A Guide to Active Citizenship*. Toronto: Gage Learning, 2002.

Lee, Wing On and Sai Wing Leung. "Global Citizenship Education in Hong Kong and Shanghai Secondary Schools: Ideals, Realities, and Expectations." *Citizenship Teaching and Learning* 2, no. 2 (2006): 68–84.

*Mundy, Karen and others. *Charting Global Education in Canada's Elementary Schools: Provincial, District and School Level Perspectives*. Toronto: UNICEF Canada, 2007. www.unicef.ca/portal/Secure/Community/508/WCM/EDUCATION/Global_Education_in_Canada_UNICEF_OISE.pdf.

Pike, Graham. "Global Education and National Identity: In Pursuit of Meaning." *Theory into Practice* 39, no. 2 (2000): 64–73.

*Pike, Graham and David Selby. *In the Global Classroom 2*. Toronto: Pippin, 2000.

Endnotes

Chapter One: Introduction to Comparative and International Education: Why Study Comparative Education?

1. Edmund King, *Other Schools and Ours* (London: Holt, Rinehart, and Winston, 1973).
2. Phillip E. Jones, *Comparative Education: Purpose and Method* (St. Lucia: University of Queensland Press, 1971), 31–56; A. R. Trethewey, *Introducing Comparative Education* (Oxford: Pergamon Press, 1976), 12–23.
3. William Theodore de Bary, *East Asian Civilizations: A Dialogue in Five Stages* (Cambridge, MA: Harvard University Press, 1988).
4. Ruth Hayhoe and Julia Pan, eds., *Knowledge across Cultures: A Contribution to Dialogue among Civilizations* (Hong Kong: Comparative Education Research Centre, University of Hong Kong, 2001).
5. Stewart Fraser, *Jullien's Plan for Comparative Education 1816–1817* (New York: Teachers College, Columbia University, 1964), 39.
6. Ibid., 40.
7. Ibid., 40–1.
8. Walter V. Brewer, *Victor Cousin as a Comparative Educator* (New York: Teachers College Press, 1971).
9. Jones, *Comparative Education: Purpose and Method*, 40–52.
10. George Bereday, "Sir Michael Sadler's 'Study of Foreign Systems of Education,'" *Comparative Education Review* 7, no. 3 (1964): 307–14.
11. Shigeru Nakayama, "Independence and Choice: Western Impacts on Japanese Higher Education," in *From Dependence to Autonomy: The Development of Asian Universities*, ed. Phillip Altbach and Viswanathan Selveratnam (Dordecht, The Netherlands: Kluwer Academic Publishers, 1989), 100.
12. Bob White, "Talk about School: Education and the Colonial Project in French and British Africa, 1860–1960," *Comparative Education* 32, no. 1 (1996): 9–25; Advisory Committee on Native Education in British Tropical African Dependencies, *Education Policy in British Tropical Africa* (London: Her Majesty's Stationary Office, 1925).
13. Nicholas Hans, *Comparative Education* (London: Routledge and Kegan Paul, 1967).
14. Isaac Kandel, *Comparative Education* (Boston: Houghton Mifflin Co., 1933).

15. In his preface, Kandel argued that "education systems are dominated by national ends, and that it is the duty of educators and teachers to understand the meaning of nationalism and all the forces that contribute to it." Kandel, *Comparative Education,* xxiv.

16. The IBE was merged with UNESCO in 1969. Bogdan Suchodolski and others, *The International Bureau of Education in the Service of Educational Development* (Paris: UNESCO, 1979).

17. Jing Shi-bo and Zhou Nan-zhao, "Comparative Education in China," *Comparative Education Review* 29, no. 2 (1985): 241, footnote 3.

18. Vandra Masemann, Mark Bray, and Maria Manzon, eds., *Common Interests, Uncommon Goals: Histories of the World Council of Comparative Education Societies and its Members,* CERC Studies in Comparative Education 21 (Hong Kong: Comparative Education Research Centre, University of Hong Kong and Springer, 2007).

19. George Bereday, *Comparative Method in Education* (New York: Holt Rinehart and Winston, 1964)

20. Harold Noah and Max Eckstein, *Towards a Science of Comparative Education* (London: MacMillan, 1969).

21. King, *Other Schools and Ours,* 20.

22. Ibid.

23. Edmund King, *Post-Compulsory Education: A New Analysis in Western Europe* (London: Sage, 1974); Edmund King, *Post-Compulsory Education II: The Way Ahead* (London: Sage, 1975).

24. Vandra Masemann, "Culture and Education," in *Comparative Education: The Dialectic of the Global and the Local,* ed. Robert F. Arnove and Carlos Torres (Lanham, MD: Rowman and Littlefield, 1999), 115–33.

25. Vandra Masemann, "Critical Ethnography in the Study of Comparative Education," *Comparative Education Review* 26, no. 1 (1982): 1–15.

26. Karl Popper, *Conjectures and Refutations: The Growth of Scientific Knowledge* (London: Routledge and Kegan Paul, 1963).

27. Brian Holmes, *Comparative Education: Some Considerations of Method* (London: George Allen and Unwin, 1981).

28. Lê Thàn Khôi, "Toward a General Theory of Education," *Comparative Education Review* 30, no. 1 (1986): 12–29.

29. Ruth Hayhoe, "Introduction," in *Education in China and Abroad: Perspectives from a Lifetime in Comparative Education,* ed. Mingyuan Gu (Hong Kong: Comparative Education Research Centre, University of Hong Kong, 2001), 5–24.

30. Gu Mingyuan, "Modern Production and Modern Education," in *Education in China and Abroad,* 27–51.

31. Fraser, *Jullien's Plan for Comparative Education,* 40–1.

32. Gu Mingyuan, "Modernisation and Education in China's Cultural Traditions," in *Education in China and Abroad,* 101–10.

33. Martin Carnoy, *Education as Cultural Imperialism* (New York: D. McKay Co., 1974), 56–7.

34. Paulo Freire, *Pedagogy of the Oppressed* (New York: Continuum, 1970).

35. Daniel Schugurensky, "The Legacy of Paulo Freire," *Convergence* 31, no. 1–2 (1998): 17–29.
36. Robert F. Arnove, "Comparative Education and World Systems Analysis," *Comparative Education Review* 24, no. 1 (1980): 48–62.
37. Philip Altbach and Gail P. Kelly, *Education and the Colonial Experience* (New Brunswick, NJ: Transaction Books, 1984).
38. Gail P. Kelly and Carolyn M. Elliot, *Women's Education in the Third World: Comparative Perspectives* (Albany, NY: State University of New York Press, 1982); David Kelly, ed., *International Feminist Perspectives on Educational Reform: The Work of Gail P. Kelly* (New York: Garland Publishing, 1996).
39. Nelly Stromquist, "Romancing the State: Gender and Power in Education," *Comparative Education Review* 39, no. 4 (1995): 423–54; Nelly Stromquist, "Determinants of Educational Participation and Achievement of Women in the Third World: A Review of Evidence and a Theoretical Critique," *Review of Educational Research* 59, no. 2 (1989): 143–83; Nelly Stromquist, "What Poverty Does to Girls Education: The Intersection of Class, Gender and Policy in Latin America," *Compare* 31, no. 1 (2001): 39–56.
40. Grace Mak, *Women, Education and Development in Asia: Cross-National Perspectives* (New York: Garland Publishing, 1996).
41. Kelly, *International Feminist Perspectives*, 37.
42. Johan Galtung, "A Structural Theory of Imperialism," *Journal of Peace Research* 8, no. 2 (1971): 81–117.
43. Ali Mazrui, "The African University as a Multinational Corporation," *Harvard Educational Review* 45, no. 2 (1975): 191–210.
44. George J. S. Dei, "Learning Culture, Spirituality, and Local Knowledge: Implications for African Schooling," *International Review of Education* 48, no. 5 (2002): 335–60; George J. S. Dei, "Afrocentricity: A Cornerstone of Pedagogy," *Anthropology and Education Quarterly* 25, no. 1 (1994): 3–28.
45. Karen Mundy, "Globalization and Educational Change: New Policy Worlds," in *International Handbook of Educational Policy, Part II*, ed. Nina Bascia and others (The Netherlands: Springer, 2005), 3–17.
46. Martin Carnoy, *Globalization and Educational Reform: What Planners Need to Know* (Paris: International Institute for Education Planning, 1999).
47. Andy Green, *Education, Globalization, and the Role of Comparative Research* (professional lecture, London: Institute of Education, University of London, December 2002).
48. Stephen Ball, "Big Policies/Small World: An Introduction to International Perspectives in Education Policy," *Comparative Education* 34, no. 2 (1998): 119–30; Gita Steiner-Khamsi, ed., *The Global Politics of Educational Borrowing and Lending* (New York: Teachers College Press, 2004).
49. See, for example, Miriam Henry and others, *The OECD, Globalisation, and Education Policy* (Oxford: Pergamon Press, 2001), 39–105; Karen Mundy, "Educational Multilateralism and World (Dis)order," *Comparative Education Review* 42, no. 4 (1998): 448–78; Susan Robertson, Xavier Bonal, and Roger Dale, "GATS and the Education Service Industry: Politics of Scale and

Global Reterritorialisation," *Comparative Education Review* 46, no. 3 (2002): 472–96; Roger Dale and Susan Robertson, "The Varying Effects of Regional Organizations as Subjects of Globalization of Education," *Comparative Education Review* 46, no. 1 (2002): 10–36.

50. Karen Mundy and Lynn Murphy, "Transnational Advocacy, Global Civil Society: Emerging Evidence from the Field of Education," *Comparative Education Review* 45, no. 1 (2001): 85–126.

51. Michael Crossley and Leon Tikly, "Postcolonial Perspectives and Comparative and International Research in Education: A Critical Introduction," *Comparative Education Review* 40, no. 2 (2004): 147–56. See also Rolland Paulston, ed., *Social Cartography: Mapping Ways of Seeing Social and Educational Change* (New York: Garland Publishing, 1996, republished as a paper in 2000).

52. Anne Hickling-Hudson, "Cultural Complexity, Post-Colonialism and Educational Change: Challenges for Comparative Educators," *International Review of Education* 52, no. 1 (2006): 201–18.

53. Kathryn Anderson-Levitt, *Local Meanings, Global Schooling: Anthropology and World Culture Theory* (New York: Palgrave Macmillan, 2003).

54. Arnove and Torres, *Comparative Education: The Dialectic of the Global and the Local.*

55. David Baker and Gerry LeTendre, *National Differences, Global Similarities: World Cuture and the Future of Schooling* (Palo Alto, CA: Stanford University Press, 2005); Francisco Ramirez and John Boli, "Global Patterns of Educational Institutionalization," in *Institutional Structure: Constituting State, Society, and the Individual,* ed. George M. Thomas and others (Newbury Park, CA: Sage, 1987), 150–72.

56. Green, *Education, Globalization.*

57. See also, Gita Steiner-Khamsi, Judith Torney-Purta, and Jack Schwille, eds., *New Paradigms and Recurring Paradoxes in Education for Citizenship* (Oxford: Elsevier Science Ltd., 2002).

Chapter Two: Philosophy and Comparative Education: What Can We Learn from East Asia?

1. Max Weber, *Sociological Writings,* ed. Wolf Heydebrand (New York: Continuum, 1994), 266.

2. Ezra Vogel, *The Four Little Dragons: The Spread of Industrialization in East Asia* (Cambridge, MA: Harvard University Press, 1991).

3. Brian Holmes, *Comparative Education: Some Considerations of Method* (London: George Allen and Unwin, 1981), 111–175.

4. Benjamin Schwartz, *The World of Thought in Ancient China* (Cambridge, MA: Harvard University Press, 1985), 70.

5. William Boyd and Edmund J. King, *The History of Western Education* (London: Adam and Charles Black, 1975), 32–36.

6. Schwartz, *The World of Thought in Ancient China,* 69.

7. Ibid., 95.

8.   Tu Wei-ming, "Beyond the Enlightenment Mentality," in *Confucianism and Ecology: The Interrelation of Heaven, Earth and Humans*, eds. Mary Evelyn Tucker and John Berthrong (Cambridge, MA: Harvard University Centre for the Study of World Religions, distributed by Harvard University Press, 1998), 13–14.

9.   Lee Wing On, "The Cultural Context for Chinese Learners: Conceptions of Learning in the Confucian Tradition," in *The Chinese Learner: Cultural, Psychological and Contextual Influences*, eds. David A. Watkins and John B. Biggs (Hong Kong: Comparative Education Research Centre, University of Hong Kong, 1996), 30.

10.   Boyd and King, *The History of Western Education*, 36.

11.   Roger T. Ames and David L. Hall, *Daodejing: "Making this Life Significant": A Philosophical Translation* (New York: Ballantine Books, 2004).

12.   Henry Weerasinghe, *Education for Peace: The Buddha's Way* (Ratmalana, Sri Lanka: Aarvodaya Book Publishing Services, 1992), 49–50.

13.   Lee Wing On, "The Cultural Context for Chinese Learners," 38.

14.   Ruth Hayhoe, *Portraits of Influential Chinese Educators* (Hong Kong: Comparative Education Research Centre, University of Hong Kong, 2006), 21.

15.   Isabelle Llasera, "Confucian Education through European Eyes," in *China's Education and the Industrialized World: Studies in Cultural Transfer*, eds. Ruth Hayhoe and Marianne Bastid (New York: M.E. Sharpe, 1987), 21–32.

16.   Holmes, *Comparative Education*, 146.

17.   Ibid., 148.

18.   Ibid., 145.

19.   Ibid., 156.

20.   Ibid., 162–172.

21.   Horio Teruhisa and Steven Platzer, *Educational Thought and Ideology in Modern Japan: State Authority and Intellectual Freedom* (Tokyo: University of Tokyo Press, 1988), 399.

22.   Julia Ching, "East Asian Religions," in *World Religions: Eastern Traditions*, ed. William Oxtoby (Toronto, New York, Oxford: Oxford University Press, 1996), 379.

23.   George Bereday, *Universities for All* (San Francisco: Jossey Bass, 1973).

24.   Nobuo K. Shimihara, "Teacher Education Reform in Japan: Ideological and Control Issues," in *Teacher Education in Industrialized Nations: Issues in Changing Social Contexts*, eds. Nobuo K. Shimihara and Ivan Z. Holowinsky (New York and London: Garland Publishing Inc., 1995), 169–179.

25.   Horio Teruhisa, *Educational Thought and Ideology*, 171–279.

26.   Miyazaki Ichisada, *China's Examination Hell: The Civil Service Examinations of Imperial China* (New York and Tokyo: Weatherhill, 1971).

27.   William Cummings, "The Institutions of Education: Compare, Compare, Compare!," *Comparative Education Review* 43, no. 4 (1999): 425.

28.   Douglas Reynolds, *China 1898-1912: The Xinzheng Revolution and Japan* (Cambridge, MA: Council on East Asian Studies, Harvard University, 1993).

29.   Ruth Hayhoe, "The Evolution of Modern Educational Institutions," in *Contemporary Chinese Education*, ed. Ruth Hayhoe (New York: M.E. Sharpe, 1984), 38.

30. Barry Keenan, *The Dewey Experiment in China: Educational Reform and Political Power in the Early Republic* (Cambridge, MA: Harvard University Press, 1977).

31. Douglas C. Smith, "Foundations of Modern Chinese Education and the Taiwan Experience," and Liao-wen Mao and Stanley E. Bourgeault, "Early Childhood Education and Elementary Education in Taiwan," in *The Confucian Continuum: Educational Modernization in Taiwan*, ed. Douglas C. Smith (New York: Praeger Publishers, 1991), 1–98.

32. Ronald Price, "Convergence or Copying? China and the Soviet Union," in Hayhoe and Bastid, *China's Education and the Industrialized World*, 166.

33. Leo A. Orleans, "Soviet Influences on China's Higher Education," in Hayhoe and Bastid, *China's Education and the Industrialized World*, 184–195.

34. Ruth Hayhoe, *China's Universities 1895–1995: A Century of Cultural Conflict* (Hong Kong: Comparative Education Research Centre, University of Hong Kong, 1999), 99–100.

35. Ruth Hayhoe, *Portraits of Influential Chinese Educators*, 69.

36. Gu Mingyuan, "Modernization and Education in China's Cultural Traditions," in *Education in China and Abroad: Perspectives from a Lifetime in Comparative Education*, ed. Gu Mingyuan (Hong Kong: Comparative Education Research Centre, University of Hong Kong, 2001), 101–110.

37. Jonathan London, "Rethinking Vietnam's Mass Education and Health Systems," and Doan Hue Dung, "Centralism—the Dilemma of Educational Reforms in Vietnam," in *Rethinking Vietnam*, ed. Duncan McCargo (London and New York: RoutledgeCurzon, 2004); Pham Minh Hac, "The Educational System of Vietnam," in *Higher Education in Vietnam*, eds. David Sloper and Le Thac Can (New York: St Martin's Press, 1995), 41–61.

38. Michael J. Seth, *Education Fever: Society, Politics, and the Pursuit of Schooling in South Korea* (Honolulu: University of Hawaii Press, 2002).

39. Jason Tan, S. Gopinathan, and Ho Wah Kam, *Challenges Facing the Singapore Education System Today* (Singapore: Prentice Hall, 2001).

40. Gavin Sanderson, "International Education Developments in Singapore," *International Education Journal* 3, no. 2 (2002): 85–103.

41. Mark Bray and Ramsey Koo, eds., *Education and Society in Hong Kong and Macao: Comparative Perspectives on Continuity and Change* (Hong Kong: Comparative Education Research Centre, University of Hong Kong, 1999).

42. Lee Wing On, "Citizenship Education in Hong Kong: Development and Challenges," in *Citizenship Education in Asia and the Pacific: Concepts and Issues*, eds. Wing On Lee and others, 59–80 (Hong Kong: Comparative Education Research Centre, University of Hong Kong, 2004).

43. Ruth Hayhoe, "Creating a Vision for Teacher Education between East and West: The Case of the Hong Kong Institute of Education," *Compare* 31, no. 3 (2001): 329–45.

44. Gu Mingyuan, "Modern Education and Modern Production," in Mingyuan, *Education in China and Abroad*, 37.

45. Harold W. Stevenson and James W. Stigler, *The Learning Gap: Why our Schools are Failing and What We Can Learn from Japanese and Chinese Education* (New York: Simon and Schuster, 1992).
46. Ibid., 70–1.
47. Ibid., 71.
48. Ibid., 80.
49. Ibid., 83.
50. Ibid., 111.
51. Ibid., 141.
52. Ibid., 166–7.
53. Ibid., 167–8. It should be noted that Stigler and Stevenson's portrayal of East Asian teachers and learners has come under considerable criticism from social and cultural psychologists. See, for example, Giyoo Hatano and Kayoko Inagaki, "Cultural Contexts of Schooling Revisited: A Review of The Learning Gap from a Cultural Psychology Perspective," in *Global Prospects for Education: Development, Culture and Schooling*, eds. Scott G. Paris and Henry M. Wellman (Washington, DC: American Psychological Association, 1998), 79–104.

Chapter Three: "Education for All," Africa, and the Comparative Sociology of Schooling

1. General Assembly of the United Nations, *Universal Declaration of Human Rights*, Article 26, 1948, www.un.org/Overview/rights.html.
2. Samuel Bowles and Herbert Gintis, *Schooling in Capitalist America; Educational Reform and the Contradictions of Economic Life* (London: Routledge and Kegan Paul, 1977); Detlef Muller, Fritz Ringer, and Brian Simon, *The Rise of the Modern Educational System: Structural Change and Social Reproduction 1870–1920* (New York: Cambridge University Press, 1989).
3. Bruce Fuller, *Growing up Modern: The Western State Builds Third World Schools* (New York: Routledge, 1991); Bruce Fuller and Richard Rubinson, *The Political Construction of Education : the State, School Expansion, and Economic Change* (New York: Praeger, 1992); Randall Collins, "Comparative and Historical Patterns of Education," in *Handbook of the Sociology of Education*, ed. Maureen T. Hallinan (New York: Kluwer Academic and Plenum, 2000), 213–40.
4. Thomas Marshall, *Citizenship and Social Class* (Cambridge: Cambridge University Press, 1950); Roger Dale, *The State and Education Policy* (Milton Keynes: Open University Press, 1989).
5. Francisco Ramirez and John Boli, "Global Patterns of Educational Institutionalization," in *Institutional Structure: Constituting the State, Society and the Individual*, eds. George M. Thomas and others (Beverly Hills, California: Sage, 1987), 150–72; John W. Meyer and others, "World Society and the Nation-State," *American Journal of Sociology* 103, no. 1 (1997): 144–81.
6. Joseph P. Farrell, "Changing Conceptions of Equality of Education: 40 Years of Comparative Evidence," in *Comparative Education: The Dialectic of the Global and the Local*, eds. Robert F. Arnove and Carlos A. Torres (New York: Rowman and Littlefield, 1999), 149–78.

7. Aaron Benavot and Julia Resnik, "Towards a Comparative Socio-Historical Analysis of Universal Basic and Secondary Education," in *Educating All the Children: A Global Agenda*, eds. Joel Cohen, David Bloom, and Martin Malin (Cambridge, MA: American Academy of Arts and Sciences and MIT Press, 2006), 123–231.

8. Karen Mundy, "Educational Multilateralism and World (Dis)Order," *Comparative Education Review* 42, no. 4 (1998): 448–78.

9. Alex Inkeles and Donald Holsinger, *Education and Individual Modernity in Developing Countries* (Leiden: Brill, 1974); David McClelland, *The Achieving Society* (Princeton: D. Van Nostrand, 1961).

10. Theodore Schultz, "Capital Formulation by Education," *Journal of Political Economy* 68, no. 6 (1960): 571–83; Gary Becker, "Investment in Human Capital: A Theoretical Analysis," *Journal of Political Economy* 70, no. 5 (1962): 9–49; Frederick Harbison and Charles Meyers, *Education, Manpower, and Economic Growth: Strategies of Human Resource Development* (New York: McGraw-Hill, 1964).

11. Farrell, "Changing Conceptions of Equality."

12. David Abernathy, *The Political Dilemma of Popular Education: An African Case* (Stanford, CA: Stanford University Press, 1969); Philip Foster, *Education and Social Change in Ghana* (London: Routledge, 1965).

13. Samuel Huntington, *Political Order in Changing Societies* (New Haven: Yale University Press, 1968).

14. Emily Hannum and Claudia Buchmann, "Global Education Expansion and Socio-Economic Development: An Assessment of Findings from the Social Sciences," *World Development* 33, no. 3 (2005): 333–54.

15. Ibid., 345.

16. James Coleman and others, *Equality of Educational Opportunity* (Washington, DC: US Department of Health, Education and Welfare, 1966); Anthony Halsey, Anthony Heath, and John Ridge, *Origins and Destinations: Family, Class and Education in Modern Britain* (Oxford: Clarendon, 1980).

17. Farrell, "Changing Conceptions of Equality."

18. Emily Hannum and Claudia Buchmann, *The Consequences of Global Educational Expansion: Social Science Perspectives* (Cambridge, MA: American Academy of Arts and Sciences, 2003).

19. Nelly Stromquist, "Women's Education in the Twenty-First Century," in Arnove and Torres, *The Global and the Local*, 176–203; Hannum and Buchmann, *The Consequences of Global Educational Expansion*.

20. Bowles and Gintis, *Schooling in Capitalist America*; Paul Willis, *Learning to Labor: How Working Class Kids Get Working Class Jobs* (New York: Columbia University Press, 1981); Martin Carnoy and Henry Levin, *Schooling and Work in the Democratic State* (Stanford, CA: Stanford University Press, 1985).

21. Robert F. Arnove, "Comparative Education and World Systems Analysis," *Comparative Education Review* 24, no. 1 (1980): 48–62.

22. Ivan Illich, *Deschooling Society* (New York: Harper and Row, 1971); Fuller, *Growing up Modern*.

23. Kwame Nkrumah, *Consciencism; Philosophy and Ideology for De-colonization* (New York: Monthly Review Press, 1970); Julius Nyerere, *Freedom and Socialism:*

Uhuru na Ujamaa; A Selection from Writings and Speeches, 1965–1967 (Dar es Salaam: Oxford University Press, 1969).

24. Franz Fanon, *The Wretched of the Earth*, trans. Constance Farrington (New York: Grove Press, 1963); Ngugi wa Thiong'o, *A Grain of Wheat* (Oxford Heinemann, 1986); Ngugi wa Thiong'o, *Decolonising the Mind: The Politics of Language in African Literature* (New Hampshire: Heinemann, 1986); Stromquist, "Women's Education in the Twenty-First Century."

25. George J. S. Dei, "African Development: The Relevance and Implications of 'Indigenousness,'" in *Indigenous Knowledges in Global Contexts: Multiple Readings of Our World*, eds. George J. S. Dei, Budd L. Hall, and Dorothy G. Rosenberg (Toronto: University of Toronto Press, 2000), 72; See also Ali Abdi, "African Philosophies of Education: Counter-Colonial Criticisms," in *Issues in African Education: Sociological Perspectives*, eds. Ali Abdi and Ailie Cleghorn (New York: Palgrave Macmillan, 2005), 25–42.

26. Julius Nyerere, "Education for Self Reliance," in *Ujamaa: Essays on Socialism* (Dar es Salaam, Tanzania: Oxford University Press, 1967), 1–12.

27. Joel Samoff, "No Teacher Guide, No Textbooks, No Chairs: Contending with Crisis in African Education," in Arnove and Torres, *The Global and the Local*, 409–445.

28. Yusuf Kassam, "Julius Nyerere," in *Thinkers on Education*, ed. Zaghloul Morsy (Paris: UNESCO Publishing, 1995), www.ibe.unesco.org/publications/ThinkersPdf/nyereree.pdf; Karen Mundy, "Towards a Critical Analysis of Literacy in Southern Africa," *Comparative Education Review* 37, no. 4 (1993): 389–411.

29. Paulo Freire, *Pedagogy of the Oppressed* (New York: Continuum, 1970).

30. Ibid., 95.

31. Mundy, "Educational Multilateralism and World (Dis)Order".

32. Samoff, "No Teacher Guide."

33. Frances Vavrus, "Adjusting Inequality: Education and Structural Adjustment Policies in Tanzania," *Harvard Educational Review* 75, no. 2 (2005): 174–201.

34. Samoff, "No Teacher Guide," 6.

35. Ibid., 7.

36. Ibid., 13.

37. Fernando Reimers, "Education and Structural Adjustment in Latin America and Sub-Saharan Africa," *International Journal of Educational Development* 14, no. 2 (1994): 119–29.

38. Martin Carnoy, *Globalization and Educational Reform: What Planners Need to Know* (Paris: UNESCO, International Institute for Educational Planning, 1999).

39. Eric Hanushek, "Interpreting Recent Research on Schooling in Developing Countries," *The World Bank Research Observer* 10, no. 2 (1995): 22–46.

40. Stephen Ball, "Big Policies/Small World: An Introduction to International Perspectives in Education Policy," *Comparative Education* 34, no. 2 (1998): 119–130; Roger Dale, "Globalization and Education: Demonstrating a 'Common World Educational Culture' or Locating a 'Globally Structured Educational Agenda'?" *Educational Theory* 50, no. 4 (2000): 427–48.

41. Martin Carnoy, "Structural Adjustment and the Changing Face of Education," *International Labour Review* 134, no. 6 (1995): 653–73; Christopher Colclough, "Who Should Learn to Pay? An Assessment of Neo-Liberal Approaches to Education Policy," in *States or Markets? Neo-Liberalism and the Development Policy Debate*, eds. Christopher Colclough and James Manor (Oxford: Clarendon Press, 1991), 197–213; Reimers, "Education and Structural Adjustment," 119–129.

42. Keith Hinchcliffe, "Neo-Liberal Prescriptions for Education Finance: Unfortunately Necessary or Inherently Desirable?" *International Journal of Educational Development* 13, no. 2 (1993): 183–7; Colclough, "Who Should Learn to Pay?"

43. Jeanne Moulton and others, *Education Reforms in Sub-Saharan Africa: Paradigm Lost?* (Westport, Connecticut: Greenwood Press, 2002).

44. Vavrus, "Adjusting Inequality," 183.

45. UN Resolution A/RES/55/2, *United Nations Millennium Declaration* (New York: United Nations, 2000); The Millennium Development Declaration sets out eight Millennium Development Goals (MDGs) with time bound, measurable targets. These targets, set for 2015, include reducing world poverty, the spread of HIV/AIDS, and the number of people without safe drinking water by 50 percent; reducing infant mortality by 66 percent; combating malaria; and promoting gender equity and environmental sustainability. Universal primary education and gender equity in education are MDGs numbers two and three.

46. Karen Mundy, "Education for All and the New Development Compact," *International Review of Education* 52, no. 1 (2006): 23–48; Karen Mundy, "Education in a Reformed World Bank," *International Journal of Educational Development* 22, no. 5 (2002): 483–508.

47. Rose-Marie Torres, *One Decade of Education for All: The Challenge Ahead* (Buenos Aires: International Institute of Educational Planning, 2000); Colette Chabbott, *Constructing Education for Development: International Organizations and Education for All* (New York: Routledge/Falmer, 2003).

48. Joseph Stiglitz, *Globalization and Its Discontents* (New York: W.W. Norton, 2003).

49. Alain Noel, *The New Politics of Global Poverty* (unpublished manuscript, Université de Montréal, December 2005).

50. Jean-Phillipe Therien, "The Politics of International Development: Towards a New Grand Compromise?" *Economic Policy and Law: Journal of Trade and Environmental Studies,* (special issue, September 2004); John G. Ruggie, "The United Nations and Globalization: Patterns and Limits of Institutional Adaptation," *Global Governance* 9, no. 3 (2003): 301–22.

51. World Bank, *Achieving Education for All By 2015, Simulation Results for 47 Low Income Countries* (Washington, DC: World Bank, 2002).

52. Simon Maxwell, "The Washington Consensus is Dead! Long Live the Meta-Narrative!" (working paper WP/243, London: Overseas Development Institute, 2005), www.odi.org.uk/publications/working_papers/wp243.pdf.

53. Gene Sperling, "Toward Universal Education: Making a Promise and Keeping It," *Foreign Affairs* 80, no. 5 (2001): 7–13; Nancy Birdsall and Milan Vaishnav,

"Education and the MDGs: Realizing the Millennium Compact," *Columbia Journal of International Affairs* 58, no. 2 (2005): 257–64.

54. UN Millennium Project, *Toward Universal Primary Education: Investments, Incentives and Institutions*, prepared by the Task Force on Education and Gender Equality (London: Earthscan and the UN Millennium Project, 2005), www. unmillenniumproject.org/documents/Education-complete.pdf.

55. UNESCO, *Education for All Global Monitoring Report 2005: The Quality Imperative* (Paris: UNESCO, 2005), 208.

56. Karen Mundy and Lynn Murphy, "Transnational Advocacy, Global Civil Society? Emerging Evidence from the Field of Education," *Comparative Education Review* 45, no. 1 (2001): 85–126.

57. The Group of Eight (G8) is an international forum for the governments of Canada, France, Germany, Italy, Japan, Russia, the United Kingdom and the United States. Together, these countries represent about 65 percent of the world economy.

58. Mundy, "Education for All and the New Development Compact," 23–48.

59. David Stasavage, "Democracy and Education Spending in Africa," *American Journal of Political Science* 49, no. 2 (2005): 343–58.

60. In 1961, Kenya had roughly 10 primary and middle school students for every six in Tanzania. See Brian Cooksey, David Court, and Ben Makau, "Education for Self-Reliance and Harambee," in *Beyond Capitalism and Socialism in Kenya and Tanzania*, ed. Joel Barkan (London: Lynne Rienner, 1994), 201–33.

61. Cooksey, Court, and Makau, "Education for Self-Reliance"; Malini Sivasubramaniam and Karen Mundy, *Kenya: Civil Society Participation and the Governance of Educational Systems in the Context of Sector Wide Approaches to Basic Education* (mimeo, Toronto: OISE/University of Toronto, 2006).

62. Claudia Buchmann, "The State and Schooling in Kenya: Historical Developments and Current Challenges," *Africa Today* 46, no. 1 (1999): 95–115.

63. Joel Samoff, "'Modernizing' a Socialist Vision: Education in Tanzania", in *Education and Social Transition in the Third World*, ed. Martin Carnoy and Joel Samoff (Princeton: Princeton University Press, 1990), 209–73.

64. Maarifa ni Ufunguo, *Cost Sharing: A Case Study of Education in Kilimanjaro* (Arusha, Tanzania: Maarifa ni Ufunguo, 2000); Jeanette L. Kuder, "The Formulation of Primary Education Policy in Tanzania within a Global Governance Approach to Aid and Development" (PhD dissertation, University of Bristol, 2004).

65. Megan Haggerty and Karen Mundy, *Tanzania: Civil Society Participation and the Governance of Educational Systems in the Context of Sector Wide Approaches to Basic Education* (working paper, Toronto: OISE/University of Toronto, 2006).

66. While the government is broadly favourable to civil society, it also reacts aggressively to criticism. In 2005, the government banned the influential education advocacy NGO Haki Elimu from publicizing its research in print or broadcast media because it was critical of the government's EFA efforts.

67. Dickson Khainga and others, *United Republic of Tanzania: Education Sector Public Expenditure Review (PER)*, (2nd draft report, Madrid, Spain: Altair Asesores, Neimacro Group, 2005).

68. Joel Samoff, "From Funding Projects to Supporting Sectors? Observations on the Aid Relationship in Burkina Faso," *International Journal of Educational Development* 24, no. 4 (2004): 397–427.
69. World Bank, "EdStats," devdata.worldbank.org/edstats; United Nations Development Programme, *Human Development Report 2006,* Table 18 (2007), hdr. undp.org/en/media/hdr06-complete.pdf; UNESCO, *EFA Global Monitoring Report: GMR Data* (2007), gmr.uis.unesco.org.
70. Robert Serpell, "Local Accountability to Rural Communities: A Challenge to Educational Planning in Africa," in *Education, Cultures and Economics: Dilemmas for Development*, eds. Fiona Leach and Angela Little (New York: Garland, 1999), 107–35.

Chapter Four: Comparative Indigenous Ways of Knowing and Learning

1. Vandra Masemann, "Educational Reform: Impact of Indigenous Knowledge," in *Encyclopedia of International Education* (2nd ed.), eds. Torsten Husén and T. Neville Postlewaite (Oxford: Pergamon, 1994), 1848–52.
2. As per the Royal Commission on Aboriginal Peoples, *Indigenous* and other such terms are capitalized in this chapter wherever they are used as proper names for a collective group of people, such as would be used in identifying the French or Chinese, as well as when used as a modifier for those groups (for example, French cuisine; Aboriginal traditions).
3. Although the scope of this chapter encompasses Indigenous peoples worldwide, it primarily focuses on the Indigenous peoples of Canada, the United States, Australia, and New Zealand. This is due in part to the concentration of scholarship that has emerged from those countries on Indigenous topics and by Indigenous scholars, as well as to the background and experience base of the authors.
4. Indian and Northern Affairs Canada, *An Evolving Terminology Relating to Aboriginal Peoples in Canada* (Canada: Indian and Northern Affairs Communications Branch, 2002), 166; Leanne Simpson, "Anishinaabe Ways of Knowing," in *Aboriginal Health, Identity, and Resources*, eds. Jill Oakes, and others (Winnipeg, MB: Aboriginal Issues Press, University of Manitoba, 2000), 165–85.
5. The presence of well-developed Aboriginal pedagogies prior to colonial contact is documented by many sources, including Lenore A. Stiffarm, ed., *As We See ... : Aboriginal Pedagogy* (Saskatoon, SK: University Extension Press, University of Saskatchewan, 1998); Willie Ermine, "Aboriginal Epistemology," in *First Nations Education in Canada: The Circle Unfolds*, ed. Marie Battiste and Jean Barman (Vancouver, BC: University of British Columbia Press, 1995), 101–12; Gregory Cajete, *Look to the Mountain: An Ecology of Indigenous Education* (Durango, CO: Kivaki Press, 1994).
6. Wendy Brady, "Indigenous Australian Education and Globalisation," in *Tradition, Modernity and Post-Modernity in Comparative Education*, ed. Vandra

Masemann and Anthony Welch (Dordrecht, The Netherlands: Kluwer Academic Publishers, 1997), 421.

7. There is wide documentation on the negative impacts of colonization and practices such as enforced residential schooling on Aboriginal peoples. Challenges such as breakdown in family structures, family violence, alcoholism, and high suicide rates are often linked to ruptures caused by the residential schooling experience. See, for example, Kevin Annett and the Truth Commission's film *Unrepentant: Kevin Annett and Canada's Genocide*, video. google.com/videoplay?docid=-6637396204037343133.

8. Marie Battiste, *Indigenous Knowledge and Pedagogy in First Nations Education: A Literature Review with Recommendations*, Report Commissioned by the Minister's National Working Group on Education (Ottawa, ON: Indian and Northern Affairs Canada, 2002).

9. Masemann, "Educational Reform," 1849.

10. Leroy Little Bear, "Jagged Worldviews Colliding," in *Reclaiming Indigenous Voice and Vision*, ed. Marie Battiste (Vancouver, BC: University of British Columbia Press, 2000), 77–85; Eber Hampton, "Toward a Redefinition of Indian Education," in Battiste and Barman, *First Nations Education*, 5–46; Battiste, *Indigenous Knowledge and Pedagogy*; Masemann, "Educational Reform."

11. Battiste, *Indigenous Knowledge and Pedagogy*, 6.

12. Ibid., 4.

13. Ibid., 13.

14. Joseph Couture, "The Role of Native Elders: Emergent Issues," in *The Cultural Maze: Complex Questions on Native Destiny in Western Canada*, ed. John W. Friesen (Calgary, AB: Detselig Enterprises Ltd, 1991), 201–17.

15. Ermine, "Aboriginal Epistemology," 107.

16. Hampton, "Redefinition of Indian Education," 19.

17. Battiste, *Indigenous Knowledge and Pedagogy*, 13.

18. Little Bear, "Jagged Worldviews," 77.

19. Ermine, "Aboriginal Epistemology," 107.

20. Ibid., 101.

21. Hampton, "Redefinition of Indian Education," 19.

22. Taima Moeke-Pickering and others, "Keeping our Fire Alive: Towards Decolonising Research in the Academic Setting," *World Indigenous Nations Higher Education Consortium Journal* (2006): 5.

23. Marlene Brant Castellano, "Updating Aboriginal Traditions of Knowledge," in *Indigenous Knowledges in Global Contexts: Multiple Readings of Our World*, eds. George J. Sefa Dei, Budd L. Hall, and Dorothy Goldin Rosenberg (Toronto: OISE/University of Toronto Press), 21–36.

24. See, for example, Lillian E. Dyck, "An Analysis of Western, Feminist and Aboriginal Science Using the Medicine Wheel of the Plains Indians," in Stiffarm, *As We See*, 87–102.

25. Interpretations of the medicine wheel vary widely according to each Indigenous culture and tradition; for example, in some cultures black is not used as one of the four colors since in those cultures it represents death. The wheel depicted also only represents a few of the potential aspects of each direction.

26. Judie Bopp and others, *The Sacred Tree*, 3rd ed. (Twin Lakes, WI: Lotus Light Publications, 1989).

27. Little Bear, "Jagged Worldviews," 78.

28. Gregory Cajete, "Indigenous Knowledge: The Pueblo Metaphor of Indigenous Education," in Battiste, *Reclaiming Indigenous Voice*, 183.

29. George J. Sefa Dei, "African Development: The Relevance and Implications of 'Indigenousness,'" in Dei, Hall, and Rosenberg, *Indigenous Knowledges*, 70–86.

30. Royal Commission on Aboriginal Peoples, *Report of the Royal Commission on Aboriginal Peoples, Vol. 1*.Ottawa, ON: Canada, 1996, 622–3.

31. Vine Deloria, Jr., *Red Earth, White Lies: Native Americans and the Myth of Scientific Fact*, (Golden, BC: Fulcrum Publishing, 1997); Theresa Smith, *The Island of the Anishnaabeg: Thunderers and Water Monsters in the Traditional Ojibwe Life-World* (Toronto, ON: University of Toronto Press, 1995).

32. Ermine, "Aboriginal Epistemology," 104.

33. MaryAnne Lanigan, "Aboriginal Pedagogy: Storytelling," in Stiffarm, *As We See*, 106.

34. David A. Lertzman, "Rediscovering Rites of Passage: Education, Transformation, and the Transition to Sustainability," *Conservation Ecology* 5, no. 2 (2002), www.consecol.org/vol5/iss2/art30.

35. Fhulu Nekhwevha, "No Matter How Long the Night, the Day is Sure to Come: Culture and Educational Transformation in Post-Colonial Namibia and Post-Apartheid South Africa," in *Education, Equity, and Transformation*, eds. Crain Soudien and Peter Kallaway (Dordrecht, The Netherlands: Kluwer Academic Publishers, 1999), 491–506.

36. Battiste, *Indigenous Knowledge and Pedagogy*, 13.

37. Castellano, "Updating Aboriginal Traditions," 23–24.

38. Ibid., 24.

39. Castellano, "Updating Aboriginal Traditions," 31; Little Bear, "Jagged Worldviews," 81.

40. Cajete, *Look to the Mountain*, 112.

41. Lanigan, "Storytelling," 113.

42. Cajete, *Look to the Mountain*, 68.

43. Simpson, "Anishinaabe Ways," 257.

44. Ida Swan, "Modelling: An Aboriginal Approach," in Stiffarm, *As We See*, 51–2.

45. Lertzman, "Rites of Passage," 4.

46. Little Bear, "Jagged Worldviews," 78.

47. Ermine, "Aboriginal Epistemology," 110.

48. Ibid.

49. James (Sákéj) Youngblood Henderson, "*Ayukpachi*: Empowering Aboriginal Thought," in Battiste, *Reclaiming Indigenous Voice*, 263.

50. Hampton, "Redefinition of Indian Education," 2.

51. Henderson, "*Ayukpachi*," p. 263.

52. Douglas Cardinal, "Dancing with Chaos: An Interview with Douglas Cardinal," quoted in Dennis H. McPherson and J. Douglas Rabb, *Indian from the Inside: A*

Study in Ethno-Metaphysics (occasional paper 14, Thunder Bay, ON: Lakehead University Centre for Northern Studies, 1993).

53. The potlatch is a complex ceremony practised primarily by Northwest coastal peoples in North America (such as Haida, Haisla, Coast Salish, and Kwakiutl). A form of political, economic, and social exchange, it is a vital part of these cultures' way of life. Although protocol differs among the Indigenous nations, the potlatch could involve a feast, with music, dance, and spiritual ceremonies. Gifts are given by the host to establish or uphold status positions in society; gifting also serves to redistribute resources throughout the community. Potlatches often mark a significant event, such as the celebration of births, rites of passages, weddings, funerals, puberty, and honouring of the deceased. Potlatches are also the venue in which ownership to economic and ceremonial privileges is asserted, displayed, and formally transferred to heirs.

54. Battiste, *Indigenous Knowledge and Pedagogy*, 15.

55. Ermine, "Aboriginal Epistemology," 110.

56. Lanigan, "Storytelling," 112.

57. Ermine, "Aboriginal Epistemology," 108.

58. Battiste, *Indigenous Knowledge and Pedagogy*, 14.

59. Little Bear, "Jagged Worldviews," 81.

60. Royal Commission on Aboriginal Peoples, "Elders' Perspectives," in *Report of the Royal Commission on Aboriginal Peoples, Vol. 4,* (Ottawa, ON: Canada, 1996), www.ainc-inac.gc.ca/ch/rcap/sg/sjm3_e.html.

61. Hampton, "Redefinition of Indian Education," 19.

62. Deborah McGregor, "Coming Full Circle: Indigenous Knowledge, Environment and our Future," *American Indian Quarterly*, 28, no. 3 and 4 (2004): 385–410.

63. Ibid.

64. Battiste, *Indigenous Knowledge and Pedagogy*, 14.

65. Hampton, "Redefinition of Indian Education," 21.

66. Vandra Masemann, "Contextualising the Dialogue," in G. Robert Teasdale and Zane Ma Rhea, *Local Knowledge and Wisdom in Higher Education* (Oxford, England: Elsevier Science, 2000).

67. Philip Altbach and Gail P. Kelly, *Education and the Colonial Experience* (New Brunswick, NJ: Transaction Books, 1984)

68. Vandra Masemann, "Ways of Knowing: Implications for Comparative Education," *Comparative Education Review* 34, no. 4 (1990): 465–73.

69. Masemann and Welch, *Tradition, Modernity, and Postmodernity*.

70. Teasdale and Ma Rhea, *Local Knowledge and Wisdom in Higher Education*.

71. See, for example, Claudia Zaslavsky, *Africa Counts: Number and Pattern in African Culture*, 3rd ed. (Chicago: Lawrence Hill Books, 1999); Anne R. Hickling-Hudson, "'White', 'Ethnic' and 'Indigenous.' Pre-service Teachers Reflect on Discourses of Ethnicity in Australian Culture," *Policy Futures in Education* 3, no. 4 (2005): 340–58; Anne R. Hickling-Hudson and Roberta Ahlquist, "Contesting the Curriculum in the Schooling of Indigenous Children in Australia and the USA: from Eurocentrism to Culturally Powerful Pedagogies," *Comparative Education Review* 47, no. 1(2003): 64–89.

72. Coalition for the Advancement of Aboriginal Studies, *Learning about Walking in Beauty: Placing Aboriginal Perspectives in Canadian Classrooms* (report presented to the Canadian Race Relations Foundation, 2002), www.crr.ca.

73. Minister's National Working Group on Education, *Our Children: Keepers of the Sacred Knowledge* (report prepared for the Minister of Indian Affairs and Northern Development, Canada, 2002), www.ainc-inac.gc.ca/ps/edu/finre/ouchi_e.pdf.

74. Frances B. Stancavage and others, *National Indian Education Study: Part II: The Educational Experiences of Fourth- and Eighth-Grade American Indian and Alaska Native Students* (NCES 2007–454), U.S. Department of Education, National Center for Education Statistics (Washington, DC: U.S. Government Printing Office, 2006).

75. Akwesasne Freedom School, "The Thanksgiving Address," pages.slic.com/mohawkna/prayer.htm.

76. Indian and Northern Affairs Canada, *Report of the Royal Commission on Aboriginal Peoples* (Hull, Quebec: Canada Commission Group, 1996).

77. Brenda Tsioniaon LaFrance, "Culturally Negotiated Education in First Nations Communities: Empowering Ourselves for Future Generations," in *Aboriginal Education: Fulfilling the Promise*, eds. Marlene Brant Castellano, Lynne Davis, and Louise Lahache (Vancouver: University of British Columbia Press, 2000), 101–13; Jean-Paul Restoule, "Walking on One Earth: The Akwesasne Science and Math Pilot Project," *Environments*, 28, no. 2 (2000): 37–48.

78. See, for example, Four Worlds International Institute for Human and Community Development, "Indigenous People Lead Path to Sustainable Global Security and Development at Action Summit," *Kahtou News Online*, (2001), www.kahtou.com/images/IndigenouSummit.html; Otomi First Nation, *The Reunion of the Condor and the Eagle International Indigenous Trade and Social Agreement Pact* (Estado de Mexico, Mexico: Ndongu, Otomi First Nation, May 5, 1999), www.unitedindians.com/pdf/downloads/reunion_condor_eagle.pdf; Laverne Beech, "The Eagle and the Condor Join Together in Ceremony," *Wellbriety Magazine* 4, no. 21 *(Summer/Fall 2003),* www.whitebison.org/magazine/2003/volume4/vol4no21.html.

79. Foreign Affairs and International Trade Canada, "Intern Chronicles with Nunavut Youth Abroad: Arctic Youth Tell Their Stories," *Aboriginal Planet* (January 2005), www.dfaitmaeci.gc.ca/aboriginalplanet/750/archives/january2005/art6_main-en.asp.

80. Information about Ghost River Rediscovery's Youth Leadership Program can be viewed at www.ghostriverrediscovery.com/youth_ldshp.htm.

81. Information about the University of Calgary International Indigenous Studies Program can be viewed at www.ss.ucalgary.ca/INDG.

82. Hilom Banteyerga, "An Alternative Model in Teacher Education: The Classroom in Focus," (paper presented at the Pan-African Colloquium, September 1994, 1–2), as cited in Nekhweha, "No Matter How Long."

83. See, for example, Peter Sacks, *Standardized Minds: The High Price of America's Testing Culture and What We Can Do to Change It* (New York: Perseus, 2000);

Marita Moll, ed., *Passing the Test: The False Promises of Standardized Testing* (Ottawa: Canadian Centre for Policy Alternatives, 2004).

84. Enrique Salmón, "Decolonizing our Voices," *Winds of Change*, (1996): 70–2.
85. Masemann, "Ways of Knowing," 471.
86. Four Worlds International and United Indians of All Tribes Foundation, *The Fourth Way: An Indigenous Contribution for Building Sustainable and Harmonious Prosperity in the Americas*, (Seattle, WA: United Indians, 2006).
87. Castellano, "Updating Aboriginal Traditions," 33.
88. Couture, "The Role of Native Elders," 202.
89. Cathy Wheaton, "An Aboriginal Pedagogical Model: Recovering an Aboriginal Pedagogy from the Woodlands Cree," *Voice of the Drum*, ed. Roger Neil (Brandon, MB: Kingfisher Publications, 2000), 151–66.
90. Battiste, *Indigenous Knowledge and Pedagogy*, 28–9.
91. We suggest the "Rediscovery in the Schools" handbook produced by Ghost River Rediscovery; please see Appendix B for more information.
92. Masemann, "Educational Reform."
93. Daniel Justice, *Bringing Great Minds Together as One: How Aboriginal Worldviews Can Enhance Learning in the Academy* (panel presentation for workshop held at Emmanuel College, University of Toronto, November 26, 2004).

Chapter Five: Teaching and Learning to Teach: Successful Radical Alternatives from the Developing World

1. Stephen Anderson, ed., *School Improvement in the Developing World: Case Studies of the Aga Khan Foundation Projects* (Amsterdam: Swets and Zeitlinger, 2002); Fernando Reimers, ed., *Unequal Schools, Unequal Chances: The Challenges to Equal Opportunity in the Americas* (Cambridge, MA: Harvard University Press, 2000).
2. J. D. Bransford, Ann L. Brown, and Rodney R. Cocking, eds., *How People Learn: Brain, Mind, Experience and Schooling* (Washington, DC: Commission on Behavioral and Social Sciences, National Research Council, National Academy Press, 2000); David Olson, *Psychological Theory and Educational Reform: How School Remakes Mind and Society* (Cambridge: Cambridge University Press, 2003).
3. Joseph P. Farrell, "International Lessons for School Effectiveness: The View from the Third World," in *Policy for Effective Schools*, eds. Mark Holmes, Kenneth Leithwood, and Donald Mussela (New York: Teachers College Press and OISE Press, 1989), 131–53; Joseph P. Farrell, "Improving Learning: Perspectives for Primary Education in Rural Africa" (core comparative background paper prepared for the UNESCO/World Bank seminar on Improving Rural Primary Education in Africa, Lusaka, Zambia, 1998); Joseph P. Farrell, "Alternative Pedagogies and Learning in Alternative Schooling Systems in Developing Nations" (paper presented at the annual meeting of the Comparative and International Education Society, Salt Lake City, Utah, 2004); John Abbott and Terry Ryan, *The Unfinished Revolution: Learning, Human Behavior, Communities and Political Paradox* (Alexandria, VA: Association for Supervision and Curriculum Development, 2001); Renate N. Caine and Geoffrey Caine,

Education on the Edge of Possibility (Alexandria, VA: Association for Supervision and Curriculum Development, 1997); Francoise Caillods, ed., *The Prospects for Educational Planning* (Paris: International Institute for Educational Planning, 1989); Ingemar Fagerlind and Britt Sjostedt, *Review and Prospects of Educational Planning and Management in Europe* (Paris: UNESCO/International Congress on Planning and Management in Europe, 1990); Lynn Davies, "The Management and Mismanagement of School Effectiveness," in *The State and the School: An International Perspective,* ed. John D. Turner (London: Falmer Press, 1996), 91–107; Eleoussa Polyzoi, Michael Fullan, and John P. Anchan, *Change Forces in Post-Communist Eastern Europe: Education in Transition* (London: Routledge/Falmer, 2003).

4. David Tyack and Larry Cuban, *Tinkering Toward Utopia: A Century of Public School Reform* (Cambridge, MA: Harvard University Press, 1995); Diane Ravitsch and Maris Vinovskis, eds., *Learning from the Past: What History Teaches Us About School Reform* (Baltimore: Johns Hopkins University Press, 1995); for an essay review of both books see Joseph P. Farrell, "Why is Educational Reform So Difficult? Similar Descriptions, Different Prescriptions, Failed Explanations," *Curriculum Inquiry* 30, no. 1 (2000): 83–103.

5. Joseph P. Farrell, "A Retrospective on Educational Planning in Comparative Education," *Comparative Education Review* 41, no. 3 (1997): 298.

6. See, for example, the following websites: New Horizons for Learning, www.newhorizons.org; Sudbury Valley School, www.sudval.org; The Education Revolution, www.educationrevolution.org; Paths of Learning, www.pathsoflearning.net.

7. Kurt J. Bauman, "One Million Homeschooled Students," *Teachers College Record,* February 16, 2005, www.tcrecord.org/Content.asp?ContentID=11756.

8. Theodore Sizer, "Forum Discussion," *Harper's Magazine,* September 2001, 56; See also John T. Gatto, "Against School: How Public Education Cripples Our Kids, and Why," *Harper's Magazine,* September 2003, 33–40.

9. Olson, *Psychological Theory and Education Reform,* ix.

10. Michael Fullan and Nancy Watson, *School-Based Management: Reconceptualizing to Improve Learning Outcomes* (paper prepared for the World Bank seminar on Improving Learning Outcomes in the Caribbean, 1999).

11. Atelia Melaville, Amy C. Berg, and Martin J. Blank, *Community Based Learning: Engaging Students for Success and Citizenship* (Washington DC: Coalition for Community Schools, 2006).

12. Gouvernement du Québec, Ministère de l'Éducation, *Québec Education Program: Elementary Education* (Québec City, Canada: Ministère de l'Éducation, 2000).

13. UNICEF, *Annual Report on the State of the World's Children 2006,* (New York: UNICEF, 2006), 98–100, www.unicef.org/sowc06.

14. Vicky Colbert and Jairo Arboleda, *Universalization of Primary Education in Colombia: The New School Program* (paper presented at the World Conference on Education for All, Jomtien, Thailand, 1990); Ernesto Schiefelbein, *In Search of the School of the 21st Century: Is Colombia's Escuela Nueva the Right Pathfinder?* (Santiago, Chile: UNESCO Regional Office for Latin America

and the Carribbean, 1991); R.C. Siabato, *Educación Básica Primaria en Zonas Rurales: La Escuela Nueva y su Relación de la Plan de Universalación de la Educación Básica Primaria* (Bogota: Ministerio de la Educacion Nacional, 1997); Patrick J. Benveniste and Luis McEwan, "The Politics of Rural School Reform: Escuela Nueva in Colombia," *Journal of Education Policy* 16, no. 6 (2001): 547–99; Jennifer Pitt, "Civic Education and Citizenship in Escuela Nueva Schools in Colombia" (unpublished master's thesis, Ontario Institute for Studies in Education/University of Toronto, 2002); Jennifer Pitt, *Case Study for Escuela Nueva Program* (Washington, DC: Academy for Educational Development, 2004); Joseph P. Farrell, "Transformación de las Formas de Educación en el Mundo en Desarrollo. La Aparación de un Model de Educación Radicalmente Alternativo: El Papel Transformador de la 'Escuela Nueva' de Colombia," in *Memorias del Primer Congreso Internacional de Escuelas Nuevas* (Armenia, Colombia: Colombia National Ministry of Education, 2003), 71–103.

15. Manzoor Ahmed, *Primary Education for All: Learning from the BRAC Experience: A Case Study* (Dhaka: Abel Press, 1993); Suzanne Scott, "Education for Child Garment Workers in Bangladesh" (unpublished master's thesis, Ontario Institute for Studies in Education/University of Toronto, 1996); Anne T. Sweetser, *Lessons from the BRAC Non-formal Primary Education Program* (Washington, DC: Academy for Educational Development, 1999); Brenda Haiplik, *BRAC's Non-Formal Education Program (NFEP)* (Washington, DC: Academy for International Development, 2004).

16. Mallak Zaalouk, *The Children on the Nile: The Community Schools Project in Upper Egypt* (Paris: UNICEF, 1995); *The Pedagogy of Empowerment: Community Schools as a Social Movement in Egypt* (Cairo: The American University in Cairo Press, 2004); Ash Hartwell, *Review of Egypt's Community Schools Project* (Cairo: UNICEF-Egypt, 1995); Joseph P. Farrell and F. M. Connelly, *Final Retrospective Report: Forum Workshops on Educational Reform in Egypt* (Report to UNICEF-Egypt and the Ministry of Education, Egypt, 1998); Joseph P. Farrell, *The Egyptian Community Schools Program: A Case Study* (Washington, DC: Academy for Educational Development, 2004).

17. Joseph DeStafeno and others, *Meeting EFA: Cost-Effectiveness of Complementary Approaches* (Washington, DC: Academy for Educational Development, 2005).

18. Ernesto Schiefelbein, "School Performance Problems in Latin America: The Potential Role of the Escuela Nueva System" (paper prepared for the 2nd International New Schools Conference, Medellin, Colombia, 2006).

19. Farrell, *The Egyptian Community Schools Program*, 15.

20. Haiplik, *BRAC's NFEP*.

21. Jean Clandinin and F.M. Connelly, "Stories to Live By: Narrative Understandings of School Reform," *Curriculum Inquiry* 28, no. 2 (1998): 149–64.

22. Manzoor Ahmed, *The Economics of Non-Formal Education: Resources, Costs and Benefits* (New York: Praeger, 1975); Philip Coombs and Manzoor Ahmed, *Attacking Rural Poverty: How Non-formal Education Can Help* (Baltimore: Johns Hopkins University Press, 1974); Philip Coombs, "Non-Formal Education: Myths, Realities and Opportunities," *Comparative Education Review* 20, no.

3 (1976): 281–93; David Evans, *The Planning of Non-Formal Education* (Paris: International Institute for Educational Planning, 1981).

23. Alan Rogers, *Non-Formal Education: Flexible Schooling or Participatory Education?* (Hong Kong: Comparative Education Research Centre, University of Hong Kong, 2004).

24. For a much more comprehensive discussion of the topics raised in this chapter, please see, Joseph P. Farrell, "Community Education in Developing Countries: The Quiet Revolution in Schooling," in *Sage International Handbook on Curriculum and Instruction*, ed. F. M. Connelly and others (Thousand Oaks, CA: Sage Publications, forthcoming), chap. 21.

Chapter Six: Understanding Pedagogy: Cross-cultural and Comparative Insights from Central Asia

1. Sarfaroz Niyozov, *Understanding Teaching in Post-Soviet, Rural, Mountainous Tajikistan: Case Studies of Teachers' Life and Work* (PhD dissertation, University of Toronto, 2001); Duishon Shamatov, *Beginning Teachers' Professional Socialization in Post-Soviet Kyrgyzstan: Challenges and Coping Strategies* (PhD dissertation, University of Toronto, 2005); Alan De Young, Madeline Reeves, and Galina Valyaeva, *Surviving the Transition? Case Studies of Schools and Schooling in the Kyrgyz Republic since Independence* (Greenwich, CT: Information Age Publishing, 2006).

2. Phillip W. Jackson, *Life in Classrooms* (New York: Holt, Reinhart and Winston, 1968); Linda Dove, *Teachers and Teacher Education in Developing Countries* (London: Croom Helm, 1986); Beatrice Avalos, "Training for Better Teaching in the Third World: Lessons from Research," *Teaching and Teacher Education* 1, no. 4 (1985): 289–99; M. Kazim Bacchus, "The Role of Teacher Education in the Development of Southern Countries," *The Alberta Journal of Educational Research* 42, no. 2 (1996): 77–86; Niyozov, *Understanding Teaching*, 27–53.

3. Ivor Goodson and Andy Hargreaves, *Teachers' Professional Lives: Aspirations and Actualities* (New York: Falmer Press, 1996); Val D. Rust and Per Dalin, eds., *Teachers and Teaching in the Developing World* (New York: Garland Publishing Inc, 1990).

4. David Tyack and Larry Cuban, *Tinkering Toward Utopia: A Century of Public School Reform* (Cambridge, Massachusetts: Harvard University Press, 1995).

5. James Calderhead, ed., *Exploring Teachers' Thinking* (London: Cassell, 1987); Virginia Richardson, ed., *Handbook of Research on Teaching*, 4th ed. (Washington, DC: AERA, 2001).

6. Hargreaves and Goodson, *Teachers' Professional Lives*.

7. Nadine M. Lambert and Barbara L. McComb, eds., *How Students Learn. Reforming Schools through Learner-Centred Education* (Washington, DC: American Psychological Association, 1998).

8. Gerard Guthrie, "To the Defense of Traditional Teaching in Lesser-Developed Countries," in Rust and Dalin, *Teachers and Teaching in the Developing World*, 119–232. While he refers specifically to the United States his observations are

applicable to Canada and other developed nations; Annette Henry, "Five Black Women Teachers' Critique Child-Centered Pedagogy: Possibilities and Limitations of Opposing Standpoints," *Curriculum Inquiry* 26, no.4 (1996): 363–384; Yatta Kanu, "Tensions and Dilemmas of Cross-Cultural Transfer of Knowledge: Post-Structural/Postcolonial Reflections on an Innovative Teacher Education in Pakistan," *International Journal of Educational Development* 25, no. 5 (2006), 493–513.

9. Naomi Norquay, "Social Difference and the Problem of the 'Unique Individual': An Uneasy Legacy of Child-Centred Pedagogy," *Canadian Journal of Education* 24, no. 2, (1999):183–196; John Darling, *Child-Centred Education and its Critics* (London: Paul Chapman Publishing Ltd, 1994).

10. Robin Alexander, *Culture and Pedagogy. International Comparisons in Primary Education* (Maiden, MA: Blackwell Publishers Inc, 2000), 540.

11. Peter Mortimore, ed., *Understanding Pedagogy and its Impact on Learning* (London: Paul Chapman Publishing, 1990).

12. Gregory Gleason, "Introduction to Central Asia: Ancient Societies and the New Millennium," in *The Challenges of Education in Central Asia,* ed. Stephen Heyneman and Alan De Young (Greenwich, CT: Information Age Publishing, 2004), 11–20.

13. Arne Haugen, *The Establishment of National Republics in Soviet Central Asia* (New York and Hampshire: Macmillan, 2003).

14. De Young and others, *Surviving the Transition.*

15. Jamila Jalilova, *Sotsiokultur'naya Traditsiya Islama v Kontekste Etnopedagogiki.* [Islamic Socio-Cultural Tradition in the Context of Ethno-Pedagogy] (Dushanbe: Irfon, 2006); Maria Zvereva, "Razvivayushayasya Systema Obuchenia Zankova: O Didacticheskikh Printsipakh" [Zankov's Evolving Education System: On His Didactic Principles], *Praktika Obrazovaniya* [Educational Practice] 3, (2005), www.zankov.ru/article.asp.

16. De Young and others, *Surviving the Transition.*

17. UNICEF, *Annual Report on the State of the World's Children 2006* (Paris: UNICEF, 2006), 98–116; UNDP, *Human Development Report 2005: International Cooperation at a Crossroads; Aid, Trade and Security in an Unequal World* (New York: United Nations Development Programme), hdr.undp.org.

18. Jack Miller, *The Holistic Curriculum* (Toronto: University of Toronto Press, 1988), 4.

19. Jim Cummins, *Negotiating Identities: Education for Empowerment in a Diverse Society* (Los Angeles: California Association for Bilingual Education, 1996), 1–26.

20. Shamatov, *Beginning Teachers' Professional Socialization in Post-Soviet Kyrgyzstan,* 187.

21. Stephen T. Kerr, "Will Glasnost Lead to Perestroika? Directions of Educational Reform in the USSR," *Educational Researcher* 19, No. 7 (1990): 27.

22. Avalos, *Training for Better Teaching,* 211; see also Rust and Dalin, *Teachers and Teaching in the Developing World.*

23. Cummins, *Negotiating Identities,* 8.

24. Robin Alexander, "In Search of Good Primary Practice," in *Contemporary Issues in Teaching and Learning,* ed. Peter Woods (London and New York: Routledge, 2006), 57–72.

25. Alexander, *Culture and Pedagogy,* 557–58.

26. Niyozov, *Understanding Teaching in Tajikistan,* 129.

27. Miller, *The Holistic Curriculum,* 6.

28. Jerome Bruner, *The Culture of Education* (Cambridge, MA: Harvard University Press, 1996).

29. James Muckle, *Portrait of a Soviet School under Glasnost* (London: Macmillan, 1990); Sh. Amonashvili et al., "The Methodology of Reform," *Soviet Education* 31, No. 7 (1989): 44–76.

30. Ubaid Zubaidov, *Tafriqa Nerui Peshbari Ta'lim* [Differentiation as the Force of Education Improvement] (Dushanbe: Sarparast Publishing, 2003); Ainura Akulova, ed., *Antologiya Pedagogicheskoi Mysli Kirgizskoi SSR* [Anthology of Pedagogical Thoughts in Kyrgyz SSR] (Moscow: Prosveshenie Publishing House, 1988), 1–28.

31. Alexander, *Culture and Pedagogy,* 265–80.

32. Bruce Fuller and Conrad Snyder, "Vocal Teachers, Silent Pupils? Life in Botswana Classrooms," *Comparative Education Review* 35, no. 2 (1991): 274–294; Stephen Anderson, *Improving Schools through Teacher Development: Case Studies of the Aga Khan Foundation Projects in East Africa* (Swets and Zeitlinger, 2001).

33. Huhua Ouyang, "One-Way Ticket: A Story of an Innovative Teacher in Mainland China," *Anthropology and Education Quarterly* 31, no. 4 (2000): 397–425.

34. Alexander, *Culture and Pedagogy,* 461–73.

35. Niyozov, *Understanding Teaching in Tajikistan,* 321.

36. Ibid., 163.

37. Shamatov, *Beginning Teachers' Professional Socialization,* 186–7.

38. Nel Noddings, *The Challenge to Care in Schools: An Alternative Approach to Education* (New York: Teachers College Press, 1992).

39. Niyozov, *Understanding Teaching in Tajikistan,* 185.

40. Ibid., 244.

41. Shamatov, *Beginning Teachers' Professional Socialization,* 168.

42. Niyozov, *Understanding Teaching in Tajikistan,* 102–3.

43. Ibid., 187.

44. Ibid., 242.

45. Ibid., 159.

46. Ibid., 178.

47. Ibid.

48. Ibid., 288.

49. Ibid., 162.

50. Ibid., 145.

51. Michael Apple, ed., *Cultural and Economic Reproduction in Education: Essays on Class, Ideology, and the State* (London: Routledge and Kegan Paul, 1982).

52. Gerard Guthrie, "To the Defense of Traditional Teaching in Lesser-Developed Countries," in Rust and Dalin, eds., *Teachers and Teaching in the Developing*

World, 119–232; Richard Tabulawa, "Pedagogical Classroom Practice and the Social Context: the Case of Botswana," *International Journal of Educational Development* 17, no. 2 (1997): 189–204.

53. Alice Hunsberger, *Nasir Khusraw:The Ruby of Badakhshan. A Portrait of Persian Poet, Traveler, and Philosopher* (London: I. B. Tauris, 2000).

54. Sarfaroz Niyozov, "Nasir Khusraw: An Introduction," in *Nasir Khusraw: Yesterday, Today, Tomorrow*, eds. Sarfaroz Niyozov and Ramazon Nazariev (Khujand: Noshir Publishing House, 2005), 16.

55. Hunsberger, *Nasir Khusaw: The Ruby of Badakhshan*, 61.

56. Khairulloh Afzalov and Bayon Rahimov, *Ta'rikhi Pedagogikai Khalqi Tojik* [History of the Pedagogy of Tajik People] (Dushanbe: Irfon Publishing House, 1994), 30.

57. Sarfraz Khan, *Muslim Reformist Political Thought: Revivalists, Modernists, and Free Will* (London and New York: Routledge Curzon, 2003); Adib Khalid, *The Politics of Muslim Cultural Reform: Jadidism in Central Asia* (Berkeley: University of California Press, 1998).

58. George Makdisi, *The Rise of College: Institutions of Learning in Islam and the West* (Edinburgh: Edinburgh University Press, 1981); Helen Boyle, *Quranic Schools: Agents of Preservation and Change* (New York: Routledge Falmer, 2004).

59. Niyozov, *Understanding Teaching in Tajikistan*, 276.

60. Ruth Hayhoe and Julia Pan, eds., *Knowledge across Cultures: A Contribution to Dialogue among Civilizations* (Hong Kong: Comparative Education Research Institute, University of Hong Kong, 2001).

61. Iveta Silova, *From Sites of Occupation to Symbols of Multiculturalism. Reconceptualizing Minority Education in Post-Soviet Latvia* (Greenwich: Information Age Publishing, 2006).

62. Deborah Britzman, *Practice Makes Practice: A Critical Study of Learning to Teach* (New York: Albany, 1991), 8.

63. Andy Hargreaves, *Changing Teachers Changing Times: Teachers' Work and Culture in the Postmodern Age* (London: Falmer Press, 1994).

Chapter Seven: Comparative Perspectives on School Improvement

1. See, for example, Michael Fullan, *The New Meaning of Educational Change, 3rd Edition* (New York: Teachers College Press, 2001).

2. See, for example, Paul Berman, "Educational Change: An Implementation Paradigm," in *Improving Schools: Using What We Know*, eds. Rolf Lehming and Michael Kane (Beverly Hills, CA: Sage Publications, 1981), 253–286.

3. See, for example, Fullan, *The New Meaning*; Gene Hall and Shirley Hord, *Implementing Change: Patterns, Principles, and Potholes, 2nd Edition* (Boston, MA: Pearson Education, Inc., 2006).

4. See, for example, Ronald Havelock and Michael Huberman, *Solving Educational Problems: The Theory and Reality of Innovation in Developing Countries* (Paris, FR: UNESCO, 1978).

5. See, for example, Keith Lewin with Janet Stuart, *Educational Innovation in Developing Countries: Case Studies of Changemakers* (London: MacMillan Press

Ltd., 1991); Val Rust and Per Dalin, *Teachers and Teaching in the Developing World* (New York: Garland, 1990); Adrian Verspoor, *Pathways to Change: Improving the Quality of Education in Developing Countries*, World Bank Discussion Papers #53 (Washington, DC: The World Bank, 1989).

6. Verspoor, *Pathways to Change*.
7. Verspoor, *Pathways to Change*, 99.
8. Richard Elmore, "Getting to Scale with Good Educational Practice," *Harvard Educational Review* 66, no. 1 (1996): 1–26.
9. Reviewed in Daniel Levine and Lawrence Lezotte, *Unusually Effective Schools: A Review and Analysis of Research and Practice* (Madison, WI: The National Center for Effective Schools Research and Development, 1990).
10. Stewart Purkey and Marshall Smith, "Effective Schools: A Review," *The Elementary School Journal* 83, no. 4 (1983): 427–52.
11. David Reynolds and others, *World Class Schools: International Perspectives on School Effectiveness* (London and New York: RoutledgeFalmer, 2002).
12. For example, David Reynolds and Charles Teddlie with David Hopkins and Sam Stringfield, "Linking School Effectiveness and School Improvement," in *The International Handbook of School Effectiveness Research*, ed. Charles Teddlie and David Reynolds (New York: Falmer Press, 2000), 206–31.
13. Beatrice Avalos, "Teacher Effectiveness: Research in the Third World, Highlights of a Review," *Comparative Education*, 16, no. 1 (1980): 45–54; Bruce Fuller, "What School Factors Raise Achievement in the Third World?" *Review of Educational Research*, 57, no. 3 (1987): 255–92.
14. See, for example, Henry Levin and Marlaine Lockheed, eds., *Effective Schools in Developing Countries* (London: Falmer Press 1993); Reynolds and others, *World Class Schools*; Teddlie and Reynolds, *International Handbook of School Effectiveness*.
15. Fuller, *School Factors*.
16. Levin and Lockheed, *Effective Schools*.
17. Cited in David Reynolds, "School Effectiveness: The International Dimension," in Teddlie and Reynolds, *International Handbook of School Effectiveness*, 232–56.
18. Reynolds, *World Class Schools*, 279.
19. Task Force on Education and Gender Equity, *Towards Universal Primary Education: Investments, Incentives and Institutions. A United Nations Millennium Project Report* (New York: United Nations Millennium Project, 2006).
20. Joseph Patrick Godson Chimombo, "Quantity Versus Quality in Education: Case Studies in Malawi," *International Review of Education* 51 (2005):155–72.
21. Liz Higgins and Rosemary Rwanyange, "Ownership in the Education Reform Process in Uganda," *Compare* 15 no. 1 (2005): 7–26.
22. Reynolds et al., *World Class Schools*.
23. James Stiegler and James Hiebert, *The Teaching Gap: Best Ideas from the World's Teachers for Improving Education in the Classroom* (New York: The Free Press, 1999).
24. See, for example, Louise Stoll and Dean Fink, *Changing Our Schools: Linking School Effectiveness and School Improvement* (Buckingham, UK: Open University Press, 1996).

25. For a review of the restructuring phenomenon, see Joseph Murphy and Philip Hallinger, *Restructuring Schooling: Learning from Ongoing Efforts* (Newbury Park, CA: Corwin Press, 1993).

26. Kenneth Leithwood and Teresa Menzies, "A Review of Research Concerning the Implementation of Site-Based Management," *School Effectiveness and School Improvement* 9, no. 3 (1998): 233–85.

27. See, for example, Barbara Eason-Watkins, "Implementing PLCs in the Chicago Public Schools," in *On Common Ground: The Power of Professional Learning Communities*, eds. Richard DuFour, Robert Eaker, and Rebecca DuFour (Bloomington, IN: National Education Service, 2005), 193–207.

28. For syntheses of this research, see Task Force on Education, *Towards Universal Primary Education*.

29. Ibid.

30. Levin and Lockheed, *Effective Schools*, 11.

31. For an overview of the CSR movement see Joseph Murphy and Amanda Datnow, *Leadership Lessons for Comprehensive School Reform* (Thousand Oaks, CA: Corwin Press, 2003).

32. Vicky Colbert, Clemencia Chiappe, and Jairo Arboleda, "The New School Program: More and Better Primary Education for Children in Rural Areas in Colombia," in Levin and Lockheed, *Effective Schools in Developing Countries*, 52–68.

33. Stephen Anderson, ed., *Improving Schools Through Teacher Development: Case Studies of the Aga Khan Foundation Projects in East Africa* (Lisse, The Netherlands: Swets and Zeitlinger Publishers, 2002).

34. Gulzar Kanji and Takbir Ali, "School Improvement: A Case from the Northern Areas in Pakistan," in *Partnerships in Educational Development*, ed. Iffat Farah and Barbara Jaworski, (Oxford, UK: Symposium Books, 2006), 193–206.

35. For a review of school choice in the United States, see R. Kenneth Godwin and Frank Kemerer, *School Choice Tradeoffs: Liberty, Equity, and Diversity* (Austin, TX: University of Texas Press, 2002).

36. For a comparative analysis of choice policies in Chile, New Zealand, Australia, England and Wales, Sweden, South Africa, China, the Czech Republic, and Hungary, see David Plank and Gary Sykes, *Choosing Choice: School Choice in International Perspective* (New York: Teachers College Press, 2003).

37. Anderson, *Improving Schools.*

38. Godwin and Kemerer, *School Choice*; Plank and Sykes, *Choosing Choice.*

39. See, for example, Anthony Bryk, Valerie Lee, and Peter Holland, *Catholic Schools and the Common Good* (Cambridge, MA: Harvard University Press, 1993).

40. Plank and Sykes, *Choosing Choice.*

41. For an overview, see Susan Fuhrman, ed., *From the Capitol to the Classroom: Standards-Based Reform in the States. One Hundredth Yearbook of the National Society for the Study of Education* (Chicago: University of Chicago Press (2001).

42. See, for example, Michael Fullan, Al Bertani, and Joanne Quinn, "New Lessons for Districtwide Reform," *Educational Leadership* 61, no. 7 (2004): 42–46.

43. Fuhrman, ed., *From the Capitol to the Classroom*, 6.
44. Verspoor, *Pathways to Change*.
45. See, for example, James Scheurich and Linda Skrla, *Leadership for Equity and Excellence: Creating High Achievement Classrooms, Schools, and Districts* (Thousand Oaks, CA: Corwin Press, 2003).
46. Michael Fullan, *Leadership and Sustainability: System Thinkers in Action* (Thousand Oaks, CA: Corwin Press, 2005).
47. Michael Fullan, *Educational Change*, 92.
48. Du Four, Eaker, and DuFour, *On Common Ground*.
49. Wendy Togneri and Stephen Anderson, *Beyond Islands of Excellence: What Districts Can Do to Improve Instruction and Achievement in All Schools* (Washington, DC: The Learning First Alliance, 2003).

Chapter Eight: International Educational Indicators and Assessments: Issues for Teachers

1. Darrell Huff and Irving Geis, *How to Lie with Statistics* (New York: WW Norton and Company, 1954).
2. For an overview of the IBE's *International Education Yearbook*, see *UNESCO 50 Years for Education* (Paris: UNESCO, 1997), 56, www.unesco.org/education/educprog/50y/brochure/unintwo/56.htm.
3. See the UNESCO Institute of Statistics, *Global Education Digest: Comparing Education Statistics around the World* (Montreal, QC: UNESCO Institute of Statistics, 2006), www.uis.unesco.org. The UNESCO Institute of Statistics also maintains an online database of educational statistics.
4. Jeffrey Puryear, "International Education Statistics and Research: Status and Problems," *International Journal of Educational Development* 15, no. 1 (1995): 79–91.
5. Available electronically at: www.unicef.org and www.worldbank.org.
6. Adapted from Brian Holmes and Saul Robinsohn, *Relevant Data in Comparative Education* (Hamburg, Germany: UNESCO Institute for Education, 1963), 57; see also UNESCO, *International Standard Classification of Education ISCE97* (Paris: UNESCO, 1997), www.uis.unesco.org.
7. Joseph P. Farrell, "Literacy and International Development: Education and Literacy as Basic Human Rights," in *Cambridge Handbook of Literacy*, eds. David R. Olsen and Nancy Torrance (Cambridge, UK: Cambridge University Press, 2007).
8. Ernesto Schiefelbein, "School Performance Problems in Latin America: The Potential Role of the Escuela Nueva System" (paper presented at the Second International New Schools Congress. Medellin, Colombia, 2006).
9. UNICEF, "Child Poverty in Perspective: An Overview of Child-Wellbeing in Rich Countries," *Innocenti Report Card 7* (Florence, Italy: UNICEF Innocenti Research Centre, 2007); UNESCO, *Education for All Global Monitoring Report* (Paris: UNESCO, 2007).
10. Stephen P. Heyneman, "The Use of Cross-National Comparisons for Local Education Policy," *Curriculum Inquiry* 34, no. 3 (2004): 345–52.

11. For example, a study of the use of the Scholastic Aptitude Test (SAT) in the United States found that it was no better as a predictor of post-secondary success than were the average secondary school grades assigned by teachers. Daryl G. Smith and Gwen Garrison, "The Impending Loss of Talent: An Exploratory Study Challenging Assumptions about Testing and Merit," *Teachers College Record* 107, no.4 (2005): 629–53.

12. IEA, *Brief History of the IEA* (Amsterdam: IEA, 2005), www.iea.nl/brief_history_of_iea.html.

13 Torsten Husén, *International Study of Achievement in Mathematics: A Comparison of Twelve Countries* (Stockholm: Almqvist and Wiksell, 1967) 1: 30–1.

14. Ibid., 2:288.

15. Ibid., 1:31.

16. Harold J. Noah, and Max A. Eckstein, *Doing Comparative Education: Three Decades of Collaboration* (Hong Kong: Comparative Education Research Centre, University of Hong Kong, 1998).

17. Lawrence A. Cremin, *The Genius of American Education* (New York: Vintage Books, 1966) 88–122; Geraldine Jonçich Clifford, *The Shape of American Education* (Englewood Cliffs, NJ: Prentice Hall, 1975) 129–64.

18. National Commission on Excellence in Education, *A Nation at Risk: The Imperative for Educational Reform* (Washington, DC: Government Printing Office, 1983).

19. Benjamin Levin, "An Epidemic of Education Policy: (What) Can We Learn from Each Other?" *Comparative Education* 34, no. 2 (1998):131–41; Gerald K. LeTendre and David P. Baker, "International Comparisons and Educational Research Policy," in *Competitor or Ally? Japan's Role in American Educational Debates,* ed. Gerald K. LeTendre (New York: Falmer Press, 1999).

20. Stephen J. Ball, "Big Policies/Small World: An Introduction to International Perspectives on Education Policy," *Comparative Education Review* 34, no. 2 (1998): 119–30; Luis Benveniste, "The Political Structuration of Assessment: Negotiating State Power and Legitimacy," *Comparative Education Review* 46, no.1 (2002): 89–118.

21. Roser Cussó and Sabrina D'Amico, "From Development Comparatism to Globalization Comparativism: Towards More Normative International Statistics," *Comparative Education Review* 41, no. 2 (2005): 199–266.

22. Kenneth A. Leithwood, "Programs and Politics: The Local Uses of International Tests," *Curriculum Inquiry* 34, no. 3 (2004): 363–77, 374–75.

23. Miriam Henry, Bob Lingard, Fazal Rizvi, and Sandra Taylor. *The OECD, Globalisation and Education Policy* (Oxford: Pergamon Press, 2001); George Papadopoulos, *The OECD and Education, 1960–1990* (Paris: OECD, 1994).

24. OECD, *The OECD Programme for International Student Assessment* (Paris: OECD, 2007), www.pisa.oecd.org/dataoecd/51/27/37474503.pdf.

25. OECD, *First Results from PISA: Executive Summary. Programme for International Student Assessment* (Paris: OECD, 2006), www.oecd.org/dataoecd/1/63/34002454.pdf; OECD, *Education at a Glance 2006* (Paris: OECD, 2006.

26. World Conference on Education for All, *Meeting Basic Learning Needs: A Vision for the 1990s* (New York: Inter-Agency Commission for World Conference on Education for All, 1990), 36, unesdoc.unesco.org/images/0009/000975/097552e.pdf.

27. Benveniste, "The Political Structuration of Assessment," *Comparative Education Review*, 91.

28. Information about the SACMEQ and the OREALC programs can be found online at: www.sacmeq.org/; www.unesco.cl/ing.

29. Deon Filmer, Amer Hasan, and Lant Pritchett, "A Millennium Learning Goal: Measuring Real Progress in Education," *Centre for Global Development Working Paper*, No. 97 (2006), www.cgdev.org/content/publications/detail/9815.

30. Larry Kuehn, "Globalization and the Control of Teachers' Work: The Role of the OECD Indicators," *Standardized Testing in Canada* (2004), www.maritamoll.ca/webmom/content/pisa-oecd.htm.

31. A detailed introduction to both policy and technical measurement issues can be found in Joseph P. Farrell, "The Use and Abuse of Comparative Studies of Educational Achievement," *Curriculum Inquiry* 34, no. 3 (2004):256–65

32. Michelle Stack, "Testing, Testing, Read All About It: Canadian Press Coverage of the PISA Results," *Canadian Journal of Education* 29, no. 1 (2006): 49–69.

33. H. Howard Russell, "Connections among Factors in Education," *Curriculum Inquiry*. 34, no. 3 (2004): 268–69.

34. Graham Nuthall, "The Cultural Myths and Realities of Classroom Teaching and Learning: A Personal Journey," *Teachers College Record* 107, no. 5 (2005): 895–934, 900–01.

35. Levin, "An Epidemic of Education Policy," *Comparative Education* 34, no.2 (1998): 131–41.

36. See for example, Karen Bogard Givvin, James Hiebert, Jennifer K. Jacobs, Hilary Hollingsworth, and Ronald Gallimore, "Are there National Patterns of Teaching? Evidence from the TIMSS 1999 Video Study," *Comparative Education Review* 49, no.3 (2005): 311–42; David P. Baker and Gerald K. LeTendre, *National Differences, Global Similarities: World Culture and the Future of Schooling* (Stanford, CA: Stanford University Press, 2005).

37. Bogard and others, "Are There National Patterns of Teaching?" 311.

38. Judith Torney-Purta, Rainer Lehmann, Hans Oswald, and Wolfram Schultz, *Citizenship and Education in Twenty-Eight Countries: Civic Knowledge and Engagement at Age Fourteen* (Amsterdam: International Association for Educational Achievement, 2001); Gita Steiner-Khamsi, Judith Torney-Purta, and Jack Schwille, *New Paradigms and Recurring Paradoxes in Education for Citizenship: An International Comparison* (Amsterdam: Elsevier Press, 2002)

39. See for example, OECD, "Executive Summary," in *First Results from PISA 2003* (Paris: OECD, 2006) 18–24; OECD, *Where Immigrant Students Succeed. A Comparative Review of Performance and Engagement in PISA 2003* (Paris: OECD, 2006).

40. OECD, *The OECD Programme for International Student Assessment* 1.

41. See the Council of Ministers of Education Canada (CMEC), *PISA Fact Sheet* (Ottawa, ON: CMEC), 6, www.cmec.ca/pisa/2003/indexe.stm.

42. Ibid., 3–5.
43. Sample PISA questions and marking guides are available at pisa-sq.acer.edu. au.
44. OECD, Draft Briefing Note for Canada: Education at a Glance 2006 (Paris: OECD, 2006), 2–3, www.oecd.org/dataoecd/52/1/37392733.pdf.
45. Ibid., 3; HRSDC and Statistics Canada, "Measuring Up: Canadian Results of the OECD PISA Study: The Performance of Canada's Youth in Mathematics, Reading, Science and Problem Solving?" (Ottawa, ON: HRSDC, 2004).
46. Ibid., 3
47. See OECD, *Where Immigrant Students Succeed. A Comparative Review of Performance and Engagement in PISA 2003* (Paris: OECD, 2006); HRSDC, *Reading Achievement in Canada and the United States: Findings from the OECD Programme of International Student Assessment* (Ottawa, ON: HRSDC, May 2004); and Statistics Canada, "Children of Immigrants: How Well Do They Do in School?" *Education Matters Online*, no. 4 (2004), www.statcan.ca/english/freepub/81-004-XIE/200410/immi.htm.
48. Ibid., 6–7.
49. HRSDC, *Reading Achievement in Canada and the United States*; Statistics Canada, "Children of Immigrants," 5; OECD, *Where Immigrant Students Succeed*; Statistics Canada, "Children of Immigrants," 2.
50. OECD, *Where Immigrant Students Succeed*; Statistics Canada, "Children of Immigrants," 7.
51. OECD, *Where Immigrant Students Succeed*; Statistics Canada, "Children of Immigrants," 3.
52. Stack, "Testing, Testing, Read All About It," 65.
53. The Economist, "Clever Red-Necks: It's Not Just the Economy that is Booming, the Schools are Too," *The Economist*, September 21, 2006, www.economist.com/world/la/displaystory.cfm?story_id=7945805.
54. Stack, "Testing, Testing, Read All About It," 65.

Chapter Nine: Gender and Education

1. Elaine Unterhalter, *Gender, Schooling and Global Social Justice* (London and New York: Routledge, 2007).
2. Stewart Fraser, *Jullien's Plan for Comparative Education 1816-1817* (New York: Teachers College, Columbia University, 1964).
3. Vandra Masemann, Mark Bray, and Maria Manzon, eds, *Common Interests, Uncommon Goals: Histories of the World Council of Comparative Education Societies and Its Members* (Hong Kong: Comparative Education Research Centre, University of Hong Kong and Springer, 2007).
4. See the historian's page on the CIES website, www.cies.us.
5. David H. Kelly, *International Feminist Perspectives on Educational Reform: The Work of Gail Paradise Kelly* (New York: Garland Publishing, 1996).
6. UNESCO, *Education For All (EFA) International Coordination, Goal 5* (Paris: UNESCO, 2007), www.unesco.org.

7. 185 countries (more than 90 percent of the members of the United Nations) have signed and ratified this Convention. "Countries that have ratified or acceded to the Convention are legally bound to put its provisions into practice. They are also committed to submit national reports, at least every four years, on measures they have taken to comply with their treaty obligations." United Nations, *Convention on the Elimination of All Forms of Discrimination Against Women States Parties* (New York: UN, 2007), www.un.org/womenwatch/daw/cedaw/states.htm.

8. UNHCHR, *Convention on the Elimination of All Forms of Discrimination Against Women* (Geneva, Switzerland: UNHCHR, 1981), www.unhchr.ch/html/menu3/b/e1cedaw.htm.

9. Maureen Lewis and Marlaine Lockheed, *Inexcusable Absence: Why 60 Million Girls Still Aren't In School and What to Do About It* (Baltimore, MD: United Book Press, 2006).

10. Robert K. Merton, *Social Theory and Social Structure* (Toronto, ON: Collier-Macmillan Canada Ltd., 1957).

11. Theodore W. Schultz, *Investment in Human Capital: The Role of Education and of Research* (New York: The Free Press, 1971), 48–49, as cited in Elaine Unterhalter, *Gender, Schooling and Global Social Justice* (London and New York: Routledge, 2007), 40.

12. Rosa Braidotti, and others, *Women, the Environment and Sustainable Development: Towards a Theoretical Synthesis* (London: Zed Books with INSTRAW, 1994), 44.

13. Linda Jean Shepherd, *Lifting the Veil: The Feminine Face of Science* (Boston: Shambhala Publications Inc., 1993).

14. Philip Foster, *Education and Social Change in Ghana* (London: Routledge and Kegan Paul Ltd., 1965).

15. Vandra Masemann, *Motivation and Aspirations in a West African Girls' Boarding School* (PhD thesis, University of Toronto, 1972).

16. Martin, Jane Roland, *Changing the Educational Landscape: Philosophy, Women, and Curriculum* (New York: Routledge, 1994).

17. Chandra Mohanty, "Under Western Eyes: Feminist Scholarship and Colonial Discourses," *Feminist Review*, no. 30 (1988): 61–88, 61.

18. Madan Sarup, *Marxism and Education* (London and Boston: Routledge and Kegan Paul, 1978).

19. Rosa Braidotti and others, *Women, the Environment and Sustainable Development*, 48.

20. Ibid., 48-9.

21. UNESCO, *Education for All Global Monitoring Report 2007: Strong Foundations* (Paris: UNESCO, 2006), 1.

22. Ibid., 30. UNESCO uses the term *South and West Asia* as a region that includes Afghanistan, Bangladesh, Bhutan, India, Islamic Republic of Iran Maldives, Nepal, Pakistan, and Sri Lanka.

23. Ibid.

24. Ibid., 351.

25. Ibid., 266–69.

26. Ibid., 30.

27. Ibid., 31.

28. Ibid., 1.

29. UNESCO, *Education for All Global Monitoring Report 2007*, 1.

30. Ibid., 30.

31. Ibid., 2.

32. Ibid., 33.

33. Ibid., 31.

34. Ibid.

35. Ibid., 33.

36. Ibid., 1.

37. Ibid., 39.

38. Ibid., 33.

39. Maureen Lewis and Marlaine Lockheed, *Inexcusable Absence,* 1.

40. Ibid., 3.

41. Mary Chamie, *National, Institutional, and Household Factors Affecting Young Girls' School Attendance in Developing Societies* (Washington, DC: United States Agency for International Development, International Center for Research on Women and Office of Human Resources, 1983) as cited in Marlaine E. Lockheed, and others, *Improving Primary Education in Developing Countries* (New York and Washington DC: Oxford University Press and World Bank, 1991), 148.

42. UNESCO, *Education for All Global Monitoring Report 2007*, 36.

43. Ibid., 37.

44. Ibid., 36.

45. Ibid., 40.

46. Ibid.

47. Ibid.

48. Ibid., 44.

49. Ibid., 81.

50. Ibid., 44.

51. Ibid.

52. UNESCO, *Education for All Global Monitoring Report 2007*, 58.

53. Ibid., 60.

54. Ibid.

55. Ibid., 196.

56. UNICEF, *State of the World's Children 2007* (New York: UNICEF, 2007), 5.

57. Kara Janigan, *Defying the Odds: A Study of Female Students in Grade 11 in Eritrea* (master's thesis, Ontario Studies in Education/University of Toronto, 2002). All data and primary quotations in this section are taken from this thesis, unless otherwise referenced.

58. World Bank, *Eritrea Country Brief* (Washington DC: World Bank, 2007), www. worldbank.org.

59. UNICEF, *Eritrea: Frontlines of a Different Struggle* (Namibia: UNICEF, 1996), 35.

60. Gross Enrolment Ratio (GER) refers to the "total enrolment in a specific level of education, regardless of age, expressed as a percentage of the population in the official age group corresponding to this level of education." UNESCO, *EFA Global Monitoring Report 2007* (Paris: UNESCO, 2007), 349.

61. Eritrean Ministry of Education, *Eritrea: Essential Education Indicators 1998/99* (Asmara, Eritrea: Ministry of Education, 1999), 20.

62. Ibid., 21.

63. Eritrean Ministry of Education, *Girls' Education in Eritrea* (Asmara, Eritrea: Ministry of Education, 1997), 65.

64. Eritrean Ministry of Education, *Eritrea: Essential Education Indicators 1998/99*, 25.

65. Kara Janigan, *Defying the Odds*, 176.

66. Alison Prentice, *The School Promoters: Education and Social Class in Mid-Nineteenth Century Upper Canada* (Toronto, ON: McClelland and Stewart, 1977), 15–16.

67. Ibid., 143.

68. Ibid., 17.

69. Ibid., 112.

70. Ibid., 115.

71. Ibid., 113.

72. Ibid.

73. Ibid., 113–14.

74. Ibid., 111.

75. Ibid., 153.

76. Rebecca Priegert Coulter, "Gender Equity and Schooling: Linking Research and Policy," *Canadian Journal of Education* 21, no. 4 (1996): 433–52, 434.

77. Vandra Lea Masemann, "Culture and Education," in *Comparative Education: the Dialectic of the Global and the Local*, eds. Robert F. Arnove and Carlos Torres (Lanham, MD: Rowman and Littlefield, 1999), 115–33.

78. Celia Haig-Brown, *Resistance and Renewal: Surviving the Indian Residential School* (Vancouver, BC: Tillacum Library, 1988).

79. Today, the result of this abuse through generations is still being dealt with, in part through legal claims by aboriginal groups. Linda Otway, "Women in First Nations Politics," *CBC News Online*, November 22, 2005, www.cbc.ca/news/background/aboriginals/roleofwomen.html.

80. Status of Women, Canada, "Canada and the United Nations General Assembly: Special Session: Beijing +5: Factsheets" (Ottawa, ON: Status of Women, 2003), www.swc-cfc.gc.ca/pubs/b5_factsheets/b5_factsheets_4_e.html.

81. Coulter, *Gender Equity and Schooling*, 434.

82. Ibid., 437.

83. Status of Women, Canada, "Canada and the United Nations General Assembly."

84. Status of Women, Canada, "Canada and the United Nations General Assembly."

85. In 1999, 89 percent of women in Canada had high school or higher education: 28 percent held a post-secondary diploma; 14 percent held a university degree. In 1997–98, women made up 52 percent of college enrolment and 55 percent

of university enrolment; 51 percent master's and 43 percent of doctoral ranks. See Status of Women, Canada, "Canada and the United Nations General Assembly."

86. Coulter, *Gender Equity and Schooling*, 436.

87. Coulter, *Gender Equity and Schooling*, 439.

88. Statistics Canada, "The Gap in Achievement between Boys and Girls," *Education Matters Online*, no. 4 (2004), www.statcan.ca.

89. Becky Francis and Christine Skelton, *Reassessing Gender and Achievement: Questioning Contemporary Key Debates* (New York: Routledge, 2005), 76.

90. Susan Ormiston, "Boy's Own Story," *CBC News Online*, November 25, 2003, www.cbc.ca/news/background/gendergap.

91. Francis and Skelton, *Reassessing Gender and Achievement*, 83.

92. Bernie Froese-Germain, "Educating Boys: Tempering Rhetoric with Research," *McGill Journal of Education* 41, no.2 (2006): 145–54, 149; Francis and Skelton, *Reassessing Gender and Achievement*, 88.

93. Froese-Germain, *Educating Boys*, 148–49; Francis and Skelton, *Reassessing Gender and Achievement*, 55–74.

94. Ontario Ministry of Education, "Stamping Out Bullying in Ontario Schools," *CNW Group Ontario Newsroom*, November 16, 2007, ogov.newswire.ca/ontario/GPOE/2005/11/16/c5874.html?lmatch=&lang=_e.html.

95. Wendy M. Craig and Debra J. Pepler, "Identifying and Targeting Risk for Involvement in Bullying and Victimization," *Canadian Journal of Psychiatry* 48, No. 9 (2003): 577–82, 579.

96. Coulter, *Gender Equity and Schooling*, 439; See Roots of Empathy Program at www.rootsofempathy.org.

97. David Sadker, "Gender Equity: Still Knocking at the Classroom Door," *Educational Leadership* 56, no.7 (1999): 22–6, 24.

Chapter Ten: Education for Conflict Resolution and Peacebuilding in Plural Societies: Approaches from Around the World

1. Chadwick Alger, "Building Peace: A Global Learning Process," in *Teaching about International Conflict and Peace*, eds. Merry Merryfield and Richard Remy (Albany: SUNY Press, 1995), 128.

2. Marc Ross, *The Culture of Conflict: Interpretations and Interests in Comparative Practice* (New Haven, CT: Yale University Press, 1993); Marc Ross, *The Management of Conflict: Interpretations and Interests in Comparative Perspective* (New Haven: Yale University Press, 1993).

3. Kenneth Bush and Diana Saltarelli, *The Two Faces of Education in Ethnic Conflict: Towards a Peacebuilding Education for Children* (Florence, Italy: UNICEF Innocenti Research Centre, 2000); Lynn Davies, *Education and Conflict: Complexity and Chaos* (London: Routledge/Falmer, 2004); Clive Harber, "Not Quite the Revolution: Citizenship Education in England," in *Learning Democracy and Citizenship: International Experiences*, eds. Michele Schweisfurth, Lynn Davies, and Clive Harber (Oxford, UK: Symposium Books, 2000), 225–37.

4. Sarah Graham-Brown, *Education in the Developing World: Conflict and Crisis*, (Essex, UK: Longman Group/World University Service, 1991); Fiona Leach, "Gender Violence in Schools: What is it and Why Does it Happen?" *Gender Violence in Schools Newsletter*, no. 1. (March 2004), www.sussex.ac.uk/education/documents/gvschools1.pdf.

5. James Williams, "Civil Conflict, Education, and the Work of Schools: Twelve Propositions," *Conflict Resolution Quarterly* 21, no. 4 (2004): 479.

6. Davies, *Education and Conflict*; Kathryn Tomlinson and Pauline Benefield, *Education and Conflict: Research and Research Possibilities* (UK: National Foundation for Educational Research, 2005).

7. Martin Carnoy and Joel Samoff, "Education and Social Transformation: Theory and Practice," in *Education and Social Transition in the Third World*, ed. Martin Carnoy and Joel Samoff (Princeton: Princeton University Press, 1990), 315–59; Graham-Brown, *Education in the Developing World*.

8. Helen Ware and others, *The No-Nonsense Guide to Conflict and Peace* (Oxford, UK and Toronto: New Internationalist Publications/Between the Lines, 2005), 129.

9. Ibid.

10. Adam Curle and Maire Dugan, "Peacemaking: Stages and Sequence," *Peace and Change: A Journal of Peace Research* 8, no. 2–3 (1982): 19–28; Adam Curle, Paulo Freire, and Johan Galtung, "What Can Education Contribute towards Peace and Social Justice?" in *Education for Peace: Reflection and Action*, ed. Magnus Haavelsrud (Keele, UK: University of Keele, 1974), 64–97.

11. Motoko Akiba and others, "Student Victimization: National and School System Effects on School Violence in 37 Nations," *American Educational Research Journal* 39, no. 4 (Winter 2003): 829–53.

12. Samie Ikechi Ihejirika, "The Role of Peace Education in Peace Building in Africa," in *Three Decades of Peace Education around the World: An Anthology*, ed. Robin Burns and Robert Aspeslagh (New York: Garland Publishing, 1996), 223–35.

13. Lillian Moncada-Davidson, "Education and its Limitations in the Maintenance of Peace in El Salvador," *Comparative Education Review* 39, no. 1 (2005): 54–75.

14. Marc Sommers, "Peace Education and Refugee Youth," in *Learning for a Future: Refugee Education in Developing Countries*, ed. Jeff Crisp, Christopher Talbot, and Daiana Cipollone (Geneva: UN High Commission for Refugees, 2001), 14–21; Tony Waters and Kim LeBlanc, "Refugees and Education: Mass Public Schooling without a Nation-state," *Comparative Education Review* 49, no. 2 (2005): 129–47.

15. Jeaniene Spink, "Education and Politics in Afghanistan: The Importance of an Education System in Peacebuilding and Reconstruction," *Journal of Peace Education* 2, no. 2 (2005): 195–207.

16. Ernest Gellner, *Nations and Nationalism* (Oxford: Basil Blackwell, 1983) as cited in Sobhi Tawil and Alexandra Harley, eds., *Education, Conflict, and Social Cohesion* (Geneva: UNESCO/International Bureau of Education, 2004), 11.

17. Daniel Bar-Tal, "The Elusive Nature of Peace Education," in *Peace Education: The Concept, Principles, and Practices around the World*, eds. Gavriel Salomon and Baruch Nevo (Mahwah, NJ: Lawrence Erlbaum Associates, 2002), 31.

18. Johan Galtung, "Violence, Peace, and Peace Research," *Journal of Peace Research* 6, no. 3 (1969): 167–92; Johan Galtung, *Peace: Research- Education- Action* (Copenhagen: Ejlers, 1975).

19. Johan Galtung, *Peace by Peaceful Means: Peace and Conflict, Development, and Civilization* (London: Sage Publications and International Peace Research Association, 1996).

20. Johan Galtung, "Is Peaceful Research Possible? On the Methodology of Peace Research," in *Peace: Research - Education - Action*, ed. Johan Galtung (Copenhagen: Chrsitan Ejlers, 1975), 279.

21. Kathy Bickmore, "Education for Peacebuilding Citizenship: Teaching the Dimensions of Conflict Resolution in Social Studies," in *Challenges and Prospects for Canadian Social Studies*, eds. Adam Sears and Ian Wright (Vancouver: Pacific Educational Press, 2004), 187–201.

22. Kathy Bickmore, "Foundations for Peacebuilding and Discursive Peacekeeping: Infusion and Exclusion of Conflict in Canadian Public School Curricula," *Journal of Peace Education* 2, no. 2 (2005): 161–81.

23. Richard Merelman, "The Role of Conflict in Children's Political Learning," in *Political Socialization, Citizenship Education, and Democracy*, ed. Orit Ichilov (New York: Teachers College Press, 1990), 47–65.

24. Hague Appeal, "UN Referendum A/54/98," *The Hague Agenda for Peace and Justice for the 21st Century* (Geneva: UNESCO, 1999), www.haguepeace.org.

25. Burns and Aspeslagh, *Three Decades of Peace Education*; Swee-Hin Toh and Virginia Floresca-Cawagas, "Educating Towards a Culture of Peace," in *Weaving Connections: Educating for Peace, Social and Environmental Justice*, ed. Tara Goldstein and David Selby (Toronto: Sumach Press, 2000), 365–87.

26. Hague Appeal, *The Hague Agenda*.

27. Betty Reardon, *Comprehensive Peace Education: Educating for Global Responsibility* (New York: Teachers College Press, 1988); Betty Reardon, "Militarism and Sexism: Influences on Education for War," in Burns and Aspeslagh, *Three Decades of Peace Education*, 143–60.

28. Galtung, *Peace by Peaceful Means*.

29. Clark McCauley, "Head First Versus Feet First in Peace Education," in Salomon and Nevo, *Peace Education*, 247–58.

30. Paulo Freire, *Pedagogy of the Oppressed* (New York: Continuum, 1970); Joel Spring, *Pedagogies of Globalization: The Rise of the Educational Security State* (Mahwah, NJ: Lawrence Erlbaum Associates, 2006).

31. Paulo Freire, *Pedagogy of the Heart* (NY: Continuum, 1996), 26.

32. Freire, *Pedagogy of the Oppressed*, 73.

33. Robert F. Arnove, "Reframing Comparative Education: The Dialectic of the Global and the Local," in *Comparative Education: The Dialectic of the Global and the Local*, ed. and Carlos A. Torres (Lanham, MD: Rowman and Littlefield, 1999), 1–23; Spring, *Pedagogies of Globalization*; Paulo Freire, *Pedagogy in Process: The Letters to Guinea-Bissau* (New York: Seabury, 1978).

34. Katherine Madjidi, "Revolucão Humana: Stories of Struggle and Human Transformation within the Movimento Sem Terra" (thesis, Stanford University, 2000).

35. Ware and others, *The No-Nonsense Guide to Conflict and Peace*.

36. Clive Harber, *Schooling as Violence: How Schools Harm Pupils and Societies* (London, UK: Routledge-Falmer, 2004), 85–96.

37. Maria Hadjipavlou, "Cyprus: A Partnership between Conflict Resolution and Peace Education," in Salomon and Nevo, *Peace Education*, 193–208; Spyros Spyrou, "Images of 'the Other': The Turk in Greek Cypriot Children's Imaginations," *Race, Ethnicity and Education*, 5, no. 3 (2002): 255–72; Harber, *Schooling as Violence*.

38. Nemer Frayha, "Developing Curriculum as a Means to Bridging National Divisions in Lebanon," in Tawil and Harley, *Education, Conflict, and Social Cohesion*, 159–206; Phillip Stabback, "Curriculum Development, Diversity and Division in Bosnia and Herzegovina," in Tawil and Harley, *Education, Conflict, and Social Cohesion*, 37–84.

39. Bush and Saltarelli, *The Two Faces of Education*; Harber, *Schooling as Violence*, 85–96.

40. John Rutayisire, John Kabano, and Jolly Rubagiza, "Redefining Rwanda's Future: The Role of Curriculum in Social Reconstruction," in Tawil and Harley, *Education, Conflict, and Social Cohesion*, 315–74.

41. Anna Obura, *Never Again: Educational Reconstruction in Rwanda* (Paris: UNESCO International Institute for Educational Planning, 2003), 18, www.unesco.org/iiep.

42. Zsuzsa Mátrai, "National Identity Conflicts and Civic Education: A Comparison of Five Countries," in *New Paradigms and Recurring Paradoxes in Education for Citizenship: An International Comparison*, eds. Gita Steiner-Khamsi, Judith Torney-Purta, and John Schwille (Amsterdam: JAI/Elsevier Science, 2002), 85–104.

43. Hillel Wahrman, "Is Silencing Conflicts a Peace Education Strategy? The Case of the 'Jewish State' Topic in Israeli Civics Textbooks," in *Education of Minorities and Peace Education in Pluralistic Societies*, eds. Yaacov Iram and Hillel Wahrman (Westport, CT: Praeger Publishers, 2003), 230.

44. Leslie Limage, "Education and Muslim Identity: The Case of France," in *Comparative Education Reader*, ed. Edward Beauchamp (New York: Routledge-Falmer, 2003); Jeffrey Milligan, "Teaching Between the Cross and the Crescent Moon: Islamic Identity, Postcoloniality, and Public Education in the Southern Philippines," *Comparative Education Review* 47, no. 4 (2003): 468–92.

45. Aziz Haidar, "Minority Education in the Palestinian Authority," in Iram and Wahrman, *Education of Minorities and Peace Education*, 149–67.

46. Gita Steiner-Khamsi, "Cultural Recognition or Social Redistribution: Predicaments of Minority Education," in Iram and Wahrman, *Education of Minorities and Peace Education*, 15–28.

47. Nathan C. Funk and Abdul Aziz Said, "Islam and the West: Narratives of Conflict and Conflict Transformation," *International Journal of Peace Studies* 9,

no. 1 (2004): 1–28; Marc Ross, *The Management of Conflict: Interpretations and Interests in Comparative Perspective* (New Haven: Yale University Press, 1993).

48. Keith Barton and Alan McCully, "History, Identity, and the School Curriculum in Northern Ireland: An Empirical Study of Secondary Students' Ideas and Perspectives," *Journal of Curriculum Studies* 37, no. 1 (2005): 85–116.

49. Orit Ichilov, "Pride in One's Country and Citizenship Orientations in a Divided Society," *Comparative Education Review* 49, no. 1 (2005): 44–61.

50. Ruth Firer, "The Gordian Knot between Peace Education and War Education," in Salomon and Nevo, *Peace Education*, 55–61.

51. Majid Al-Haj, "National Ethos, Multicultural Education, and the New History Textbooks in Israel," *Curriculum Inquiry* 35, no. 1 (2005): 47–71.

52. Lal Perera, Swarna Wijetunge, and A.S. Balasooriya, "Education Reform and Political Violence in Sri Lanka," in Tawil and Harley, *Education, Conflict, and Social Cohesion*, 375–433.

53. Joseph Zajda and Rea Zajda, "Reinventing the Past to Create the Future: The Rewriting of School History Textbooks in Post-Communist Russia," in Schweisfurth, Davies, and Harber, *Learning Democracy and Citizenship*, ed., 211–24.

54. Ruth Hayhoe, "Dilemmas in Japan's Intellectual Culture," *Minerva* 36 (1998): 1–19; Zheng Wang, "Situating History and Values in Peacebuilding" (paper presented at International Peace Research Association, Calgary, Alberta, July 2006).

55. Salazar Tetzagülc, Manuel de Jesús, and Katherine Grigsby, "Curriculum Change and Social Cohesion in Multicultural Guatemala," in Tawil and Harley, *Education, Conflict, and Social Cohesion*, 85–158.

56. Andrea Bear-Nicholas, "Citizenship Education and Aboriginal People: The Humanitarian Art of Cultural Genocide," *Canadian and International Education* 25, no. 2 (1996): 59–107.

57. John Bond, "From Saying 'Sorry' to a Journey of Healing: National Sorry Day in Australia," in *People Building Peace II: Successful Stories of Civil Society*, ed. Paul Van Tongeren, Marte Hellema, and Juliette Verhoeven (London, UK: Lynne Rienner Publishers, 2005), 647–53.

58. Crain Soudien, "Memory Work and the Remaking of the Future: A Critical Look at the Pedagogical Value of the Truth and Reconciliation Commission for Peace," in Salomon and Nevo, *Peace Education*, 155–61.

59. Penny Enslin, "South Africa: The Truth and Reconciliation Commission as a Model of Peace Education," in Salomon and Nevo, *Peace Education*, 237–43.

60. Ware and others, *The No-Nonsense Guide to Conflict and Peace*, 51.

61. Walter Stephan, *Reducing Prejudice and Stereotyping in Schools* (New York: Teachers College Press, 1999); Nurit Tal-Or, David Boninger, and Faith Gleicher, "Understanding the Conditions Necessary for Inter-group Contact to Reduce Prejudice," in Salomon and Nevo, *Peace Education*, 89–107.

62. Cheyanne Church, Anna Visser, and Laurie Shepherd Johnson, "A Path to Peace or Persistence? The 'Single Identity' Approach to Conflict Resolution in Northern Ireland," *Conflict Resolution Quarterly* 21 no. 3 (2004): 273–93; Tal-Or, Boninger, and Gleicher in "Understanding the Conditions."

63. For example, see Michael Arlow, "Citizenship Education in a Divided Society: The Case of Northern Ireland," in Tawil and Harley, *Education, Conflict, and Social Cohesion*, 255–313.

64. Davies, *Education and Conflict*, 137–39.

65. Davies, *Education and Conflict*, 223.

66. Yaacov Katz and Yaacov Yablon, "Promoting Intergroup Attitudes in Israel through Internet Technology," in Iram and Wahrman, *Education of Minorities and Peace Education*, 169–79.

67. Allan McCully, Marian O'Doherty, and Paul Smyth, "The Speak Your Piece Project: Exploring Controversial Issues in Northern Ireland," in *Peacebuilding for Adolescents: Strategies for Educators and Community Leaders*, ed. Linda Forcey and Ian Harris (New York: Peter Lang, 1999), 119–35, 126.

68. Corinne Bloch, "Listen to Understand: The Listening Project in Croatia," in van Tongeren and others, *People Building Peace II*, 654–60.

69. Rachel Hertz-Lazarowitz and Devorah Eden, "Israel: Empowering Arab and Jew—School Leadership in Acre," in Salomon and Nevo, *Peace Education*, 209–16.

70. Aaron Barnea, "Building Trust, Promoting Hope: The Families Forum Hello Peace Project in Israel and Palestine," in van Tongeren and others, *People Building Peace II*, 495–500.

71. For example, Miro Cernetig, "Mideast Tensions Divide Sesame Street," *Globe and Mail*, July 31, 2002; Peter Scowen, "The United Nations of Muppetry," *Toronto Star*, November 6, 2005.

72. Lisa Shochat, "'Our Neighborhood': Using Entertaining Children's Television to Promote Interethnic Understanding in Macedonia," *Conflict Resolution Quarterly* 21, no. 1 (2003): 79–93.

73. Claire McGlynn and Zvi Bekerman, "The Challenges of Initiatives for Catholic-Protestant and Palestinian-Jewish Integrated Education in Northern Ireland and Israel," (paper presented at the annual meeting of the American Educational Research Association, San Francisco, CA, April 7–11, 2006).

74. See also Grace Feuerverger, *Oasis of Dreams: Teaching and Learning Peace in a Jewish-Palestinian Village in Israel* (New York/London: Routledge/Falmer, 2001) and Chris Moffat, ed., *Education Together for a Change: Integrated Education and Community Relations in Northern Ireland* (Belfast: Fortnight Educational Trust, 1993).

75. Ed Cairns and Miles Hewstone, "Northern Ireland: The Impact of Peacemaking on Intergroup Behavior," in Salomon and Nevo, *Peace Education*, 217–28.

76. Edy Kaufman, "Dialogue-Based Processes: A Vehicle for Peacebuilding," in van Tongeren and others, *People Building Peace II*, 473–87.

77. Hizkias Assefa, "Reconciliation: Challenges, Responses, and the Role of Civil Society," in van Tongeren and others, *People Building Peace II*, 637–44.

78. John Paul Lederach, "The Arts and Peacebuilding: Using Imagination and Creativity" in van Tongeren and others, *People Building Peace II*, 283–92; Antonella Verdiani, ed., *Best Practices of Non-Violent Conflict Resolution in*

and Out of School: Some Examples (Paris: UNESCO, 2002), www.unesco.org/ education/nved/index.html.

79. L. Randolph Carter and Michael Shipler, "Youth: Protagonists for Peace," and Emma Kamara and Keith Neil, "Food, Education, and Peacebuilding: Children's Learning Services in Sierra Leone," in van Tongeren and others, *People Building Peace II.*

80. Kay Pranis, Barry Stuart, and Mark Wedge, eds., *Peacemaking Circles: From Crime to Community* (St. Paul, MN: Living Justice Press, 2003).

81. De Palazzo and Bob Hosea, "Restorative Justice in Schools: A Review of History and Current Practices," *The Fourth R: Newsletter of the Education Section (Association for Conflict Resolution)* (Winter 2004): 1 and 7–8.

82. John Paul Lederach, *Preparing for Peace: Conflict Transformation across Cultures* (Syracuse: Syracuse University Press, 1995).

83. John Paul Lederach, *Beyond Prescription: New Lenses for Conflict Resolution Training Across Cultures* (commissioned by the Inter-racial and Cross-cultural Conflict Resolution Project Waterloo, ON, 1991), 40.

84. Jean-Paul Restoule and Kathy Madjidi, personal correspondence, May 29, 2007.

Chapter Eleven: Educating for "Global Citizenship" in Schools: Emerging Understandings

1. Carole Hahn, *Becoming Political: Comparative Perspectives on Citizenship Education,* (Albany: State University of New York Press, 1998); Orit Ichilov, "Patterns of Citizenship in a Changing World," in *Citizenship and Citizenship Education in a Changing World,* ed. Orit Ichilov (London: The Woburn Press, 1998), 11–27; Eleanor Ireland and others, eds. *Active Citizenship and Young People: Opportunities, Experiences and Challenges in and Beyond School* (London: DfES, 2006); David Kerr, *Citizenship Education: An International Comparison across 16 Countries,* (paper presented at the annual conference of the American Educational Research Association, New Orleans, LA, April 2000); David Kerr, Elizabeth Cleaver, Eleanor Ireland, and Sarah Blenkinsop, *Citizenship Educational Longitudinal Study First Cross-Sectional Survey 2001–2002,* (Research Report 416 for the Department for Education and Skills, London: DfES, 2003); Julie Nelson and David Kerr, *Active Citizenship in INCA Countries: Definitions, Policies, Practices and Outcomes.* (Berkshire, UK: QCA/NFER International Review of Curriculum and Assessment Frameworks; 2006); Judith Torney-Purta, John Schwille, and Jo-Ann Amadeo, eds., *Civic Education Across Countries: Twenty-four National Case Studies from the IEA Civic Education Project* (Amsterdam: International Association for the Evaluation of Educational Achievement, 1999); Wing On Lee, "Emerging Concepts of Citizenship in the Asian Context," in *Citizenship Education in Asia and the Pacific: Concepts and Issues,* ed. Wing On Lee, David Grossman, Kerry Kennedy, and Gregory Fairbrother (Boston: Kluwer Academic Publishers, 2004), 25–36; The Council of Europe designated 2005 as the *European Year of Citizenship through Education* and the European Commission

launched a new program of activities entitled *Citizens for Europe* to run from 2007 to 2013 to support active European citizenship. At the international level, the United Nations (UN) Decade on Human Rights is ongoing and the IEA announced plans for a further International Civics and Citizenship Education Study (ICCES) to run from 2006 to 2010.

2. For additional information about these various conceptions and purposes of citizenship education, see: Roland Case and Penny Clark, "Four Purposes of Citizenship Education," in *The Canadian Anthology of Social Studies: Issues and Strategies for Teachers*, ed. Penny Clark and Roland Case (Vancouver: Simon Fraser University Press, 1997), 17–27; Lynn Davies, "Comparing Definitions of Democracy in Education," *Compare* 29, no. 2 (1999): 127–40; Derek Heater, *What Is Citizenship?* (Cambridge: Polity Press, 2000); Yvonne Hébert and Alan Sears, *Citizenship Education* (Toronto: Canadian Education Association, 2001), www.cea-ace.ca/media/en/Citizenship_Education.pdf; Orit Ichilov, "Patterns of Citizenship in a Changing World," in Ichilov, *Citizenship and Citizenship Education*, 11–27; Will Kymlicka, "Multicultural Citizenship," in *The Citizenship Debates*, ed. Gershon Shafir (Minneapolis: University of Minnesota Press, 1998), 167–88; Lee, Grossman, Kennedy, and Fairbrother, *Citizenship Education in Asia and the Pacific*, 25–36; Daniel Schugurensky, "Citizenship and Citizenship Education: Canada in an International Context," *AEC 3131: Citizenship Learning and Participatory Democracy, OISE/UT* (Toronto, ON: University of Toronto, 2005). Shafir, *The Citizenship Debates*; Joel Westheimer and Joe Kahne, "What Kind of Citizen? The Politics of Educating for Democracy," *American Educational Research Journal* 41, no. 2 (2004): 237–69.

3. T.H. McLaughlin, "Citizenship, Diversity and Education: A Philosophical Perspective," *Journal of Moral Education* 21, 3 (1992): 235–47.

4. Heater, *What Is Citizenship?*, 175.

5. James Banks, "Educating Global Citizens in a Diverse World," (Seattle, WA: New Horizons for Learning, 2004), www.newhorizons.org/strategies/multicultural/banks2.htm; Ian Davies, Mark Evans, and Alan Reid, "Globalising Citizenship Education? A Critique of 'Global Education' and 'Citizenship Education'," *British Journal of Educational Studies* 53, no. 1 (2005), 66–87; Audrey Osler and Hugh Starkey, *Changing Citizenship: Democracy and Inclusion in Education* (London: Open University Press, 2005); Audrey Osler and Kerry Vincent, *Citizenship and the Challenge of Global Education* (Stoke on Trent, UK: Trentham Books, 2002); Mary Joy Pigozzi, "A UNESCO View of Global Citizenship Education," *Educational Review* 58, no.1 (2006): 1–4; Michele Schweisfurth, Lynn Davies, and Clive Harber, *Learning Democracy and Citizenship: International Experiences* (Oxford: Symposium Books, 2002).

6. Linda Darling-Hammond, "Teachers and Teaching: Testing Hypotheses from a National Commission Report," *Educational Researcher* 27, no. 1(1998): 5–15.

7. Robin Alexander, "Comparing Classrooms and Schools," in *Learning from Comparing: New Directions in Comparative International Research: Volume 1. Contexts, Classrooms, and Outcomes*, eds. Robin Alexander, Patricia Broadfoot, and David Phillips (Wallingford, Oxford: Symposium Books, 1999), 109–12;

Michael Crossley, "Comparative and International Education: Contemporary Challenges, Reconceptualisation and New Directions for the Field," *Current Issues in Comparative Education* 4, no. 2 (2002): 81–6.

8. Luis Albala-Bertrand, "What Education for What Citizenship? First Lessons from the Research Phase," *Educational Innovation and Information,* 82, (1995): 2–8; Elise Boulding, *Building a Global Civic Culture: Education for an Interdependent World* (New York: Teachers College Press, 1988); Heater, *What Is Citizenship?*; David Held, "The Transformation of Political Community: Rethinking Democracy in the Context of Globalization," in *Democracy's Edges,* ed. Ian Shapiro and Casiano Hacker-Cordón (Cambridge: Cambridge University Press, 1999); George Richardson, "Global Education and the Challenge of Globalization," in *Challenges and Prospects in Canadian Social Studies,* ed. Alan Sears and Ian Wright (Vancouver, BC: Pacific Education Press, 2004), 138–49.

9. Audrey Osler, "Learning to Live Together: Citizenship Education in an Interdependent World," *Global Citizenship Supplement* (Leicester, UK: Centre for Citizenship Studies in Education, University of Leicester, 2002), 2–6.

10. Graham Pike and David Selby, *In the Global Classroom 2* (Toronto: Pippin, 2000), 11.

11. Merry Merryfield, Elaine Jarchow, and Sarah Pickett, eds., *Preparing Teachers to Teach Global Perspectives: A Handbook for Teacher Educators* (London: Sage Publications, 1997), 1–24.

12. Ibid., 12.

13. Heater, *What Is Citizenship?*, 116.

14. Heater, *What Is Citizenship?*, 164.

15. Lynn Davies, "Global Citizenship: Abstraction or Framework for Action," *Educational Review* 58, 1 (2006): 5–25, 6.

16. Oxfam, *What Is Global Citizenship?* (London: Oxfam, 2006), www.oxfam.org.uk/education/gc.

17. Roland Case and Penny Clark, "Four Purposes of Citizenship Education," in Clark and Case, *The Canadian Anthology,* 17–27; Hébert and Sears, *Citizenship Education*; A.B. Hodgetts, *What Culture? What Heritage? A Study of Civic Education in Canada,* (Toronto: OISE Press, 1969); Reva Joshee, "Citizenship and Multicultural Education in Canada: From Assimilation to Social Cohesion," in *Diversity and Citizenship Education: Global Perspectives,* ed. James Banks (San Francisco: Jossey-Bass, 2004), 127–58; Keith A. McLeod, "Exploring Citizenship Education: Education for Citizenship" in *Canada and Citizenship Education,* (Toronto: Canadian Education Association, 1989); Ken Osborne, "Education is the Best National Insurance: Citizenship Education in Canadian Schools, Past and Present," *Canadian and International Education* 25, no. 2 (1996): 33–58.

18. Richardson proposes five distinct and overlapping perspectives that have been emphasized over the last century in Canada: the imperial imaginary, the bipolar imaginary, the multi-polar imaginary, the ecological imaginary, and the mono-polar imaginary. See, George Richardson, "Global Education," in Sears and Wright, *Canadian Social Studies,* 138–49.

19. Dick Holland, "Hope for a New Vision: The Emergence of Global Citizenship in Ontario," (master's thesis, Ontario Institute for Studies in Education/University of Toronto, 2004).

20. Council of Ministers of Education, *Education for Peace, Human Rights, Democracy, International Understanding, and Tolerance* (Ottawa, ON: UNESCO and Council of Ministers of Education, 2001).

21. Kymlicka, "Multicultural Citizenship."

22. Ken Osborne, "Democracy, Democratic Citizenship, and Education," in *The Erosion of Democracy in Education: From Critique to Possibilities*, eds. John P. Portelli and Rovell P. Solomon (Calgary: Detselig Enterprises, 2001), 29–61.

23. Alan Sears, "Something Different to Everyone: Conceptions of Citizenship and Citizenship Education," *Canadian and International Education* 25, no. 2 (1996): 1–15.

24. Veronica Strong-Boag, "Claiming a Place in the Nation: Citizenship Education and the Challenge of Feminists, Natives, and Workers in Post Confederation Canada," *Canadian and International Education* 25, no. 2 (1996): 128–45.

25. British Columbia Ministry of Education, *Civic Studies 11: Integrated Resource Package 2005* (Victoria, BC: Ministry of Education, 2005), 12, www.bced.gov.bc.ca/irp/civic11.pdf.

26. Gouvernement du Québec, Ministère de l'Éducation, du Loisir et du Sport, *Education in Québec: An Overview* (Montréal: Gouvernement du Québec, 2005), 11, www.mels.gouv.qc.ca/GR-PUB/m_englis.htm.

27. Ontario Ministry of Education and Training (MET), *Canadian and World Studies, Grades 9 and 10* (Toronto: MET, 1999, 2005), 65–6; Ontario Ministry of Education and Training, *Canadian and World Studies, Grades 11 and 12* (Toronto, ON: MET, 2000); Ontario Ministry of Education and Training, *Social Studies, Grades 1–6; History and Geography, Grades 7 and 8* (Toronto, ON: MET, 1998).

28. See Derek Heater, *World Citizenship: Cosmopolitan Thinking and its Opponents* (London: Continuum, 2002); Osler and Vincent, *Challenge of Global Education.*

29. Further details can be seen at www.teachernet.gov.uk/pshe/curriculum.cfm?sectionId=76.

30. Further details can be seen at the website for the Post-16 Citizenship Support Programme, www.post16citizenship.org.

31. Department for International Development (DfID), *The Rough Guide to a Better World, and How You Can Make a Difference* (London: DfID, 2003).

32. Further details can be seen on the Oxfam website: www.oxfam.org.uk/education/gc.

33. David Kerr and Ted Huddleston, *Making Sense of Citizenship: A Continuing Professional Development Handbook* (London: Hodder Murray, 2006).

34. See the following examples: Cathie Holden and Nick Clough, *Education for Citizenship: Ideas into Action* (London: RoutledgeFalmer, 2002); Bhavani Algarra, *Activate: Enquiries into Global Citizenship* (Cheltenham, UK: Nelson Thornes, 2002); Tony Thorpe and David Marsh, *Citizenship Studies for OCR GCSE Short Course* (London: Citizenship Foundation and Hodder and Stoughton, 2002).

35. Davies, Evans, and Reid, "Globalising Citizenship Education?" 66–89.
36. Government of Pakistan, *The Education Policy 1998–2010* (Islamabad, Pakistan: Ministry of Education, 1998).
37. Ministry of Education, *Social Studies Curriculum for Classes VI–VIII* (Islamabad: Government of Pakistan, 2002), 5.
38. Department of Education (DoE), *White Paper on Education and Training* (Pretoria, South Africa: Government Printers, 1995).
39. The Constitution of the Republic of South Africa, Annotated Version (Wynberg, South Africa: HN Communications, 1996).
40. DoE, *Annual Report* (Pretoria: Government Printers, 1999).
41. Ibid., 66–7.
42. DoE, *Values, Education and Democracy* (report of the Working Group on Values in Education, Pretoria, South Africa: Government Printers, 2000).
43. John Rawls, *A Theory of Justice.* (Cambridge, MA: Harvard University Press, 1971); David Miller, *Citizenship and National Identity,* (Oxford: Polity Press, 2000).
44. DoE, *Saamtrek: Values, Education and Democracy in the 21st Century,* (Pretoria, South Africa: Government Printers, 2001).
45. DoE, *Manifesto on Values, Education and Democracy* (Cape Town, South Africa: Cape Argus Teach Fund, 2001), www.education.gov.za.
46. William Galston, *Liberal Purposes: Goods, Virtues, and Diversity in the Liberal State,* (Cambridge, MA: Cambridge University Press, 1991); Stephen Macedo, *Liberal Virtues: Citizenship, Virtue, and Community in Liberal Constitutionalism* (Oxford: Oxford University Press, 1990); Kymlicka, "Multicultural Citizenship."
47. DoE, *Manifesto on Values.*
48. Lesiba Teffo, "Moral Renewal and African Experience(s)," in *African Renaissance: The New Struggle,* ed. Malegapuru W. Makgoba (Cape Town, South Africa: Mafube and Tafelberg Publishers, 1999) 149–72.
49. Lynn Davies, "Abstraction or Framework for Action," 5–25; Davies, Evans, and Reid, "Globalising Citizenship Education?" 66–89.
50. Heater, *What Is Citizenship?,* 136.
51. Graham Pike, "Global Education and National Identity: In Pursuit of Meaning," *Theory Into Practice* 39, no. 2 (2000): 64–73, 71.
52. George Richardson, "Global Education," in Sears and Wright, *Canadian Social Studies,* 144.
53. Heater, *What Is Citizenship?,* 15.

Appendix A

Suggested Audio-visual Resources, with Discussion Questions

CHAPTER ONE: INTRODUCTION TO COMPARATIVE AND INTERNATIONAL EDUCATION: WHY STUDY COMPARATIVE EDUCATION?

Film: *Going to the Sea*, **by Jocelyn Cullity and Prakash Younger**
This film is a documentary of two Canadians living in Dalian, China, in 1993. As English instructors to teacher candidates at Liaoning Normal University, Jocelyn Cullity and Prakash Younger find during their year-long stay that the university and the city are undergoing major economic and social changes. The shift from Maoist Marxism to a market economy in China plays a serious role in the futures of the students and fellow faculty at Liaoning Normal University.
48 minutes

Questions for Reflection and Discussion
1. Although the film is over a decade old, did you see any similarities between the students' experiences and yours?
2. What is the philosophy of education at Liaoning Normal University? How does this philosophy differ from yours? How is it similar?
3. Dalian made many changes during the time of this documentary. Can you identify social, civic, economic, or educational policy changes in your local area, province, or country that could affect your profession as a teacher?
4. What can Canadian and American teachers learn from China? What can Chinese teachers learn from Canada and the United States?

How to Obtain the Film
Distributor: Jocelyn Cullity (filmmaker)
Contact Information: 1-905-889-1165 (Eastern Time)
Email address: jcullity@fsu.edu

CHAPTER TWO: PHILOSOPHY AND COMPARATIVE EDUCATION: WHAT CAN WE LEARN FROM EAST ASIA?

Film: *Preschool in Three Cultures: Japan, China and the United States,* by Joseph Tobin

This video is a supplement to the book *Three Cultures: Japan, China and the United States* by Joseph Tobin, David Wu, and Dana Davidson. Observing one day in the life of preschool children and teachers from these three countries, Tobin explores the similarities and differences between these cultures. Viewers watch preschool children go about their daily activities and hear Tobin explain how teachers from the other two cultures responded to the structure, discipline, and activities of one another's classes.

53 minutes

Questions for Reflection and Discussion

1. Did anything surprise you about the conduct in the preschool classrooms? Which preschool experience resonates with you? Why?
2. Using Chapter Two as your resource, please explain the different philosophical underpinnings you observed between the Japanese, Chinese, and American classrooms.
3. How would preschool lessons learned in each culture affect the child's concept of schooling?

How to Obtain the Film

Distributor: Dr. Joseph Tobin

Contact Information: Arizona State University, Mary Lou Fulton College of Education, PO Box 870211, Tempe, AZ 85287-0211 USA

Telephone: 1-480-965-1451 (Mountain Time)

Email address: joseph.tobin@asu.edu

Instructions: The film costs US$50, including shipping.

CHAPTER THREE: "EDUCATION FOR ALL," AFRICA, AND THE COMPARATIVE SOCIOLOGY OF SCHOOLING

Film: *Back to School,* part of *Wide Angle PBS* series of international documentaries

Back to School is from the PBS series *Wide Angle*, which highlights international social issues. The film follows seven children in seven

different countries, documenting their school experiences. The series will follow these children to 2015, the year the international community has targeted for universal access to primary education.
90 minutes

Questions for Reflection and Discussion
1. Why do these children want to attend school?
2. Is schooling sorting these children into different kinds of life chances?
3. What kinds of variation in the seven school experiences portrayed most surprised you?

How to Obtain the Film
Distributor: WNET, PBS Channel 13
Contact Information: 450 West 33rd Street, New York, NY 10001, USA
Telephone: 1-212-560-1313 (Eastern Time)
URL: www.pbs.org/wnet/wideangle/about/film_s5_f7.html
Instructions: Educational institutions may obtain a free copy of the *Wide Angle* series, if the department chair or full-time faculty member signs a licence agreement with WNET.

CHAPTER FOUR: COMPARATIVE INDIGENOUS WAYS OF KNOWING AND LEARNING

Note: The following two films are intended to be shown together, with *The Learning Path* shown first and *Rediscovery – The Eagle's Gift* shown second. Instructors may choose to show one film only, or to show clips or portions of each to shorten overall running time.

Film: *The Learning Path*, by Loretta Todd
The Learning Path tells the story of Aboriginal peoples' forced participation in the residential schooling system in Canada, including experiences of racism, loss of cultural identity, and of educational alienation. It then shows how Native Canadians are now regaining control over their education, highlighting the work of three Aboriginal educators in Edmonton, Alberta. Part of a five-part documentary series entitled *As Long as the Rivers Flow*, the feature-length version of this film

won a Silver Hugo award at the Chicago International Film Festival. 57 minutes (short version; part of the *As Long as the Rivers Flow* NFB series)

Questions for Reflection and Discussion

1. Share your reactions to the experiences of the residential schooling system portrayed by the individuals in this film. Thinking back to Chapter Four, compare some of the differences in ways of knowing and learning that Aboriginal children would have experienced in those schools. Have you had any experiences where you felt that your formal education contrasted with your own personal educational values or ways of knowing?

2. This film highlights the work of three Aboriginal women educators, and shares their educational experiences as young girls both in schools, in their families, and communities. Looking to Chapter Nine in this volume (Gender and Education), can you identify any similarities with the themes raised in that chapter? Why do you think women were chosen as exemplars for "the learning path" that this film describes?

3. This film focuses on efforts to transform or regain control of Aboriginal education within the formal school system. What are some of the ways this is happening, both as described in the film and in Chapter Four, and in your own experience? Did you find any limitations or points of contestation with the idea of introducing Aboriginal ways of knowing in the historically Western contexts described in the film?

How to Obtain the Film

Distributor: National Film Board of Canada

Contact Information: PO Box 6100, Station Centre-Ville, Montreal, QC H3C 3H5, Canada

Telephone in Canada: 1-800-267-7710 or 1-514-283-9450 (Eastern Time)

Telephone in the United States: 1-800-542-2164.

Fax: 1-514-296-1895

Email: international@nfb.ca

URL: www.nfb.ca/collection/films

Film: *Rediscovery—The Eagle's Gift,* by Peter Prince
This documentary describes a cultural "rediscovery" program of the Haida peoples in the Queen Charlotte Islands, British Columbia. Native and non-Native children from the area participate in a two-week camp, in which they learn about themselves, one another, and the natural world. The program is based on traditional Haida practices and ways of knowing. The film documents the experience of a group of youth, Haida leaders and Elders, and educators as they take part in this two-week camp program.
29 minutes

Questions for Reflection and Discussion
1. How do the educational experiences and "ways of knowing and learning" presented in this film compare and contrast with those highlighted in *The Learning Path*? Which pedagogies presented appeal most to you, as both a teacher and a learner?
2. A common *Rediscovery* saying is, "I hear, I forget. I see, I remember. I do, I understand." Considering your own learning experiences, both formal and informal, is this statement true for you? If so, can you see yourself implementing this educational philosophy in the classroom as a teacher, and in what ways?
3. From the beginning of the *Rediscovery* program, Haida Elders insisted that non-Native children, including children of logging families (with whom the Haidas were in dispute at the time), be included in the camps. What do you think the value might be in this, for both the Native and the non-Native children? How does this relate to the discussion in Chapter Four on the potential implications of Indigenous ways of knowing for *all* children?

How to Obtain the Film
Distributor: Vision Quest Films
Contact Information: PO Box 1542, Station E, Victoria, BC V8W 2X7, Canada
Telephone: 1-604-385-4440 (Pacific Time)
Or you can contact
Ghost River Rediscovery
Contact Information: 3359 27th Street NE, Suite 164, Calgary, AB T1Y 5E4, Canada

Telephone: 1-403-270-9351 (Mountain Time)
Email: manager@ghostriverrediscovery.com
URL: www.ghostriverrediscovery.com

CHAPTER FIVE: TEACHING AND LEARNING TO TEACH: SUCCESSFUL RADICAL ALTERNATIVES FROM THE DEVELOPING WORLD

Film: *Education Through Imagination*, by Antonia Antonopoulos
This short film explains the non-formal educational programs offered by the Bangladesh Rural Advancement Committee (BRAC). BRAC's creative response to rural community learning emphasizes the power of the imagination through child-friendly, gender-empowered, ethnically integrated, and community-participatory schooling. Viewers watch the daily school activities while the narrator explains the philosophies behind the many non-formal educational programs that BRAC supports.
17 minutes

Questions for Reflection and Discussion
1. Song, dance, and role-playing are important to Bengali culture and are used as learning tools in BRAC programs. What other arts-based teaching techniques may be appropriate to teaching in Canada or the United States? Do you know of other societies that use culture specific methods of teaching?
2. If you had only 15 days of teacher training, what important lessons would you need to learn?
3. If you were to become a teacher in your hometown, what would non-traditional schooling look like?

How to Obtain the Film
Distributor: Aga Khan Foundation, Canada
Contact Information: 360 Albert Street, Suite 1220, Ottawa, ON K1R 7X7, Canada
Telephone: 1-613-237-2532 (Eastern Time)
URL: www.akfc.ca
Filmmaker: Antonia Antonopoulos
Email address: antonia_ant@yahoo.com

CHAPTER SIX: UNDERSTANDING PEDAGOGY: CROSS-CULTURAL AND COMPARATIVE INSIGHTS FROM CENTRAL ASIA

Film: *The Teachers of the Karakorum*, by Arthur Holbrook and the Aga Khan Foundation
This video highlights an on-the-job teacher education program supported by the Aga Khan Foundation. Most teachers in the Karakorum, a rural and mountainous region of Pakistan, are poorly trained and rarely supervised. Through support from the Aga Khan Foundation, teacher trainees participate in a one-year program. The teachers take part in workshops, observe the classroom of a master teacher, and gradually incorporate what they have learned in the classroom. This field-based program helps build confidence, encourages child-centred teaching, and supports teachers in their preparation for the primary teaching certification exam.
27 minutes

Questions for Reflection and Discussion
1. In what ways do Chapter Six and *Teachers of Karakorum* reinforce and disagree with each other in terms of:
   a. Appreciating the complexity of teachers' lives and work?
   b. Approaching teacher/educational change?
   c. Related implications for teaching in Canadian or American multicultural schools?
2. How does the image of teaching and teachers in the Karakorum compare to your experience of teaching and teachers?
3. Could a teacher-training program such as the one highlighted in *Teachers of Karakorum* work in other contexts?

How to Obtain the Film
Distributor: Aga Khan Foundation
Contact Information: 360 Albert Street, Suite 1220, Ottawa, ON K1R 7X7, Canada
Telephone: 1-613-237-2532 (Eastern Time)
URL: www.akfc.ca
Instructions: For programs in Canada, there are three university libraries with this film. According to Library and Archives Canada,

the University of Calgary and Brock University offer this video on interlibrary loan. See the AMICUS catalogue for the University of Calgary, and James A. Gibson Library at Brock University. Please consult with your library about interlibrary loan services availability.

CHAPTER SEVEN: COMPARATIVE PERSPECTIVES ON SCHOOL IMPROVEMENT

Film: *Managing Change*, by Drs. Michael Fullan and John R. Champlin
Managing Change examines change as a crucial aspect of any effort for school improvement. Highlighting key initiation factors for change, the film discusses the complexities of the change process and its potential role in promoting school improvement. Part of a two-part series, this film explores some of the principles of change management and the dynamics of change as it affects schools.
30 minutes

Questions for Reflection and Discussion
1. Do you feel that the principles of change management presented in the film would apply in a Canadian or American classroom today?
2. How do you think the concept of change management varies depending on the cultural context of a school system? Draw on your own personal experiences.

How to Obtain the Film
Distributor: Video Journal of Education, National Center for Outcomes Based Education
URL: www.schoolimprovement.com/products/index.cfm?productid=204
Telephone: 1-866-835-4185 (Eastern Time)
Fax: 1-888-566-6888
Instructions: The package includes two video cassettes, a tape cassette, and workbook on managing change.

CHAPTER EIGHT: INTERNATIONAL EDUCATIONAL INDICATORS AND ASSESSMENTS: ISSUES FOR TEACHERS

Audio-visual Resource

Instead of selecting a film for this chapter, we suggest that instructors explore with students the activities and audio-visual resources provided on international assessment websites. Holding this class in a computer lab would be ideal.

a) Explore PISA questions and questionaires:
pisa-sq.acer.edu.au

b) Take sample questions from the IEA Civics Education Study:
www.wam.umd.edu/~jtpurta.

c) Review a short study, "Highlights from the TIMSS 1999 Video Study," with its video clips, from classrooms in Japan, the Netherlands, the United States, and Hong Kong:
nces.ed.gov/pubs2003/timssvideo/index.asp

d) Explore and manipulate performance data from the TIMSS and PIRLS studies. This website allows users to ask their own questions of TIMSS and PIRLS datasets, creating simple charts and tables comparing various aspects of several countries' performances:
lighthouse.air.org/timss.

e) Instructors may also wish to use selected footage from the *TIMSS 1999 Video Study: Science Public Release Lessons* or *TIMSS 1999 Video Study: Mathematics Public Release Lessons* funded by the National Center for Education Statistics. These two multi-CD sets present video footage from the math and science classrooms of Grade Eight students in Australia, Czech Republic, Japan, Netherlands, and the United States. Distributor: Pearson Achievement Solutions
URL: www.lessonlab.com/bkstore/index.cfm/action/displayby category

Questions for Reflection and Discussion:
1. How could the research data in these websites support understanding educational inequality?
2. What can Canadian teachers learn from international assessment research?
3. Can international tests be used for educational policy decisions? Under what circumstances?

CHAPTER NINE: GENDER AND EDUCATION

Film: *What's Going On? Girls' Education in India*, produced by RCN Entertainment in association with the United Nations
This film is one of a 10-part series titled *What's Going On?* to find out what is happening in children's lives. This episode highlights the educational experiences of three girls, Aarti, Geetha, and Leala. The film explores the challenges each girl faces relating to schooling.
30 minutes

Questions for Reflection and Discussion
1. Identify what you think are the most important issues raised in this film. What other things would you have liked to have known about these girls' lives?
2. What links can you make between this film and this chapter? Issues to consider include girls' access to schooling, prevailing social attitudes, and the importance of rural/urban differences.
3. How will insights you have gained from this film affect your teaching?

How to Obtain the Film
Distributor: United Nations
URL: www.socialstudies.com/c/wgo.html
Instructions: For online viewing, see: www.teachers.tv/video/20862.

CHAPTER TEN: EDUCATION FOR CONFLICT RESOLUTION AND PEACEBUILDING IN PLURAL SOCIETIES: APPROACHES FROM AROUND THE WORLD

Film: *Promises*, by Justine Shapiro and B.Z. Goldberg
This film follows four Jewish-Israeli children (from ultra-conservative to liberal-secular backgrounds) and four Palestinian children (citizens

in Jerusalem and refugees in a nearby camp) from 1999–2000. B.Z. Goldberg interviews the children about their views of the Israeli-Palestinian conflict. Goldberg eventually brings some of them together for a day of fun, relationship building, and dialogue. The film ends by showing the children two years later to find out about their views on the conflict and whether they keep in touch with the children they met through the contact program.

The film was nominated for an Academy Award for Best Documentary Film in 2002.

106 minutes

Questions for Reflection and Discussion

1. According to your understanding of this chapter, identify examples of formal or informal education depicted in this film that 1) exacerbated destructive inter-group conflict, and 2) seemed to contribute to peacebuilding. Did you see any limitations in Goldberg's approach to building community among these young people?

2. Inter-group contact involves multiple narratives and forms of communication. In the interviews of the children, what were the examples of positional (adversarial) dialogue (see the section on Identity Based Conflict in Chapter Ten)? Of human relations dialogue? Of activist and problem-solving dialogues (see the section on Learning to Hear the Other in Chapter Ten)? Did you notice any narrative representations of self and the other that would facilitate or impede mutual understanding?

How to Obtain the Film

URL:

www.promisesproject.org/dist.html

www.imdb.com

www.amazon.com

Instructions: As an Oscar-nominated film, *Promises* can be purchased through a variety of venues. The film's website offers an educational package as well as the video for home use. For classroom viewing, there is a natural starting point about 45 minutes into the film.

Film: *Teaching Peace in Time of War*, produced by Kent Martin and Peter d'Entremont

Featuring Canadian peace educator Hetty van Gurp, the film takes viewers behind the scenes of her work with a middle school in Serbia. The film shows the problems and processes of transforming teacher-to-student relationships and student-to-student relationships into peace-centred ways of learning and interacting with a particular school. The film highlights the personal life of van Gurp, as well as explores the challenges that the Serbian teachers have in adopting this method of pedagogy and practice.

56 minutes

Questions for Reflection and Discussion

1. Chapter Six discusses and analyzes the complex role of teachers. How does this film speak to the points made in that chapter? As a teacher, what aspects of classroom peace building would you adopt?

2. Do you think van Gurp's peacebuilding education process in this Serbian school will find success? Why or why not? What are the positive and negative aspects of taking a North American model of peace education and transferring it to Serbia?

3. What aspects of van Gurp's peacebuilding education have you seen in your classroom or schooling experiences?

How to Obtain the Film

Distributor: National Film Board of Canada

Contact Information: PO Box 6100, Station Centre-Ville, Montreal, QC H3C 3H5, Canada

Telephone in Canada: 1-800-267-7710 or 1-514-283-9450 (Eastern Time)

Telephone in the United States: 1-800-542-2164.

Fax: 1-514-296-1895

Email: international@nfb.ca

URL: www.nfb.ca/collection/films

CHAPTER ELEVEN: EDUCATING FOR "GLOBAL CITIZENSHIP" IN SCHOOLS: EMERGING UNDERSTANDINGS

Audio-visual Resources

We suggest that rather than showing a film, instructors explore Internet resources on citizenship education. Holding part of this class in a computer lab would be ideal.

a) Explore the Voice section of Taking It Global. This site offers tool kits on youth activism, allows youth to identify the global issues that matter to them most, and provides a list of websites and events that call for youth participation: www.takingitglobal.org/action/voice.

b) Review and perhaps conduct a classroom activity suggested in the document *Educating for Global Citizenship in a Changing World: A Teacher's Handbook*: cide.oise.utoronto.ca/globalcitizenship.php.

c) Take some of the quizzes and games on citizenship aimed specifically for children on the Cyber School Bus website sponsored by the UN for children: www.un.org/Pubs/CyberSchoolBus.

d) Instructors may also wish to use selected footage audio-visual resources on the Australian Broadcasting Corporation website, The Common Good. The website offers several websites on citizenship and democracy and highlights other online resources that may be useful to secondary school teachers: www.abc.net.au/civics.

Appendix B

Online Resources for Selected Chapters

CHAPTER THREE: "EDUCATION FOR ALL," AFRICA, AND THE COMPARATIVE SOCIOLOGY OF SCHOOLING

Organization: United Nations
Title: *Universal Declaration of Human Rights*:
URL: www.un.org/Overview/rights.html

Organization: United Nations Development Programme
Title: *Human Development Report 2006*
URL: hrd.undp.org/en/media/hdr06-complete.pdf

Organization: UNESCO
Title: *EFA Global Monitoring Report [GMR]: GMR Data*
URL: gmr.uis.unesco.org

Organization: UN Millennium Project
Title: *Toward Universal Primary Education: Investments, Incentives and Institutions*
URL: www.unmillenniumproject.org/documents/Education-complete.pdf

Organization: World Bank
Title: *EdStats* (database of education statistics)
URL: devdata.worldbank.org/edstats

CHAPTER FOUR: COMPARATIVE INDIGENOUS WAYS OF KNOWING AND LEARNING

Organization: Canadian Race Relations Foundation
Title: *Learning about Walking in Beauty: Placing Aboriginal Perspectives in Canadian Classrooms*
URL: www.crr.ca
This website offers a summary of the report *Learning about Walking in Beauty*, which uses the learning circle as a pedagogical and analytical framework for describing how to include Aboriginal culture and history in school curricula. In the report, the four directions of the medicine wheel (north, east, south, and west) are used to explain Aboriginal history and identity.

Organization: Department of Indian Affairs and Northern Development Canada
Title: *Our Children: Keepers of the Sacred Knowledge*
URL: www.ainc-inac.gc.ca
This 2002 report presents the work focusing on the education of Aboriginal youth undertaken by the National Working Group on Education and includes 27 recommendations for improvement.

Organization: Four Directions Teaching
URL: www.fourdirectionsteachings.com
Through audio-narration, this website is a resource for learning about Indigenous knowledge and philosophy from five First Nations in Canada: an excellent resource for in-classroom learning.

Organization: Ghost River Rediscovery
URL: www.ghostriverrediscovery.com
Ghost River Rediscovery is a cultural, experiential learning program based on Aboriginal traditions and values. The Teacher Manual and Student Workbooks, available under the "Rediscovery in the Schools" program, provide teachers with materials they need to introduce Aboriginal and holistic learning activities in their own classroom.

Organization: Government of Manitoba
Title: Aboriginal Education Directorate

URL: www.edu.gov.mb.ca/aed/research.html
This website provides access to documents, reports, studies, and initiatives related to Aboriginal Education in Canada.

Organization: Ministry of Education, Alberta and the University of
     Alberta
Title: *Aboriginal Education: A Research Brief for Practitioners*
URL: edc.gov.ab.ca
Description: This website provides a good starting place for curricular materials to support classroom activities that support Indigenous ways of knowing.

Organization: Otomi First Nation
Title: *The Reunion of the Condor and the Eagle International Indigenous
     Trade and Social Development Agreement and Unity Pact*
URL: www.unitedindians.com/pdf/downloads/reunion_condor_
     eagle.pdf
This pact between the Indigenous tribes and nations of the Western hemisphere lays the principles under which they will collaborate with each other on Indigenous capacity building.

Title: *Unrepentant: Kevin Annett and Canada's Genocide*
URL: video.google.com/videoplay?docid=-6637396204037343133
Awarded Best International Documentary at the 2006 Los Angeles Independent Film Festival, *Unrepentant* documents the genocide of First Nations youth in the residential school programs of Canada and includes testimonies of residential school survivors.

CHAPTER FIVE: TEACHING AND LEARNING TO TEACH: SUCCESSFUL RADICAL ALTERNATIVES FROM THE DEVELOPING WORLD

Organization: Alternative Education Resource Organization (AERO)
Title: *The Education Revolution*
URL: www.educationrevolution.org
AERO considers itself the hub for alternative education programs throughout the world. Based on learner-centred approaches to education, it offers books, online courses, networking, and research on alternative schooling.

Organization: New Horizons for Learning
URL: www.newhorizons.org
This website offers several useful tools for teachers in addressing all sorts of learning needs. The site is organized into seven sections: news from the neurosciences, transforming education, perspectives on the future, teaching and learning strategies, special needs, lifelong learning, and student voices. Within each section is a database of articles, reading lists, and research.

Organization: Paths of Learning
URL: www.pathsoflearning.net
The works of Dr. Ron Miller are highlighted on this website. Miller's research focuses on holistic education, which is an open-ended philosophy of education that embraces the complexity of learning and multiple factors that affect each learner, their community, their family, and their unique talents.

Organization: Sudbury Valley School
URL: www.sudval.org
Sudbury Valley School offers a philosophy of education that centres on independence and freedom in the learning process. Involvement within the school, particularly in its governance, is an important aspect of developing confidence and communication skills.

CHAPTER EIGHT: INTERNATIONAL EDUCATIONAL INDICATORS AND ASSESSMENTS: ISSUES FOR TEACHERS

Organization: Boston College, TIMSS/PIRLS International Study Center
URL: timss.bc.edu
The TIMSS/PIRLS Center offers publications, information, and statistical data on the last two PIRLS tests and the last four TIMSS tests.

Organization: Council of Minister of Education, Canada
URL: www.cmec.ca/stats/international.en.stm
The Council of Ministers of Education for Canada provides links to current reports about the status of Canadian education.

Organization: Education Quality and Assessment Office (EQAO)
URL: www.eqao.com
This website provides information on assessment, with both findings from, and instructions for teachers and parents about Ontario's participation in TIMSS, PIRLS, PISA, and the like. Past testing results and information on the upcoming TIMSS 2007 are also available.

Organization: IEA
Title: *IEA Civics Education Study*
URL: nces.ed.gov/surveys/cived
Through this site, information on the study is accessible, as is a chance to try answering some of the questions. This website also links to a history of IEA: its purpose, its first studies, and its networks.

Organization: OECD Department of Education
URL: www.oecd.org/department/0,2688,en_2649_33723_1_1_1_1_1,00.
html
The Directorate for Education website provides access to OECD statistics, reports, and educational information on each member country and several non-member countries.

Organization: PISA
Title: *Highlights from the TIMSS 1999 Video Study*
URL: nces.ed.gov/pubs2003/timssvideo/index.asp
This report highlights the findings from the TIMSS (Third International Mathematics and Science Study) 1999 Video Study. The 1999 study examines classroom teaching practices through in-depth analysis of videotapes of eighth-grade mathematics lessons and provides rich descriptions of mathematics teaching as it is actually experienced by eighth-grade students in seven countries (Australia, the Czech Republic, Hong Kong SAR, Japan, the Netherlands, Switzerland, and the United States).

Organization: PISA Canada
URL: www.pisa.gc.ca
The PISA Canada website offers a description of the PISA program in Canada, links PISA partners in other countries, and offers a comparative summary of Canadian students' performance on the PISA.

Organization: Statistics Canada
Title: *Children of Immigrants: How Well Do They Do in School?*
URL: www.statcan.ca/english/freepub/81-004-XIE/200410/immi.
htm
Statistics Canada offers a wealth of quantitative data on education
with this site, focusing on the 2000 PISA performance of immigrant
children in Canada.

Organization: TIMSS United States
URL: ustimss.msu.edu
Funded by the National Science Foundation, National Center for
Educational Statistics, and Michigan State University, this website links
to several publications, reports, statistical surveys, presentations, and
professional organizations.

Organization: UNESCO's Institute for Statistics
URL: www.uis.unesco.org
The UNESCO Institute for Statistics (UIS) website presents data on a
wide range of educational topics, from meeting MDGs to surveying
middle-income countries for its World Education Indicators project.
More than 1,000 indicators and raw data on education, literacy, and
science and technology are stored in the new UIS database.

Organization: Youth in Transition Canada (YITS)
URL: www.pisa.gc.ca/yits.shtml
The Youth in Transition Survey queries youth at 15 years old and
between 18 and 20 years old to learn about the transition from school
to work. Results from the first survey are available on this site.

CHAPTER NINE: GENDER AND EDUCATION

Organization: The United Nations Girls' Initiative (UNGEI)
URL: www.ungei.org
Through this site, information by country, reports, newsletters,
photoessays and other resources regarding girls' educational issues
globally are accessible.

Organization: UNIFEM (United Nations Development Fund for
  Women)
URL: www.unifem.org
This website highlights innovative programs and strategies to foster
women's empowerment and gender equality and makes available a
variety of publications.

Organization: UNESCO Bangkok
URL: www.unescobkk.org
This website provides information and reports on issues of gender
and education in Asia and the Pacific regions including materials
to implement strategies for promoting gender equality and gender
mainstreaming in education.

CHAPTER TEN: EDUCATION FOR CONFLICT RESOLUTION AND PEACEBUILDING IN PLURAL SOCIETIES: APPROACHES FROM AROUND THE WORLD

Organization: The Hague Appeal for Peace
URL: www.haguepeace.org
Through its website the Hague Appeal for Peace, an international
network of organizations and individuals dedicated to the abolition
of war and making peace a human right, provides access to peace
education activities, lesson plans, books, and CDs.

Organization: UNESCO
Title: *Best Practices of Non-Violent Conflict Resolution In and Out of School:
  Some Examples*
URL: unesdoc.unesco.org/images/0012/001266/126679e.pdf
This report highlights 14 successful conflict resolution programs, from
formal and non-formal educational contexts, as a way of providing
educators with possible pedagogical tools for violence prevention.
These programs come from various countries around the world.

CHAPTER ELEVEN: EDUCATING FOR "GLOBAL CITIZENSHIP" IN SCHOOLS: EMERGING UNDERSTANDINGS

Organization: Canadian International Development Agency (CIDA)
Title: *Youth Zone*
URL: www.acdi-cida.gc.ca/youthzone
Youth Zone encourages young people to engage in global issues by publishing articles written by teens, linking to youth development organizations, and through the Youth Speakers Project.

Organization: Citizenship Education Research Network (CERN)
URL: canada.metropolis.net/research-policy/cern-pub
Based in Canada, CERN's goal is to establish a long-term citizenship education research.

Organization: Classroom Connections
URL: www.classroomconnections.ca/en/takingaction.php
This web page offers several types of classroom modules and activities through different online publications by Classroom Connections, including *Cultivating a Culture of Peace in the 21st Century.*

Organization: Department for International Development (DFID) (United Kingdom)
Title: *Global Dimension: An Essential Tool for Teachers*
URL: www.globaldimension.org.uk
This handbook looks at school-wide approaches to citizenship education as well as classroom activities focusing on political literacy, social and moral responsibility, and community involvement. The handbook's activities are appropriate for students 11 years of age and older.

Organization: Global Youth Action Network (GYAN)
URL: www.youthlink.org/gyanv5/index.htm
GYAN is a youth driven organization with several global initiatives. There are several youth focused publications on this site, including books, posters, movies, online games, e-cards, and the like.

Organization: Ontario Institute for Studies in Education at the
    University of Toronto
Title: *Educating for Global Citizenship in a Changing World: A Teacher's
    Resource Handbook*
URL: cide.oise.utoronto.ca/globalcitizenship.php
This handbook offers a wealth of classroom activities and web resources
on global citizenship.

Organization: The Common Good (Australia)
URL: www.abc.net.au/civics
Based in Australia, this site offers audio-visual as well as text-based
resources for students on civics and citizenship education. Professional
development opportunities for teachers, games for students, and
research on citizenship education are accessible through this site.

Organization: Quality Improvement Agency (United Kingdom)
URL: www.post16citizenship.org
The emphasis of this website is to help support youth over 16 years
old to engage with their community. This website announces training
opportunities, lists networks of post-16 groups in the United Kingdom,
and work-based learning resources.

Organization: Oxfam
URL: www.oxfam.org.uk/education/gc
Oxfam supports two citizenship education sites, one for teachers and
one for children. The teacher's site offers multiple ways to obtain
curriculum materials for citizenship learning, whereas the children's
site has games and fun activities.

Organization: Oxfam Canada
URL: www.oxfam.ca
Oxfam Canada is a branch of Oxfam UK. This website offers curriculum
materials, PowerPoint presentations, lesson plans, and student
participation activities for Canadian and American teachers.

Organization: Oxfam Hong Kong
URL: www.cyberschool.oxfam.org.hk
The Hong Kong office of Oxfam links to several programs that support
teacher and student learning about global issues.

Organization: Teacher Net
URL: www.teachernet.gov.uk/pshe
Teacher Net has three distinct programs to support teachers: Teachers
TV, Teachers Magazine, and Schools Email. This particular page teams
up Teacher Net publications with learning objectives for citizenship
education.

Organization: United Nations
Title: Global Teaching and Learning Project Cyber School Bus
URL: www.un.org/Pubs/CyberSchoolBus
The Cyber School Bus is a global teaching and learning project which
includes resources, curriculum, as well as games and quizzes for
children and youth. This site links to UN resources for kindergarten
to Grade 12.

About the Editors and Contributors

Stephen Anderson is an associate professor in the Department of Theory and Policy Studies in Education at OISE-UT. Dr. Anderson's areas of specialization include planned educational change, school improvement, initial and in-service teacher development, comparative and development education, and program evaluation. His research and consulting experiences have been situated in Canada, the United States, Africa (Kenya, Tanzania, Uganda), and Pakistan. Recent publications include *Improving Schools Through Teacher Development: Case Studies of the Aga Khan Foundation Projects in East Africa; Beyond Islands of Excellence: What School Districts Can Do to Improve Instruction and Achievement in All Schools;* and articles on the district role in education change.

Kathy Bickmore is an associate professor in the Department of Curriculum, Teaching, and Learning at OISE-UT. Her areas of specialization include international and comparative perspectives on conflict resolution and controversial issues in education, and education for democracy, peace, and social justice/equity. Dr. Bickmore's current research, "Safe and Inclusive Schools: A Comparative Analysis of Anti-violence Policies and Programs," examines the citizenship and equity implications of intervention and prevention programs for handling student conflict and reducing violence in urban Canadian schools. Recent international collaborative work includes an anti-bullying initiative with Japan, a democratic civic education project with Tula, Russia, and the Peace Education Council of the International Peace Research Association. Recent publications appear in *Handbook of Research in Social Studies, The Challenge of Teaching Controversial Issues, Conflict Resolution Quarterly, Theory and Research in Social Education, Curriculum Inquiry, Canadian Journal of Education,* and *Journal of Peace Education.*

Mark Evans is a senior lecturer in the Department of Curriculum, Teaching, and Learning (CTL) and former Director of the Secondary Teacher Education Program at OISE-UT. Dr. Evans' areas of specialization include: teacher education, approaches to professional learning, education for citizenship in democratic contexts, education for global understanding, and social studies education. He has been involved in a variety of curriculum reform initiatives, teacher education projects, and research studies with teachers and schools locally and internationally (Toronto, Ottawa, England, Pakistan). Most recently, his work focuses on "teaching for deep understanding" and "citizenship education pedagogy" in Canada and the United Kingdom. His funded research includes: "Civic Education and Democracy in Russia"; "Education for Citizenship in a Changing World: Perspectives and Classroom Practices"; and "Education for Citizenship through Teacher Education: An International Mobility Programme." He is the recipient of the University of Toronto Teaching Award, the Student Teacher Union's OISE/UT Professor of the Year Award, and numerous Certificates of Teaching Excellence.

Joseph P. Farrell is a professor emeritus in the Department of Curriculum, Teaching, and Learning at OISE-UT. Dr. Farrell's areas of specialization include comparative and international education; planning education for social development, especially in developing countries; comparative teacher development; education policy studies; and evaluation of reform projects. He is a co-founder of the Comparative, International, and Development Education program at OISE and an Honorary Fellow of the Comparative, International and Education Society of the United States. Recent publications include *The National Unified School in Allende's Chile: The Role of Education in the Destruction of a Revolution; Textbooks in Developing Countries: Pedagogical and Economic Issues* (with Stephen Heyneman); and *Teachers in Developing Nations.*

Ruth Hayhoe is a professor in the Department of Theory and Policy Studies in Education at OISE-UT as well as president emerita of the Hong Kong Institute of Education. Dr. Hayhoe's areas of specialization include comparative higher education, international academic relations, and higher education in Asia. She has written extensively on higher education in China and educational relations between China and the

West, and has received a number of honours and awards, including Honorary Fellow of the University of London Institute of Education (1998), the Silver Bauhinia Star of the Hong Kong SAR Government (2002), Honorary Doctorate in Education, the Hong Kong Institute of Education (2002), and Commandeur dans l'ordre des Palmes académiques by the Government of France.

Kara Janigan is a PhD student in the Department of Curriculum, Teaching, and Learning at OISE-UT. Her previous work includes primary teaching, teacher training, and curriculum development in Canada, Eritrea, Ethiopia, and Malawi. Her areas of specialization include gender and education, teacher development, curriculum development, comparative and international education, and Southern and Northeast Africa.

Meggan Madden is a PhD student in the Department of Theory and Policy Studies at OISE-UT. She is currently studying comparative higher education. Her areas of interest include quality assurance, the internationalization of higher education, and international academic relations.

Katherine Madjidi is a PhD student in the Department of Adult Learning and Community Development at OISE-UT. She has extensive experience working in international community development and non-formal educational programming, particularly in Indigenous communities in both North and South America. Her areas of specialization include Indigenous ways of knowing, transformative and holistic education, participatory development, Latin America, and comparative and international education.

Vandra Lea Masemann is an adjunct associate professor in the Department of Adult Education and Counselling Psychology at OISE-UT. Her areas of specialization include comparative and international education, girls' education, multicultural and bilingual education, and historical perspectives on comparative education societies. She was president of the World Council of Comparative Education Societies (1987–1991) and its secretary general (1996–2000), president of the Comparative and International Education Society (1990–1991), and president of the Comparative and International Education Society of Canada (1985–1987). Her PhD thesis was an ethnography of a girls' boarding school in West Africa, and she has devoted a considerable portion of her career to advocating the uses of ethnographic and other qualitative methods in research in comparative education.

Karen Mundy is an associate professor in the Department of Adult Education and Counselling Psychology and Director of the Comparative, International, and Development Education Centre at OISE-UT. She also holds the Canada Research Chair in Global Governance and Comparative Educational Change. Her areas of specialization include comparative and international education, educational policy and reform in sub-Saharan Africa, Canadian development aid policies in education, the politics of international cooperation in the field of education, Education For All initiatives, and international organizations with education mandates.

Sarfaroz Niyozov is an assistant professor in the Department of Curriculum, Teaching and Learning at OISE-UT. His doctoral dissertation, entitled *Understanding Teaching in the Post-Soviet Rural and Mountainous Tajikistan*, received the 2002 Best Dissertation Award by the American Educational Research Association and the 2002 Best Dissertation Award by the Comparative International Education Society. His areas of specialization include curriculum studies and teacher development, diversity and commonalities in education, global education, and cultural and social practices in developing, Muslim, and post-Soviet societies.

Jean-Paul Restoule is Anishinaabe and a member of the Dokis First Nation. He is an assistant professor of Aboriginal Education at the Ontario Institute for Studies in Education of the University of Toronto. His research has included Aboriginal identity development in urban areas and the application of Indigenous knowledge in academic and urban settings. He is currently researching traditional Anishinaabek teachings for ethical research and access to post-secondary education for Aboriginal peoples. Dr. Restoule is actively involved in creating a network and support program for Aboriginal graduate students in Ontario (Supporting Aboriginal Graduate Enhancement).

Index